*f*P

THE
SELF MANAGING ORGANIZATION

HOW LEADING COMPANIES ARE TRANSFORMING THE WORK OF TEAMS FOR REAL IMPACT

Ronald E. Purser

Steven Cabana

THE FREE PRESS

THE FREE PRESS
A Division of Simon & Schuster Inc.
1230 Avenue of the Americas
New York, NY 10020

Designed by MM Design 2000 Inc.

Manufactured in the United States of America

10 9 8 7 6 5 4 3 2 1

Library of Congress Cataloging-in-Publication Data

Purser, Ronald E., 1956–
    The self managing organization : how leading companies are transforming the work of teams for
real impact / Ronald E. Purser, Steven Cabana.
        p.   cm.
    Includes bibliographical references and index.
    ISBN 0-684-83734-X (alk. paper)
        1. Employee empowerment.   2. Industrial management—Employee participation.
3. Employee empowerment—Case studies.   4. Industrial management—Employee participation—
Case studies.   I. Cabana, Steven.   II. Title.
HD50.5.P87   1998
658.3'152—dc21   98-27061
                                                                                                              CIP

ISBN 0-684-83734-X

This book is dedicated to the late Fred Emery,
who showed us how democracy could be put to work.

CONTENTS

FOREWORD

Once there were pyramids, departments, leaders, troops; now there are webs, nodes, communities, networks. Once there was continuous improvement and incremental change; now we see continuous discontinuous change. We've shifted from economies of scale to economies of time; from fixed boundaries to open spaces. Information and knowledge have redefined our economy, and technology has compressed the time needed to obtain information, innovate, make decisions, and initiate action. In this new world of high-velocity businesses and market economies, new forms of organizational design are emerging. They are fundamentally altering the nature and agenda of management.

While industrialized nations are shifting quickly to a new market economy, many companies are having to play catch up. The command-and-control paradigm is alive and well in most organizations today, perhaps disguised in more participative management styles, but still entrenched nevertheless. This is why many senior managers get frustrated when the marketplace demands change and the organization is inept at meeting the challenge. Today's tuned-in executives want the company to adapt to the marketplace as fast as the marketplace changes. These executives know that the traditional model of organization is a recipe for disaster. A new model of the *self-managing organization* operating under similar principles as the new economy and the new information technologies is what they need for their competitive strategy.

Organizations that fail to replace bureaucracy and command-and-control hierarchy with responsive market mechanisms and self-managing, self-organizing network structures will be replaced themselves; they will not survive. As technology networks spread, so will social networks, which will supplant hierarchy and become the means by which the organization does its work. This book is about building organizations that align with the new knowledge economy and reconfigure themselves as fast as the economy changes. It is about providing individuals the power, knowledge, and skills to adapt to the changes taking place in the business around them. It is about people learning to self-organize in order to respond to the demands of the marketplace.

The notion of a self-managing organization is not new, but its time has definitely come. A half century ago, two pioneering social scientists, Eric Trist and Fred Emery, articulated the principles and design of self-managing teams as alternatives to the command-and-control work structures of Taylorist theory. There have been decades of experimentation and slow migration to this new form of work organization. Although positive performance differences when compared to traditional work systems are well substantiated, it has taken the widespread use of information technology for the self-managing work structure to be recognized as the new organizational paradigm of the network age.

Ron Purser and Steven Cabana provide both theory and practice for designing the self-managing organization. They have for the first time combined a substantive explanation of the design principles underlying self-managing organizations with two primary planning and design approaches, the Participative Design and Search Conference methodologies. These approaches have gained widespread appeal and usage due to the success they have experienced with organizations around the world. *The Self-Managing Organization* is an important contribution for those seeking to transform traditional command-and-control organizations to new high-performance work systems.

This is not yet another book about teams, as the authors make an important distinction between self-managed teams and the self-managing organization. In the self-managing organization a multitude of structural configurations can be creatively designed to align with the firm's strategy that are not limited to what many envision as the self-managing team typically found in manufacturing environments. Moreover, the self-managing organization has the ability to self-organize or reconfigure according to market demands, respond flexibly based on principles of redundancy and variety, and gain commitment from its members. The design principles presented in this book are the "DNA" of the organization design; they may result in various structural forms, such as global virtual customer solution teams.

As we move into the future, this new form of organization will be an important source of advantage. At the enterprise level, the challenge is to design the human infrastructure for self-management that regulates its processes through market mechanisms and is enabled through information technology. How an organization develops, combines, and leverages its core competencies to support its strategy will in most cases make all the difference in the world in terms of marketplace success or failure. Self-managing organizations are future-focused, designed and oriented to satisfy the evolving needs of its customers, and have the ability to demonstrate flexibility with speed. In many cases the search for advantage through fast and flexible structures will be a search to overcome the inadequacies of the current hierarchical organization.

Self-managing, self-organizing network structures are adaptive to the market. Decision making is not bottlenecked at the top, but is in the hands of the people who manage the work and are closest to the customer. This is the secret, intangible, and untapped source of competitive advantage. Reconfigurable organizational capabilities—self-managing network structures that are matched to the needs of the customer—will inevitably surpass traditional organizational forms. People who have the power, knowledge, information, and skill to manage these networks will also be the ones who enable fast, flexible decision making. Indeed, *The Self-Managing Organization* may in the long run be the only real sustainable source of competitive advantage.

Stu Winby
Director, Strategic Change Services
Hewlett-Packard
Palo Alto, California

PREFACE

Everything changes, nothing remains without change.
                                        —The Buddha

Over the last decade, we have witnessed many companies struggling to fundamentally change their structures and work processes in order to compete in a turbulent environment. Numerous techniques and approaches—Empowerment, Teams, Total Quality Management (TQM), and Reengineering—were common nostrums executives tried in their search to improve business performance in the global economy. Some companies achieved significant results from these improvement methods, while the benefits derived in many other firms were short-lived. As we watched this trend repeat itself again and again, we began to wonder why such tools, techniques, and methods are often quickly tried and just as quickly relegated to the fad dustbin. We began to question why these contemporary-change-management and continuous-improvement methods fail to truly and fundamentally transform organizations. We became increasingly concerned that employees in thousands of corporations were becoming more cynical about programs that espoused employee participation, teams, empowerment, and the like. We were also sympathetic toward managers who were being forced to reengineer their organizations from the top down, often without their informed consent and approval.

We soon realized that many companies which adopted such methods were caught in the middle between two competing organizational paradigms: the bureaucratic and democratic. In our analysis, these methods failed to transform the DNA, or fundamental design principle, that informs how organizations are structured and managed. The bureaucratic organization design—structured as a machine with its command-and-control hierarchy—was still too firmly entrenched to allow for the complete emergence of flexible, adaptive, self-managing, democratic organizations. Although many change management methods were billed as "radical," we soon discovered that they were simply phenotypical variations from the same gene pool which produced the industrial revolution.

When we understood that these two diametrically opposed traditions for designing and managing organizations were competing for dominance, it became clear to us why managers and employees were often being bombarded by mixed messages and a confusing mishmash of structures, management styles, and techniques. The bureaucratic and democratic design principles are based on different logics; each constitutes a distinct class with a specific genetic order. Our phenotypic choices (i.e., tools, techniques, methods, and structures) are derived from one gene pool (bureaucracy) or the other (self-managing organization). When these logics are mixed together in efforts to shore up the failings of bureaucracy, empowerment and reengineering efforts often fizzle because the basic tenets of a traditional hierarchy have not been uprooted. Until there is a fundamental change in the design principles underlying organizations, executives will keep searching for the next panacea. Like unsuspecting sheep, the consulting wolves will descend upon their paradigm paralysis.

The self-managing organization challenges long-established beliefs and practices about the distribution of power and authority in private enterprises. Indeed, the shift and evolution toward self-management has been a struggle and long in coming. Touted by management consultants and business school academics, the call for a veritable "paradigm shift" has unfortunately become just another cliché. Consultants have tried to arouse managers to action by splattering them with exhortations to embrace a new holy paradigm of organizational redemption, but rarely have they bothered to articulate the principles and practical realities that lie behind it.

This book describes the principles and methods for designing the self-managing organization. We show how companies in any industry can change and evolve to become fully self-managing organizations. We provide a simple but powerful set of tools that can be used at all levels to transform rigid bureaucracies into flexible work systems, using self-managing work groups as the basic building block. We explain in simple language the concepts underlying the Participative Design (PD) and Search Conference methods, and a step-by-step blueprint for immediate application.

We wrote this book primarily for executives, middle managers, and front-line supervisors, each of whom will find these methods to be extremely useful and practical in their efforts to design and implement fundamental change. Professional change agents—external and internal consultants, organization development and training specialists, quality directors, and human resource managers—will also find the concepts and techniques to be helpful and relevant to their practice.

Companies that are well on their way to becoming self-managing organizations—American Express, Charles Schwab, Hewlett-Packard, Lockheed Martin, Microsoft, Motorola, Sequa Chemicals, Sybase, Syncrude—are featured as case studies throughout the book. Most of these companies have used Participative Design and Search Conferences as methods for transforming various parts of their business, and in some cases their entire enterprise, to self-managing organizations. Participative Design and Search Conferences have been applied successfully in a wide variety of industries: petrochemicals, financial services, airlines, food and beverages, professional services, computers, electronics, forest and paper products, health care, hotels, mining, and software companies. In addition, many agencies within the U.S. government have used our methods— the federal circuit courts, the Environmental Protection Agency, and the Department of Agriculture's Forest Service.

On the one hand we are excited and encouraged by the rapid diffusion of these innovative methods to workplaces throughout the world. On the other hand, we recognize that Participative Design and Search Conferences are not the only methods for effecting a transformative change toward self-management. There are other viable methods, and multiple evolutionary paths to the same goal: to relocate responsibility and authority for work in the hands of those who do the work. Rather than staking our claim in a particular method or technique, we believe it is wiser to search for a sound theory and set of core principles for designing the self-managing organization. Much of the confusion and failures in the field stem from the fact that methods and tools for redesigning organizations are often applied with no conscious awareness of the principles behind them. Many methods are shrouded in the rhetoric of organizational transformation, but in practice, these methods tiptoe around the tough issues of changing the hierarchical power structure. Simply mouthing the empowerment doublespeak does nobody any good. Further, many consultants are becoming overly dependent upon their tools and techniques—to the extent that they are unable to adapt them to the situation and needs of each unique company. This trend—a mechanical fixation and dogmatic dependence on technique—

has become a poor substitute for the creative thinking and deep under-standing required for the resolution of complex problems in organizations today.

In our view, theories and principles are a wiser investment, since they are always open to being challenged, tested, refined, and even discarded if they fail to provide a coherent basis for guiding action and informing prac-tice. Such a scientific spirit is necessary if we are to continue to learn how to effect systemic and transformative change toward self-management. The world needs fewer parrots and followers of the latest management guru, and more independent thinkers who can offer fresh insights that challenge the existing order of business. Indeed, when theories become enshrined in a particular method, creativity and innovation cease. We have been led to believe that all business problems could be solved if only we had the right method, tool, or technique. And while this book offers new methods and techniques for designing self-managing organizations, we recognize that an evolution toward ever greater capabilities for self-management must eventually rely on the creativity of people. Certain results can be achieved and kick-started by techniques and methods, but creativity and genuine self-management are not among these.

While we are pleased to have written this book, we realize that self-managing organizations are a new corporate species and there is still so much to learn. We stand on the shoulders of giants like Fred Emery, Eric Trist, Calvin Pava, Bill Pasmore, and Kurt Lewin. We have developed theo-ries, experimented with the methods, and documented how companies have failed and succeeded. All during the process, we listened to the people in the trenches, who taught us a great deal about what works and what doesn't. This action research caused us to reflect on our ideas, and to mod-ify the methods, and each time we keep discovering increasingly subtle dis-tinctions to make self-management more attainable. We now appreciate the myriad paths toward self-management that can occur once a company has internalized the principles and logic described in this book.

We have a request for our readers intent on applying what they have learned. As you use the principles, logic, and perhaps the methods, described in this book, call or write us and let us know what you have learned from your efforts. On the West Coast, Ron Purser can be reached at (415) 338-2380, or e-mail him at rpurser@sfsu.edu. On the East Coast, Steven Cabana can be reached at (978) 466-6884; his e-mail is StevCa-bana@aol.com.

The evolution to more self-managing forms of organization is an exciting and timely development, coemergent with the knowledge work economy. It is our bet that the logic and principles underlying the self-managing organization will likely stand the test of time, but we fully expect the methods and tools congruent with those principles to get stronger and more numerous with reflective application. Every organization will need to find its own path. We want to know what you and other pioneers are doing to create organizations where people can experience dignity, caring, and meaning in work, while at the same time achieving world class quality and performance.

STRUCTURE OF THE BOOK

In this book, we explain and demonstrate how organizations can create social learning contexts—communities of trust—where people can engage in open dialogue to chart the future and redesign their own work. Part One of the book examines the conceptual evolution toward self-managing forms of organizations, and the key principles which underlie this revolutionary paradigm for organizing work. Part Two of the book deals in considerable detail with the methods, tools, and step-by-step techniques for designing and developing self-managing organizations. It is in this section that we present case studies of North American companies that are early adopters of self-managing design principles and practices. The companies featured in the case studies have used Participative Design and Search Conference as methods for leading change and transformation to self-management.

This book, then, focuses on both the theory and practice of self-managing organizations. Unlike many other "bullet point" books that offer simple cookie-cutter approaches, we first provide some conceptual grounding in the design principles that make self-managing organizations work. We also take a critical look at some of the "pseudo-empowerment" approaches and management fads that have caused a great deal of confusion in the field and have impeded efforts at fundamental organizational transformation. One of our intentions in this book is to make the reader become a more informed consumer of management techniques, better able to differentiate fad from substance. To do this, we deal in considerable detail with the concepts and issues of changing the fundamental organization paradigm, or design principle, from one based on a dominant, command-and-control hierarchy to one based on a democratic, self-managing structure.

Chapter 1 argues that conventional management as we have known it for the last century is coming to an end. Textbook descriptions of management as planning, directing, controlling, and organizing the work of others is being replaced by a new, self-managing organization paradigm that allows people to take responsibility for controlling and coordinating their own work.

In Chapter 2, we provide an inside look at a self-managing organization in action at Lockheed Martin's Government Electronic Systems (GES) division. There are many paths to creating self-managing organizations, and this story describes the path Lockheed Martin took to build a world-class organization that has gone on to win many esteemed industry awards. The case provides a concrete description of the issues and processes involved in the design, development, and evolution of a self-managing organization. Chapter 3 evaluates the merits of the Participative Design method, noting its advantages over more expert-oriented methods such as Reengineering and Socio-Technical Systems. This chapter ends with a minicase of how Participative Design was used to facilitate the implementation of SAP R/3 software at CELGARD, L.L.C., a subsidiary of Hoechst Celanese. In Chapter 4, we discuss how the self-managing organization differs from traditional organizations, and how these differences are rooted in a fundamentally different design principle. Then, in Chapter 5, we show how companies that lack conscious knowledge of design principles often get stuck in the middle between two opposing paradigms of organization.

In Chapter 6, we discuss why a new process for strategy creation is needed, one that involves hundreds, if not thousands of new voices from the organization in strategic conversations using the Search Conference methodology. This chapter features a case study and step-by-step illustration of how Motorola's wireless minichip business unit used the Search Conference to create and implement a global product strategy with its technical professionals around the globe. We continue along those lines in Chapter 7 by showing how Microsoft and Charles Schwab used the Search Conference as a participative engine for rapid strategy creation.

In Chapter 8, we present and explain the critical steps in the Participative Design process, from the preparation required for getting senior management on board, all the way to running Participative Design sessions. That leads directly to the real-life issues and challenges involved in changing a whole enterprise to self-management, which we address in Chapters 9 and 10. In Chapter 9, we describe how Sequa Chemicals used both Participative Design and Search Conferences to stimulate innovation and growth by creating a self-managing workforce. In Chapter 10, we examine and analyze how Syncrude Canada used these same methods with over 3,500 employees, redesigning a large and complex enterprise to become self-managing. Chapter 11 discusses how the role of management must change in self-managing organizations, and explains the importance that each level plays in a self-managing enterprise. The Epilogue concludes the book by speculating on the future of democracy at work in the twenty-first century.

ACKNOWLEDGMENTS

Some meetings are fateful encounters that by happenstance can change the course of one's life and career. The authors experienced several meetings of this auspicious nature, triggering a series of events that led to this book. The first such meeting occurred in June 1991, when Ron Purser met with the late Eric Trist at his home in Gainesville, Florida. For those that do not know him, Trist was an unassuming man, who is credited with having discovered self-managing work teams and the principles behind them in the early 1950s. His seminal work led to the development of a whole new field and action research discipline within management science and organizational behavior, known as the Socio-Technical System (STS) approach to organization design.

At our Gainesville meeting, we were surprised to see that Trist was dismayed that his work had not resulted in the timely diffusion of self-managing organizations on the scale that he had hoped to see in his lifetime. Our meeting was also of significance because Trist was helping us to plan for a gathering to be held in San Francisco later that year among concerned consultants, academics, line managers, and unionists who wanted to take the discipline of redesigning high-performance organizations to a new level. We had hoped this round-table gathering would lead to a fruitful dialogue between practitioners and socially engaged social scientists on how existing change methods could be improved to help organizations cope with future challenges. The outcomes of our efforts, we hoped, would lead to new ideas, new collaborations, and new possibilities for moving the field of organization design into the twenty-first century. Unfortunately, Trist became ill and could not be present for the round-table gathering which was also to be held in his honor. He passed away in June 1993.

During the round-table meeting in San Francisco, Ron Purser had the opportunity to meet Fred and Merrelyn Emery, who had flown from their home in Australia without advance notice to participate in this event. Fred Emery was Trist's longtime intellectual partner, dating back to their joint work at the Tavistock Institute in London in the 1950s. The Tavistock Institute was a unique center that coupled social science research with action-based field work to solve organizational problems. Because they were a dynamic intellectual duo, their productive collaboration over the years produced a series of seminal works in Socio-Technical Systems theory, industrial democracy, and the changing social ecology of organizations. As a senior staff member at Tavistock, Emery did groundbreaking work, developing the key concepts of Socio-Technical Systems design. From 1962 to 1969, Emery worked with Einar Thorsrud on the Norwegian Industrial Democracy Project, a national program geared toward increasing employee participation in decision making to improve the quality of work life and industrial productivity. It was during this period of experimentation that Emery achieved many practical and theoretical advances in Socio-Technical Systems methods. By 1970, Emery had moved back to Australia, where he worked with the Australian Royal Air Force and ICI using the Participative Design methodology, a faster and more democratic approach to Socio-Technical Systems design. Emery was an internationally renowned systems scientist, making the rounds as a visiting scholar at the Center for Advanced Studies in Palo Alto, and as a visiting professor at Wharton's Department of Social Systems Sciences. A prolific writer, Emery authored hundreds of articles and dozens of books dealing with organization design, Socio-Technical Systems, semi-autonomous work groups, industrial democracy, economics and society, creativity, social ecology, long-range planning, and systems theory. Fred Emery was to have written an Epilogue for this book, but he unfortunately passed away in April 1997.

The chance meeting with the Emerys in San Francisco was a godsend. Our collaboration with Fred and Merrelyn Emery over the years has been instrumental in understanding the fundamental theory behind the self-managing organization, and the democratic ideals that drive the quest for more humane and productive organizations. Since 1991, we have continued to test, adapt, and refine the conceptual and practical contributions of the Emerys. Ron Purser and Merrelyn Emery began introducing North America to these innovative methods for democratizing work when they coauthored *The Search Conference* (Jossey-Bass, 1996), a book that enjoyed wide acceptance among organization development practitioners, academics, and management consultants. Steve Cabana began disseminating the practical utility of the Participative Design method to a North American managerial audience by publishing articles in a number of practitioner-based outlets, including the *Journal for Quality and Participation*, and the trade journal for the Association for Manufacturing Excellence, *Target*. It was during this time that it became apparent to us that a more contemporary and practical book which described the concepts, tools, and methods for designing self-managing organizations was needed for a wider managerial audience.

After the San Francisco round-table meeting, late one night in a bar Ron also met with Calvin Pava, a Harvard Business School professor who had been Trist's student at Wharton. At that time, Pava was the leading thinker in the field on redesigning knowledge work organizations, having published a watershed book, *Managing New Office Technology* (The Free Press, 1983). At that time, Pava was in remission from brain cancer. Pava had a laser-like intensity about him. He felt that the future success and growth of knowledge-based organizations depended on managing deliberations—the way people come together to create, share, and utilize knowledge. Bureaucratic organizations—built on the premise of fixed formal offices, where authority is based on one's position in a hierarchy—were antithetical to effective knowledge creation and knowledge utilization. Self-managing forms of organization would be needed to tap the creativity and talents of professional knowledge workers. Pava's remission from brain cancer didn't last; he also passed away shortly after the San Francisco meeting.

Three of our mentors—Eric Trist, Fred Emery, and Cal Pava—are now gone. In many ways, the San Francisco round-table meeting was an intellectual initiation, a peak professional experience that planted the seeds for this book. We are especially grateful to Merrelyn Emery, who has been a close friend and mentor, and who has profoundly shaped our thinking and practice on designing self-managing organizations through Participative Design. She has generously allowed us to build on her work. Indeed, the Participative Design and Search Conference methodology—the conerstone methods for designing the self-managing organization—come directly from Merrelyn. Without her help, support, and criticism, the ideas here would never have made it into print. She deserves full and total credit for her crusading efforts to diffuse these innovative methods all over the world.

We want to make it very clear that this book is a product of many creative and professional collaborations. Many of the chapters, concepts, and cases would never have materialized if it were not for the friends and colleagues who have contributed directly to our efforts. Many of the case studies in this book of the leading-edge companies that are on the forefront of designing self-managing organizations are the result of their commitments.

We would first like to thank John Duncan, who is, in our opinion, one of the most competent consultants around on using the methods that are described in this book. John gave so much of his time and energy in helping us get access to Sequa Chemicals, which appears as a case study in this book. Because John was the principal consultant for Sequa Chemicals and other companies that have adopted the methods in this book, his expertise was an invaluable resource. John went out of his way to make himself available for us, serving as a constant critic and advisor to the project. In this regard, we would like to also thank Jack Cabrey, president of Sequa Chemicals, for allowing us full and unfettered access to Sequa's operations. Cabrey has been an enthusiastic supporter and advocate for our ideas, and has collaborated with us in making numerous presentations at professional conferences. We also would like to extend our thanks to Wes Reid, Glen Pellet, Jim Craig, Michele Kesler, and all the enthusiastic and thoughtful people we came in contact with at Sequa.

The largest organizational transformation effort to date that we are aware of in North America—one where a whole enterprise has engaged its entire workforce in Participative Design—is at Syncrude, Ltd., Canada's second largest oil company, located in northern Alberta. The mastermind and leader of that enterprise-wide redesign effort is Don de Guerre, Director of Organizational Effectiveness. Don paved the way for us to visit with workers and managers at the Syncrude facility, and has been a close and supportive colleague. Don provided us countless hours of support throughout the project. His exceptional staff of internal consultants—Mike Noon, Debbie Kalinin, Sam Salter—were also instrumental in our efforts. We would also like to thank all of the managers at Syncrude who were willing to share their time and thoughts with us. The honest dialogues we had with cross-sections of the workforce, and the extraordinary willingness of all the work teams to share both their positive and negative experiences with us strengthened our account of Syncrude's large-scale change process. We are particularly grateful to Mike Rogers for his many lengthy phone conversations, which gave us useful insights into understanding middle management's role in self-managed work settings.

We are indebted to the people at Lockheed Martin's Government Electronic Systems (GES) division for being so generous with their time. In particular, we would like to thank Jack Irving, Vice President of Production and Life Cycle Programs, Carmen Valentino, Director of AEGIS Programs, and Charlie Louie, Director of Quality and Mission Success, who shepherded our visit and briefed us on their evolution toward self-management. John Shelton was our liaison to the company and was instrumental in organizing our site visit. Rob McClusky, a national Baldrige Award examiner, and Stu Noble, an independent consultant, assisted us on the site visit to Lockheed Martin's GES division. We appreciate their perspectives and insights, which helped shape the second chapter of the book.

We are very grateful to Janet Fiero, who was the principal consultant on the Motorola project. Janet is a highly skilled practitioner of the methods described in this book. We have benefited from her insights and experience. We express our sincere gratitude to Cynthia Scott, a principal consultant at ChangeWorks in San Francisco, who generously provided the case material on Charles Schwab. Cynthia and her collaborator, Steve Rosell, managed and facilitated a strategic search conference for Charles Schwab's Information Technology organization. Over many extended dinners at some of San Francisco's best restaurants, Steve provided us valuable feedback on our early drafts, which was instrumental to improving the clarity of our ideas. In addition, special thanks is in order for Dennis Jaffe, our friend and colleague, who also provided helpful comments, and who kept egging us on to finish the book. We also owe a very special debt to our friend and colleague for many years, Bob Rehm. Bob agreed to serve as a collaborator with us on this book, and his feedback and comments on the manuscript were invaluable. During the course of many revisions, he gave us helpful suggestions and advice for shaping the presentation of our arguments. Bob is perhaps the first consultant to begin using Search Conferences and Participative Design methods with North American companies. He has been a constant source of support.

The ideas on social creativity and jazz are really the result of our collaboration with Alfonso Montuori over these last seven years. Monty, as we call him, has been our constant cheerleader, and has helped us articulate our ideas on social creativity as they apply to knowledge workers. We are also grateful to Craig McGee, who allowed us to retell his story about his consulting work with Sybase that is based on the methods in this book.

Special thanks go to Patricia Moody, editor of *Target*, who provided us useful insights and criticism. We would also like to extend our thanks to numerous people who encouraged us along the way as the manuscript evolved—Billy Alban, Mike Albert, Rossana Alvarez, Peter Aughton, Michael Beyerlein, Richard Castaldi, Nancy Cebula, Kristin Cobble, Kathy Dannemiller, Alan Davies, Stan Day, Joel Diemer, Bunny Duhl, Ed Ericson, Nick Gurney, Bob Hall, Ned Hamson, Frank Harrison, David Hurst, Homer Johnson, Paul Judy, Jon Katzenbach, Gary Kissler, Stan Kowalczyk, Joseph Macchiarulo, Charles Parry, Bill Pasmore, Monique Pelletier, Tom Petzinger, George Roth, Vilma Ruddock, Edgar Schein, Peter Senge, John Shibley, Peter Sorensen, John Spencer, Gil Steil, Steven Wheelwright, Steven Williamson, and Yim Yu Wong.

We owe a great deal to our editor, Robert Wallace, who has been very patient with us as the structure, outline, and content of the book kept changing and evolving over the last two years. We also want to acknowledge Jeanne Glasser, at John Wiley and Sons, and Nikki Foster and Nan Stone, at the Harvard Business School Press. Their avid interest in the book proposal and initial suggestions inspired us to push the limits of our thinking to create a more readable work. Obviously we had to choose one publisher.

Finally, we reserve our greatest debt to our families, whose support and patience helped to see us through the ups and downs of a long and lonely book project. At the same time that Ron was beginning to work on the book, his son Pauli was born. Not enough thanks can be expressed to Fay Purser, for tolerating and putting up with the near-monastic lifestyle of her husband. Steve would like to especially thank his parents, Edmond and Vanda Cabana, who taught him about integrity and doing work that is a service to fellow human beings.

Ronald E. Purser
Steven Cabana
San Francisco
Boston
June 1998

PART

ONE

CHAPTER 1

THE END OF MANAGEMENT AND THE RISE OF THE SELF MANAGING ORGANIZATION

What we call the beginning is often the end. And to
make an end is to make a beginning. The end is where
we start from.

—T. S. Eliot

Management is coming to an end. We might liken the end of management
to the fall of communism. When institutions get out of synch with the
movement of history, they go into decline—whether they are national governments or private enterprises. We believe that conventional management
will be the next domino to fall.

Conventionally, management has been focused on planning, organizing, directing, coordinating, and controlling human efforts. Managers
were seen as the exclusive stewards of the business, occupying a distinct
social role and fixed position in a bureaucratic hierarchy. For many years
managers were internally focused, absorbed in operational details, controlling and coordinating the work of their subordinates and dealing with
office politics. Management was sucked into acting as a troubleshooter and
firefighter for the level below. This all just seemed like the natural order of
things. And from such a perspective, it didn't make sense to question what
seemed to be well-established dogma. Management meant controlling the
work of other people. Over the course of this century, management had
established its own interests, and to question this was to risk deconstruct-
ing what had been carefully constructed.

Yet as the foundation of bureaucracy started to crack, the frailties of
the traditional management approach became more and more apparent.
No matter how dedicated internally focused managers were, their interme-

diary role did not directly contribute to output or add value to customers. Managers were fixated on control, order, and prediction, but they themselves did not produce anything real or useful. Like a cancer, management spread as it became associated with the external supervision of internal work processes. Layers upon layers of management were added, and a costly support staff proliferated, making organizations into bureaucratic labyrinths. As organizations became more complex, this justified the call for more managers, more supervisors, and more administrators to wade through the maze and barrage of paperwork, memoranda, endless sign-offs, and bureaucratic approvals.

Excess management put a stranglehold on the real producers—the people who actually produce a product or provide a value-added service. Most jobs in manufacturing and service industries were narrowly designed and subject to close supervision. In the absence of intrinsically motivating and interesting work, employee alienation led to a loss of commitment. Symptoms of employee alienation showed up in high turnover, absenteeism, labor disputes, poor product quality, and increased downtime—all of which added to the costs of production. In short, tall hierarchies, a control-oriented management, and poor work design resulted in an unresponsive, self-serving bureaucratic monster. Management, as we have known it in this sense, is coming to an end.

SELF-MANAGEMENT AND THE KNOWLEDGE REVOLUTION

The knowledge revolution is making conventional management obsolete. The unprecedented and rapid advancements in information technology, telecommunications, and artificial intelligence are transforming both the context and content of work. Organizations on the leading edge of this change are creating network-like virtual organizations that undermine our whole notion of conventional managerial roles in a bureaucratic hierarchy. Intranets, electronic spreadsheets, groupware, and teleconferencing are obliterating Max Weber's "files" and offices—the raw materials of a bureaucracy.

Clearly, the magnitude of this transformation is pervasive. Despite the continual decline and exodus of heavy U.S. manufacturing, innovations in technology and knowledge-based products have brought about the transition to a white-collar professional and service economy, which now accounts for 75 percent of private employment. Although the growth of the service sector, along with the concomitant emergence of the "knowledge worker," is as dramatic a change as was the disappearance of farm hands and the replacement of agrarian work with that of mass assembly-line production, productivity in the white-collar sector has remained relatively flat. This is why the principles and practices of self-management increasingly make sense if organizations are to tap the creative talents of their knowledge workers. Indeed, quality and productivity improvements in knowledge-based work will not be derived solely from installations of new technology, but will require substantial changes in business processes and organizational arrangements.

The environmental conditions that once made a traditional command-and-control hierarchy viable are rapidly decreasing. Under conditions of rising uncertainty, bureaucratic organizations simply do not have the requisite learning and information processing capacity to cope with the accelerating rate of technological and social change. Turbulence has forced organizations to develop or strengthen their ability to scan the environment and respond to it through the acquisition, development, and application of knowledge (Purser and Pasmore, 1992). In fact, organizations must now devote a more significant proportion of their resources to apprehending, thinking, learning, and innovating—the basic elements of knowledge work. Put more simply, the changes we are experiencing are causing organizations to employ more people who think for a living rather than simply following directions.

Further, the infusion of new information technology into corporations is eliminating the need for redundant managerial positions whose only purpose is to collect and process information, relay messages up and down the hierarchy, monitor performance, and measure results. Traditional status and power relationships that are the cornerstones of a dominant hierarchy are being shattered by new information technology that can break down barriers between levels and functions. Secrecy is the enemy of trust, and new technology makes it possible to share greater amounts of information with the workforce. Rather than expropriating information from workers so that it can be utilized and controlled by management (the stuff that Taylorism is made of), new technology is being used to democratize work. When shop-floor operators and front-line employees can access information about their performance instantaneously, what need is there for a human intermediary whose only task is to collect and disseminate information to others? The knowledge revolution has the potential of turning every employee into a "self-manager."

Moreover, as work centered around production processes continues to shift to work that is dependent upon employees to generate knowledge, as well as to deliver products and services fast, reliably, and at the lowest possible cost, organizations require highly committed and well-educated employees. Organizations can no longer survive if their workforce is alienated, poorly trained, and unresponsive to the shifting demands of the marketplace. Perhaps most importantly, hierarchies based on personal superiority—that is, organizations that align authority with position—are becoming increasingly ill suited to knowledge-intensive companies. These types of organizations—high-technology companies, software houses, professional service firms, and science-based industries—must rely on the creativity and commitment of knowledge workers who are specialists or professionals in their fields. Knowledge workers are more autonomous, more specialized, and are quite capable of controlling and coordinating their own work. Conventional "command-and-control" management is a kiss of death in knowledge-based firms, as knowledge workers place a high value on their autonomy and freedom to make their own decisions. However, in most traditional organizations, authority of position overshadows expertise in decision making. Conventional management often decides, unilaterally, what knowledge will be used and how. Experts who have the most relevant knowledge are frequently excluded from discussions where key strategic decisions are made.

We are quite certain that if companies are going to improve their knowledge development capabilities, it will require a fundamentally different set of social dynamics and structural logic for designing organizations. Indeed, if the primary goal is to improve the development and application of useful knowledge—to unleash human intelligence to serve customers— then the self-managing organization seems to be a logical and rational choice for managers in the twenty-first century. But the inertia of the old paradigm is still with us. For almost a century, bureaucratic organizations limped along under the protection of stable domestic markets. Under these conditions, it was possible to tolerate such dynamics as hoarding knowledge for political gain; secrecy; one-upmanship; conflict among functions or departments; the exercise of power in decision making unrelated to knowledge or expertise; a lack of cooperative behavior; and a reluctance to change practices or procedures. Rather than improving competitiveness and enhancing the competencies of the firm, a great deal of time and energy is often wasted on these debilitating distractions. Most organizations nowadays cannot afford such distractions; they must focus their attention in more productive and fruitful ways.

Companies that must compete in a rapidly changing and unpredictable environment, especially if they rely on knowledge workers, can derive great benefits by focusing their design efforts in the direction of greater self-management. We are witnessing a conscious evolution to a new, more adaptive form of corporate species—the self-managing organization. This trend is clearly the wave of the future. The question is: will companies wake up in time to ride the crest of the wave, rather than being left behind in its wake?

THE SELF-MANAGING ORGANIZATION

Based on a new design principle, the self-managing organization eradicates the need for external supervision and costly bureaucratic overhead. A self-managing organization places the control of the work process in the hands of the people who actually touch a product or provide the service. People can control their own work, participating directly in decisions that affect the outcomes of their unit. Self-managing organizations by design prevent persons from centralizing authority or embedding power in fixed roles, allowing the organization to remain flexible and adaptive to changing circumstances.

Self-management, then, implies more than simply a cosmetic change in management style that leaves asymmetrical power arrangements intact. Self-managing organizations redistribute the power to make decisions to people who have the strategic knowhow, or to groups who are responsible for a whole work process. Under such new arrangements, the traditional tasks of management—planning, controlling, organizing, and coordinating the work of others—no longer makes sense. Rather, it is management's responsibility to create the conditions that allow people to plan, control, organize, and coordinate their own work. This is a big paradigm shift.

But the paradigm shift has been underway for some time now. *Fortune* magazine's 1998 assessment of the 100 best companies to work for in America found that many companies have been moving toward the self-management paradigm. For example, at the company at the top of their list—Southwest Airlines—employees are treated with utmost respect, are paid well, and their ideas are used to solve problems on a regular basis. Similarly, *Wall Street Journal* columnist Tom Petzinger's (1997) annual forecast of business strategies found that the key emerging trend was toward restructuring organizations toward self-management. Leading-edge companies are finding ways to tap the contributions of their employees through self-managing work systems, freeing talented knowledge workers from the bastions of central planning and autocratic control. Petzinger says the dominant theme in the hundreds of interviews he conducted and the thousands of e-mails he has received is the need to rethink our antiquated definitions of management and the way we structure work.

At W. L. Gore, the manufactuer of Gore-Tex fabrics and many other high-tech materials, the traditional hierarchy has been replaced by a broad-based system of empowerment which is unique and unduplicated elsewhere. Consider the way it operates: There are no fixed positions of formal authority (people have sponsors, not bosses), lines of communication are direct, objectives are set by those who make them happen, teams are formed when the need arises, tasks and functions are organized through commitments, not compliance.

At Synovus Financial in Columbus, Georgia, we find a bank where people actually enjoy working because they are able to learn, grow, and have fun. At one of the most profitable enterprises, the major Wall Street investment firm Goldman Sachs, in New York, employees perceive that their teamwork is better than on most professional sports teams. The Whole Foods supermarket chain in Austin, Texas, was recently featured in a PBS special as having an empowered workforce which caps CEO compensation at 10 times the average that team members are paid. As we go through the list of *Fortune*'s 100 best companies to work for in America, we find over thirty that have been working with the principles behind self-management for many years.

And we can see why. Self-management can rev up the workforce and boost performance. Meet the workers at CIG Gas Cylinders in Sydney, Australia, a unionized facility where technicians work without bosses breathing down their necks. Technicians at CIG have even started taking on tasks that were once reserved for top-level management. For example, technicians interviewed candidates for the general manager of a business that will turn over $43 million this year. After the interviews they came to the conclusion that they really didn't need to fill the general-manager position—they would do the job themselves! John Buis, the only remaining manager at CIG Gas Cylinders, supported the technicians but admitted that such autonomy depends on the maturity of the people and teams. "The decision is not irreversible," says Buis. "But the role of management in this business is in promoting change, business development, and improvement."

The technicians designed a new structure that would redistribute the work of the traditional general manager's role to themselves and the professional support staff. "We are saying we are going to self-managing teams that are accountable for what they do," says technician Larry Smith. "If we hire a general manager we would be being hypocritical." CIG has been on the journey toward self-management for over a decade. CIG's teams have received training, equivalent in some years to 10 percent of total payroll costs, to allow them to take on greater responsibilities from their immediate managers gradually.

"We have just watched our people blossom," says Buis. CIG Gas Cylinders has seen productivity rise by more than 240 percent, and the benefits are shared under a gain-sharing scheme. As the result of significant productivity improvements, technicians have been able to earn monthly bonuses of up to 20 percent of their pay. The number of gas cylinders produced per man-hour worked has nearly tripled, from 0.6 to 1.7. Rising productivity and quality have allowed CIG to break into the Japanese market for high-pressure aluminum gas cylinders for beer and soft-drink dispensing.

Self-management, however, isn't just for the operatives. Self-managing organizations also liberate senior and middle-level managers from their enslavement to internal administrative tasks. Management's role dramatically shifts to lead the search for value creation, facilitating processes that can improve the organization's capability to detect, create, and satisfy customer needs. Managers become strategic architects who focus their attention on building organizational capabilities that can foster continuous growth and innovation.

For example, Harley-Davidson Chairman Richard F. Teerlink is moving the company toward self-management and decentralizing decision making at the strategic level of the business. The leadership role has been dispersed throughout the top and middle of the enterprise with an innovative management structure consisting of three circles that meet in the middle. (They nominate a rotating leadership council to mediate issues not settled by consensus in circle meetings.) Numerous functions, such as business development, customer service, and marketing, comprise the "create demand" circle-team. Engineering, powertrain operations, purchasing, and logistics are part of the "produce product" circle-team. Finance, human resources, legal, information systems, and other staff groups are now all located together in a "provide support" circle-team. Within each circle-team, leadership moves from person to person, depending on the issue at hand. These collaborative, interdependent teams may not move as fast as individuals, but they are proving the worth of self-management at the strategic level of the business by being more innovative and resourceful.

MICROSOFT: A SELF-MANAGING ORGANIZATION IN ACTION

"Hiring smart people who can learn on the job," says Doug McKenna, head of Human Resources Planning, is one of the key ingredients that makes self-management work at Microsoft. "We give new people tasks as broad as they can handle, and let them work alongside mentors that can guide them through the informal networks," he points out. Once people are working as members of a project team, they learn to make their own decisions regarding such things as setting their performance objectives, defining the scope of their jobs, hiring new people, and training the people they hire.

Bill Gates and his twelve or so senior executives, top developers, and managers run the critical product areas, seek out new initiatives, and oversee what everyone else is doing. Gates focuses much of his attention on exploring possibilities for strategic new products in high-growth areas and ideas for new versions of existing products. With the help of his brain trust, Gates keeps a strategic eye on the entire product line to make sure that it is aligned with the vision, he reflects on his competitors' moves, and considers the business-versus-technology tradeoffs. Microsoft's managers know their technology and markets and use that expertise to decide when to enter new markets, replace obsolete technology, or shift their competitive focus.

The way management decisions get made in Microsoft is by putting expertise where it can have the most impact. Bill Gates has this to say about decision making in his company:

> There's no one path at Microsoft. We have a very flat organization. Sometimes ideas flow down, sometimes they flow up, or horizontally. Usually someone will get an idea or identify a problem and send e-mail to someone else. That may kick off a swat team to deal with it. At some point the decision gets made face-to-face or over e-mail. On strategic decisions, it may go up to a senior VP or to me. By and large we empower people to make decisions themselves. I try to identify major decisions and work with my staff to make sure they are focused on them. (From "A Conversation with Bill Gates," *Information Outlook* 1:5 (May 1997), p. 23.)

Because Microsoft's survival and market success depend on new products, product development is central to everything it does. Microsoft is really a collection of small development centers with approximately three or four hundred people in a typical product-development group. These product groups are intensely competitive in the marketplace because responsibility and authority are pushed into small multifunctional teams that work as part of larger project teams. This approach keeps turf battles, detailed procedures, unnecessary documents, or formalized hierarchical modes of communication out of the picture.

Each development center has software development, testing, specification, user education, and product-planning expertise. Projects are subdivided into feature and component teams. These small multifunctional teams have overlapping responsibilities to avoid functional animosity and political gamesmanship. At the same time, strong functional skills are maintained by having pay scales based on the levels of technical competency that a knowledge worker attains. When developers, program managers, and testers work side-by-side they can effectively coordinate and synchronize the development of their components and incrementally evolve product features to target specific user activities.

Gates believes that when managers begin to believe that their responsibility is to control the work of subordinates, they quickly lose sight of real problems and issues. For this reason the company places authority and responsibility in the hands of the people who demonstrate the most competence. For example, the team leader in a small development group still writes code. They must have higher code writing skills than the rest of their team so they can be free to act as a dispatcher and troubleshooter. The technical leader on a development project is expected to have the most comprehensive understanding of how the product works.

If Microsoft had faith in bureaucracy, it would give a lot of authority and responsibility to its managers, who would closely direct people's work in the project teams. Instead, product development teams at Microsoft and the individuals on them are free to alter specifications and designs. Groups of teams coordinate their work across a project with daily builds, continuous testing of critical interdependencies, and intermediate milestone deadlines.

Autonomous teams at Microsoft are much clearer about their own goals than a traditional manager ever could be. They act much more quickly and with highly flexible behavior to incrementally evolve features targeting what customers actually do with their computers. Microsoft's management practices are not perfect. For example, there aren't enough middle managers. While every middle manager has strong technical skills and understands how to help Microsoft make money, many have weak management skills. Until recently, technical competencies have received a lot of emphasis and people skills have not. But middle managers are given roles where their knowledge is aligned with their authority and their expertise is put where it belongs.

Program managers, for example, act as coordinators, not bosses. They oversee an entire product-development process making sure developers (who write the code), product managers (who oversee marketing and sales), testers (who fix bugs in the code), customer support engineers (who keep tabs on users' problems, needs, and priorities), and senior executives (who point them toward the opportunities) keep talking with each other. Program managers see to it that the features users want are shipped in the product, and they ensure the product hits the market with optimal timing.

The product-management role is also democratized. Product managers handle the marketing and sales process. These managers oversee a software product and are empowered to run it like an independent business. Their organizations have the resources and freedom they need to recognize and pursue market opportunities. They operate independently and check in with higher-ups occasionally to ensure that they are fighting for the good of the whole enterprise. These are the people who led the rapid strategy-creation process at Microsoft, which is featured in Chapter 7.

In a bureaucratic organization, middle managers rarely meet with their peers to learn from each other and share information across business-unit boundaries. At Microsoft, test managers from Word, Excel, and Project will meet over lunch with their colleagues to discuss common concerns. Education managers from different product groups will sit down with their peers and talk about their products, technological developments, and human-resource concerns. We have seen that Microsoft has the ability to move people around, reorganizing or adding groups as technology and markets shift. These changes occur in a contentious intellectual atmosphere where people have emotionally intense dialogue until they get right down to the heart of an issue. Gates values frequent communication, openness about errors or slips in schedules, constructive criticism, and learning how to do things better. Microsoft's people act quickly on issues they feel are important.This kind of openness to sound ideas helps keep the company flexible and responsive to sudden changes.

But what about organizations in entirely different industries? Can a more mature business, with people who are true believers in command-and-control, learn how to democratize the way it manages itself as parts of Microsoft have done? What does a business have to do to make it possible for self-management to succeed over time? How does a traditional management hierarchy escape from the turf battles and narrow mindsets to create strategic leadership throughout the enterprise?

DESIGNING ORGANIZATIONS FOR SELF-MANAGEMENT

A key feature of all self-managing organizations is an underlying *design principle,* which requires restructuring work so that responsibility for control and coordination is located at the level where the work is actually done. In self-managing organizations, teams are responsible for controlling and coordinating their own work process and are held accountable for results. For example, at GE Canada's Pooled Financial Services, the End User Support team now does many of the tasks that were traditionally reserved for management. The team does its own hiring, budgeting, expense-tracking, buying decisions, and performance reviews. And at the strategic level, as the Harley-Davidson example illustrates, self-management entails defining the roles and responsibilities of each management circle and ensuring effective coordination across functional boundaries to achieve strategic objectives. For Harley-Davidson's senior managers, this means coming together to think systematically about strategic issues, coordinating efforts across functional boundaries, and leading change throughout the organization.

This basic insight—that work can be controlled and coordinated by self-managing groups—is the radical paradigm shift that Fred Emery initiated with his pioneering action research that took place in the fifties and sixties. Self-managing organizations are dynamic and capable of continuous organizational learning and self-renewal because of several essential design features:

- employees have knowledge, information, and skills to make all decisions that concern them;
- authority and responsibility for control and coordination are located as close as possible to the people actually in contact with the work process or customers;
- authority is based on expertise and competence, not hierarchical position or status;
- management and leadership are shared functions widely distributed across levels and departments;
- access to information and feedback is instantaneous and transparent;
- support systems are congruent and synergistic with the requirements of self-managing work structures;
- the role of management is redesigned to focus on value creation for key stakeholders—customers, shareholders, and employees.

COMPLEX ADAPTIVE SYSTEMS

Self-managing organizations are a new paradigm for organizing work. They display all the properties and features of what scientists call "complex adaptive systems." Some of the most successful complex adaptive systems can be found in nature—such as tropical rain forests, ant colonies, and the human brain. A common feature of all these systems is that they do not rely on centralized structures of control or a hierarchy of supervision. In other words, in complex adaptive systems, there is no single agent that issues commands or directives for organizing. Rather, what we see are self-managing structures where the functions and capabilities of each agent or part are extended—what Fred Emery refers to as "redundancy of functions." This design principle increases the capacity and range of functions that each part can perform. Complex adaptive systems are capable of a high degree of cooperative behavior, where self-managing groups of agents can produce higher-order behaviors that no single agent could accomplish on its own. Our human brain is organized this way. Millions of neurons are self-organizing, clustering in particular regions of the brain to control such complex functions as language, visual perception, and motor coordination.

Biologists are now arguing that redundancies in nature play a major evolutionary role. Redundant functions have a "variety-increasing" effect on the organism's potential for responding adaptively to environmental demands. In examining the history of organs, the noted paleontologist Stephen Jay Gould points out that ". . . evolution is a messy process brimming with redundancy. An organ might be molded by natural selection for advantages in one role, but anything complex has a range of other potential uses by virtue of inherited structure. . . . Any vital function restricted to one organ gives a lineage little prospect for long-term evolutionary persistence; redundancy itself should possess an enormous advantage" (Gould, 1993). Gould also discusses the possibility that apparently useless molecules in DNA may in fact be crucial redundancies that enable genes to evolve. At the level of biological systems, building redundancy into the parts creates a superior evolutionary advantage.

Similarly, self-managing organizations have a superior competitive advantage because they build redundancy by extending the skills and functions of their people and by relocating responsibility for the control and coordination of work to the level at which the work is actually performed. This design principle is the underlying DNA of self-managing organizations. Does management simply go away in self-managing organizations? No, of course not. The function of management doesn't disappear. Rather, *management as a function* is absorbed into self-managing work teams which have direct responsibility for achieving measurable results. In self-managing organizations, teams are responsible for controlling and coordinating their own work process and are held accountable for results.

Effective adaptation to turbulence requires deep, systemic, and whole-systems change—a fundamental shift to a self-managing organization design. Consider the fundamental changes made by SEI Investments in Oaks, Pennsylvania, when they decided to flatten the hierarchy and become more team oriented. The company formed customer-support teams, asking employees to participate in groups formed for a few days, weeks, or months as customer needs arose. SEI redesigned its office space into light-filled open floors (no more cubicles, no more secretaries), and put desks—loaded with technology—on wheels. They designed their own software so a paperless office could be created and data would get to you when your team rearranges itself to deal with the next critical set of customer relationships. Unfortunately, SEI is more the exception than the rule.

BEYOND TEAMS, REENGINEERING, AND TQM

There has been a major wave of activity to redesign organizations for improving productivity, quality, and organizational effectiveness. Business process reengineering (BPR), total quality management (TQM), and self-directed work teams are some of the more recent approaches that have been tried by thousands of companies. While these techniques have been immensely popular, there is a growing recognition that such methods often fail to deliver on their promise. According to a survey conducted by *Fortune* magazine, 70 percent of change efforts fail. We have observed a number of problems and shortcomings associated with current expert-driven change management approaches:

- Long, drawn-out enterprise-wide projects in pursuit of "the one best design" often lose energy, momentum, and relevance in a fast-changing business environment.
- Rehashing of competitor ideas (a.k.a. "industry best practices") and benchmarking often amounts to little more than imitation and copy-cat behavior, where companies attempt to transplant "best practices" out of context. However, real competitive advantage comes from creating capabilities that can't be copied easily, practices that are embedded within, and grow out of the uniqueness of, a company's corporate culture. This requires creativity, not more of the same "me too" thinking.
- Many change efforts to "transform the organization" focus their attention on the middle and lower levels of the company, often ignoring the

importance of executive involvement and support. In addition, senior management often consider themselves exempt from and "above" the need to transform their own roles and behaviors. This elitism and aloofness is the number one cause of transformational-effort failures.

- Many consulting firms that specialize in reengineering focus almost exclusively on implementing new technology or redesigning the work process, which may achieve nothing more than incremental benefits, despite the hype. Further, cutting costs through reengineering doesn't build an organizational capability for growth and innovation.

Now let's look at some of the more specific problems associated with some of these recent techniques.

The Problems of Teams. Over the last decade, corporations experimented with the "team concept" in droves. Katzenbach and Smith's (1994) best-selling Harvard Business School Press book, *The Wisdom of Teams*, attests to the popularity of teams in the workplace. Further, the widespread adoption of Total Quality Management (TQM) in the United States opened the doors to more team-based work arrangements. A KPMG Peat Marwick study found that among organizations with more than five years of experience with TQM, almost 50 percent were utilizing work teams. More and more, organizations are shifting to team-based structures.

Despite this growing trend, many organizations are struggling with the process of implementing team-based designs. In a 1994 *Fortune* article entitled "The Trouble with Teams," Brian Dumaine points out that only 10 percent of workers in Fortune 500 companies are in self-managing teams and that such teams are more of a hassle than their fans let on. "When teams are introduced as an isolated practice, they fail. My gut feeling is most are introduced in isolation. The very thing that often gives rise to teams—reengineering—often has a devastating impact on team spirit. And time and time again teams fall short on their promise because companies don't know how to make them work together with other teams."

The Reengineering Emperor Has No Clothes. The painful cries of the downsized, right-sized, and reengineered indicate that the human side of change has been short shrifted. Something has gone awry. After lots of data gathering and consultation by reengineering experts, a new blueprint for change is imposed on the organization. Employees affected by proposed organizational changes are not directly involved in the reengineering process. They may be consulted, they may fill out surveys, and their input may be solicited, but employees are not directly in control of the effort. Change is done *to* them rather than *with* them. Partial results may be achieved in this manner, but usually such heavy-handed approaches trigger resistance and resentment on the part of those whose work lives are affected. We would be wise to heed the advice of author and management theorist David Hurst, who says, "It is the objectivity which frameworks such as reengineering give their users that undermines the social dynamics leading to fundamental change. Indeed, the intellectual detachment of the designers and managers of change from the process itself should be identified as a leading cause of the failure of such change efforts" (Hurst, 1997).

Besides ignoring the human side, recent studies have shown that reengineering doesn't deliver the financial results it promises. Why not? In a recent interview in *Across the Board* (Vogel, 1997), Margaret Wheatley, author of the best-selling book *Leadership and the New Science*, stated, "I'm talking to companies who are in deep fury when they actually assess how much they spent on reengineering—in one case $300 million. And they just got nowhere with it. So you can make all these reengineering diagrams about work flow and what each person should deliver, but you're not capturing the real efficiencies of the organization. In many cases, I would argue, you're destroying them because of what happens to people's desire to work for you." Cost cutting is appealing, but it fails to build organizational capability for growth and innovation. Reengineering success stories are more the exception than the rule. Even the popularized success story of Ford's accounts-payable department, which reduced its staff by 75 percent, fails to mention that this reengineering effort took five years to complete. Davenport goes on to report that a study by CSC Index—the management consulting firm that is a leading proponent of Reengineering—found that 67 percent of reengineering initiatives that were completed "were judged as producing mediocre, marginal or failed results."

The problems with teams, Reengineering, TQM, and other programs is that they are too piecemeal—each program focuses on different aspects of organizational improvement. These piecemeal initiatives rarely succeed because the underlying logic and design principle for the enterprise hasn't fundamentally changed. Teams are too limited in their scope to effect systemic change, while Reengineering and TQM focus mainly on improving the technical work process. None of these programs is really that radical, in the sense of going down to roots and changing the fundamental design principle that underlies the structures and systems of the organization.

The self-managing organization goes beyond simply implementing teams at lower levels of the business, or experimenting with teams on a limited basis in select areas of a corporation. Teams are usually seen as something that may work for workers on the shop floor or for front-line employees at the service counter, but not for middle managers, and certainly not for senior executives. In other words, it is one thing to implement teams at lower operational levels, and quite another to radically redesign the entire enterprise to be self-managing. The shift to a self-managing organization requires a complete and total redesign of the entire system, from operational levels to the strategic apex of the firm.

Underlying all of the numerous failures and pitfalls with these methods is a common Achilles heel: conventional change efforts are guided by an elite few who control the destiny of the many. More often than not, the change process used for redesigning organizations is conducted in an authoritarian and top-down manner. Many of these authoritarian change processes are cloaked in the guise of participation, which is used as a way of coopting employees to accept policies and structures that have already been decided by management. So-called employee involvement programs are usually nothing more than a managerial wolf in a cooperative sheep's clothing.

CREATING THE SELF-MANAGING ORGANIZATION: PARTICIPATIVE DESIGN AND SEARCH CONFERENCES

We have to be honest. Fully self-managing organizations that have been redesigned from top to bottom are rarely seen. The concept is too new and truly radical. Yet numerous companies are in the process of transforming their enterprise to self-managing forms of organization. The early adopters of self-management in North America that are ahead of the learning curve are featured in this book. We have found that companies that are on the leading edge of the self-managing organization revolution—American Express, Microsoft, Motorola, Hewlett-Packard, Charles Schwab, Sequa Chemicals, StorageTek, Sybase, and Syncrude—have engaged in significant and system-wide initiatives that have transformed entire businesses to become fully self-managing. These companies have discovered how to rapidly design self-managing work systems by involving employees directly in the process.

Participative Design has been used for rapid business redesign, while another breakthrough method, the Search Conference, has been used for rapid strategy creation. Used in tandem, Search Conferences and Participative Design can democratize the entire strategy creation and organization design process. These methods are built on the natural principle that transformation of a whole enterprise requires direct and widespread employee participation, where those that will be affected by change can have more control and a direct say in deciding how their work will be structured to achieve organizational goals.

The Search Conference method democratizes the strategy creation process, supplanting the old Soviet-style approach to planning, where the top twenty executives in the business go off on a retreat and come back to dump their newly minted vision statement on the employees. As Margaret Wheatley points out, "If we want employees to feel the same kind of connection to their work that the executives feel at their retreat, then we have to get them involved. One of the things we've discovered is that when employees are engaged in creating a vision or mission, the statements they come up with create a much broader meaning to why they are doing their work than any leader would give them" (Vogel, 1997).

Monsanto CEO Robert Shapiro has learned this lesson in spades. In a recent interview in the *Harvard Business Review* (Magretta, 1997), Shapiro discusses the challenge of growth through global sustainability. Sustainable development will be an organizing principle for responding to global environmental degradation, and Monsanto had to dramatically change by creating a sustainability strategy. The top twenty-five critical thinkers within Monsanto—up-and-coming leaders from the business units, board members, manufacturing, policy, safety and health personnel—gathered together at an off-site retreat to search for new possibilities, taking into account emerging future trends in the world and the role Monsanto could play toward making the world better. As a result, eighty Monsanto employees coalesced and organized themselves into project teams that focused on a number of strategic new global sustainability initiatives.

The Participative Design method democratizes the redesign of business processes. This method overcomes many of the pitfalls described above, helping organizations to become self-managing faster and more effectively. This revolutionary methodology has no need for high-powered consultants, elite design teams and steering committees, or reengineering czars. Instead, Participative Design provides employees with conceptual and practical tools for doing the hard design and organizational change work that is normally the province of internal experts and external consultants. Because employees are empowered to design and make changes that fit their unique set of circumstances, the Participative Design process elicits trust and collaboration and fosters an environment for continuous organizational learning.

The Participative Design (PD) method enables employees and managers to participate directly in the task of redesigning the entire organization from the ground up. Participative Design is applied to all levels of the organization—the strategic, middle, and operational—and in all functions, from manufacturing to R&D. Participation is the fractal, or base element of an alchemical process that transforms a bureaucratic organization into an empowered workforce aligned for high performance. Indeed, participation is the best, and perhaps the only method for transforming a workforce from mere employees to strategic partners that have a stake in the business. The outcomes to be expected are leaner, flatter, team-based organizations with fewer people, new challenging roles, better communications, and higher performance.

A cardinal rule of the Participative Design method is that *no designs are ever imposed.* The basic assumption behind Participative Design is that the most adequate and effective designs come from those closest to the work process—the people actually doing the work. The methodology is fast and doesn't involve a lengthy and time-consuming analytical process. Organizational change and transformation is smoother and changes are sustained because employees are truly architects of the design process. Why resist or be opposed to your own creations?

The following quotations illustrate the versatility and benefits of the Search Conference and Participative Design methods. More detailed and in-depth case studies will follow throughout the book.

Syncrude, the second-largest oil producer in Canada, used Participative Design and Search Conference methods throughout the entire enterprise, transforming the shale-oil production facility over to self-managing operations. Don de Guerre, Director of the Organizational Effectiveness at Syncrude, notes, "The challenge was to get the cost of producing a barrel of oil down to be competitive with traditional oil. The result of using Search Conferences and Participative Design methods was a 75-percent improvement in productivity—the major variable affecting conversion cost." These are truly remarkable results, given that Syncrude achieved this with no significant changes or investments in new technology. The only things that changed were organizational structures, work processes, and power relationships.

Jim Heckel, production manager at Hewlett-Packard's Greeley, Colorado, facility recalled, "We held a Search Conference to create a strategy and shared vision for building manufacturing flexibility in our workforce. Our vision called for creating a manufacturing facility where employees would act more like owners of the business. We brought together all the managers in manufacturing and a selected cross-section of employees to establish six key goals to make this happen. One of those goals was to redesign the workplace so employees could act more like owners. Employees were already making significant progress, and we wanted to formalize the path we were on. We used the Participative Design method because it is fast and leads to higher commitment and much less resistance than other more traditional approaches to design. It is also less consultant-dependent, and the boundary of analysis can be very small (a single team) or very large (a whole division or one facility), which gives us tremendous flexibility. The design process was new for us, but not its philosophy. We were already a 'Theory Z' organization. I believe that Participative Design will help us operate smarter by giving our people the ability to control and coordinate their work from the perspective of being owners" (Cabana, 1995).

Walt Grady reflects on the redesign effort at the Greeley HP facility: "My experience is a team that develops their own work design will consistently outperform a team with a great work design which has been imposed upon them—even if the group's own design is still in need of more work. It's their own creation. They've used their own creative talents and simply won't let it fail" (Cabana, 1995). The PD session creates a deep impression with participants because it's a democratic process that is congruent with its democratic result—a self-managing organization.

Nick Crawford, an internal consultant at the Champion International paper mill in Pensacola, Florida, notes the challenges his company faces:

"Margins will continue to decrease in our industry, forcing us to respond with increases in productivity, efficiency, and cost reductions in operations. I believe PD has helped us cut costs out of the system and improve service levels to customers. The plant has used PD to redesign eleven departments into four independently operating business units. Each business now operates as its own profit-and-loss center. Champion was involved early on with setting up team-based organizations, but PD is different. With PD, people know where the boundaries lie, who is responsible for what, what they can and cannot do. PD offered us a way to formalize the team structure, making it clear to people what it meant to be a self-managing team, defining the responsibilities of each team and team member."

David Weiss, the CEO at StorageTek, says he expects leaders to be accountable, to honor their commitments, and to promote teamwork. "Those three things are the cornerstone of a successful organization," asserts Weiss (Jesitus, 1997). Storage Technology is a leading supplier of tape-drive and library storage systems for mainframe and midrange computers. At its main facility in Boulder, Colorado, StorageTek used PD to improve the design of its functional groups and cut a year off their cycle time for redesigning work. For example, the Logistics department was redesigned in less than two months, with full participation of all 110 of its members. Even the corporate legal department was redesigned. Lawyers found that they were organized in silos, which caused an uneven distribution of work and poor communication. As a result of going through PD, the corporate counsel's role was substantially redefined, resulting in a better utilization of the skills and talents of the legal professionals.

A Levi Strauss manufacturing facility in Harlingen, Texas, used PD after previous participation efforts had failed. Ron Martz, formerly the plant manager for the Harlingen facility, recalls, "We had tried involving everyone in redesigning the plant by bringing hundreds of people together at the same time and it didn't work." Martz wanted to involve the entire workforce in redesigning the plant, but he soon realized that the complexity of such a task required a more focused approach. Martz noted, "Participative Design gave our people more of an understanding of what needed to be done. . . . We redesigned the reward system, the technical system, the work flow, the method of work . . . the whole system. . . . Plant efficiency was running at 70 percent before we did PD. Now it's at 110 percent." Quality also improved. What did Martz think of PD? "It was fun watching the light bulbs go on for people," he says. "We did an initial design and then revised it, had reevaluation meetings. You could see the change in people's thinking. It was fantastic."

PARTICIPATIVE DESIGN AT AMERICAN EXPRESS

Two hundred seventy people work in Travel Financial Capture (TFC) inside consumer credit giant American Express. The TFC business handles transactions with the airline industry, financial reconciliation, billing, and accounting related to airline ticketing around the world.

In late 1997, the leadership team discovered fragmented business processes that created errors and losses, fragmented groups that didn't work together, and a workforce that was disconnected from the business strategy. Significant changes in information technology were underway to keep the business more competitive. These technological changes would alter core business processes—which the TFC was hardly ready to tackle. In addition, the workforce was reeling from ongoing reengineering, reduction in force, outsourcing, and resource shortages. In short, the TFC was unprepared for the tremendous changes facing it.

The leadership team decided that a top-down change initiative would take too long and further alienate the workforce. These leaders wanted to accelerate the change process, generate commitment and buy-in, and access the knowledge and talent of all the employees. They brought in consultant Mark LaScola to help them design a process to engage the entire TFC organization.

Participative Design was chosen to create a big picture design for a business owner. Rather than creating a strategic organization design behind closed doors, the new TFC leadership team believed that TFC's members were up to the challenge. Employees would utilize their relevant knowledge to generate a macro-organization design framework and then engage in a dialogue with the leadership team to generate design alternatives. Once a macro design was in place, individual teams would use Participative Design again, to create their own local designs. LaScola helped them through a process to build organizational capacity for change, and linked the change process to a shared TFC business strategy. The design focus was on integrating, aligning, and redesigning human and technical aspects of the business. Five major objectives were established for the design project:

- Design an organizational structure to achieve the TFC vision that leverages system and technology changes.
- Build meaningful and respectful relationships among all TFC management and employees, both within and between functions, and within and between all levels of the business.
- Create a well-functioning business where all TFC management and employees feel like business owners.
- Reduce/eliminate the sense among all TFC management and employees that they are being "beaten up."
- Create a flexible organization capable of changing job roles, and embracing change.

The senior leadership team sponsored the project and set criteria for team membership. Those selected to be team members needed to represent multiple levels and functions, be trusted by their peers, and possess relevant knowledge about the business process. The role of the sponsors was to champion the TFC vision and to select design alternatives which supported the strategic objectives. Three teams were chartered to drive project results. A fourteen-member "People Team" worked on designing alternatives to strengthen the social system. The "Structure Team" identified alternatives for how TFC could be organized to achieve the TFC vision, given the software system changes which were in the pipeline. A third "Linking Team" worked to synthesize, integrate, align, and support the alternatives provided by the People and Structure Teams and to test them against the business strategy.

The People Team interviewed employees to discover factors in the work environment that motivated them to work at their best. The Structure Team used the Participative Design method to map the work flow and redesign the organizational structure. Both teams gathered baseline "current state" data and created desired-future-state benchmarks, which allowed them to conduct a "gap analysis." After every step in the process, data was posted in the work area and run by the whole workforce before proceeding to the next step.

In other words, these employee-led Macro-Participative Design teams took their peers (in their natural work groups) and the leadership team on tours to view the charts and provide feedback to the teams. For example, in reviewing current state data, they asked them: Is this our organization? Is anything missing from our diagnosis and process maps? A lot of light bulbs went on during all these dialogue sessions. Heidi Oberman, a team associate, commented: "People would look at the wall quietly for a while. Then you'd hear, 'Wow! Is that our organization? I didn't know these groups [who were at opposite ends of the building] had an impact on each other's work.'"

The Structure, People, and Linking Teams worked collaboratively to put together a workable and comprehensive organizational design. The key questions they kept asking were: Will this design option further our business strategy? Do our human needs and our software components fit well together? Are we designing the work system for optimal human performance? Does our design provide opportunities for multiskilling, more variety, and a view of the whole process? Once the teams agreed on the alternatives for the new design for TFC, they presented their design proposals to the senior leadership team. The business owner culture grew right before their eyes. You could close your eyes and it wasn't possible to tell which roles people held in the operation. Every voice was speaking for what was best for the whole business. Matt Wilson, a project analyst, commented: "In every business I've ever been in, the employees always felt that they could run the business better, but were never given the chance. Leadership was always top-down. The way this process was run, we were all equals. The most important thing is that leadership was brought to everyone in the business."

The senior leadership team collaborated with the employees on the three Macro-Participative Design Teams as peers and equals. When employees presented their design alternatives to the senior leadership team, they spoke passionately about their proposals, but they also had plenty of facts and analyses to back up their recommendations. There was considerable dialogue around each design alternative. Key design decisions were made on the spot, and a new strategic organization design for TFC was approved by senior leaders. The new design would eliminate functional silos, increase interdependence, and require multi-skilled workers. Teams that focused on market segments would be organized in an end-to-end process that provided enhanced customer service. As customer volume increased or decreased, the team structure could contract or expand like an accordion.

The implementation phase for the new design is just beginning and Participative Design is also being used to orchestrate that process. Customer-focused teams are now using Participative Design to develop their micro-team structure.

One of the unique aspects of this project was that the design process focused not just on deficiencies and things that were broke in the system, but also on positive experiences of business successes that people carry in their memories. This positive, appreciative focus helped to reduce defensiveness and increase receptivity to change. Members of the Macro-change team felt this more appreciative approach to organizational design created synergy and facilitated the overall Participative Design process. Perhaps Juan Benitez, a team leader, said it best, "On the walls in every conference room at American Express hang a set of values we all believe in, about how to treat people. Every day we've worked together on this process, we have lived those values."

GENESIS OF THE METHODS

The genesis of these innovative methods and concepts traces back to the pioneering work of two eminent social scientists, Fred Emery and Eric Trist. Based at the Tavistock Institute in London in the late 1950s, Emery and Trist invented a method known as Socio-Technical Systems (STS) design. Their work is a landmark in the field as they offered industries a practical method to improve both productivity and the quality of the work life of employees. Many U.S. companies—like Procter & Gamble, General Foods, TRW, Cummins Engine, and Corning—redesigned entire manufacturing facilities based on STS principles. These innovatively designed plants often resulted in flatter organizations composed of multiskilled, self-managing work teams that performed many of the tasks that had been traditionally reserved for management: quality control, scheduling, hiring and firing, performance reviews, etc. However, self-management in these plants was seen as something for the operatives; management and technical-support functions remained fairly traditional and bureaucratic.

While many STS-designed facilities achieved significant performance improvements, the concept failed to diffuse to the rest of the corporation. A sea of traditional corporate bureaucracy surrounded these islands of innovation. Senior managers in the corporate centers didn't know what to make of these STS-designed plants. Some managers ignored the results achieved by the renegade plants, treating such examples as anomalies; managers who worked at these innovative plants were seen as heretics who couldn't be trusted. Some senior-level managers and corporate staff groups were downright hostile to innovative plants. These new work systems ran counter to the rules and traditions of a control-oriented management.

A classic example of such corporate misunderstanding and mistrust toward these pockets of innovation is the Topeka Gaines pet-foods plant, which was owned in the early 1970s by General Foods. Consider the results: the Topeka pet-foods plant outperformed its more traditional counterpart and had the greatest year-to-year productivity increase of any General Foods plant since its inception, holding that record consistently for seventeen years before the plant was sold to Quaker Oats. Despite its unequivocal superior performance, the Topeka plant was a target of much hostility, ridicule, and ill treatment from managers in other plants and among senior managers at corporate. Without consistent support and commitment from corporate headquarters, many STS-designed operations have suffered from slow regression back to traditional work systems, eventually becoming encapsulated by the corporate bureaucracy.

When Fred Emery returned to his native Australia in the early 1970s, he was swamped with requests for projects similar to those he carried out when at the Tavistock. Emery recognized the problem of diffusion with the expert-driven approach to socio-technical design based on his consulting experiences with Shell in the U.K. and projects in Norwegian industry. He reinvented STS by creating a faster and more participative method for designing organizations to be self-managing. He called his new approach Participative Design.

MAKING A CASE FOR THE
SELF-MANAGING ORGANIZATION

Almost half a century has passed since Eric Trist and his colleagues at the Tavistock Institute made the original discovery of self-managing work teams operating in the British coal mines. After that, Fred Emery and other applied social scientists began accumulating evidence and building claims for a serious alternative to modern bureaucratic organizations. Many of these claims and arguments are not new; they have been around for decades. But we are now at a point in history where the accumulation of evidence and the pressures of a turbulent environment are making self-management appear to be a practical necessity for survival. A case for the self-managing organization can be made on several grounds, including the following:

The Economic Imperative. Arguments in favor of the self-managing organization can be made on economic grounds, since such organizations have a potential and track record for achieving superior business performance. As all firms are concerned with maximizing their long-term profitability and financial returns through the efficient and effective use of resources, the self-managing organization provides a clear advantage in this respect. Overhead and personnel costs are lower in self-managing organizations because they require far fewer middle managers, supervisors, and employees. Staffing levels are 25 percent to 40 percent less than in traditional bureaucratic organizations.

In addition to lower staffing levels, self-managing organizations are more productive. The empirical research on new production facilities that have been designed from the outset using self-managing (PD/STS) principles shows that productivity is on average 38 percent higher than plants using the same or comparable technology. Procter & Gamble, an early adopter of STS design concepts, for many years leveraged "high-performance work systems" as a proprietary manufacturing strategy and a source of competitive advantage for many of its production facilities. Managers and engineers were trained in the concepts and then took leadership for designing and managing these innovative plants. According to a 1986 *Business Week* report, productivity is 30 percent to 40 percent higher in P&G's high-performance production facilities than in its sister plants within the corporation. As Margaret Wheatley points out, "The fact is that workers who are involved in the design of their work are 35 percent more productive. That's a minimum improvement when you are into self-management. We have plenty of case histories over the years to document this increase. . . . It's not about show-me-the-cases anymore. There is something more profound going on. It's about control and power, and frankly I don't know whether we'll choose now for effectiveness over control. That is the choice. We've been confronted with it in the past and rejected it for 50 years now" (Vogel, 1997).

These sites, however, are not even fully self-managing, since redesign efforts are usually limited to mostly nonexempt operational-level employees. In many cases, these "high-performance work systems" have resulted in team-based organizations but have failed to change the remaining crucial support systems and ancillary functions—human resources, accounting, finance, logistics, and so on. Productivity improvements on the order of 50–100 percent are entirely possible when a whole enterprise—plant operations, business units, divisions, staff groups, and senior management functions—are also included in a total transformation to self-management.

The Organization Effectiveness Imperative. Self-managing organizations are not only more productive and efficient than traditional organizations, they also have the capacity to be more effective. By effective, we mean a set of organizational capabilities for continuously improving products and services, for rapid innovation, for being flexible and responsive to changing market demands, for rapid strategy creation and participative design.

These capabilities—continuous quality improvement; radical reinvention; and creativity, flexibility, speed, strategic thinking, and rapid redesign—are distinctly human capabilities that can only be developed through the way in which an organization is designed and managed. The self-managing organization is designed to tap, develop, and leverage human capability in conjunction with advanced information technology that provides the source of a competitive advantage that can't be copied easily by competitors. Recent *Industry Week* (Taninecz, 1997) census data support this. According to the report, world-class manufacturing plants were more likely to have self-directed teams and innovative human-resource practices which were used to build a more intelligent, involved workforce. These innovative plants tended to provide more training per employee, had a strong emphasis on cross-training, and offered employees payment incentives for learning new skills.

Self-managing organizations are more effective in providing employees more freedom and autonomy, while at the same time increasing the degree of control and accountability throughout the system. In a turbulent environment, effective organizations must have a capacity that allows them to embrace dilemmas and paradoxes, reconciling what seemingly appear as opposite polarities. Management theorist Charles Handy (1992) argues for balancing corporate power with a new federalism which "deals with the paradox of power and control: the need to make things big by keeping them small; to encourage autonomy but within bounds; to combine variety and shared purpose, individuality and partnership, local and global, tribal region and nation state, nation state and regional bloc."

One reason why self-managing organizations are more effective is because both human needs and technical requirements for getting the work done are taken into account in the design of the whole organization. The technical system (machines, equipment, work process, physical layout, information flow) and the social system (people, their psychological needs, and the way they are organized) work together in congruence. This concept is based on the socio-technical approach to designing organizations, where a best match, or balance, between people and technology is achieved.

In traditional organizations, the technical system (jobs, work flow, production line) is designed or reengineered in isolation from the people who have to operate it. The technical system is optimized first, and employees are mostly an afterthought; they are expected to adapt to their jobs as given. Rather than fitting people to technology, self-managing organizations attempt to address the requirements of the social and technical systems simultaneously—they are "jointly optimized" to provide the best fit between the two. Because these two systems—people and technology—are interdependent, they have to be considered together. Reengineering business processes or redesigning work systems independently of those who have an intimate knowledge of those processes and have to live with the consequences of a new design is alienating, foolhardy, and destined to fail. Similarly, simply improving team relations, changing managerial styles, or making people feel better while ignoring the technical aspects of work rarely leads to the desired bottom-line results and also misses the mark.

Only by matching the human requirements and capabilities of the social system with the requirements and capabilities of the technical system can the best overall result be obtained. This means designing jobs, work systems, and organizational structures so that human as well as technical needs can be met.

The Commitment Imperative. As the nature of work has changed from tasks involving manual labor to tasks involving the processing of information, so has the need for greater employee involvement, responsibility, and commitment. The trend toward generating commitment in the workforce began in continuous process and science-based industries where the work processes were more interdependent, making safety and high reliability a primary concern. Many jobs required operators to detect and correct errors in real time, without the luxury of consulting with a supervisor. If an error or problem occurred, there simply was no time to wait for a decision to be made in a traditional bureaucratic fashion. Downtime could result in a significant loss of productivity. Thus the successful and safe operation of the technical system now depended a great deal on the quality of attention of the ordinary worker and his commitment to the job at hand. Since work in knowledge-based industries involves interpreting, analyzing, and responding to information, commitment is crucial to avoiding costly and even catastrophic errors.

Now that intellectual capital has emerged as the most critical element in organizational success, the desire to generate commitment in an increasingly knowledge-based workforce has accelerated. The transformation of information into value-added knowledge for products and services depends on how committed people are to their work. Companies that will be able to attract and retain talented knowledge workers will be those that provide a meaningful, engaging, and autonomous work environment—a culture of self-management. Commitment to one's work is the result of high involvement and an experience of the conditions that satisfy a set of human needs. The self-managing organization is designed to create these conditions of high involvement, with human needs in mind. It does so by designing work systems that meet the critical psychological requirements that people have to experience responsible, fulfilling, and meaningful work.

This requires a total system change in the way the structure of work is designed. Simply installing teams doesn't bring about a change in the conditions under which people experience a sense of commitment—or don't. Rather, the critical human requirements that lead to high commitment must be participatively designed into the work itself. People must be able to redesign their tasks so that each individual within a team has:

1. *Autonomy and discretion.* Engaging work provides a blend of opportunities that allow an individual to make their decisions without close supervision, but also provides a set of guidelines that define an individual's scope of authority and decision-making rights. Individuals

need an adequate degree of freedom in the way tasks are carried out, but they also need to know the prescribed limits and boundaries in which they may exercise their autonomy and discretion.

2. *Opportunity to learn and continue learning on the job.* Engaging work provides ample opportunity for developing and sharing knowledge and skills, and opportunities for applying what one has learned that has positive consequences for the individual and organization. This form of action learning is possible when there are opportunities for (a) setting reasonably challenging goals and (b) receiving timely feedback on one's actions that provides the opportunity to question assumptions, reflect on and learn from mistakes, and correct and modify one's actions.

3. *Optimal level of variety.* Work that engages and involves people is neither too demanding nor too easy, but somewhere in between. This usually means that people can coordinate tasks within their unit, allowing them to engage in an optimal variety of activities. Too much variety leads to stress and burnout; too little variety results in apathy, boredom, and fatigue.

4. *Need for social support and an opportunity to exchange help and respect.* Conditions must be created that provide the opportunity for people to give and receive support and assistance from others in carrying out their work. The formation of teams often provides an opportunity for exchanging help and respect, but conditions for collaboration may also be created through more informal networks. A strong social support system based on mutual respect also fosters the recognition of individual achievement within a collaborative context.

5. *Sense of meaningful contribution.* Engaging work provides employees and managers with a sense that their contributions are worthwhile and socially useful. Commitment is likely to be enhanced if people feel the objectives of the company are also seen to fulfill some worthwhile purpose for society. Engaging work derives from a sense of working for a larger purpose, of knowing how one's job contributes to the whole product. Individuals working in highly fractionated jobs often feel their jobs are relatively meaningless since they cannot perceive how what they do fits into the larger scheme of things.

6. *Prospects of a desirable future.* Engaging work offers the prospect of advancement, higher compensation, learning new skills, and personal growth. What is considered to be a "desirable future" will vary widely among individuals; it might mean a degree of job security that allows

one to plan ahead; ample opportunities for promotion and advancement; opportunities to increase one's skills and knowledge; acquiring greater levels of responsibility; taking on more complex and challenging assignments.

This is not an exhaustive list by any means, but the research on work design has shown that these six criteria are the major aspects that provide people with conditions for being committed to their work. From coal mines to clean rooms, there appears to be a remarkable consistency among the set of human needs that must be fulfilled if work is to be psychologically enriching, personally meaningful, dignified, and worthy of respect. Traditional organizations are only running on a couple of cylinders, rather than all six. Self-managing organizations are designed to provide the motivational horsepower that produces higher performance, in terms of both business results and human satisfaction.

The Creativity Imperative. In a world where the future is becoming increasingly uncertain and more complex, organizations that can foster creativity will have an easier time reinventing themselves as shifting discontinuities demand new responses, new thinking, new strategies, and new products. Yes, people will have to learn and unlearn, reflecting on what they do, and diffusing what they learn throughout the organization. However, organizational learning will not be enough. People will also have to learn to deal with the unforeseen, to improvise in real time, and to *create the future* rather than becoming too attached to their historical success. In other words, *organizational creativity* will be key to thriving in the new environment (Woodman, Sawyer, and Griffin, 1993).

Continuous improvement of existing products and services will still be important, of course—and even that requires creativity. But the real source of competitive advantage will be based on the capacity for continuous invention of new products and services. Warren Bennis, coauthor of *Organizational Genius*, knows the value of a creative workforce. Says Bennis, "I am convinced that the key to competitive advantage in the 1990s and beyond will be the capacity of leadership to create the social architecture that generates intellectual capital. Success will belong to those who unfetter greatness within their organizations and find ways to keep it there" (Bennis, 1997).

Organizational creativity can't be forced or engineered into systems—

we can't order people to be creative or simply pull a tool off the shelf for people to use, expecting creativity to flow on demand. Instead, self-managing organizations are designed in ways that allow *social creativity* to flourish. Organizing for social creativity means developing work environments that promote creative collaborations and interactive learning (Purser and Montuori, 1998).

New product development is increasingly being performed by multidisciplinary teams of cross-functional groups that have front-to-back end responsibility for bringing the product to market. Yet, most knowledge workers often resent working in teams because there are pressures to achieve unity and a semblance of harmony through suppression of minority and divergent opinions. Many teams fall into the trap of operating like totalitarian regimes, which demand conformity rather than spirited dialogue and debate, forcing individuals to abide by "group norms" and policing deviant members who threaten to rock the boat. Thought police at Storage Technology used to reinforce the "hammer all the nails down" norm with a slogan that had become popular there, "There is no 'I' in T-E-A-M."

The self-managing organization is designed to enhance social creativity and collective entrepreneurship, as well as everyday creativity—the kind of creativity that has escaped our attention in our hero-worshiping culture. This means developing a culture of improvisation, where people can share their knowledge and express divergent views in an atmosphere of trust. It is a culture where people tolerate ambiguity and actually seek out complexity, relying on colleagues for support and encouragement which provide the essential safety net that allows people to rally from setbacks. In self-managing organizations, people have more freedom of expression and movement, and aren't afraid of expressing dissent; employees are encouraged to vigorously challenge authority, customs, and tradition. The democratization of strategy creation and work processes in self-managing organizations gives employees more power and more voice, putting those with critical knowledge, expertise, and technical competence into positions where they can influence the outcomes of key decisions. Cultivating a culture of improvisation requires a spirit of play as well as a dedication to hard work, all held together by a larger sense of purpose and a compelling vision of the future.

The Partnership Imperative. Building effective partnerships will be a critical success factor in the global economy. Partnerships are emerging in many shapes and forms: creating strategic alliances, entering joint ventures, forming R&D consortia, building networks and linkages in a virtual organization, partnering with customers and suppliers, and treating employees as strategic partners in the business. As Rosabeth Moss Kanter puts it, more and more companies are becoming PALs, "pooling, allying and linking" (Kanter, 1997). Companies are discovering that there is a deep connection between building quality relationships based on a "high trust" partnership culture and building quality products.

Partnership, participation—these words come from the same root—*pars,* which means *to partake.* When we build effective partnerships, we build relationships that are based on equal participation, mutual regard, and trust. Partnerships have the give and take between equals. There is a mutuality of interests between parties that provides common ground, allowing the partners to collaborate toward shared goals. Effective partnerships drive out fear, because each party trusts that the other party will act in their best interests. There is no coercion, manipulation, or attempts to dominate or overpower the other party. In a partnership system, power is shared rather than wielded over others, which creates a "high trust" culture.

Traditional organizations are based on just the opposite—systems that legitimize domination—where a person at "higher levels" has been given the right to exercise *power over* others, unilaterally, without their consent. It's a system predicated on the inequitable distribution of power and authority that is fundamentally "antidemocratic." Hierarchies of personal dominance are built into traditional organizations like a fractal pattern that is replicated at every level and in every function. Shareholders have power over senior managers. Senior managers have power over middle managers. The middle level has power over the first line. First-line supervisors have power over employees. As everyone is organized to look down rather than out, all this power meddling and micromanaging leads to an inward focus. Customer requirements are ignored and forgotten. Opportunities for growth and innovation are missed. Human capabilities are squandered and wasted.

In traditional organizations, responsibility for control and coordination is always located at a higher level of authority. Indeed, the design principle is based on centralizing authority, which leads to an authoritarian, fear-based culture. The hierarchical order that is put in place in traditional organizations is held together by a pattern of behavior based on deference to authority. Those on the lower end of the totem pole bow down and kiss up to those at higher levels. This authoritarian arrangement is dangerous since those on top can willfully ignore and deflect any information coming from subordinates. Authority of position gives managers immunity from competence. As Philip Slater (1992) points out, "this is one of the many reasons power so inevitably corrupts."

Authoritarian leaders become more and more insulated from the real world of the organization. Those at the top rarely have a clear or accurate idea of what is really happening below them because subordinates will distort and filter information as it travels up the hierarchy. Subordinates, wanting to look good in the eyes of their superiors, will tell those in command what they want to hear. "Things are going great, everything is under control." Indeed, the higher one moves up the hierarchy, the more things look good. And, after all, since *I* am in charge, things *must* be going well.

As one might suspect, genuine and effective partnerships can never really develop and mature in a traditional hierarchy. Shifting from a dominator to a partnership system requires a deep change in the organization's design principle—the genetic code that instructs how structures and processes should be organized to achieve its goals. The self-managing organization is built on the democratic design principle, shifting from a command-and-control hierarchy to a *partnership work system,* where equality between levels and individuals becomes the norm. In a partnership work system, different groups and individuals may perform different functions, but no one is considered "superior" or above anyone else. It is only by fostering norms of equality that real trust and genuine partnership can emerge.

But let's be realistic. If individuals and groups are going to be given more latitude, more autonomy and responsibility for making their own decisions, as well as more freedom to be creative, we can't just throw control and order out the door. The result would be complete anarchy, total chaos, and too much disorder—as people would be working at cross-purposes with each other. There would be no sense of alignment or social coherence. Because the self-managing organization *is* designed to provide people more autonomy and creative latitude (raising the level of disorder), *the level of order must be raised too* to prevent the system from spinning out of control. But that order is not imposed from above or through a traditional command-and-control hierarchy that suppresses differences and makes everyone slavishly follow the rules. Rather, the order emerges as partnership and trust are established—indeed, partnership and trust are the social glue that keeps the system coherent.

A RADICAL CHANGE

The self-managing organization requires a radical change in the design and management of the enterprise. The shift to self-management involves uprooting work arrangements and authority structures that have enjoyed immunity from fundamental change under the protection of a dominant hierarchy. Deep, system-wide, and democratic change can cause distress, anger, and resistance among those who have become accustomed to the status quo. Yet in a world where discontinuities and unexpected change are the norm, attachment to the status quo and complacency with past success can be suicidal.

Self-managing organizations are designed to be dynamic and open to change. They are designed to strengthen the competitive advantage of the enterprise by enhancing the knowledge, skills, and investment of all employees. In self-managing organizations, there are no clear-cut divisions between those who manage and those who are the managed. Rather, everyone in the enterprise community is viewed as having full membership status, with a real share of the voice, and with a legitimate right to fully participate in the management of his or her own work.

CHAPTER 2

THE ROAD LESS TRAVELED

Lockheed Martin's Journey Toward Self Management

> The purpose of an organization is to enable ordinary people to do extraordinary things.
>
> —Peter Drucker

Lockheed Martin Government Electronic Systems (GES), a billion-dollar business with 3,700 employees, is an example of an organization evolving out of its bureaucratic past. GES designs, integrates, and tests complete shipborne radar-array systems for guided-missile-carrying cruisers, destroyers, and frigates. Eighty such ships are currently either operating (in the U.S. or Japanese navies) or in production. GES has a one-million-square-foot facility located on 400 acres in Moorestown, New Jersey, near Philadelphia. The workforce of GES is represented by the following bargaining unions: the International Union of Electrical Workers (IUE), the International Federation of Professional Engineering Personnel (IFPTE), and the Association of Scientists and Professional Engineering Personnel (ASPEP). The U.S. Navy is the primary customer of GES, along with Japan, Spain, Australia, and other NATO countries. A principal U.S. competitor is Raytheon; worldwide, GES faces Thomson-CSF/Signaal, Alenia, CelsiusTech, GEC-Marconi, and others.

What did managers in this radar-array business do to position their organization so they could learn, adapt, and evolve with the changing world? They renewed their strategy, benchmarked the "best-in-class," developed the business systems to support self-management, allowed employees to participate in the design of their own work, and established clear, simple goals and built on them.

Managers and employees at GES understand that cultural change is hard work, with ups and downs that require flexibility, patience, and a learning organization. Their evolution toward self-management began when managers realized they had to let go of their quick-fix mentality—there was no cookbook solution to transformation. They discovered that the journey is tough, that employees have to be directly involved in designing their own work, and that it takes a long time to fit all the pieces together. Everyone has to blaze their own trail.

Despite being one of the most successful programs in the Navy's history, GES was like many successful organizations, insulated and self-absorbed. The military build-up of the Reagan years had made the company prosper. The 25-year success of the sole-source AEGIS program did not facilitate a hungry, competitive environment. GES offered jobs for life, producing and evolving its mainline product—the AEGIS weapons system. High-quality products and technological leadership kept the company on a roll.

Beginning in 1990, after the breakup of the Soviet Union, the United States began to reduce defense spending and downsize its armed forces. Department of Defense (DOD) orders for new hardware were cut in half. The combination of a demanding customer and a declining defense budget was a wake-up call: American business needed to change the way the defense business was run. Norm Augustine, Martin Marietta's visionary CEO, foresaw the decline in defense spending and how it would profoundly affect the aerospace industry. Through a series of acquisitions and mergers, he built today's Lockheed Martin Corporation, an aerospace giant that leverages the best practices of its Martin Marietta, Lockheed, GE, and Loral heritage.

In 1990, GES was part of GE. (It was sold in 1993 to Martin Marietta, which later merged with Lockheed.) Jack Welch, GE's dynamic CEO, launched "WorkOut," a program designed to improve quality and reduce costs by streamlining business processes to eliminate waste. This program involved GES employees in the design and planning of their own work for the first time.

Jack Irving, a GE manager and pioneer of employee self-direction, was sent to GES to strengthen and streamline operations. One of his first accomplishments was to flatten the organization by removing layers of management. GES then began to cut operating costs by outsourcing work and closing some of its facilities. Gene Marozzi, member of the International Union of Electrical Workers, Local 106, says of that period, "We were losing 1,400 jobs because of outsourcing. They closed the plant in Gibbsboro, New Jersey, and laid off eight hundred people. That was GE's corporate mentality at the time. They bought, they sold, they traded. They didn't care about people, just profits."

Relations between GES's three unions and management became tense and uncomfortable. "It was war!" quips Jack Irving. "I was called things in public I'm not even sure I would even say to someone in private. We were at each other's throats every minute of every day!" Those were the dark days of the business.

In 1991, the GES phoenix rose from the ashes in the form of the Competitive Initiative, an IUE–management agreement designed to save the plant and the jobs of its employees. Management and the union developed an initiative that would offer GE corporate management the same competitive advantages then being realized through outsourcing, by keeping the work in house. In effect, GES would reinvent itself by using cooperation and self-direction to reduce manufacturing cycle times by 50 percent and costs by 25 percent in the first year. Oh, and while all of this was going on, GES would maintain or improve its product quality and already near-perfect reliability record. Union and management took this "50/25" initiative to GE CEO Jack Welch and Electronics Sector President Tom Corcoran. Welch and Corcoran agreed that if GES met these goals, the plant and the jobs would be saved. GES not only met, they exceeded these targets. The next year, goals were set to reduce both scrap and defects by 40 percent; both goals were exceeded. These milestones mark the beginning of the GES Business Improvement Journey, which goes on today.

BUILDING A PARTNERSHIP WITH THE WORKFORCE

In early 1993, Joseph Threston, then president of GES, faced several difficult challenges and choices. Defense markets were shrinking and new contracts were unlikely. Price increases were not an option; in fact, competition required GES to drive prices down each year. The only viable choice was to focus on improving productivity and lowering costs. To survive, GES had to get more productivity out of the workforce. "To get cost competitive," recalls Threston, "we went to our people for help." Jack Irving, today Vice President of Production and Life Cycle Programs, is proud of the progress made since the defense downturn. Jobs are actually being added and plenty of work will be available for at least the next five years.

A third of the GES workforce works in areas that manufacture and test advanced micro-electronic packages, surface mount and through-hole modules, cabinet assemblies and radar systems. By 1995, self-management was strong in these manufacturing areas, where the focus is on cost competitiveness. GES management began to apply these lessons learned in the engineering, program management, and support departments with positive results. More importantly, interdepartmental cooperation began to improve as GES personnel all across the business learned to work together.

Although there is less pressure for change today, people are still improving the business. And they aren't ready to stop. Helene Marinella, an operator in the High Density Interconnect Facility, has views echoed all over the Moorestown site: "In 1991, I was one of the original six union members who went out to the workforce to get the union-management partnership going. Our colleagues (front-line workers) threw a lot of rocks at us back then! Today, our members' mindset is different. Management wants people capable of making decisions on their own. For example, I am involved in process improvement, costs, cycle time reduction, quality, and interfacing with the customer. It will be over my dead body that any negative things get in my way. I am going to make this work and take care of things ASAP."

These benefits and results aren't achievable by piecemeal solutions like stealing tasks away from one person to enrich another employee's job, or by training supervisors to be warm and friendly while they continue to order subordinates around, or even by training people in TQM, Just-in-Time, or ERP. Sophisticated technological solutions or reengineered business processes won't make people any smarter or more interested in improving their performance. Altering the behavior of an entire workforce is a culture change. It can only happen over time, and only by empowering employees to design their own work processes and control the variables that affect their success.

Today, LM GES is run by teams. In manufacturing, every team has both a management and a union coleader. All teams decide their purpose, document best practices, and publish their minutes. Each team is also in the process of creating a web page. Peers from all the teams meet periodically to support communication across all the groups. Engineers and operators are learning to collaborate to turn designs into reliable products at a pace which challenges the endurance of competitors.

Now, everyone at GES—the employees in the work centers, technical professionals, team leaders, union members, and managers at all levels— understand first hand the global competition they are facing. After seven years of partnership between union and management, GES is a completely different company. Formerly stovepipe departments have learned to work together and cooperate. Before redesign, 550 million GES dollars used to be tied up in inventory. Today inventory is not even in the 20-million-dollar range, and the inventory turnover rate has almost quadrupled.

Employees in the Inventory Management Group (IMG) redesigned the reorder-point system to save time and improve efficiency, and they changed the printing process to cut costs in half. Jim Robbins, one IMG team member, sees himself as an important part of the whole company, not just a clock puncher. Robbins noticed that many of GES's employees didn't use regional public transportation because of inconvenient bus schedules: those who did use it arrived at the plant fifteen minutes late. His solution: Contact the Southern New Jersey Transit coordinator and convince him to change the bus schedules. Now, everyone can arrive at their work station on time. When another team member found a cheaper color printer to work in the network, he convinced management to spend the money to buy it for the whole site, not just the work center. The whole IMG group is self-managing and proud of it.

GES's move toward self-management has not gone unrecognized. Initiatives spearheaded by Jack Irving and the GES Moorestown team gained GES significant recognition. Charlie Louie led GES's efforts to be recognized as one of *Industry Week* magazine's "America's Best Plants" in 1994, and won them the Baldrige-based New Jersey State Quality Achievement Award in 1995. More recently, and again led by Louie, GES was a finalist for the 1997 Malcolm Baldrige National Quality Award. "GES's continued use of the Baldrige process and criteria has been one of the key catalysts to improving the business," indicates John Shelton, Facilitator, National Malcolm Baldrige Effort.

Public recognition is nice, but it's not what enables a company to prosper and grow—business performance based on employee participation does that. It used to take over a year to produce antenna arrays at GES; now it takes less than six months. GES business groups now redesign themselves numerous times with the full participation of employees. A world-class partnership has replaced the war with the union. The rumor mill has been sacked for a communications process that other companies try to emulate.

A lack of metrics has been replaced by an obsession to measure absolutely everything. Even so-called soft measures—which are often the most difficult to quantify—are tracked with utmost precision. But it is also important to point out that managers don't impose metrics anymore. Micro-business units (more on this later), which consist of numerous self-managing teams, now have the skills and internal support to develop their own metrics. Middle managers are involved in setting and negotiating objectives with the teams instead of giving marching orders from on high.

What is even more amazing is people aren't forced to participate on teams; voluntary participation is the norm at GES, and more than two-thirds of the workforce have chosen to participate. Go out on the manufacturing floor and walk casually around and ask people about cash flow, budgets, economic value added, and so on, and intelligent answers will be offered. Sam Dedonatis was chosen by his team as its facilitator. He has been with the company since 1987, when there was nothing outstanding in any of GES's business practices. Says Dedonatis: "Just seven years ago, you would come into work, you'd punch the clock, and you'd go home. It was as simple as that."

Joe Charitonchick, a team member in Dedonatis' group, feels that an open organization developed because people were involved in everything. "We were involved in planning for dozens of initiatives, work changes, how to move the process along, new things to learn, all kinds of stuff," he points out.

SELF-MANAGEMENT STARTS AT THE TOP

Threston and the rest of his management staff spent a great deal of time soul searching before they decided to move the whole enterprise in the direction of self-management. One of the key issues was that they themselves were not working together as a team to coordinate business goals across functions. The division leadership team was adamant that if they didn't learn to coordinate work across functional boundaries, then how could the rest of the organization learn to do it?

As Jon Katzenbach (1998), in his book *Teams at the Top*, points out, the litmus test of a *real* team at the top (or any level for that matter) is "mutual accountability for group results, collective work products (defined as the tangible result of several members of a group applying different skills to produce a performance improvement not achievable by any one member alone) and a sharing or shifting of leadership role among the members" (p. 15). GES's leaders have learned to work in various subgroups when that is needed while still making decisive decisions as individual functional leaders. "In a true self-managing organization," Fred Emery told us, "functional managers are rewarded (or punished) as much for their effective coordination as for the ability to propose and implement policies in their division of the organization."

Bob Coutts, the new president of GES, feels that many of the executives who come to GES to benchmark their innovative practices consider themselves exempt from having to work together to optimize the business as a whole. That's unfortunate. Keeping a bunch of independent actors in place at the top confuses the employees and doesn't lead to focused, coordinated, and committed actions. While it's true that a single leader can act swiftly and decisively, a real team at the top can be just as decisive once executives have put the principles behind self-management to work.

During this soul-searching period, Irving and his staff in Operations visited a lot of "leading edge" organizations that were aggressively exhorting teams to improve their quality orientation. They saw a number of well-run teams existing at one or two levels of an organization that were managing their own work, but above them the management didn't look much different. There were still a bunch of individuals with strong egos managing their little pieces of the business like independent fiefdoms. Senior managers in these firms didn't have any experience working together to coordinate initiatives across functions.

GES's senior leadership team (Coutts' staff) believes that managers need to take the lead and build a cohesive, integrated system for self-management to be effective. In order to improve the performance of the whole organization, self-management has to start at the top. GES management feel that this is essential, but very difficult. Bureaucracies are often most entrenched at the top of an organization and, initially at least, it is at the top that the idea of team autonomy meets the most resistance.

What are the benefits when the team at the top learns to work together to achieve common goals? An example is the establishment in 1993 of the Materials Acquisition Center—Mid-Atlantic Region (MAC-MAR). A shrinking orders base demanded a more focused purchasing strategy.

James Thomas, then Vice President of Sourcing, set up and guided a team that expanded the original idea and created a regional purchasing center which now leverages buying power across eight businesses in Lockheed Martin's Electronics Sector—a nine-billion-dollar business unit.

From the senior leadership team's perspective, the idea is to look out as far as people can see to create a bold, hard-to-achieve vision, then back up and say, "Okay, where do we need to be in a couple of years?" Then back up again and say, "What do we need to do to get to that intermediate step?" The role of senior leaders is to define initiatives, charter cross-functional improvement teams, establish measures of success, and determine what work processes need to be realigned to make it happen.

To accomplish this, GES employees need access to a lot of information. In Operations, Irving and his staff created ownership by opening the books, showing their people how to use financial information, and entrusting them with greater responsibility. When it came time for managers to relinquish their traditional roles and transfer authority to the teams, they had already been well prepared. When managers became role models for the rest of the organization, it only added credibility to the team concept.

What do managers do, now that teams are self-managing? Joe is a manager in the Analog Chassis Micro Business, where he plans production schedules, deals with supply problems, sets up white boards with a week's worth of tasks, and makes sure employees have the proper training to keep their technical, business, and people skills current. When the team has a roadblock, they'll come to Joe to expedite things. If the team needs methods or test equipment or has an engineering-related issue, they turn to Joe and he gets it resolved for them.

Now, Joe makes sure that team members are involved in meetings with engineers to work out design issues before they become problems. The antenna group, for example, sends team representatives off the floor to concurrent engineering meetings. As they learn how the product is being developed, they might say to engineers, "I'm out there building it, maybe you could make this change." As Joe put it, "Before we never had those meetings until it was too late. Now we address the issues and fix them before the designs get in our hands."

Just as senior leaders are learning to cooperate and manage across functional boundaries, engineers at GES are learning to listen and make adjustments. As James Melton, VP of Engineering, puts it, "With the kind of work environment we have created, if you aren't having fun running around on teams (over five hundred engineers are on them), you are doing something wrong." Just ask Joe Iannocone, an engineering project manager leading a twenty-person team to reduce cycle time by 33 percent, increase first test yields to 90 percent, and reduce engineering change orders on new programs by 50 percent.

Iannocone's work is taken very seriously by senior management. Melton and his colleagues create forums that give integrated product teams "face-time" with the senior leadership team to discuss their progress and to get critical support. The management team at GES has worked very hard to look at themselves honestly and drive this philosophy throughout the business. In other words, they don't shoot the messengers in these face-time sessions. GES's leaders believe that a genuine reality check means not lying to themselves.

Openness, trust, honesty, and truthfulness emerged slowly and deliberately at GES. According to Jack Irving, "Nowadays there is truly very little conflict on business direction and priorities." One important part of this senior leadership vision was to establish boundaries within which business center teams would be free to act. As Michael DelRossi, the Human Resource VP at GES, puts it: "Our role is to establish the context within which people can solve problems on their own and be responsible for them." Problem–solution boundaries, or empowerment guidelines, can be reviewed and sometimes revised as the business evolves and people's knowledge and skills increase.

At GES, people aren't afraid to come up to any executive to drive home a point that the executive may not want to hear. People understand that the leadership group has to make the call on strategic issues, and when there are competing ideas—but they expect to be consulted, be involved, and hear an explanation of why the decision was made. GES has learned that you can deflate the whole damn thing, the honesty and trust, very quickly if you go against these expectations.

Self-management is a high-maintenance system. It requires a rigorous communications process and constant attention from the top: build the bridges; knock down the walls. Learn to think about and model connectivity instead of isolation. Focus on the end goals you want to achieve. Remember what is driving it—the customer, the market—and empower employees to design appropriate processes to accomplish those goals.

Building around teams changes all the human-resource practices such as selection, recruitment, training, appraisal, communication processes,

Table 2.1 Empowerment Guidelines at LM GES

Empowerment is . . .
"The freedom, responsibility and accountability to act within a set of guidelines that define your authority to make decisions and generate actions that you know will be supported."

CAN DO	CANNOT DO
• Understand your customers' needs	• Deviate from process/compliance
• Organize teams, select members & leaders, determine objectives, create a plan & obtain support needed to reach work-center goals	• Hire, fire, discipline
	• Choose vendors
	• Change pay scale
• Assume responsibility for achieving workcenter performance objectives	• Refuse work
	• Be cost ineffective
• Control cost, manpower, work flow	• Adversely impact schedule, quality, or integrity
• Communicate thoroughly	
• Focus on the process and design	
• Improve or cross skill sets with training	
• Change layout of workcenter	
• Improve cycle time	
• Control schedule, work-in-process, material input	
• Recommend equipment changes	

career development, and compensation. If you don't want a bunch of people who like to work one on one, then your selection criteria have to change. If teams are going to form, you can't have people who are averse to change or unwilling to keep on learning. At GES, training programs are requested by employees and designed to meet their requirements; they are not imposed by an HR bureaucracy.

THE ROLE OF THE UNION AT GES

Once GES shifted to a self-managing organization, the role of every union in the division was redefined. Unions originally grew up to fight the bureaucracy and protect the worker. In a self-managing organization, what is the role of the steward and the union hierarchy? Like the roles of first-line supervisors, these traditional union roles have to change as well. The magnitude of the organizational shift is difficult for people to envision. Managers and union representatives, at all levels, need a productive justification for their existence with new roles and responsibilities and a new set of values.

At GES, a permanent union-management steering committee was formed to tackle bold bottom-line competitive initiatives one at a time. For example, an onerous set of twenty-six narrow job classifications was compressed down to four bands, with cross-training within bands to facilitate broader skill sets and greater flexibility. Gene Marozzi, member of IUE local 106, has the spirit for business success rarely found in union-management settings. "These improvement efforts are never over," says Gene. "Once it's over, people celebrate their success and lay back down."

Many modern business leaders have grown up expecting unions to thwart management's efforts for innovative change. But that doesn't have to be the case. Joe DiCarlo, president of IUE Local 106, has only added value to the business. Regarding all the change initiatives and the high involvement culture, DiCarlo remarked, "All our initiatives had the support of the grassroots leaders people trusted. And we had an agreement only normal attrition would be used instead of layoffs." It seems that previously the people who worked on improvement teams were managers' "pets." The workers didn't trust them to have their best interests in mind.

We've said so many good things about GES that readers might think their seven-years-plus journey happened with a minimum of trauma. Actually, the reverse is true. There were lots of pitfalls and missteps along the way. For example, management's early efforts at change hit a credibility gap. GES produced a quality product in 1990, but it wasn't cheap. A $15-million-a-year pile of scrap and an equally costly rework/repair loop were addressed by an aggressive group of cross-functional operations teams. Process control engineers were hired to teach the workforce statistical process control (SPC) and continuous process improvement (CPI) techniques. The idea was to use workcenter teams to drive operational improvements in cycle time, productivity, and waste reduction. Trend data in defects, scrap, and characteristic verification would be collected by each workcenter. Only a handful of quality inspectors would be needed and they would be used in a training role, not as policemen. Nice idea. Except the union rank and file saw it as "another bullshit plan to cut our jobs and force us out the door." The effort initially faltered.

Just the traumas and travails of getting the union–management cooperation going could fill an entire book. High-level air cover had to be provided for both camps. Jack Welch provided it for GES managers and the
head of the national IUE provided it for the local union president. To help
them learn to work together, the former adversaries searched for unions
and managers who were already getting along to find out how in the hell
they did it. They found an example of union–management partnership in
another GE division—which, in an ironic twist of fate, sought GES's advice
as its own partnership was faltering.

Because of the Competitive Initiative, it has become commonplace for
GES's workcenters to redesign their own work with the help of internal
expertise. When employees manage this trick once, management scholars
call it a "shift to radically different frames and processes causing a change
in the status quo." When it happens repeatedly academics call it "third-
order change, the creation of the capability to change in a broad group of
people." That's what GES was after. For example, the ISEM workcenter
came up with a manufacturing-cell concept and revised the layout of the
entire workcenter. The cabinet workcenter was moved and then redesigned
itself. Combiner and antenna workcenters have done it several times. "It
turns out better every time a workcenter redesigns itself," says Steve Piro,
Director Business Services. "Now we are looking at the phase-shifter area."
The phase shifters' workcenter is a major high-population area performing
an intricate process. The teams have been meeting and have already gone
through several revisions of their design.

The ASSETS Group, a cabinet-level test facility, designed an entire
room and a complex shielding structure, a very sophisticated facility. Jack
Irving feels the self-design piece is a major part of how GES goes about
improving the business. GES doesn't bother to quantify the benefits of self-
design because its value is self-evident. "You can go almost line by line,"
says Irving, "and look at all the things which were done in each of those
facilities and know that one or two smart industrial engineers would not
be able to think of that stuff. We would have ended up with an entirely different facility . . . probably a lot less efficient. I know, I did all those jobs in
the past."

OPEN COMMUNICATIONS

Form follows function at GES. Managers look at what they need to do and then find the form to get it accomplished. The standard practice to create new systems is to put a cross-functional team together that manages itself, then disbands when it completes its charter. For example, early on, a communications-process team was set up to open up communications. Members discussed their ideas on what was needed to improve the process and talked with functional VP's.

Prior to this effort, management used surveys and a focus group to reveal that, despite reducing the levels of managers from seven down to three, 67 percent of GES's employees were still getting their information from informal channels. This is one of the hallmarks of an entrenched bureaucracy and it had to go. GES had had it with bureaucracy.

The way this was handled is instructive. Rather than blame managers, supervisors, and team leaders, senior leaders took responsibility for creating a strong communications system. The way it works is this: there are monthly "KeyComm" meetings where GES gathers together its managers, team leaders, and union leaders—about 200 people all told. It started out as just an effort to get middle managers and supervisors together for the first time, but like anything useful at GES it was tweaked, refined, and massaged until it was a benchmark-worthy program in its own right.

Today, KeyComm meetings are part of an extensive communication network that leaves no one out of the loop. The KeyComm meeting is designed to flow information down to the entire workforce in forty-eight hours. If employees are going to be empowered to make decisions, then critical information needs to be in their hands with minimal delays. Charlie Louie, the Director of Quality and Mission Success, says, "The executive staffs meets at one o'clock in the afternoon on Monday. Our KeyComm meeting is at nine o'clock in the morning on Tuesday. After that, I meet with my staff at eleven o'clock. The information is going to reach the Quality and Mission Success team before noon, and then they'll let me know what they think about it." This gets management and the workcenter teams all aligned and on the same page within forty-eight hours.

This may sound like a top-down process, but it isn't. Let's visit a KeyComm meeting. Jack Irving happens to be hosting this month's KeyComm meeting (hosting duties are rotated). The rest of the senior management team covers different parts of the agenda, which includes a review of the

International Program, the business financials, the Northrop-Grumman merger, ethics, environmental health and safety issues, and the facilities-development plan. Things like the facilities-development plan are a big deal to the workforce. GES has grown to the extent that now there are too many people crammed into too little space. So space has to be sourced, a decision has to be made concerning who goes where, a schedule has to be created for the move, and lots of people will want to have input into that. And they will.

The teams feed information back up to management. And there's a few other wrinkles to this one. Consider this. Early in the change process, workcenters called town-hall meetings anytime they wanted to and management would come running. Jack Irving and the union-management steering committee were gluttons for punishment. Says Irving, "Town-hall meetings are my favorite. We go to a workcenter, stand at the center of a firestorm of questions, get beat up real good, learn a hell of a lot, make much better decisions, and end up with a highly motivated workcenter that has its competitive act together."

There are other aspects of the whole communication system. For example, the union-management leadership team goes on what are called "walkarounds." During our visit to GES, we went on one with them and saw that people were very willing to make their opinions and ideas known about the resources they needed, or the impediments they wanted removed. Bob Coutts, the president of GES, doesn't stay in the background, either. GES's president holds regular "skip-level meetings," where he skips a layer or two (of management) to find out what's on people's minds.

All of GES's communication systems reinforce each other. Many engineers, for example, prefer the written forms like the *Wave,* an employee-edited publication, or the "official" GES newsletter, *Up Front,* or the IUE-sponsored publication, *Initiative Ink.* The messages from the Key-Comm meetings are circulated in a publication called *Face-to-Face.* There are twenty video monitors all over the plant that are used as electronic bulletin boards, called the Employee News Network (ENN). There is the usual intranet message system as well.

Oral communication provides a check-and-balance process between the three layers of management, and with people in workcenter teams. Each member of the senior leadership team has a responsibility to go around and talk to the workforce one on one. People bring managers issues that aren't getting resolved, tell managers what's going on, and describe the help they need. "We know what is going on," says James Melton, Vice President of Engineering. "People aren't shy here." Questions and issues flow out of these meetings. Senior leaders respond to them and are held accountable by employees for the actions they commit to take.

By asking workcenters and functional groups what the issues are, and what the business needs are, managers open up an ongoing dialogue. And, as trust grows and employees' competence increases, the whole communications process keeps evolving. Subtle changes in people's sense of ownership are evident every few months. For example, at first, when issues came up, executives assigned someone to deal with them. The time wasn't right yet to let go of the reins and delegate that aspect of the management function to the workcenters. Now the Micro-Businesses take ownership of issues and handle them by themselves.

JUST-IN-TIME TRAINING

Initiatives like Integrated Product Development, team-based management, and a world-class quality program are supported with extensive training. GES spends roughly double the industry average on training. To enable employees to build the skills necessary to manage their expanded roles, training opportunities are provided to all categories of employees, not just managers.

GES knows that a flexible workforce must have the knowledge, skills, and competencies to succeed in a self-managing environment. Several thousand employees have been educated in cycle-time reduction, team-based management, performance measurement, and characteristic-verification processes, to name just a few.

Remember the Micro-Business concept we mentioned earlier? It seems GES wasn't satisfied with the static nature of the Baldrige criteria. They made this nationally recognized standard come alive by using it as a template to build curricula so that newly chartered Micro-Businesses could manage themselves as miniature businesses. One of the Baldrige examiners was so impressed he wondered why people weren't already beating down GES's doors to see what has been done. He believes that the Baldrige staff ought to visit GES and consider altering the criteria to make them even more useful.

Typically, in a bureaucratic organization training departments provide courses that are often disconnected from people's real jobs. It's no wonder that training staff often have to fight managers to justify their existence. GES lets the employees decide what they need in terms of training and education. The employees also give feedback on whether the training was useful, and suggest improvements. And training needs are determined by teams that have all the stakeholders on them, so it's tough to go off track.

AN INTEGRATED SYSTEM OF SELF-MANAGEMENT

GES has advice for anyone wanting to journey toward self-management. Individual change initiatives—whatever they are—have a half-life of six months before things slowly start regressing back toward an inflexible bureaucracy. "That's why we've worked so hard and so long to create an integrated system of self-management," says President Bob Coutts. "And we're not done yet. We'll never be done. And neither will anyone else, if they want to succeed."

At GES, if a manager is not positively focused, employees will let that manager know about it. Likewise, employees who detract from the team's goals will hear about it from a manager or the other team members. Each keeps the others in the partnership on track. Learning is an ongoing process. When a new piece is added to strengthen the whole system, things get messy and uncomfortable for a while, and then come back into focus.

The Micro-Business team concept is a case in point. The approach was designed by a cross-functional team and launched in 1995. What is it? It's a business excellence process based on the seven criteria of the Malcolm Baldrige National Quality Award. Its objective: Continue to maximize business performance in a labor-intensive environment by making employees business owners.

The Micro-Business approach instills an intimate knowledge of business processes across a broad range of the plant population. It standardizes GES's business systems across workcenters and implements a compensation system based on involvement. In other words, GES adapted the quality process to support their objectives of having grassroots employees act as business owners—a program which is congruent with the democratic mindset of self-management. The Micro-Businesses keep learning and growing by examining best practices outside the company and learning from each other inside the company.

It's still new and it's not all up and running yet, so a whole bunch of teams are working to make sure it will be. For example, the union-management steering committee has its eye on this program. They remove impediments and roadblocks, encouraging "growing pains" (mistakes) so employees can learn how to run their own show.

When Micro-Business teams experience negative dynamics, another team is there to throw them a life preserver and pull them to shore. Every team has members with good facilitation skills that help the team with consensus decision making. There are lots of support teams to help them with self-auditing, communications, human resource practices, business metrics, customer satisfaction, and public responsibility.

The Competitive Initiative at GES is never over. To make sure of that, the Next Step team sets goals and objectives for the next step in the Competitive Initiative. This team reports to the union-management steering committee on its efforts to strengthen the foundation of self-management. The Next Step team is working on increasing flexibility, expanding the breadth of nontraditional roles, and a compatible design for a broad, team-based compensation system at GES.

SUMMARY

GES offers many lessons for modern corporations. Self-management is hard, challenging, and forces members of management to be exceedingly honest with themselves as well as to learn how to work together. Many will run away kicking and screaming from this requirement alone. The process is unique to the particular corporation. You can't copy something from someone else or rely on a big consulting firm to put it in place for you. It has to be home grown. It's based on trust and having established credibility with the workforce. It can be crushed in an instant by old-style autocratic managers. Trust is hard to build and easy to destroy.

As Harvard Business School Professor Nitin Nohria points out, "All it takes to destroy trust is a few people who are driven to acquire power-over as opposed to power-with. Organizations based on the principle of power-with will always remain fragile and especially susceptible to reversal to a command-and-control system during times of change in leadership." For this reason careful attention has to be paid to select senior leaders who will work to preserve and strengthen a hard-won culture of self-management.

The top group must be the guardians and warriors who protect the self-managing system and must fight to keep out tools, techniques, processes, and unenlightened managers that attempt to sneak bureaucratic control back into the system. GES's leaders do this by asking a few simple questions over and over again: Can this idea help us make our system of employee ownership stronger and more cohesive? Does this method work in a self-managing context? Is the technique internally consistent with our approach to self-management? How can our business use it? Can we adapt a tool or method and make it our own? (Notice what they did with the Baldrige criteria.) Will it fit with what we have done so far and make the whole system stronger?

It takes a long time to reach the point of development which is in place at GES. Additionally, GES would not be so successful today if it did not have the teamwork and cooperation of the on-site customer (U.S. Navy) and customer representatives (DCMC, DCAA). The relationship has proven to be extremely fruitful. Putting self-management in place is a deliberate, methodical journey, but it leads to a powerful competitive result. There are many such journeys going on now in America and around the world. We invite you to start down your own path.

CHAPTER 3

AWAY WITH EXPERTS

Participative Design

The real voyage of discovery consists not in seeing new
landscapes but in having new eyes.

—Marcel Proust

Participative Design (PD) is based on the assumption that the best solutions for redesigning organizations come directly from those who have intimate knowledge of their own workplace. Rather than using outside experts to analyze and design the work of others, the Participative Design method employs workers directly in analyzing and redesigning their own work. The method relocates the responsibility for design with those who will have to make it work in practice. The tools and concepts are simple but powerful, allowing employees to develop new designs for their own units. This user-friendly methodology enables employees and managers to collaboratively self-manage their way through the redesign process. With PD, the means—the process of redesign—are congruent with the ends the organization is trying to achieve—a fully self-managing organization. In other words, PD uses a democratic process to create democratic structures. This way, the knowledge and wisdom of all employees at every level of the organization is used in the formulation of self-managing work structures. In essence, PD democratizes the process of redesigning organizations.

Existing redesign methods such as Reengineering and Socio-Technical Systems rely upon *representative forms of participation*, which leave the bulk of decisions on how a new work system shall be designed to experts and traditional design teams. In contrast, the PD method strives for *direct* or *full participation*, involving all members continuously throughout the system in the redesign process.

SHORTCOMINGS OF REENGINEERING AND STS

Participative Design seeks to overcome many of the shortcomings that plague existing redesign methods, particularly Reengineering and STS. As pointed out earlier in our brief historical account, expert-oriented methods contain a number of pitfalls that have retarded efforts to design and diffuse self-managing work systems in organizations. The limitations and problems with Reengineering and STS are reviewed in more detail below.

1. **An Elite Few Design the Future for the Many.** A common feature of both STS and Reengineering methods is to establish a small team from within the organization to lead the redesign effort. In the case of STS, a "design team" is assembled by drawing from a "vertical slice" of the organization. A typical design team may be composed of six to twelve members, usually including several supervisors, professional staff, and workers from different functional areas. Often a special room is provided to the design team, and members may work together in close quarters for six to eighteen months. The design team is charged with the task of conducting the analytical work that is used to assess the functioning of the social and technical systems of the organization. The design team uses the data gathered from these analyses to develop proposals for redesigning the target organization. As the design process progresses, the design team assumes an expert role. After conducting all their detailed analytical work, they are faced with the monumental task of coming up with the "one best design" for the whole organization.

Reengineering also borrows this format but is much less participative than STS. Hammer and Champy (1993) believe reengineering can't be done from the bottom up and can never be a democratic process. The group that does the designing is composed mainly of senior managers— the Business Process Reengineering (BPR) team. The BPR team analyzes and redesigns each core work process, such as order fulfillment, logistics, materials management, and so on. Many BPR teams end up papering their walls with detailed workflow diagrams and complicated charts of business processes. Cloistered together in a secure room, the team scrutinizes the process to find out where they might be able to save some money, reduce headcount, or increase margins.

Hammer and Champy (1993) concede that front-line managers and rank-and-file employees do not have a broad enough perspective to redesign a whole process. Process improvement can only occur across organizational functions. Most managers on the front lines are struggling to optimize their little functional piece of the pie. Even if front-line managers were to get together and redesign the process from beginning to end, middle management—intent on protecting its own vested interests—would shut it down as fast as they could. The only positions that are not vulnerable to being reengineered lie at the organizational apex—the CEO or division general manager. For Hammer and Champy, it is only the upper echelon that can look objectively down upon the whole work process and that has the clout and power to require a forced march. Only those at the very top should possess the authority to change sensitive systems like compensation, approve structural changes, and redesign jobs so that people will focus on processes instead of functions. The role of front-line and middle managers is merely to provide pertinent information to the BPR team.

Jack Cabrey, CEO of Sequa Chemicals, isn't comfortable with the elite role Hammer and Champy would have him and his senior management team play. Cabrey contends, "This is where we part company with Michael Hammer. He thinks management should be driving the whole process. Our experience is that if senior management leads the process improvement group or any kind of group, then they are going to get their way. And that means we won't get the best thinking or the best design. It also means that when you get down to implementation someone is going to feel shortchanged and then the leader will end up feeling like Julius Caesar on the Ides of March. He gets stabbed in the back by covert resistance: *Et tu, Brute.* This approach (Participative Design) slows you down a bit until everyone is on board; then it's like the Millennium Falcon in *Star Wars* when they hit the hyperdrive."

As one might suspect, there are a number of problems with both STS and Reengineering, where an elite few are designing the future for the many. The fact that Design/BPR teams are isolated from the rest of the organization as they are conducting their analytical and design activities contributes to a lack of trust and a great deal of suspicion among those whose jobs may be affected by the work of the Design/BPR team. The expert and elite status of the Design/BPR team, coupled with its power to make irreversible design decisions without the consent of those whose jobs may be affected, generates resistance. An elite group that has carte blanche authority to change everyone else's job is rarely able to engender enough trust and ownership in the larger organization to make acceptance of a new design workable. Design/BPR teams often become pariahs in the eyes of employees fearful of losing their jobs. In the face of such resistance, the Design/BPR team has to go to great lengths in an attempt to "sell" their redesign/reengineering proposals.

Another problem related to the Design/BPR team approach is that its expert orientation to redesign often fails to comprehend the subtleties and cultural idiosyncrasies that exist within each unique work system. STS and Reengineering methods are often alienating to those who are excluded from participating directly in the redesign process. This generates further resistance, which raises its ugly head during the implementation phase. It is not surprising then why both STS and Reengineering have such poor track records for implementing sustainable solutions.

2. Overreliance and Dependency on Consultants. Instead of developing a widely distributed capability for self-management, as expert-driven methods STS and Reengineering foster dependency on outside experts and consultants. Indeed, it is in a consultant's self-interest to foster client dependency—after all, their livelihood depends on it. Most consultants would be reluctant to adopt a method that would make the client less dependent on their expertise. The complicated and lengthy methodology is self-serving to some STS consultants, who have been known to stretch out their projects as long as they possibly can. Reengineering consultants do not fare much better.

3. Obfuscating Language and Academic Jargon. One of the pitfalls of the STS method is its off-putting academic jargon. As much of the STS literature was written by academics for academics, translation of the theory into practice has proven difficult. The esoteric flavor of STS has inevitably impeded its diffusion and acceptance as a method among managers and practitioners. Further, such obfuscating language has only served to preserve its expert-based status. This expert-led, consultant-centered orientation keeps it out of the hands of those that can put it to best use: the employees actually doing the work.

4. Piecemeal Approach to Redesign. Reengineering initiatives focus on parts of the organization to make them leaner and meaner, but fail to appreciate that the whole is greater than the sum of the parts. Reengineering as a method is based on reductionistic thinking—not systems thinking. Each work process is optimized separately as if it existed in a vacuum. The narrow business-process focal setting of Reengineering doesn't take into account the interdependencies between the organization's parts, and the interactions between the entire business and its ever-changing competitive environment. As Womack and Jones (1996) point out in *Lean Thinking,*

> Typically a reengineering approach concentrates on information flow rather than production operations or product development (because functional resistance is much lower for these office activities formerly organized by department). Reengineering rarely looks beyond the firm to delve into the operations of customers or distributors, even when these account for the great majority of costs and lead times. (p. 252)

This reductionist way of doing things is so strongly ingrained in our thinking that it pervades both the way we ask questions and the questions we ask. As Russell Ackoff (1994) aptly put it, "We fail more often because we solve the wrong problem than because we get the wrong solution to the right problem. . . . The problems we select for solution and the way we formulate them depends more on our philosophy and world view than on our science and technology."

Reengineering attempts to take the pieces of the machine bureaucracy apart to understand what's really essential in the work process that adds value. Once this analytic work is accomplished, some redundant pieces are discarded, others are replaced with information technology, and the core pieces that remain are put back together in a new, reengineered organization. Sounds logical and simple enough. However, this mechanistic approach to design and change is overly simplistic when dealing with social systems. When a social system is taken apart, it often loses many essential properties that emerge from the interaction of the system's parts. Consider a social system such as that of a basketball team. Every team has its own norms, values, and ways of working together. Imagine matching up the 1998 NBA champions—the Chicago Bulls—against an all-star team whose players are selected based on their superior individual performance. Star players like Carl Malone, Grant Hill, Kobe Bryant, Gary Payton, and Patrick Ewing will be paired up against Michael Jordan, Scotty Pippen, Dennis Rodman, Tony Kukoc, and Luc Longley. The all-stars will have a couple of weeks to practice before they play the Bulls. Given their individual superior performance, would you place your bets on the all-star team? Does the individual performance of star athletes from different teams equal stronger collective performance against the best team in the NBA?

Reductionistic thinking ignores the synergistic properties that are inherent in social systems. Reengineering is based on the assumption that organizations can be socially engineered to a set of rational specifications. However, social systems can't be analyzed, taken apart, and rebuilt in the same way that machines can be. Reengineering is an apt term for what its advocates attempt to do. While the engineering metaphor is appealing, it fails to explain or take into account the complexity of social systems. It also failed long ago when time-and-motion studies overlooked the fact that workers had an informal system for circumventing productivity improvement schemes. Hammer and other expert-oriented consultants seem somewhat naïve when it comes to understanding how to change social systems.

5. Slow and Cumbersome Processes. STS and Reengineering are too slow, cumbersome, and alienating to those not directly involved in the upstream analytical work. Only the Design/BPR teams are trained in the analytical methods (usually by external consultants). The STS method involves a long and arduous data-gathering process, often taking anywhere between six months to a year. During this process, the design team engages in cumbersome and detailed analyses of the organization's external environment, and social and technical systems. Only after all of the analytical work is completed does the design team begin to explore redesign alternatives. Based on its findings, the design team attempts to develop a more balanced organizational design, one that will jointly optimize the social system with new or existing technology.

Many STS design teams often lose energy and patience as they are wading through the complicated variances matrices and control charts, social-survey data, interviews, and other research tasks. While most design teams get bogged down and become bored with the analytical work, others over-invest in it and produce reports that resemble doctoral dissertations. During this lengthy and tedious analysis phase, design teams become isolated from the rest of the organization. Other employees in the organization begin to look at the design team as another group of experts cloistered together for a long period of time—up to something big—"but they won't tell us."

The appeal of Reengineering is the speed at which its advocates claim improvement is possible. However, executive sponsors tend to overesti-mate the speed at which top-down change can happen. In theory, the fact that the BPR team is primarily staffed by senior managers should enable speedy progress toward mapping and implementing a new process design. In reality, once the new design is "rolled out" to the rest of the organization, resistance surfaces and implementation slows down. In fact, an MIT study of reengineering initiatives in the telecommunications and medical-products industries found that projects averaged eighteen months in dura-tion, and in several firms the implementation phase was dragged out over three years. Evidently Hammer and Champy's promise of speedy imple-mentation is an overinflated claim.

6. Partial Versus Fundamental Change. Experts redesign work processes without fundamentally changing from a bureaucratic to a democratic structure, a failing that comes back to haunt them. Often this is because those doing the designing don't understand that fundamental change requires uprooting and unlearning long-held beliefs about hierarchy, authority, and how work should be designed. The mental models experts carry around in their heads still reflect powerful and deep-seated assump-tions that reinforce bureaucratic organization. Those doing the designing also lack practical theories and internally consistent principles for putting together the structural building blocks that make self-managing organiza-tions work. The presence of these unexplored assumptions creates the illu-sion of fundamental change while merely rearranging the deckchairs on the bureaucratic *Titanic*. Reengineering, like STS, often leaves in place an organization caught between two competing paradigms—management by control at the top and team-based management at the bottom. This design resembles the political situation Hong Kong people face under China's rule: two systems, one country. Under Reengineering and STS initiatives, an elite dominant hierarchy is left intact while the masses are supposedly told they are empowered. Emery calls this a mixed-mode design, which breeds confusion and cynicism. Reengineering and STS both fail to achieve fun-damental and permanent structural change because very few people in the organization really have a clear understanding of what the redesign process is all about. While STS does seek to create a more democratic and high-performance workplace, the design team rarely has a conscious and shared understanding of the design principles underlying self-managing organi-zations.

7. Assumption of Common Interests and Avoidance of Conflict. Both STS and Reengineering make light of the fact that different groups and individuals in organizations have different interests, and this usually results in some form of conflict. With STS, the focus is on achieving a harmonious balance, or joint optimization, of the social and technical systems. The organismic language of open systems theory is invoked to emphasize "the system's" goals—high performance, joint optimization, quality, productivity, and so on. However, this emphasis speaks of "the organization" as if it were an independent biological organism or social collective that has a welfare over and above the welfares of participating individuals. It assumes that organizations have aims and goals of their own, and that the behavior of individual members is directed toward them. This focus on harmony and common interests obscures the fact that apparent organizational goals may simply reflect (or conceal) the personal goals of a dominant coalition (senior management and expert consultants) who have the power to impose their design preferences on others. STS and Reengineering methods redesign the division of labor, which usually results in semiautonomous work teams designed around business processes. STS and Reengineering do not redesign the *division of power* or structure of authority in organizations. These methods have shied away from designs that raise questions and issues about *who has what rights to do which things*.

8. Ignoring the Human Side of Change. It's a cardinal rule among change-management gurus that successful implementation of a new organization design depends on the support and commitment of the people who will be most affected. Like any other large-scale change effort that affects hundreds or even thousands of people, reengineering is also culturally dependent. A Coopers & Lybrand study found that one of the major causes of reengineering failures could be attributed to a lack of understanding regarding change management. Reengineers tend to look at the world through a mechanistic lens, thinking that their designs will function like clockwork without any need to manage the human side of change. Widespread fear and anxiety running rampant through the organization can make it difficult for the BPR team's message to be heard. Three years after initiating the reengineering juggernaut, Hammer himself admitted in a *Wall Street Journal* interview (Lancaster, 1995) that he "wasn't smart enough" when it came to the human dimension in process redesign.

The rush to reengineer corporations is but a modern-day form of Taylorism, only now those affected by the scheme are not dumb turn-of-the-century immigrants but educated, motivated, and aware professionals. The engineering mindset of eradicating inefficiency that industrial engineers once so coolly applied to the laborer on the assembly line has now trickled up—the engineers now find themselves designed out of a job. The threat of economic insecurity for the "survivors" of reengineering is very much similar to the threat immigrants, thanks to scientific management, once faced. Both groups found that they were easily replaced—redundant parts. Like scientific management, reengineering ignored the human side of the equation.

9. Resistance at the Implementation Stage. Reengineering and STS succeed or fail during the implementation stage. All the painstaking analysis and elegant design proposals amount to naught if implementation falters. Many STS projects produce great designs on paper, but have a difficult time getting them implemented in practice. Reengineering projects don't fare much better. Even the so-called success stories—Hallmark, Capital Holding Corporation, Mutual Benefit Life—held up as exemplary cases in Hammer and Champy's book have lost their luster. Enid Mumford and her associates (1996) reported how Davenport found many cases of unfulfilled promises at these companies—increased costs, new business processes that were more difficult to manage than previous ones, poorer return on assets and equity, and demoralized employees. During implementation, BPR teams and Reengineering Steering Committees often spend a lot of time cajoling middle managers (what's left of them) to embrace the new system. Turf battles can grind things to a halt at any moment. Resistance should be expected at the implementation stage when change is driven by higher-ups and employees are simply told to get with the program. Resistance to implementation should come as no surprise when an elite Design/BPR team has cloistered itself for up to a year while it collected and analyzed data, meanwhile keeping affected employees in the dark. When the Design/BPR team suddenly emerges—like Moses with the tablets from the mountaintop—to announce the details of what will happen to every employee, resistance should be expected. When half-hearted promises of participation are used to get "buy-in" to the redesign, resistance should be expected. And when the people whose work and jobs will change are kept out of the give-and-take of generating alternative solutions, the only rational response is—in fact—resistance.

ADVANTAGES AND BENEFITS OF PARTICIPATIVE DESIGN

Our interest is shifting from totalitarian administration to Participative Design, from representative democracy to full participation. Participative Design overcomes the problems and shortcomings associated with expert-driven redesign methods and has very little use for high-powered consultants, elite design teams, or so-called reengineering czars. Instead, Participative Design provides employees with the conceptual and practical tools for doing the hard design and organizational change work that has traditionally been the task of experts. Because Participative Design treats employees as experts in their own right, allowing them to design changes that fit their unique set of circumstances, an atmosphere of trust is created. And because no designs are ever imposed, employees are more inclined to participate and take an active part in the design process. As their interests are taken into account, and as people become more directly involved in the design work, powerful feelings of psychological ownership are evoked. In this respect, Participative Design goes a long way toward overcoming the problems of resistance and diffusion of the self-managing work systems to the whole corporation.

Given the elegance and simplicity of the PD method, along with the fact that the methodology is fast and doesn't involve a lengthy and time-consuming analytical process, employees can redesign their own departments and sections. Large organizations—like Syncrude Canada and Foster's Brewing—have redesigned to self-managing work systems in less than year. The transition to self-managing work teams is also smoother as such changes are sustained and maintained, because employees are the architects of the process. After all, why should anyone resist or be opposed to his or her own creations? Indeed, PD is based on the common sense idea that employees are more willing to embrace change and own new methods of working when the process is "home grown" and is protected by a commitment to democratic mechanisms of decision making.

The benefits and advantages of the PD method over STS, Reengineering, and human relations–oriented methods can be summarized as follows:

Table 3.1 Comparisons Between Reengineering, STS, and Participative Design Methods

Issues	Reengineering	STS	PD
Locus of Design	BPR team	Design team	Local units
Design Orientation	Expert-oriented	Expert-oriented	Participant-oriented
Design Focus	Technical: Redesign organization around business processes, eliminate non-value-added work	Social & Technical: Redesign organization to create a better match between people and technology	Structural: Redesign to organization to relocate responsibility for control and coordination in self-managing teams
Governance Structure	A secret team does the design work, without direct participation by those affected.	A representative team does the design work with some solicitation of input and feedback.	Employees themselves do the design work for each unit. Participation is direct and immediate.
Implementation Time	Lengthy (1–3 years)	Lengthy (1–3 years)	Fast (3–12 months)
Track Record	70 percent failure rate	Successful for well-bounded units, but poor diffusion record	With proper preparation, widespread diffusion and acceptance

1. PD Focuses on Making Systemic, Structural Change. Making a fundamental shift to self-management requires systemic, structural change throughout the organization. Participative Design is not merely an "employee involvement" method or a program that is limited to the lower operational levels. PD produces major structural changes that shift and redistribute power throughout the organization. And since significant changes in the power structure are inevitable with successful Participative Design projects, everyone's job and role is affected: the tasks and functions of senior executives, middle management, and operational level employees are all radically transformed.

Participative Design is focused on changing the systems and structures within which people work, rather than engaging in a futile attempt to alter people to work differently in the same system. The latter, the behavioral-science approach, has been quite popular over the decades and has deep roots in the human relations school. Most of what has been propagated under the rubric of team-based training, management-skill-building courses, and leadership development programs, is simply old wine in new bottles—repackaged for resale by shrewd consultants out to make a quick buck. Despite the fact that these fads have proven to be terribly ineffective in demonstrating tangible and bottom-line results, they are still popular and in demand, according to research by Barry Macy and associates (1993). As in reengineering, the problem with piecemeal approaches is that they fail to consider organizations as complex systems. Specialized tools or training programs are created to deal with each component of an organization as a separate entity. These approaches break large complex systems down by separating them out into smaller elements. Indeed, a whole industry of specialized "change agents" has emerged to work with various elements of the organization. There are consultants of all stripes and varieties specializing in team-building, leadership, group facilitation, culture, communication skills, conflict management, and so on, ad nauseam. Now there are even "systems thinking" specialists, which seems like an oxymoron.

2. PD Facilitates Self-Managed Learning. Based on his own observations of the Participative Design process at Sequa Chemicals, Wes Reid stated, "People learn best from their actions and involvement, not from being told something as an intellectual concept. You can't just go out and do team building disconnected from the real work people do. People need to participate in change projects for things to become real for them and for meaningful changes to occur in how they go about doing their work." He's right. Self-managed learning is very different from traditional approaches to training and development. Too much money has been wasted on countless hours of training, while the pillars of bureaucracy are left untouched. As everyone knows, training sessions are frequently used as a way to introduce the latest management fad. Most people shrink when they learn that they must take time away from their jobs to sit through yet another flavor-of-the-month training session. Take TQM for example. In many organizations TQM was implemented by using a training-and-education model. Droves of employees were sent to mandatory training sessions to learn about quality concepts, methods, and philosophy. Yet TQM training didn't provide employees a systematic approach to get rid of bureaucracy, or a way to redesign the whole organization. Benchmarking is yet another example. Many organizations who jumped on the benchmarking bandwagon had trouble importing and implementing the "best practices" that they had studied at other firms.

Conventional training robs people of the opportunity to take responsibility and control for their own learning. Instead, the unspoken assumption among educators, trainers, and consultants is that people are basically incapable of making sense out of their own worlds, that such a task must be subjugated to packaged instructions that impose the wisdom of the expert. This assumption is based on an educational paradigm that conceives people as lacking the perceptual capacities to learn from their own experience; rather, one must learn and acquire knowledge by memorizing facts, through rote instruction, or assimilating the knowledge that has been accumulated by experts. Most learning in the real world, however, happens not in the artificial and sterile classroom but in "communities of practice," on the job, and in many cases, in spite of teachers or formal trainers. The hidden curriculum of conventional training programs conveys the subliminal message that people must depend upon qualified experts or "certified instructors" in order to learn something new, even if that means learning to be creative. What really underlies this pedagogy is the urge to exercise, and belief in the necessity for, social control.

In contrast, the PD method enables employees and managers at all levels of the business to change their own organizations in real time through self-managed learning. Self-managed learning makes people more confident to trust their instincts and creativity, since there aren't any high-powered experts dictating the "one best way" for doing their work. Consequently, self-managed learning progressively decreases dependency on formal expert authorities.

Participative Design is a systematic do-it-yourself method that uses consultants only as resources to the learning process. Indeed, it has been well demonstrated that techniques that put consultants at center stage, where they become indispensable to sustaining the change process, impede implementation and diffusion. The accumulated experience and expertise of those participating in the redesign of their own work is what fuels the self-managed learning process. Self-managed learning is emancipating. Participative Design sessions provide people, empowered as experts in their own right, with a real-time glimpse of what it means to work in a self-managing group without traditional supervisors, trainers, or consultants hovering over their shoulders.

Self-managed learning also helps people to take risks and to act on the knowledge and expertise they already possess. During the Participative Design process employees *learn by doing*. By sharing their tacit knowledge and hard-won operational experience, employees develop a more enriched understanding of existing work practices while exploring possibilities for fundamental improvement. The PD process provides a legitimate forum in which employees can articulate their demands and wishes in a concrete way by actually producing prototypes of various operational designs. The merits of these various "alternative designs" or "design prototypes" are thoroughly discussed and evaluated before a collectively agreed-upon decision to select a final, optimal design is made.

But don't be fooled: self-managed learning doesn't happen automatically. The conditions have to be right. Participative Design sessions are structured so that people are provided accurate and complete information about the environment, the driving forces leading to the redesign, a statement of vision and purpose for the business. They also need a milieu that is free from coercion and manipulation, and where everyone has an equal opportunity to participate. With these conditions in place, employees will be much more open to considering alternative perspectives. People will be more likely to learn from others, while at the same time being able to critically evaluate arguments and proposals for new designs. Under these ideal conditions, self-managed learning helps people to make informed, objective and rational decisions for the good of the whole.

3. PD Pools Knowledge and Initiatives for Change. It is often the case that employees within a department may have only a partial understanding of the problems in their functional area, especially if their work is interdependent with that of other groups within the organization. Their knowledge is fragmented because they cannot see the big picture. Nor do they possess the authority to collectively develop local solutions and act to solve the complicated problems that they encounter. Turf battles often prevent managers and employees from collaborating with their peers who have the critical knowledge necessary to resolve problems and conflicts. Similarly, senior management may have the power to act, but are too far removed from local problems to contribute in a meaningful way. An exclusive top-down approach to design doesn't work because it fails to engender people's commitment. Nor does a bottom-up approach, which often lacks both a big-picture focus and top-management support. The chronic problems for any organization always seem to occur between boundaries. These problems tend to grow worse as the business environment changes. In most cases, employees are aware of these problems but haven't had the time, authority, or resources to correct them. When employees come together in a Participative Design session they begin by examining: Where are problems currently occurring? Are the groupings that delineate the work of different departments correctly drawn? How can interactions and linkages between departments be modified to speed up the workflow and improve responsiveness to customer demands? In a new work configuration, where are problems likely to occur? How can a new work design minimize those problems? Where are the opportunities to drive down total costs in the whole value stream?

The PD process has also been used to pool and integrate the knowledge of various functional groups. For example, if the task is to redesign and improve the way new products are developed, employees from R&D, marketing, sales, production, and technical service are grouped together to redesign the integrative linkages between them. Participants from various functions pool their perceptions about how systems, processes, methods, and technologies can be redesigned to improve their collective work. The PD process enables people to achieve in joint activity what they could never achieve alone (or in homogenous functions). By pooling knowledge and initiatives for change, employees and management together can create, for themselves, new organizational arrangements, new explanations of why things are as they are, and therefore new possibilities for committed action.

4. PD Creates Optimal Conditions for Mutual Trust. One of the cardinal rules that differentiates PD from other redesign approaches is that *no designs may ever be imposed*. Totalitarian change management techniques are incompatible with PD. Each employee needs to be assured from the beginning that senior management doesn't have a preconceived design in mind that is being imposed on him or her. Similarly, employees must have absolute confidence that PD is not a cooptive process for merely soliciting their input or securing their "buy-in" to management's agenda. And since any major redesign effort usually evokes fear, anxiety, and suspicion, it is essential that management sincerely convey their adherence to the cardinal rule of "no designs imposed." Adherence to this rule implies that various interests must be taken into account and be given equal parity and a legitimate voice in the design process. The PD process therefore acknowledges that there will always be conflicts of interest during any major change, which may not be solely between management and employees, but can also occur between different functional groups that might be fearful of losing their power base or status in the company. Since the PD method brings differences and conflicts of interest into the open, setting up conditions for mutual trust is critical.

With the PD approach, all information about the design process is shared widely and openly. There are no design teams cloistered away from the rest of the organization, or outside consultants running around conducting confidential interviews. In other words, all the information-gathering and analysis activity is conducted with employees present. There is no master plan, hidden agendas, or secret deals going on behind the scenes—all information is directly available. We have to be straight with people. Wes Reid, an engineering manager at Sequa Chemicals who was instrumental in their Participative Design effort, emphasized the importance of openness: "We can't candy coat information when the news isn't so great. All we can do to remain credible is to let everyone have the facts about what is going on and then they will start to believe it. People need the information that is important to them. If they don't get it, they will be anxious, fearful, and eventually shut down and burn out."

Mutual trust is also enhanced during the Participative Design process as official status differences are minimized by working within self-managing groups governed by a ground-rule where all perceptions are allowed equal air time. The sharing of perceptions related to the past, present, and future of the enterprise, especially the focus on shared ideals, establishes the sense that members of the organization—from CEO to janitor—are psychologically similar and share similar concerns. Once conditions for mutual trust are established, conflicts can be acknowledged, and a design can be developed which satisfies mutual interests of all participants.

5. PD Is the Conscious Application of the Democratic Design Principle.
When the Founding Fathers drafted the U.S. Constitution they sidestepped an important issue in the Bill of Rights. This issue was so contentious, it threatened to break apart the Union. Eventually a civil war was fought over this issue—slavery. We as a people had to confront the tenet that all men (and, we later conceded, all women) are created equal and have certain inalienable rights. Similarly, a conceptual form of civil war is often fought inside organizations that customarily implement self-management in a

piecemeal fashion, underestimating the power of a bureaucracy and how it enslaves people. Those interested and supportive of self-management on the periphery are often pitted against the elites in the corporate power center. Since most change management programs don't confront bureaucracy head-on, centralized authority may persist for many years. Even companies that have ruthlessly eliminated layers of management and put self-directed teams in place may still find themselves fighting their own version of a corporate civil war. The die-hard traditionalists that have a vested interest in protecting the status quo are at odds with the advocates pushing for workplace reform.

One way to bring unity to the organization is to educate the whole organization up front in the principles that underlie self-managing work systems. People need to have a clear understanding of the redesign process, its rationale, and the goals the organization is trying to achieve. Before the Participative Design process gets off the ground, every employee learns about the differences between the bureaucratic and democratic design principles. These principles are introduced and discussed up front, so people can consciously apply them as they go about the process of redesigning their sections and departments. Moreover, once people grasp these principles, they can then use them to critically evaluate the merits of new designs proposals and test to see whether such designs truly reflect and embody a revolutionary democratic organization. Such an acid test is necessary to sort out genuine self-managing work designs from those that are simply variations of the old bureaucratic paradigms in disguise.

If people don't have conscious knowledge and understanding of the differences between these two fundamental design principles, problems are likely to occur. Compromises are likely to be made during the design process that result in a confusing mixture of the design principles. Teams may be formed, but supervisors will still hold the reins of authority and control. The result is "managed teams," not "self-managing teams." Even in instances where self-managing teams are created, the designers of these systems won't be able to fully articulate why their system works, or why such democratic structures are necessary. This makes their system vulnerable to outright attacks from corporate headquarters, dismantling by new incoming management who don't understand it, and regression over time back to the bureaucratic mean. Such systems will be subject to the changing whims and arbitrary dictums of those with more articulate arguments for getting back to the basics. In other words, if people don't have conscious knowledge of the design principles, they won't be able to clearly articulate the rationale behind the design. They won't have the conceptual horsepower to ward off attempts and appeals by those who believe democratic structures lack "management control," "accountability," and "order."

6. PD Uses Unique Designs Based on Local Knowledge. No organization can expect to succeed by copying designs that worked for another company, or by implementing a design that may be theoretically sound on paper, but in practice wouldn't be accepted by the culture. With PD, unique designs are derived from the local knowledge of employees, rather than relying solely upon the advice of outside experts and higher-level managers. Different designs can evolve that are consistent with the values, beliefs, skills, interests, and informal relationships that characterize the local culture. The Participative Design process doesn't ignore the personal idiosyncrasies, variety of needs, and special preferences of the people involved. Indeed, the design must be optimal for all those involved in the new system. In contrast, when management (along with their legions of young MBA consultants) alone attempts to redesign the work of a department or business process, the local knowledge of employees who actually do the work is usually not taken adequately into account. Social scientists have confirmed this; both experts and managers often gloss over issues and fail to notice crucial details that are obvious to employees. In fact, employees attribute half of workplace problems to local issues that could be known only to those who have become intimately familiar with day-to-day workplace realities. Unless employees participate directly in the redesign process, many problems will simply resurface as new computer systems, work processes, and organizational arrangements are put in place. Rather than having an elite group of experts clamoring to figure out how the place works and how it could be made to work better, why not tap the knowledge of the people who collectively know the ins and outs of the system already. In fact, employees already have strong views and good ideas about how things can be improved, not only for themselves, but also for their peers and colleagues and the organization as a whole.

In many respects, the PD process can compared to building a custom-designed dream home. Instead of simply purchasing a prefabricated suburban tract home where one size fits all, the builder works collaboratively with architects, contractors, interior designers, and landscapers to create a unique home that meets the needs and tastes of the owner. Similarly, PD is a powerful tool that allows employees to redesign their own workplaces in harmony with the larger organization. The power of the method lies in the conjunction of participative processes with democratic structures so that employees can become self-managing, both in the redesign and in the management of their own work. Participative Design provides capability for self-management, guided by local thinking about what is appropriate and feasible. When employees share what they know, what they have learned, and what they need to know and learn, a socially creative learning process is put into action. It is a learning process that honestly respects and draws from the local knowledge of individuals. And it is a learning process that allows the organization to update its experience, discard outdated strategies, and invent new designs that are optimal.

7. PD Uses A Broad-Front Approach. PD is an ingenious method for overcoming the problem of diffusion and resistance. Unlike STS and Reengineering, which rely on one small, isolated group (the Design/BPR team) to generate a single design for the whole organization, the PD method utilizes a broad-front approach. This approach broadly distributes redesign activities by getting everyone involved in a series of Participative Design sessions. For example, at Syncrude Canada's Mine Mobile Maintenance division, over eight hundred employees were directly involved in a series of eleven Participative Design sessions that culminated in a large town-hall meeting event where the various redesign proposals were discussed and debated before arriving at a consensus on the most optimal design (see Chapter 10). With PD, every section, department, geographic unit, and management level in the organization participates directly in generating its own designs. Some groups may work in parallel on their own areas and then compare notes for the redesign of their section. In other cases, groups from different areas (like engineering and manufacturing) may be paired in Participative Design sessions, where each group can challenge, question, and critique the other's design.

The broad-front approach increases the scope and depth of participation in the redesign process. Getting everyone involved in PD sessions creates a critical mass of people within the organization who can participate in all phases of the redesign process (planning, analysis, developing and evaluating alternatives, implementation, etc.). Rather than developing one potted plant (the design team approach), the PD approach is an intentional diffusion strategy, "letting a thousand flowers bloom." When everyone in the organization is given the opportunity to participate directly in redesigning his or her own workplace, learning, energy, and commitment spread. This is the essence of diffusion. Each person within the organization who has been a participant in a PD session becomes a potential diffuser of self-management. In contrast, the use of design teams, experimental sites, and pilot projects often encounters resistance and subsequently these do not diffuse widely to the whole organization, because those whose cooperation is required to make the new design work do not regard the changes as being in their best interest. With PD, each employee is involved as a full participant from the start, and has a direct say in shaping the contours of the design for his or her area.

HOW PARTICIPATIVE DESIGN HELPED CELGARD ADAPT RAPIDLY TO STRATEGIC SHIFTS AND NEW TECHNOLOGY

Two hundred forty people work at CELGARD, LLC., a wholly owned subsidiary of Hoechst AG. Located in Charlotte, North Carolina, CELGARD designs and manufactures membranes used in cellular batteries for computers and cell phones, hollow fibers used in blood oxygenators for heart bypass operations, and modules of hollow fibers used in ultrapure water treatment for circuit-board manufacturing processes. By the fall of 1995, the business had four product lines, three located in Charlotte and one in Wiesbaden, Germany, and a technical sales office in Tokyo. CELGARD has experienced rapid growth over the last five years.

The rapid pace of growth strained CELGARD's business systems to the breaking point. Simultaneous changes were needed in both information technology and organizational structure. In the spring of 1995 the new general manager, Milo Hassloch, focused his attention on redesigning the whole organization using Participative Design and Search Conference methods. In prior assignments, Hassloch had orchestrated organizational redesign efforts to create a team-based organization and had directed quality management efforts in the regional headquarters for Hoechst Celanese Fibers Group.

With Hassloch's executive sponsorship, a Participative Design change process was initiated that would involve all employees. Under the guidance of consultant John Duncan, the Participative Design process was broken into three stages. In the first stage, the senior management team and six middle managers and engineers created a strategic organization design, mapping out those parts of the business that gave CELGARD a distinctive competitive advantage. Senior management identified three business lines that provided CELGARD a distinct competitive advantage in the marketplace.

Seven Participative Design (PD) sessions were held, involving over 130 employees in redesigning the operating level for each of the three competitive-advantage business processes. Employees who would work in the new business lines fleshed out the details of the operating structure in these local PD sessions. The first business line was relatively small, and required only one PD session. The second business line required two PD sessions, and the third line was redesigned using three PD sessions. Stage Two was completed when the senior and middle managers, who were responsible for the total business performance of these business lines, conducted their own PD session to redesign the management hierarchy. During this PD session, managers designed a new organizational structure to operate three product lines, and also addressed roles and responsibilities for dealing with the design, manufacture, and service of product offerings.

Stage Three involved ninety more employees in the redesign of essential support processes that served the business lines. A total of five PD sessions were conducted. The first two PD sessions concentrated on developing a macro-design of business essential support processes. Physical resources, information and quality assurance, financial management, order fulfillment, and human resource management were the individual business processes defined in these macro-design sessions. Another PD session was used to work out the hierarchical arrangements. Participants in this session created middle-level-business essential-support teams (BESTs) to support the operating level teams in the five business essential-process areas.

In the next two PD sessions, professional and hourly employees who worked in the essential-support areas moved the process forward to the point of redesigning roles and identifying new skill requirements for each support area. Employees then nominated themselves, as well as their peers, to fill the positions in the new organizational architecture.

After nominations for new positions were made, the BEST reviewed employee requests and began making new work team assignments. In total, thirty-five teams were formed. Each team was responsible for developing a team charter that would be reviewed and sanctioned by management at a later date. Each team charter specified the team's mission, goals and outputs, roles and structure, unresolved issues, priorities, work plan, and performance measures. (See Chapter 9 for more details on this step.)

However, not all teams would be self-managing. In order to create a team structure, team members needed to have a common goal, a willingness to work together, joint accountability, and sufficient task interdependence. Joint accountability includes giving teams the authority to hire and fire their own members. Self-managing teams also conduct their own performance appraisals and actually make compensation decisions. Depending on the skill maturity of team members and the complexity of the task, varying authority structures were designed.

CELGARD's managers understand that joint accountability requires self-managing team structures. Otherwise, regression to a traditional command-and-control structure is inevitable. Participation in the design process proved to be so valuable and effective in generating commitment and success in the organization that such participation was extended to strategic planning activities. Senior managers, key technical leaders, and savvy business stakeholders were given a direct voice in the creation of the overall business strategy. A planning team was put in place to organize a Search Conference for January of 1998 that would involve forty strategic thinkers from Japan, Germany, and the U.S. in charting the future of CELGARD's businesses.

At the same time that all these design changes were occurring, information-systems changes also needed to be made to support business growth. At corporate headquarters, Hoechst AG had already committed to an SAP R/3 implementation worldwide. General Motors Chief Information Officer Ralph Szygenda points out, "A lot of companies buy these systems and they're worse off then they were." SAP's R/3 software ties together and automates the basic processes of business—taking orders, checking credit, verifying payments, balancing the books. CELGARD hired a consulting firm to help reconfigure SAP's R/3 software system to their business.

CELGARD couldn't afford to get entangled in a lengthy implementation nightmare. Senior managers, having learned how beneficial participation can be in redesigning work systems, paid serious attention to the human factor during the implementation of the SAP R/3 software system reconfiguration. An implementation team consisting of half CELGARD employees and half consulting personnel was assembled to work full time on customization of the R/3 system modules. Four senior managers served as sponsors for the project. "I knew SAP R/3 was so complicated most companies usually change the way their people work, rather than how the system works, but I wanted to involve people in the change effort to avoid the long-drawn-out implementations we were hearing about," says Hassloch. High-involvement methods can be used to speed up and ensure smooth implementation of SAP systems. For example, Search Conferences that employ a rapid-strategy-creation process can be used with a key group of stakeholders to chart an implementation strategy for R/3 software systems. Once a collective strategy has been agreed upon by involving all stakeholders, Participative Design sessions can be used to establish new roles to support the software. The critical success factor is to ensure that the context of the actual workplace is incorporated into implementation planning. Senior management again turned to their consultant, John Duncan, to utilize a participative approach to facilitate employee involvement in the R/3 implementation. Order fulfillment was the first targeted process.

The planning team decided CELGARD could reduce the high stress and organizational upheaval characteristic of complex software-system implementations by conducting a Search Conference to craft an organization-wide implementation strategy. The implementation plan proved to be remarkably effective. "We developed an implementation plan that went beyond the direct SAP R/3 project work," says Mack Bailey, the manager of Information and Quality. Search Conference participants acquired a greater sense of the urgency of the need for change to support the implementation of and to fully utilize the SAP R/3 systems software. "The Search Conference provided detailed plans for middle-level managers all over the organization to prepare their people for the installation of the system," says Bill Seeliger, the manufacturing-process manager. The Participative Design process was adapted for the detailed role redesign to make sure implementation occurred smoothly.

In January of 1998, another Search Conference was held for strategic thinkers from all over CELGARD to plot an overall business strategy. Two new strategic directions emerged. Management is very excited about these new strategic opportunities and is actively pursuing them. Milo Hassloch, the GM, said of this process, "The time spent here was highly valuable. Our key leadership gained a whole-systems view of this business, which is essential for our success." One of the participants remarked, "I am really surprised that we accomplished all that we set out to do in such a short period of time, especially to have the commitment to pull it off." One of the new German managers who participated in the Search Conference commented, "This was the best experience I've ever had to assimilate the nature of the business I serve." And a Japanese manager remarked, "I finally understand the bridge between strategy and why this company uses participation the way we do."

The extent of participation in planning and work design has exceeded CELGARD's expectations. A core group of strategic thinkers has spread strategic leadership throughout the business. They understand how to track changes in the business environment, and expect to be able to respond rapidly to further changes before competitors can catch their breath. CELGARD has also developed an internal capability for rapid strategy creation and rapid organizational redesign. These capabilities have diffused broadly to all employees, so that redesign can occur at will whenever it is necessary to adjust and adapt to changing circumstances.

CHAPTER 4

GOING TO THE ROOTS

Changing the Organization Design Principle

The unseen hand of Adam Smith has been replaced by
the visible hand of business bureaucracy.
—Adolf A. Berle and Gardiner Means

POLAROID'S FILM IMAGING RESEARCH DIVISION: A REDESIGN CHALLENGE[1]

Polaroid, like other high-technology companies, was started by a superbly gifted inventor and technological genius, Edwin Land, who acquired over five hundred patents during the course of his career. Land's invention of instant photography and subsequent introduction of the instant camera has made the Polaroid name a household word. Today, Polaroid manufactures instant imaging, conventional film, and digital-imaging products that are used in amateur and professional photography, industry, medicine, and education. With its headquarters in Cambridge, Massachusetts, Polaroid is a high-technology firm with subsidiaries in 35 countries. Polaroid has made a heavy investment in R&D; approximately 4,000 of its 10,000 employees work in some aspect of research, development, or engineering.

Because manufacturers are faced with having to satisfy more sophisticated and demanding customers in the instant-imaging market, the complexity of film products has increased dramatically. Further, as product complexity has increased, so has Polaroid's Film Imaging Research (FIR) organization; diverse scientific disciplines have emerged to develop the

---

[1]Material for this account was derived from a public presentation made by Polaroid employees at the "Ecology of Work" conference in Pittsburgh, Pa., June, 1991.

technical building blocks for complex film-imaging products. In the late 1980s, as both product and organizational complexity increased, the FIR division found it increasingly difficult to develop products in a timely fashion. While the majority of products developed in the past had turned out to be commercially successful, development costs were staggering. Major delays in product programs were not only common, but accepted as par for the course.

Satish Agrawal, then director of FIR, was concerned. Relatively few technical professionals were concerned with customer needs, and most lacked knowledge of the product system's architecture. One reason is that most product-development projects were organized into large, centralized functional-matrix programs. The current organizational structure and segmentation of technical disciplines had inadvertently resulted in a narrow professional focus, leading to overspecialization. Scientists sequestered in segmented departments had become increasingly out of touch with customer requirements. Instead of designing technologies with the requirements of the customer in mind, technology development, as Agrawal described it, ". . . had taken on an esoteric flavor." Identifying more with the standards of their professional disciplines, scientists often produced state-of-the-art solutions which worked flawlessly in their laboratories, but were frequently difficult to implement in product prototypes. These knowledge workers valued technical elegance, which often ran counter to requirements for manufacturability and marketing needs.

By the late 1980s, the largest new product development project in the division was in trouble. This development project was initiated as an effort to improve the overall quality of an earlier product that was still on the market. Agrawal recognized that reducing product-development cycle time would require significant and systemic changes in the way products were conceived, managed, and introduced. But he knew he faced a daunting challenge: the inertia of past history exerted a heavy influence on organizational behavior.

Edwin Land fostered an entrepreneurial spirit and inventive culture which led to Polaroid's early success and rapid growth. Built on a culture of invention, Land's Polaroid was a highly technology-driven organization. A legend in his own company, Land, even when he was CEO, was known for guarding his expert knowledge; obsessed with secrecy, he rarely relinquished control of decision making—he orchestrated projects with a benevolent iron fist.

Several significant restraining forces resulting from Land's cultural legacy were observed.

1. *Maestro Style of Management.* Most managers in the FIR division emulated the autocratic and paternalistic behavior that was so characteristic of Land. Organizational members referred to this as the "maestro model of management," symbolizing the highly dependent relationship upon the idealized leader who is looked to as the source of all commands and directives.

2. *Rewards Go to the Technological Heroes.* The technological heroes in this organization were those who had invented their way to the top. Technological genius and inventiveness were highly valued traits. Competition between professional knowledge workers was fierce. Knowledge sharing between individuals and departments was minimal. Teamwork was a misnomer within the Polaroid culture. In fact, Land had personally regarded teamwork and group cooperation as distractions from individual creativity.

3. *Top-down Communication Patterns.* Given the highly autocratic style of management, communication patterns were primarily top down. The majority of R&D professionals took their direction from one or two senior managers. For all practical purposes, the majority of R&D professionals were dependent upon the expert knowledge of these few senior managers for new product ideas, as well as for resolving product integration problems.

Today, film-imaging products are highly complex, interactive systems. The management group recognized that the Balkanized organizational structure had made it difficult for professional employees to develop an understanding of the interdependencies and complex interactions between the various technical building blocks that comprised the product system. Moreover, the product system was greater than the sum of the technical building blocks. Lacking holistic knowledge of the product system's architecture, it was difficult for knowledge workers to develop technical building blocks that fitted synergistically into the end product. Operational knowledge of the product architecture resided in the heads of a few senior managers. As one senior FIR manager put it, ". . . to the rest of the organization, the product system is an empirical mystery composed of 50,000 permutations of variables." The management team believed that for professionals to develop more of a "product orientation," the whole division would have to be redesigned from the ground up. They realized that the new FIR organization design had to be one which would enhance interdisciplinary collaboration and cross-functional communication. In the new organization, professionals developing technology would consider their work incomplete until their technology was successfully integrated into the end product.

Senior management also realized that they could no longer afford to function as the elite braintrust for the firm—that such brainpower needed to be decentralized and widely distributed through every knowledge worker in the division.

UNDERSTANDING THE DESIGN PRINCIPLES

The story of Polaroid's FIR division illustrates how autocratic management practices and bureaucratic silos are a kiss of death to complex, knowledge-based organizations. Since knowledge work constitutes a larger and more significant portion of the activities of most organizations today, we believe that quality and productivity improvement depends on self-managing organization designs. Decision making in knowledge-based organizations needs to operate differently from the way it does in a machine bureaucracy—designs that were once suitable for mass-producing Model T's and steel. For example, in manufacturing, technical understanding of the process is nearly complete, leading to tight specifications that dictate how the system is to be operated. Past experience in operating the system is directly applicable to future operations, so that those with experience are accorded greater authority in decision making. As these people rise in the system, the combination of their expertise and the tight operating specifications for the system lend strength to the traditional hierarchy. Many decisions are made in a top-down fashion, with little input required from those below in order to reach decisions of acceptable quality.

In knowledge-based organizations, expertise needs to be more widely distributed throughout the organization. Past experience may not be applicable to the development of new products, and as Ralph Katz (1978) has shown, may even inhibit creative thinking. There are few rules to govern the creative process, and yet the pieces of complex products must somehow fit together before they are transferred to manufacturing. These conditions require a more democratic self-managing enterprise, as knowledge specialists often understand more about their own work than their supervisors. Democratic structures must be combined with participative decision-making processes, allowing knowledge workers to collaborate within and between work groups to make most of the technical and operational decisions.

For example, the global sustainability initiative at agribusiness powerhouse Monsanto emerged when new teams were allowed to coalesce around critical research issues. No central authority could have directed such a thorough investigation. Monsanto's CEO, Bob Shapiro, stayed out of the way, relying instead on the information-processing power of teams of dedicated knowledge workers and managers. "The people who have been working on sustainability here have done an incredible job, not because there has been one presiding genius who organized it all and told them what to do but because they want to get it done. They care intensely about it and they organize themselves to do it," says Shapiro (cited in Magretta, 1997). When democratic structures are combined with participative decision-making processes, knowledge workers can collaborate more readily in a work environment that fosters creativity and high performance.

What's behind the freedom from centralized policies that people enjoy at Southwest Airlines? Why are employees treated like customers and their efforts celebrated when they go above and beyond the call of duty? Why is it, as CEO Herb Kelleher puts it, that "When a plane pulls into a gate our people run to meet it?"

Countless schemes and programs have been propagated by expert consultants to explain this kind of workforce commitment, but there is no universal formula, standard blueprint, or cookbook recipe for designing self-managing organizations. We have found that each self-managing organization has a unique design or phenotypical set of characteristics, displaying a variety of forms that reflect different situations and contexts. However, we also have found it to be true that every genuine self-managing organization shares a company-wide and fundamentally unique *design principle*. An organization's design principle, like human DNA, provides the structural information and serves as the operating system for the whole organization (just as MS-DOS does for the majority of IBM-compatible personal computers). In this chapter, we will decipher the genetic code that underlies the self-managing organization, to expose its DNA, or design principle, showing how it differs from that of traditional organizations.

Back to First Principles

Like a mathematician trying to solve a complicated calculus problem, those wishing to design self-managing organizations need to return to first principles. One of the defining characteristics of a first principle in math is that once you understand the principle, it becomes fairly evident if and how a mathematical operation is derived from a given principle. The same is true for organizations; once people understand the design principle underlying self-management, it provides conceptual guidance for people as they begin to redesign organizations to make them consistent with their choices. This is easier said than done, of course.

For example, Dennis W. Bakke, CEO of AES Corporation in Arlington, Virginia, and his counterpart chairman, Roger W. Sant, understand first principles. This maverick power company, which has grown 23 percent annually in its thirteen years of operation, has 1,500 people working in ten countries with only four layers of hierarchy: workers, plant managers, corporate officers, and division managers. There are no corporate departments. Plant managers assign duties like project finance, purchasing, public relations, HR issues, and operations to volunteer teams instead of corporate officers.

What are the principles AES has used to build broad-based empowerment? Are they crazy for trusting plant technicians to buy turbines and other costly supplies, engineers to arrange financing for new plants, a mechanical engineer—with only two months on the job—to negotiate a $1-billion coal contract, or an ad hoc team, including a maintenance technician, to manage a $33-million plant investment fund? Not really. At AES, principles like spreading responsibility across the workforce, fun, integrity, fairness, and social responsibility are taken very, very seriously. And these principles are rigorously defined and adhered to. Fun, for instance, equals intellectually exciting work, the struggle of learning, and the failures that go with it. Plenty of mistakes get made (there is usually a bit of a safety net) and there is tremendous peer pressure to succeed.

Conventional management practice has ignored the importance of understanding principles before leaping into action. Usually organizations feel pressured into adopting a new method because "everyone else is doing it." Reengineering is a classic example. Neither managers nor the recipients of such schemes can articulate the design principle that is driving the method. And usually the majority of organizational members don't have a clear idea of why specific changes are being made and how such changes will affect them.

Design principles are not rigid rules but instructive codes that shape our thinking about how the relationships between people, tasks, and responsibility should be structured. They reflect deep cultural assumptions having to do with issues of power, authority, and control in organizations. Design principles are equivalent to mental models that act as systemic frameworks for constructing organizations. Design principles get to the roots of how organizations are structured to get the work done. Because organizations are human and social creations, design principles provide the criteria—implicitly or explicitly—that guide how we structure and manage organizations. In this sense, design principles amount to more than just rhetoric—they go to the heart of understanding the underlying premises and the structural logic that influence management and employee behavior.

Organizations are now under pressure to increase their market share, shorten product-development cycle times, and boost the profitability of products and services. More attacks on the bureaucratic paradigm have been forthcoming. This has led to a stream of management tools and fashionable techniques, but little real questioning of the underlying assumptions, or design principle, that is at the root of the problem. The result: Employees pretend to go along with the latest slogan or management initiative, put in as little real effort as possible, and wait for the splashy launch to die down and management's attention to go elsewhere.

Most organization design efforts have not taken design principles into account. Instead, attention is primarily directed toward phenotypical characteristics—such questions as how departments will be grouped, what sort of structural linkages need to be put in place to foster better information processing, and so on. These are all very important questions and design decisions. But those issues occur in the phenotypic space of design. This is analogous to pinning wings on a caterpillar and claiming it will be able to fly. Changing a whole organization to self-management requires genetic surgery, not a facelift. Design principles help us to enter the *geno*typic space of design, deep into the DNA that informs our thinking about organizing. Ugly ducklings take time to develop into swans, and bureaucracies need time to transform into self-managing organizations.

All human beings are designers—whether they know it or not. The purposeful act toward a desired future is in essence the manifestation of design in action. Design is composing a new piece of music, developing a new software program, writing a book. But design is also part of our everyday life—planning a vacation, redecorating a house, baking an apple pie, educating a child. Design is built into our genes, and forms the underlying matrix of human systems. Through design, we construct, deconstruct, and reconstruct our social worlds on a daily basis. We are always active participants in constructing our reality. As Victor Papanek (1985) defines it, "Design is the conscious and intuitive effort to impose meaningful order" on our world.

Bureaucracy: A Meaningful Order?

Emery (1977) identified two basic but fundamentally different design principles that explain the systemic differences between bureaucratic and self-managing organizations. The order imposed by the bureaucratic design principle is built on the premise that *responsibility for control and coordination of work resides one level above where the work occurs* (see Figure 4.1).

It is the dominant design principle for modern industrial organizations. However, there is a growing recognition that this design principle no longer imposes a *meaningful* sense of order in the world of work today. Social and economic anomalies—such as the inability to quickly adapt to changes in the environment, growing employee apathy and labor unrest, and organizational inertia which slowed growth and innovation—were indications of the cracks in the foundation of bureaucracy. Even well-managed bureaucracies do not live up to their promise. It doesn't take a rocket scientist to detect the inherent flaws, contradictions, and problems of the bureaucratic model. The shortcomings of bureaucratic organizations are summarized below.

- *The Classic Peter Principle.* Authority is derived from one's position, not one's competence.
- *A Gamesman Orientation.* Subordinates selectively communicate what makes them look good and listen only to the downward communication that suits them. Similarly, managers selectively communicate what makes them look good to their superiors, and so on up the ladder.
- *The "Us vs. Them" Syndrome.* Competitive structures emerge: person versus person, group versus group, each person vying for promotion or precedence.

DESIGN PRINCIPLE 1 (DP1)

Bureaucratic structure:
Responsibility for control and coordination is located
one level above where work is actually performed.

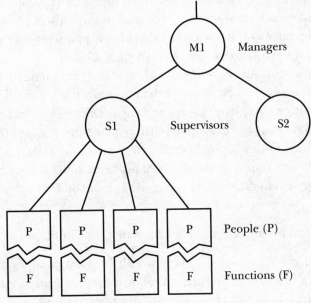

Figure 4.1

- *Looking Out for Number One.* It is not in anyone's interest to provide accurate or timely feedback, which prevents any ongoing form of meaningful learning. An individual in a bureaucracy thrives best by looking out for himself.
- *The Classic Soldiering Problem.* Employees create a shadow or informal organization (cliques and rumor mills) and seek to subvert the rules to their advantage, such as creating informal production norms.
- *The Classic Morale Problem.* Employees perform poorly in ill-designed jobs that fail to satisfy their critical psychological requirements for productive and satisfying work. The organizational fall-out can be seen in poor performance: low productivity, shoddy workmanship, and abrasive customer relations. The human consequences are inevitable: alienation, apathy, boredom, resentment, and cynicism are typical reactions to a system that is degrading to the human spirit.

Warren Bennis, one of the early critics of bureaucratic organizations, sums up such typical problems that we have all witnessed or encountered: "Bosses without technical competence and underlings with it; arbitrary and zany rules; an underworld (or informal) organization which subverts or even replaces the formal apparatus; confusion and conflict among roles; and cruel treatment of subordinates, based not upon rational or legal grounds, but upon inhumane grounds" (Bennis, 1966).

Cartoonist Scott Adams—one of our most insightful modern organizational critics—has made a career lampooning the shortcomings of bureaucracy. It's no accident that his book, *The Dilbert Principle*, has sold millions, and his comic strip (with its "bad boss" themes) adorns the walls of many office cubicles throughout North America. In 1995, his annual survey of the most annoying management practices found that "ineffective workers promoted to management" was the number one vote getter.

Extensions and Modifications of the Bureaucratic Paradigm

Despite these glaring problems, Thomas Kuhn's (1970) analysis of paradigm shifts in the natural sciences has shown that the existence of such anomalies which leads to a crisis does not automatically lead to a rejection of the existing paradigm. The same is true in our case; the bureaucratic design principle still provides a meaningful sense of order to those in positions of authority. Many managers have a great deal invested in the bureaucratic paradigm: social status and executive privilege; the need for order through layers and layers of close supervision; the illusion of unilateral control; the sacredness of managerial prerogatives; the view that people are dispensable; inequitable reward systems. Despite the evidence from numerous studies that have repeatedly shown self-managing organizations to outperform their traditional counterparts, in terms of both economic and social criteria, many managers still cling fiercely to the old bureaucratic paradigm.

However, by now most managers recognize the shortcomings of bureaucracy with its inability to compete in a fast-changing global environment. It is no surprise why the "end of bureaucracy" became a popular theme in the 1990s as *Fortune* and *Business Week* ran feature articles on the topic (Dumaine, 1991).

But instead of fully rejecting the bureaucratic paradigm, most managers have made incremental adjustments and ad-hoc improvements (cross-functional teams, problem-solving teams, pseudo-empowerment, and the like) in the hope that these solutions will compensate for the organizational handicaps of bureaucracy. So-called radical methods and innovative practices like reengineering and self-directed work teams are adapted to fit management's existing mental models of organization, which are still steeped in the bureaucratic design principle.

For example, Corning Glass Works, of Corning, New York, has self-managing teams in nearly all of its twenty-eight domestic plants. Along the way, Corning learned that they would have to jettison traditional labor–management attitudes. Decades of bureaucratic tradition, politics, and mistrust exerted a strong gravitational pull. Their initial success with TQM and self-managing teams was sucked back into the bureaucratic mire. To counteract these regressive forces, Corning took the most resistant managers, employees, and union leaders on benchmarking trips to self-directed plants. Employees under the new pay-for-skills programs received a pay raise for learning new jobs. Half of the original supervisors, who were enthusiastic early adopters, were transferred to other sites that didn't have self-managing teams. Others accepted technical positions or administrative roles, while some became team coordinators responsible for more than one team. Top management realized it was critical to the success of the transition to clarify middle management's important new role. And they did. As its transition to team-based plants progressed, Corning learned it takes a great deal of learning to develop a participative, cooperative, quality-oriented, customer-focused culture.

There is a lot of bureaucracy-bashing rhetoric in the air, but few companies have truly embraced a new paradigm of self-management, let alone implemented it. The bureaucratic design principle still exerts a strong unconscious pull on management thought. But that situation is slowly changing. An *Industry Week* census, administered by Price Waterhouse in 1997 (Taninecz, 1997) to nearly 2,800 plant executives and more than 300 corporate manufacturing executives, found that 32.6 percent of corporate executives say empowered and self-directed teams are extremely critical in enabling their companies to achieve world-class manufacturing standards. Facilities with at least 51 percent of their people in teams had productivity levels of $180,000 per employee versus $130,000 per employee for nonempowered workforces. While only 4.4 percent of plants (122 facilities) report a 100 percent self-managing workforce, 23 percent reported that a majority of their workforce was self-managing.

This slow progress is partly due to the lack of serious inquiry and questioning of the assumptions that guide traditional organization design, and it is also partly due to the lack of conscious knowledge of an alternative democratic design principle. Further, most consultants and humanistic advocates for team-based work systems have not understood the organizational dynamics behind the bureaucratic design principle, yet they have zealously adopted the "bureaucracy is bad" rhetoric, blaming managers for clinging to the only system of accountability they know. Guilt-tripping managers for their reluctance to embrace more high-involvement work systems is counterproductive. Instead, a deeper appreciation of the bureaucratic design principle is needed to understand why the transition to a new paradigm of self-management has been so difficult.

IN PRAISE OF HIERARCHY?

One of the strongest pulls of the bureaucratic design principle is its claims for efficiency. Efficiency criteria are a central tenet of the paradigm, deeply rooted in scientific management thought. Certainly the "scientific" claims of Frederick Taylor's scientific management were discredited, and his time-study methods fell out of fashion long ago. However, as a *design philosophy*, Taylorism is still alive and well within modern organizations. Consider Taylor's original principles of scientific management, which were summarized by Lou Davis in 1971.

1. The essential building block of an organization is one person assigned to one job; if the organizational designer gets these "right" (in some particular way), then the organization will function like a smooth-running machine (hence, the "machine" theory of organization).
2. Each worker is an extension of the machine, useful only for doing things that the machine cannot do.
3. The people and their jobs—the individual building blocks—are glued together by supervisors who will absorb the uncertainties and variances that arise in the work situation. Furthermore, these supervisors need supervisors, ad infinitum, until the enterprise is organized in a many-layered hierarchy. In bureaucratic organizations, the latter notion ultimately leads to situations in which a man or woman can be called a "manager" solely on the grounds that he or she supervises a

certain number of people, and without regard to the degree of judgment or decision-making responsibility such supervision requires.

4. The organization is free to use any available social mechanism to enforce compliance and ensure its own stability.

5. Job fractionation is a way of reducing costs of carrying on the work by reducing the skill contribution of the individual who performs it. Human beings are simply extensions of the machine, and obviously, the more you simplify the machine (whether its living or nonliving part), the more you lower costs.

Far from being a description of some antiquated system of the past, these principles for designing work have a contemporary ring to them. It is common practice among industrial engineers and managers to design work based on such efficiency criteria. The rationale for doing so is persuasive. Increasing the division of labor and simplifying jobs requires less training time, reduces errors, and keeps the base wage low. Increasing mechanization and standardization of work guarantees a steady work pace, even product flow, and quality. Increasing isolation among workers keeps them from talking and forming informal groups that can distract them from performing their jobs. Designing decisionless jobs is supposedly more efficient since decision making takes time and could result in errors or variances.

This design philosophy, according to Emery (1977), exemplifies the principle of designing organizations based on an ample redundancy of parts. If an individual worker on the assembly line fails to perform as expected, he can easily be replaced; he is expendable. An organization can be designed to provide redundancy in this way so long as the costs of individual parts (human labor) can be kept low, and so long as the nature of the tasks performed does not require specialized knowledge or a great investment in education and training. However, the blue-collar ferment in the early 1970s in the U.S. revealed that a high price is eventually paid for such a design philosophy, which results in the degradation of work in terms of the human costs incurred: worker discontent and alienation ("the blue-collar blues") translates into low motivation, high absenteeism and turnover, occupational stress–related diseases, poor quality, sabotage, high accident rates, and unionization.

Another strong pull and basic assumption of the bureaucratic design principle is the hierarchical structure of authority. Hierarchy, as Elliott

Jaques has argued in his *Harvard Business Review* article "In Praise of Hierarchy" (1990), provides many practical and psychological benefits to both managers and employees in traditional organizations. Advocates for more democratic forms of organizations have underestimated the sense of psychological security that is derived from a hierarchical system of responsibility. And, again, the case made for hierarchy is persuasive. Simple humanistic admonitions that participative work systems should be instituted because they are good for people—or normative statements that more democratic structures should be implemented because they are empowering—appear impotent and foolhardy when stacked up against the claims of control offered by a traditional hierarchy.

Hierarchy provides several useful functions: it serves as a conduit for communication, a bridge for coordination, and a mechanism for control. Like Jaques, we also praise hierarchy for serving these useful functions in the management of organizations. However, our agreement ends there. Jaques downplays the fact that the bureaucratic design principle leads to a dysfunctional, dehumanizing, *dominant* hierarchy. Clearly, all organizations require a hierarchy for communication, coordination, and control purposes; the question is whether the character of hierarchy needs necessarily to be one based on personal dominance. Before addressing this question, we need to understand the psychological dimensions associated with the system of responsibility that the bureaucratic design principle puts in place.

Traditional Hierarchy and Individual Accountability

One of the most appealing characteristics of the bureaucratic design principle is that it creates a system of responsibility where managers can hold *individuals* accountable for specific tasks. Individuals are assigned specific tasks with clear measures of performance. The line of accountability between superior and subordinate is clear and direct. However, for this system to work, tasks have to be subdivided and broken down into narrow assignments so that they can be delegated to specific individuals. Each individual can then be held accountable for the completion of precise assignments.

While this configuration may provide a sense of security, it is problematic in that the individuals doing the work don't have a view of the whole. Instead, the work process is fragmented into bits and pieces, with each person assigned to a narrow job. Subsequently, individuals must now depend on someone above them to oversee the task of control and coordination. It is fundamentally an authoritarian structure that limits the responsiveness and capabilities of those in direct contact with the work process. It does create a fairly predictable set of roles, responsibilities, tasks, and relationships.

Indeed, a key feature of the bureaucratic design principle is that both crucial decisions about the control and coordination of task assignments and allocation of rewards flow from a superior to subordinates. On the one hand, this structure of authority creates a sense of psychological security for the manager who has a specific point of accountability—the individual subordinate. On the other hand, this structure also increases psychological tension as one moves up the corporate hierarchy. In a traditional hierarchy, every manager is held ultimately responsible for achieving the goals of a department or work group. Yet, while the manager is held responsible, he or she does not actually perform all the work of the department but must delegate tasks to subordinates. A great deal of emphasis has been placed on the fact that a traditional hierarchy makes employees overly dependent on their bosses to tell them what to do. But this is really only half of the equation. Traditional hierarchical organization also makes the manager dependent on his or her subordinates to perform and complete their tasks successfully. A manager cannot succeed without the cooperative efforts of his or her subordinates, and often not without the cooperation of departments that are outside that manager's functional scope of authority. Formal authority for the control and coordination of work is made commensurate with one's level of responsibility, but such authority is limited, given the fact that it is so highly dependent on the cooperative efforts of other individuals. The bureaucratic design principle creates a gap between authority and responsibility that causes a great deal of stress and psychological tension in traditional hierarchical organizations.

The Responsibility–Authority Gap

To reduce stress, managers at each level of the hierarchy will feel compelled to structure the work of their subordinates in the same way. As decision making is pushed up the chain of command, the individuals closest to the problem or point of corrective action have no authority or control over their own task situation. Yet individuals will still be held accountable by their manager to get the job done. Paradoxically, the bureaucratic design principle puts both managers and employees in a double bind. While a traditional hierarchical structure may reduce managerial anxiety by establishing clear lines of accountability, i.e., by assigning specific tasks to specific individuals, it does nothing to close the design gap between responsibility and authority. If anything, the gap widens over time as employees begin to feel disaffected and alienated in a work system that leaves them little opportunity for controlling and coordinating their own affairs. This only adds to the psychological tension and anxiety that already exist within the bureaucratic organization. Intuitively sensing their employees' loss of commitment to corporate goals, and fearing that their employees may band together against the formal system or simply pursue goals of their own, managers design-in elaborate control and monitoring mechanisms. Policy manuals, rule books, electronic surveillance, performance management systems, and other types of control and monitoring mechanisms are introduced in the hope of ensuring compliance to requirements.

When these control systems fail to produce compliant behavior (which is frequently the case), the only other recourse managers have in a bureaucratic structure is to wield their authority over others. Order is imposed and maintained through coercion, cajoling, threat of sanctions, and fear—in short, through command and control. When managers resort to domination, they become autocratic. The subliminal message in a dominant hierarchy is "Do what I say, or else!" Indeed, a dominant hierarchy not only relies on the dynamics of divide and rule, it also requires elaborate schemes for doling out discipline and punishments. This is a return to the ancient past.

In his praise of hierarchy Jaques argues that this form of organization must have some intrinsic merit since it has been around for the last 3,000 years, but he fails to expose its darker side. Hierarchy is a word formed from classical Greek roots meaning "sacred order," an order established by elite groups throughout history to command and control the division of labor. Lewis Mumford reminds us that physical torture and even acts of maiming were once commonplace in the earliest days of Egyptian and Mesopotamian bureaucracies. The management practices of former times now make Frederick Taylor look like a saint. Emery points out that Taylor "simply devised new sticks and carrots so that this organization design could function within societies like the U.S.A., where the Constitution forbade 'cruel and unusual punishment' [of workers]." Authoritarian hierarchy, as Philip Slater points out, formerly had great value for the ruling class, as its original function served "to manage and control enslaved tribes—*people who would not voluntarily participate in the society or carry out its tasks*" (Slater, 1991, p. 25).

Autocracy and democracy are distinctly different accountability systems. Laissez-faire is the pure absence of accountability—a manager's worst nightmare. Gerald Kraines, president of the Boston-based Levinson Institute, is a contrarian who argues that traditional lines of authority and old-fashioned accountability are still the best way to run corporations (Lancaster, 1996). He denounces employee empowerment and work teams that form and dissolve flexibly, without regard to accountability (Kraines, 1996). Well, he's right. A lack of accountability fits our definition of laissez-faire. But Kraines doesn't understand the system of self-management that we describe in this book.

Democracy at work is frequently associated with a lack of accountability, but that is far from the case. In most traditional organizations, goals are set and monitored by management, and individuals are held accountable for their performance. In the midst of the rush to teams, many thought that empowering employees meant loosening up control mechanisms. Management therefore took a hands-off approach, allowing teams to do whatever they saw fit. In many cases, this really amounted to relaxing standards in the interest of improving morale. Relaxing controls and standards, however, has nothing to do with democracy. Lowering standards in an autocratic workplace means a shift to laissez-faire, not a change to democracy. As Kraines rightly points out, freeing people from their chains of enslavement isn't going to help them act more responsibly and creatively if it's not clear who is accountable for which decisions. Rather, democracy involves shifting from goals imposed from above to goals set by work groups in consultation with management, linking them to the business strategy.

The proposition that responsibility for the control and coordination of work can be placed in the hands of group members, that is, at the same level at which the work is actually performed, is the basis of the democratic design principle. Bureaucratic and democratic design principles reflect opposing sets of values about people and work. However, changing a design principle is not just a matter of simply espousing new values. The rhetoric of empowerment fell into this trap. Many organizations began to mouth the "E-word" without making any fundamental changes in structure.

There is another paradox: although the bureaucratic design principle is based on the premise of a separation between planning and doing, managers are more often than not involved more in the doing than in value-added planning. Since responsibility for control and coordination of tasks is not located at the subordinate level, managers are drawn into the trenches to put out fires. This explains why the management role is so often compared to that of the proverbial firefighter. But has anyone ever bothered to ask who the real arsonist is?

Excess levels of management are built into a dominant hierarchy since the *modus operandi* requires external control mechanisms to check on those who are actually doing the work. As outside pressures are bearing down on the company, the organizational dynamics are such that managers are enmeshed in all sorts of political games and non-value-added activities. What makes bureaucracy so inefficient is the long vertical chain of command, which requires successive sign-offs and approvals before a decision can be made. Corporations were able to get by with this structure when the environment was stable, but in a turbulent world a traditional hierarchy is suicidal. In this system, managers appear to act as if the employee's customer is the boss at the next level of the hierarchy, rather than those outside, in the external environment, who purchase your company's products or services. Management eventually loses sight of the real purpose of the enterprise: to satisfy customers, increase shareholder wealth, and enhance the capabilities of employees. The bureaucratic design principle produces a managerial control superstructure, bloated levels of middle management, surplus overhead, and high cost structures. Bloated corporate bureaucracies have attempted to cope by managing "head count" through downsizing. Efficiency, so it was thought, would be regained by getting back to basics.

SELF-MANAGEMENT: A DEMOCRATIC DESIGN ALTERNATIVE

Democratization of work entails a fundamental change in how work is designed. If people are to take greater responsibility for results, they must be given challenging work with real authority for making decisions. The democratic design principle relocates responsibility for control and coordination at the level at which the work is actually performed, allowing people to achieve results without being subject to external supervision and management meddling (see Figure 4.2).

Whereas the first design principle (DP1) produces complex organizations made up of simple jobs, the second design principle (DP2) generates simple organizations composed of complex jobs. People are assigned not to a single, narrow assignment but to a work team that has responsibility for a collection of tasks that make up a whole work process. Standard job descriptions are made obsolete when organizations shift to self-management. The basic building block shifts from individual job assignments to a self-managing team that shares responsibility for a logical grouping of tasks with a clear output that adds value to customers. Team members are given the management authority to make decisions about how they will organize, coordinate, and perform their tasks to achieve productive goals. At SEI Investments, highly committed self-managing teams are focused on pleasing customers, not bosses. That's why management at TBWA Chiat/Day reorganized their ad agency staff into multidisciplinary client teams. They also built client project rooms for agency and client use,

DESIGN PRINCPLE 2 (DP2)

Democratic structure:
Responsibility for control and coordination is located
at the level where work is actually performed.

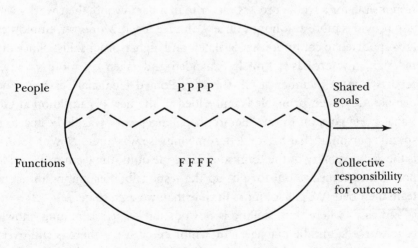

Figure 4.2

equipped with the latest computers, audiovisual equipment, lounge tables, pin-up boards, and casual seating.

Can you take people out of narrow professional roles and create a logical grouping of tasks? The *Bakersfield Californian* newspaper thinks so. It has shaken up the newsroom, merging general assignment reporters with specialists into one pool for all types of coverage. Executive editor Richard Beene sponsored this change to create a newsroom without walls in which ideas flow from department to department.

This work arrangement amounts to more than simply making utterances about empowerment. The structure of work must be fundamentally changed so that responsibility can be shared by a group of individuals. The work itself also must be redesigned so individuals working in groups have opportunities to produce a complete product or service that is perceived as socially meaningful. Typically this means employees are multiskilled; at any one time, some of the skills of a particular individual might be redundant to the task at hand. One obvious benefit of this arrangement is that when one employee is absent, another employee can easily assume the task. Team members can also evaluate their workload and assign people to high-priority tasks. But it also means much more than this. Employees share responsibility for coordination, control, and planning: they are not merely multiskilled, but more in control of the work process. Errors, problems, and deviations can be corrected in real time, right on the spot, without having to wait for authorization from supervisors. Because they are responsible for a whole process rather than a narrow job, their work itself also provides more autonomy, variety, and feedback. Moreover, employees are supported to continuously learn new and higher-order skills. "Since the redesign, my job has definitely expanded and taken on more variety," reports a team member at GE Canada's Pooled Financial Services. The democratic design principle is embedded in the new organization at GE Canada. He goes on to say, "Before the change, work was dedicated to a specific person. If that person left, someone else was hired. Now the work is the responsibility of the team so if someone quits, the team may decide not to hire someone but to split up the responsibilities among different team members. We're a lot more flexible than we used to be."

In cases where multiskilling is not possible—such as among knowledge workers, middle managers, or senior executives—there is still overlapping coordination between specialized functions. As with a senior leadership team, for example, the work as a whole is designed and organized in such a way that the work of each individual supports and facilitates the work of others in the direction of jointly negotiated goals. Instead of boss–subordinate relationships holding together a chain of links, the organization becomes an intricate web in which every part is related to other parts to achieve common business goals.

For example, the senior management team at Lockheed Martin's GES Division, described in Chapter 2, have the collective focus to work together on projects and initiatives. One successful initiative is their annual supplier conference, where five hundred people from the most critical suppliers, as well as customers, functional leaders, and senior executives, get together to discuss critical issues, deploy operational plans, and strengthen quality.

Sharing Responsibility, Sharing the Stress

If self-managing organizations are more effective—in terms of both economic performance and human satisfaction—why has the transition to this new paradigm of work been so difficult and slow in coming? Why does the democratic design principle appear so foreign or so untenable a proposition to many corporate managements? If self-managing organizations do in fact provide a better quality-of-work life, as their advocates claim, why do employees often resist the chance to participate in the design and management of these more democratic work systems? The answers to these questions are both complex and deep, but they are related to the fact that self-managing organizations utilize a fundamentally different structure of authority coupled with a system of responsibility that challenges many cherished American cultural assumptions. This paradigm shift involves substituting a traditional hierarchical authority structure with a democratic one, and changing from an autocratic, unitary system of responsibility to a more democratic, team-based system of responsibility.

Making a radical shift to this new paradigm of work is difficult, and it is usually avoided altogether or prematurely terminated because of the high levels of anxiety, stress, and tension that accompany deep genotypical change. In a traditional hierarchy, the manager is held ultimately responsible for the group, so the stress and anxiety derived from the gap between perceived responsibility and authority rest on his shoulder. However, when organizations shift to a democratic authority structure, the stress and anxiety that come with greater responsibility must be shared by all the members of a team. Further, since the team is held ultimately responsible for its own performance and authority, that stress and anxiety are more equally distributed among its members, and the level of tension is higher than it would be in a traditional hierarchy. Tension is higher because no one individual in the team has the sole authority to make decisions, thereby increasing the perceived gap between authority and responsibility. And since the whole team will be held accountable and responsible for results, the anxiety that is normally contained in a single managerial or supervisory position is now spread throughout the team. Thus, under a democratic authority structure, the potential for conflict and disagreement is heightened as more ideas are generated, divergent views and opinions are surfaced, and anxiety over issues of authority is played out.

Many organizations that have introduced team-based work systems have not been able to tolerate or successfully manage the tensions and anxieties that are generated when traditional authority structures are dismantled. For the manager working in a team-based environment, this anxiety is often experienced as a loss of control over the work system. However, it is really a loss of the managerial prerogative to assign responsibilities to individuals, who are then made accountable to their superior. The common response to the tension is "someone has to be the leader," and the knee-jerk reaction is to reappoint a designated supervisor to control and coordinate the work of the team. What initially started out as "self-directed work teams" degenerates into "managed and supervised work teams."

Motorola's Elma plant employs five hundred people outside of Buffalo, New York, manufacturing ignition and sensor equipment for the automobile industry. How did they handle these tensions? Being on the cutting edge of quality improvement, they were used to temporary cross-functional problem-solving teams, which addressed a particular quality issue and then disbanded. Self-managing teams—where groups of workers from the same department come together to improve quality and cycle time—were a natural evolution for Motorola. As team members matured in their ability to make important decisions, team leaders were able to migrate off the floor. They became trainers and liaisons to other departments.

Self-managing organizations, however, are not simply a collection of "leaderless groups." True, the responsibility that was once invested in a single leader is redistributed and widely shared by members of a work team, but strong and effective leadership is still required. The difference is that in self-managing organizations authority is not based on a formal position in the hierarchy but is contingent on the expertise required in particular tasks, situations, and contexts. In other words, leadership is situation specific. In some cases, self-managing teams may choose or appoint their own coordinator or leader, but that individual is responsible and accountable *to the team*. The team has the power to recall their appointed leader. In other cases, the leadership role may be a rotating position, or shift to different members depending on the nature of the task. Other teams may simply rely on a more spontaneous form of shared leadership.

The bottom line is that achievement of productive goals still requires control and coordination of work activity. That control and coordination is determined by a democratic structure of authority that radically changes the character of the management hierarchy, from a system based on domination to a system based on partnership. Motorola's Elma plant illustrates this point. Management supported the team approach because it promised to produce dramatic quantitative results. Management layers in the plant were reduced to three levels. A majority of the plant's workforce either is on a team or is providing support services to the teams. Teams now have significant contact with external customers. They measure their own productivity and quality, and handle discipline problems themselves. Activity-based costing was instituted because conventional accounting systems didn't work. Each self-managing team was allowed to gradually pull support functions into the team. When it came time to move to a new facility, all the teams shared responsibility for the move and did it on time, and within the budget set by management.

Whereas in a dominator system those in power take control and command others to do their jobs, in a partnership system everyone is empowered to *assume responsibility and collaborate with others* to get the job done. The role of authority and the manner in which people are rewarded is different in self-managing organizations that are based on democratic norms of equality. Does management simply disappear in self-managing organizations? No, of course not; the absence of structure and management control would be a recipe for chaos and a state of laissez-faire. Certainly there will be less of a need for managers (somewhere on the order of 40 to 50 percent less) in more mature and highly evolved self-managing organizations, but the function of management doesn't disappear. Rather, *management as a function* is absorbed into the work group, which now has direct responsibility for achieving productive goals. In self-managing organizations, teams are responsible for controlling and coordinating their own work process and they are held accountable for results. For example, at GE Canada's Pooled Financial Services, the End User Support team now does many of the tasks that were traditionally reserved for management. The team now does its own hiring, budgeting, expense tracking and buying decisions, and performance reviews.

Ranking Relationships Inhibits Teamwork

In traditional hierarchical organizations, there is a basic assumption that only individuals—not groups—can be held accountable for their actions. The bureaucratic design principle, which dictates unitary lines of responsibility from superior to individual subordinates, is predicated on a *meritocratic* ideology. Jaques' (1990) objection to self-managing organizations, ". . . group authority *with* group accountability is unacceptable," reflects a deep cultural archetype based on individualism and meritocracy. A meritocracy is designed to function exclusively on the basis of individual achievement. Individuals are sorted and ranked, allocating rewards to the most talented, hard working, and deserving. Further, a meritocratic culture assumes that individuals vary in their ability and efforts to contribute to organizational goals and should be rewarded accordingly, based of course on their merit. The assumption in a meritocracy is that individuals are motivated by competition for rewards that come with ascending to higher positions in a traditional hierarchy. Accordingly, meritocratic organizations assume that those in higher positions of authority have acquired greater knowledge and experience and therefore are more capable of assigning tasks to, and evaluating the performance of, those below them.

Upper-level managers in traditional bureaucracies believe in Darwin's theory of evolution on a personal level. Because they have survived the cutthroat competition to reach their current positions, they assume that they *must* be better qualified to make decisions of all kinds than those below them on the evolutionary (organizational) ladder. By definition there must be winners and losers in a meritocracy, or "survival of the fittest," where the whole system is based on competition to reach the top. Because roles are based on their rankings, those in higher positions command more respect and status than the "rank and file."

In bureaucratic organizations, meritocratic norms prevail: task assignments, assessment of performance, and the allocation of rewards are all administered on an individual basis. Unitary lines of responsibility and a clear chain of command from superior to subordinates not only allows a manager to make specific task assignments, but also to assess each individual's performance, allocating rewards that are commensurate with his or her merit. The focus is on *individuals,* not groups. Jaques in his defense of traditional hierarchy is also defending meritocratic norms as he argues that only individuals, not groups, can be held accountable and rewarded fairly for their performance. He explains:

> People are not employed in groups. They are employed individually, and their employment contracts—real or imagined—are individual. Group members may insist in moments of great esprit de corps that the group as such is the author of some particular accomplishment, but once the work is completed, the members of the group look for individual recognition and individual progression in their careers. And it is not groups but individuals the company will hold accountable. (Jaques, 1990, p. 128)

Jaques' position merely supports the underlying meritocratic assumptions that keep a dominant hierarchy intact. He offers a seductive, self-sealing argument in favor of the status quo. His argument also reflects the cultural bias toward individualism, the assumption that a person is a fully self-contained individual, an isolated atom and an independent actor.

However, in organizations, even individual contributors almost by definition have to work with others. Whereas painters, writers, and some scientists can, at times, work in relative physical and intellectual isolation to develop creative products, the individual in organizations works within a more structured social setting. An organization's products are typically not things that can be created without group interactions. Individuals have to work with others, for better or for worse. And despite jokes about camels being horses designed by committees, many of us have at times derived benefits from working in teams or groups, or collaborated with colleagues who somehow seemed to spark our creativity. However, most of us undoubtedly have had the experience of working in circumstances where we felt that creativity and teamwork were the last things on anybody's mind—the dull, stultifying routine of endless bickering, or just somnolent nodding in yet another meeting room. Jaques focuses only on the latter situation—

the lowest common denominator of groups—that is characteristic of bureaucratic settings.

As a deeply ingrained cultural assumption, a meritocracy assumes the individual contributor is superior to groups. Edwin Land is an American archetypal figure of the heroic lone genius. Consider his attitude toward groups, which is a good illustration of this cultural assumption. He is quoted as saying:

> I do believe wholeheartedly in the individual capacity for greatness, in one way or another, in almost any healthy human being under the *right* circumstances; but being a part of a group is, in my opinion, generally the *wrong* circumstance. Profundity and originality are attributes of a single, if not singular minds. Two minds may be better than one, provided each of the two minds is working separately while the two are working together; yet three tend to become a crowd. (Wensberg, 1987)

Land's attitude toward groups is strictly negative—hell is other people, in Sartre's words—and this mentality applies all the more to the lone, misunderstood genius. This is clearly not a mentality that is conducive to collaboration. There seems, however, to be an inherent paradox in this meritocratic view of creativity and motivation, since only certain individuals are allowed entry into higher positions, while the rest are relegated and expected to be acolytes, content with their roles as conforming subordinates. In this story, the genius as protagonist assembles a supporting cast of members who serve the function of emulating his performances. The genius-as-heroic-leader simply uses employees as handy instrumental objects for enhancing his own ideas and promoting his own creative inventions. At Polaroid, Land's personal style was often referred to as "maestro management," quite an apt image of Land the master conductor orchestrating all the different specialized segments of the product-development process.

The dichotomy between the lone individual and the conforming masses manifests itself in the literature as one reads about Whyte's "organization man," Riesman's "lonely crowd," on the one hand, and biographical and autobiographical accounts of the entrepreneurial heroes (Edwin Land, Steve Jobs, Bill Gates, etc.) or single-handed organizational reformers (Lee Iacocca, Jack Welch, John Scully) on the other. This polarization reflects our either/or mentality whereby we assume that to be creative and successful and in a leadership role we must outshine and outcompete others in a group, or alternatively, if we are to be a "team player" we must go along with the group, not rock the boat, and suppress our individuality.

Fortune columnist Thomas Stewart (1996) has put his finger on the great conundrum in American corporations: the individual versus the team. On the one hand, employees are given the message that they should be responsible for their own careers nowadays. On the other hand, organizations want individuals to work in teams. While teams can perform extraordinary work, it's often a dicey proposition for most to put the fate of their career in collectivist hands. However, the real problem does not appear to be either excessive individualism or excessive collectivism, but rather an inability to achieve a balance between the two.

But what if an individual was able to both lead *and* follow, be an organization man or woman *and* a creative entrepreneur, be self-assertive *and* cooperative? In self-managing organizations, democratic norms would encourage what Emery called "variety-increasing behavior." For example, in one situation a person may need to act as a courageous leader, to exercise independence of judgment, and to be autonomous—and yet at another time, or in a quite different situation, that person may need to act as a loyal follower, to be collaborative and supportive. This requires a more fluid design principle quite different from the underlying rigidity of bureaucratic organizations, which has a variety-reducing effect, treating people as if they were uncreative and redundant parts, limiting their capabilities to a narrow range.

Mythological Reform: The Team-as-Hero

Meritocratic organizations that emphasize task specialization and individual reward systems are falling out of synch with the changing nature of work. For example, new product development is increasingly being performed by multi-disciplinary teams and cross-functional work groups. Complex technological innovation requires a great deal of knowledge sharing and collaboration between specialists. The increasing complexity and task interdependence characteristic of knowledge work requires more than solo performances from individual contributors. Noting this trend, Robert Reich (1987) has called for a "mythological reform" of North American industry, arguing for a shift away from the myth of the lone, heroic, entrepreneur (or what we have been calling the myth of the lone genius) to a myth of collective entrepreneurship, emphasizing the *team-as-hero*. Reich's use of the term "mythological" is significant, because it points to the deeper layer of archetypal consciousness that we have been discussing.

Self-managing organizations facilitate a shift toward collective entrepreneurship, or what we referred to as "social creativity" (Purser and Montuori, 1998). Social creativity promotes an intensive exchange of know-how between specialists and cross-disciplinary contact, what James Brian Quinn (1985) calls "interactive learning." Through use of flexible organizational arrangements, fluid assignments, and overlapping boundaries, specialists can develop and share the knowledge that they need.

Peter Drucker, commenting on the "new realities" of the information-based organization, declares that:

> In information-based organizations, knowledge will lie primarily at the bottom, in the minds of specialists who do different work and direct themselves. . . . Because the players in an information-based organization are specialists, they cannot be told how to do their work. . . . The professional specialist however tends to be ever more specialized. By itself, specialized knowledge has no results unless it focuses on the needs and goals of the entire organization. The flute part is an essential part of a Beethhoven symphony, but by itself it is not music. It becomes music by becoming part of the "score". . . Yet [today] neither business nor government agency has a "score" to play by. (Drucker, 1989)

In hypercompetitive global markets and turbulent environments, the composition of the organization's "score" must be improvised in real time. While Drucker's comparison of the knowledge-based organization to a classical symphony orchestra is useful for illustrating the realities of specialization, it misses the mark. Granted, the players in a classical symphony orchestra are highly specialized, but their individual performances are all guided by a well-defined, predetermined, and certain "score." Bureaucratic organizations have much in common with symphony orchestras; both are composed of preestablished, tightly specified job descriptions, and each individual's performance is tightly controlled and orchestrated by a maestro manager. The hierarchical rank-ordering of conductor, soloists, first principal violin, second assistant principal violin, third violin, and so on, is structurally comparable to any industrial organization where the responsibility for control and coordination is located a level above where the work is actually performed. Each worker/player is required to follow a musical score, performing his or her part according to exact specifications, upheld through a hierarchy of command and control.

The maestro model of management simply won't work with knowledge workers. Knowledge workers have made a significant investment in higher education, are more self-directed, and demand special treatment. Moreover, knowledge workers define success differently, valuing personal self-expression, autonomy, and freedom of choice. Even Drucker acknowledges the fact that knowledge workers are resistant to the command-and-control model of management. Professional knowledge workers also resent and discredit performance evaluations; they prefer to be assessed on the "process integrity" of their work as defined by professional standards. Perhaps in Land's era, when products were less technically complex, customer needs and preferences were less sophisticated, and competition was less intense, maestro management sufficed. Today, even Land—undeniable genius that he was—would have difficulty composing and orchestrating new product development activities at Polaroid (or at any other high-technology organization) single-handedly from the top of the organizational pyramid.

JAZZING UP THE WORKPLACE: THE UTILITY OF THE JAZZ METAPHOR

The shift from meritocratic to democratic norms—to a team-as-hero myth—requires a new organizing metaphor, illustrating that responsibility for the control and coordination of work *can* be located at the same level where work is performed, and where accountability at the group level *does* work. On this point we concur with Jaques: the symphony orchestra is a poor analogy. A more accurate and exciting metaphor for the knowledge-based self-managing organization—also drawn from the arts—is the performance of jazz music. Jazz is, after all, a collective art form. Being a collective and improvisational art form, jazz groups exhibit a high degree of task interdependence. If any one of the players is not in good form or not up to the material, the whole sound suffers, and everybody sounds bad, no matter how individually brilliant other players may be. In jazz, the sound forms a Gestalt, a whole, which must reflect the cohesion (or lack of it) in the group. Thus, to creatively and harmoniously respond to improvisational changes occurring within the ensemble, jazz musicians have to develop enormous sensitivity to their musical environment. As Peter Senge (1990) points out, jazz ensembles have both "talent and a shared vision (even if they don't discuss it), but what really matters is that the musicians know how to *play* together" (p. 236).

There is also a redundancy of functions built into good jazz ensembles; musicians can alternate solos and back-up roles; each can provide sequential or synchronous rhythmic, melodic, or chordal contributions. Players are able to control and coordinate their own musical behavior, alternating between passages that are tightly written for ensembles and freer improvisations on shared themes, suggesting that there is a shared understanding of goals and a mutual respect, along with an optimal level of autonomy, variety, and feedback. The score that guides the performance of individual musicians in a jazz ensemble is not predetermined, but is emergent and defined in real time through synchronous interactions and individual interpretations of a common theme. Charles Savage (1990) also uses the jazz-ensemble analogy as a means for illustrating how the emergent interaction of vision and knowledge guides the performance of specialists in the knowledge-based organization:

> An enterprise's interaction with the market is not just passive listening; it is listening to and playing music at the same time, the way jazz musicians pick up a theme and work with it. The theme aligns their vision; then each musician interprets the theme based on his or her individual knowledge. As they play, they inspire and challenge each other to new combinations, new modes of expressing themselves around a basic theme. . . . The same thing can happen within a company that listens to the themes of the marketplace. As functions learn to work in parallel, they improve their timing, reduce cycle time, and improve quality and time-to-market. The alignment of their vision and knowledge allows them to discern market patterns, product design, process strategy, and service capabilities concurrently. (Savage, 1990)

The jazz ensemble embodies democratic norms that offers a direct challenge to the romantic myth that motivation and creativity are solitary processes that develop best in meritocratic social environments character-ized by hierarchical and competitive relationships. The band's music—its product—is really an emergent property of the whole system, and cannot be credited to any single member.

Overcoming the Conflict Between the Individual and the Team

The jazz ensemble is also a useful metaphor for team learning because it is an indigenous American art form that does not suppress individual cre-ativity in the service of group conformity (as, for example, the Japanese team concept tends to do). For example, members of teams often think being a good "team player" means not making waves, avoiding conflict, or conforming to group norms. In too many cases, injunctions to people to become team players to fit into the group stifle their individual initiative and true creativity. Instead, the jazz ensemble allows for a creative dialectic to exist between the individual and the group. It is the uniqueness of the six different instruments in a jazz sextet that gives the ensemble its sound and mood; the absence or suppression of even one instrument would detract from the whole. Jazz critic Nat Hentoff comments on this creative dialectic between the individual and the group:

> The high degree of individuality, together with the mutual respect and cooperation needed in a jazz ensemble, carry with them philo-sophical implications. It is as if jazz were saying to us that not only is far greater individuality possible to man than he has so far allowed himself, but that such individuality, far from being a threat to a cooperative social structure, can actually enhance soci-ety. (Hentoff, 1984)

The ideal of equality in the jazz ensemble allows individual creativity and self-expression to blossom, but it is always oriented toward enhancing the collective musical creation and emerges within the context of the group as a whole. Jazz improvisation at its best requires a knowledge that is fun-damentally different from that of classical music. In classical symphonic music, creativity is reserved for the soloist, and the conforming musicians play "second fiddle" to him. In jazz, the roles of the soloist and supporting players alternate continuously: the band is self-managing.

Dealing With the Unforeseen: Improvisation

Perhaps most importantly, jazz is about *improvisation*. The Latin origin of the word "improvise" is *improvisus*, meaning "the unforeseen." The European classical symphony orchestra is an art form of the Machine Age—a clockwork world that did not allow for the unforeseen, and *did not require the skills and competencies needed to deal with the unforeseen*. In contrast, the jazz musician is engaged in a constant process of learning how to learn. Great jazz band leaders, such as Miles Davis, allowed the music to emerge from the group members' interaction, rather than imposing his own set ideas. In other words, jazz musicians thrive on the unknown because they know that is where their future lies. Improvisation at its best is the embodiment of insecurity and evolutionary learning.

If there is any industry where the jazz metaphor readily applies, it is software development. This industry is known for being fast-paced, dynamic; innovation and improvisation are the name of the game. There is little tolerance for bureaucracy or heady management theories. Demands for speed, innovation, and flexibility require methods that can be implemented in real time, without a lot of analytical foreplay. In this volatile industry, approaches that work are improvised along the way. A good example of this is a rapid-prototyping approach to product development. The need for on-time product delivery precludes an exhaustive analysis of every contingency. Rather, a rapid-prototyping approach says, "Let's get a workable prototype into the hands of the customer, let them play with it, and then we will refine it."

The same is true for organization design. Textbook approaches and long-drawn-out methods that require a lot of up-front analysis simply won't work in fast-paced software-development companies. The industry is changing so rapidly that new organization designs must be improvised in real time. Everyone must be involved in reinventing and debugging the new design even as it is being implemented. Participative Design is ideally suited to such an industry, where a rapid-prototyping method for ramping up a new organization design is advantageous.

JAZZING UP A NEW ORGANIZATION DESIGN FOR SOFTWARE DEVELOPMENT: HOW SYBASE USED PARTICIPATIVE DESIGN AND SEARCH CONFERENCES[2]

This jazz-oriented approach to organization design had great appeal to the managers at a Sybase facility in Boulder, Colorado. This operation—now owned by Sybase—had been the entrepreneurial brainchild of two computer scientists who started the company in the late 1970s. One of their early product success stories was a product called the Database Gateway, which allowed freestanding and networked (LANs) personal computers to exchange information with mainframe systems. Sybase is the high-performance leader in database solutions, data access and data movement products, and enterprise-application-development tools for businesses seeking competitive advantage through superior technology. With a commitment to open, distributed end-to-end computing, Sybase is helping companies build advanced data warehouses and data marts, Internet-enabled applications and databases, and powerful information environments tailored to their visions of success. Started in 1984 with its headquarters in Emeryville, California, Sybase has revenues that had grown to $903 million in 1997.

As with most entrepreneurial start-ups, product development during the early years at the Boulder facility was very informal, ad-hoc, and free-wheeling. The organization operated in a high-energy, self-managing mode. The cofounders' unique understanding of the marketplace, their vision of technology, and their knowledge of the customer's needs drove development efforts. During the entrepreneurial start-up phase, highly talented individuals were hired, each possessing a high degree of initiative and self-direction. Everyone was given the freedom to plan and execute their work as he or she saw fit. Given the small size of the company, it was easy for managers to keep track of the projects that different people were on, and coordination between projects was not difficult.

At that time, the company had an innovative product with little direct

[2]The authors are very grateful to Craig McGee of Meritus Consulting for providing us material on the Sybase case.

competition. Delays in new-product releases were tolerated, since they were the only game in town. To compensate for these delays, the company developed a strong customer technical-support staff, which assisted customers with working around the glitches in existing products. As other competitors entered the marketplace, the company's technology became more of a commodity, and product planning grew more complicated. Suddenly the company faced a new challenge of developing new product features and functionalities in order to maintain its competitive advantage. However, the most important challenge facing the company was reinvention of the product planning and development process. Now resources were more limited, the technology more complex, and more people were involved in the development process. Developers needed a better sense of product-family strategy. Sales representatives needed more knowledge that could allow them to inform customers of the timing on new product introductions.

With little deliberate thinking, the Boulder operation had adopted a functional organization by default. Product development comprised separate engineering, quality assurance, and documentation departments. The development process occurred sequentially, with the typical problems associated with departmental hand-offs: lack of resource availability, lack of understanding of product features and system architecture, poor coordination across departments, and delays due to recycling to fix errors.

Rapid Prototyping from a Functional to a Product-Aligned Organization

Based on a prior cross-functional effort to study the development process, recommendations called for shifting from a functional to a horizontal organization design organized around product development teams. A rapid-business-process design approach was used that involved development staff directly in developing a new design, which consisted of five product development teams. Each team would be staffed with development engineers, quality assurance testers, and documentation writers. In addition, a new function was created—"Sustaining Engineering"—whose role was to fix bugs in newly released software. (This practice is quite commonplace. Some bugs can't be detected until the software program is actually installed and running on a customer's system. Software today is so complex that it is impossible to achieve 100 percent reliability before the program is released to the marketplace.) With the new product-aligned structure, each team had all the resources that it needed to develop a product under its direct control. Other advantages of this structural arrangement included continuity of staff across different versions of the product, continuous learning about product capabilities, and a more flexible utilization of staff, with documentation staff helping to write product specifications, developers helping to perform testing, and so on.

Revitalizing and Reclaiming a Culture of Improvisation at Sybase

While the new product-aligned structure was up and running, the new design was far from ideal. The Boulder facility continued to refine and improvise in real time. One of the historical strengths of the Boulder facility had been its cohesive, energetic, high-performance culture. Cooperation and respect for individuals were strongly valued and reinforced. Customer service and responsiveness were paramount. Individuals sacrificed their personal needs to achieve product excellence and customer satisfaction. Product quality and technical excellence were the standards. Sybase's culture supported the team-based approach. However, Sybase's rapid growth presented a tremendous challenge to maintaining the informality and creativeness of what had been a small-company culture. This was particularly true for the Boulder business unit. With an influx of new staff from different companies, along with a migration of professionals from Sybase's headquarters, the senior leadership team for the Boulder facility decided that it was time to redefine and reclaim the culture of the company. Craig McGee, an experienced consultant trained in self-managing design methods, designed and managed a Search Conference, followed by Participative Design sessions.

On the first day of the Search Conference, participants focused on setting a new strategic direction for their business unit. Participants identified and discussed trends in the business environment, including emerging changes in customers' requirements and the customer base itself. They identified potential threats from competitors and mapped out directions in which the technology was moving. From this, they deduced the critical success factors and core competencies needed to differentiate their products in the marketplace. The first day concluded with participants brainstorming possible strategies for three main areas: products and technology, organizational systems and structures, and relationships with the Sybase headquarters group. The second day focused first on formulating a set of clear, coherent strategies for each of the three areas. After reaching collective agreement on the business strategies, the conference shifted to revisiting the culture, history, and values of the company. Participants spent time defining the core values that represented the essence of their company—what attracted people to work for the company, the things that differentiated this organization from other firms in the industry. They also identified aspects and values of the "old company" that they didn't want to lose—cultural values that were important to carry forward into the future. Participants were emphatic that merely identifying core values was not enough. Day 2 of the conference also focused on identifying specific actions that individuals and managers could take to sustain the core values. Much emphasis was placed on taking *personal leadership and accountability*, rather than expecting senior managers to be keepers of the values. Day 3, the final day of the conference, focused on identifying critical actions needed to execute the strategies developed and commitments made during the conference. The conference had generated a high level of excitement and enthusiasm, but it also upped the ante and heightened expectations for solid follow-through. A number of implementation groups were formed around such projects as developing a "skunk works" for new product development, a system for rotational assignments, and a mentoring program, to develop a new employee-orientation program for inculcating the new values.

To further improvise and implement more detailed features of the new design, the Technical Services area decided to use Participative Design sessions. The consultant briefed the manager of the Technical Services area on Participative Design, and the manager strongly endorsed the approach. Participative Design sessions were conducted using mirror groups, with half the department participating in each session. During the sessions, the participants identified strengths and weaknesses of the department, as well as customer (internal and external) needs. They created a new organization structure that supported the product-aligned development teams in the rest of the organization. Participants also identified what was needed to support the new structure—training, role clarification, etc. An integration team then took the two different designs and merged them into an integrated design, which was then reviewed with the rest of the department.

What were the results? Product teams cut development time and began releasing more new products on time. Productivity also increased. Some of the programmers noted that they were now developing products with five programmers, where an IBM would have required fifty. The company earned its ISO quality certification in a lightning-fast six months. The Boulder facility is now the most profitable business unit within Sybase.

The Power of New Metaphors

We should not underestimate the power of introducing new metaphors—such as the jazz ensemble—as a method for inducing cognitive and behavioral change at the archetypal level of consciousness. Marcia Salner (1988) states that "metaphor is more than a linguistic device. The term itself becomes a metaphor for a cognitive process and a particular way of 'seeing' the world around and within us." We have, of course, idealized the world of jazz, which is not without its problems of artistic egos and personality conflicts. However, we feel that if management—as Drucker points out—is a liberal art, then we can draw from, and creatively build on, the best of this American art form.

Taking our theoretical cues from the jazz ensemble metaphor, the shift to democratic norms based on partnership is based on the following assumptions.

1. Creativity and motivation are innate human capacities which may not necessarily be equally distributed across individuals in terms of specific key traits, potentials, or propensities, but under the appropriate social conditions the human potential within each individual can be developed to a much greater extent than would be the case in a traditional bureaucratic organization.
2. Synergy between individuals can be tapped to a much greater extent when there are appropriate self-managing democratic structures, participative processes, and partnership norms that allow emergent properties to be realized.
3. The ideal of equality can be realized by providing people a democratic structure of authority that allows them meaningful participation in critical decisions that affect their work lives.
4. Potentially every person can develop multifunctional capabilities that add creative value to the organization, as well as to himself or herself in terms of continuing growth, learning, and integration.

5. Shared responsibility combined with group accountability is impeded not by lack of employee competence, but by meritocratic norms that limit the development and maturation of the self-managing organization.

The underlying principles that form the self-managing organization run directly counter to well-established and deeply held meritocratic norms. This is why it is often hard for managers to let go of their psychological and emotional attachment to traditional hierarchy. Their beliefs are shaped by their experience of working in a meritocratic social system. The democratic design principle raises a number of concerns: Without a traditional hierarchy, how will tasks be assigned? What will happen to people's motivation and commitment if traditional career ladders are kicked away? How can people be held accountable if they are working in teams? What will be the basis of allocating rewards to individuals if their primary responsibility is to a team? All of these questions still presuppose that a self-managing organization will conform to existing meritocratic norms, which is problematic.

Self-Management Requires More Democracy

The fact of the matter is that organizations cannot become self-managing until they become more democratic. We need to be careful, since *democracy* is another overused and abused word like *empowerment*. The original Greek meaning of the word is derived from the roots *demos* (the people) and *kratia* (rule), which can literally be translated, rule by the people. For organizations to become more democratic, the political ideal of equality must be built into the very structures of work, allowing individuals to participate in meaningful decisions so they can learn to rule, manage, and govern themselves. In self-managing organizations supported by democratic norms of equality, the phenotypic design will emphasize the following features.

1. A more democratic structure characterized by reduced levels of hierarchy, as well as less status and power differentials between levels.
2. Processes that allow self-managing groups to select and appoint their own leaders (if such positions are deemed necessary), and where leaders are accountable to the group that selected them.

3. Shared responsibility for group performance.
4. A more equitable distribution of rewards.

If all this sounds like a bunch of academic drivel, think twice. There is nothing academic about what is happening at Lucent Technology's Mount Olive, New Jersey, facility, where 480 self-directed associates are making digital cellular base stations. Their workforce has cut total labor costs in this brutally global market to just 3 percent of product costs. Management now sets the direction, the end game, and delegates three levels down. Professionals in cubicles now sit next to workers in assembly cells, and people solve problems in hallways, often quoting from a one-page list of working "principles" that reads like a Bill of Rights.The working principles represent a contract signed by everyone, which commits them to speed, innovation, candor, deep respect for colleagues, and other plainly stated goals. Teams have a lot of authority, and use it to constantly alter the manufacturing process and even the product design. And the yearly bonus representing 15 percent of base pay in 1996 was based equally on individual and team achievement.

TO BE OR NOT TO BE? SENIOR MANAGERS MUST MAKE AN ORGANIZATIONAL CHOICE

Senior managers are ultimately responsible for making a fundamental organizational choice: whether or not the organization should be redesigned to operationalize the democratic design principle. The decision at this stage is not about whether the organization should have teams or not have teams, or whether certain functions or departments will be combined, nor any other operational issue. The choice is whether to commit to a fundamentally different design principle for the whole organization, from top to bottom, from R&D to Manufacturing. Even not making a choice is still a choice: to uphold the status quo or to drift into laissez-faire.

Leaders need to wrestle with the implications of making the democratic design principle operational in their organizations. They need to really work through the concept, both in their own minds and through dialogue with others, before taking the plunge. Only after arriving at some shared understanding of what self-management really means for their own local situation, can a truly conscious choice be made. If people are going to be asked to "transform the organization," they have to know "Into what?" Thomas Lee at the Center for Quality Management emphasizes the link between employee involvement, self-management, and business success. His research indicates that successful results can't occur if leadership from the top is lacking. Senior management needs to personally, continuously, and consistently demonstrate the connection to employees between participation, self-management, and business results. Otherwise, resistance and inertia combine to kill attempts at meaningful change. Developing a shared understanding of the democratic design principle through dialogue about the implications of shifting meritocratic norms is also essential.

The payoff can be enormous because a fundamental change in organizational paradigm is systemic in nature. The *Industry Week* Census (Taninecz, 1997) offers a hint of what is possible. Plants with high levels of self-management are five times more likely to be using other best practices: plant-wide involvement in strategy creation and execution, customer-focused work practices, quality initiatives, the most highly regarded human-resource approaches, and supply management practices. This study goes on to show that plants that make a significant investment in technology, but fail to empower their workforce, perform no better than average. The reverse is also true. Combine investments in people and technology, and you beat a broad range of average-performance measures.

The reasons and lessons are clear: When there is no real understanding of the democratic design principle among senior levels of management, initiatives that are started will more than likely fade out in a short period of time. Attempts to introduce self-managing work teams piecemeal into an organization simply don't work. Some units may forge ahead into self-management while other units sit comfortably on the sidelines. And without a clear and agreed-upon framework to guide the redesign process, the organization begins to look like a patchwork quilt of competing initiatives that just don't add up to self-management. Employees end up cynical and confused. This is why conscious organizational choice is so important: self-management must not be seen as an optional program that is subject to cancellation.

Piecemeal approaches simply are not radical enough—they don't go down to the roots of the design principle. In order to fundamentally change the character of a dominant hierarchy, existing bureaucratic structures and support systems must also be changed. Every component of the organization must be congruent with the principles of democracy. Most importantly, if the democratic design principle is not internalized in the minds and behaviors of senior management, self-management will be alien to the dominant organizational culture. For self-management to take root, democratic structures and egalitarian norms must become part of the cultural fabric of the enterprise.

POLAROID'S FIR DIVISION REVISITED

As noted at the beginning of this chapter, Satish Agrawal, former director of Polaroid's FIR division, envisioned a learning organization in which the majority of knowledge workers would be organized in a manner that allowed them to develop products which were manufacturable, of high quality, on time, within budget, and profitable to the company. Rather than focusing narrowly and exclusively within their technical disciplines, the new organization design needed to reorient professionals to identify with both the end product and the entire development process.

Amid the chaos and turmoil that had plagued the overly bureaucratic FIR division, the emergence of a self-managing organization began with the launching of the Helios development program. Helios, a new medical-imaging system, became one of Polaroid's most successful and innovative products. Helios was developed in less than three years—a breakthrough record at Polaroid. Helios would soon become a model for how product development within FIR would be organized. In 1992, *Fortune* magazine quoted then CEO I. MacAllister Booth as saying, "Our researchers are not any smarter, but by working together they get the value of each other's intelligence almost instantaneously."

What accounts for the success of the Helios product? Unlike other projects in the division, the Helios program was organized into a self-managing product development team. The self-managing organization set up for the Helios program enabled team learning to occur. Knowledge workers met in small, informal forums; they established group norms conducive to knowledge sharing; they actively engaged in inquiry and dialogue; and they developed a mutual appreciation of product system interdependencies. The informality and the fluid arrangements among Helios project members were seen as facilitating their ability to develop new knowledge. Any project member had the authority at any time to call a meeting and make key technical decisions on the spot. Discussions of technical topics were held informally in small groups of four to five people. Comments from several Helios project members are illustrative: "Our interactions are close and continuous"; "Meetings with the team are informal affairs"; "We see each other just about every day and so we all know what others are up against."

For Helios team members, knowledge sharing was a norm. The atmosphere in the Helios project was clearly more open than what traditionally had been the case in the FIR division. As one team member stated: "There is a good exchange of perspectives among us. People aren't trying to hide things in our group." Another Helios scientist noted: "The new people are working hard and learning from each other, and not constantly reinventing the wheel." Moreover, the locus of expertise in the Helios project was widely distributed. The egalitarian climate among Helios project members was clearly evident. Ideas and knowledge were shared freely among all team members.

Team members also engaged in active inquiry. Active inquiry within Helios deliberations manifested as free-spirited dialogue, healthy debates, and open, honest discussions of the pros and cons of different technical alternatives. Prior to making a major decision to scale-up a solution, Helios team members frequently would debate the technical approach under consideration. The willingness of Helios members to engage in active inquiry was unequivocally higher than among their counterparts in the FIR division. Statements like the following were expressed: "Sometimes we get into pretty heated discussions about the merits of an approach"; "Our project manager actually invites us to state our views, even if they go against his"; "Some of us come from such different backgrounds that we don't always see eye to eye, but in the end we come out with a better solution." In sum, the enabling conditions conducive to active engagement in inquiry had a "variety amplifying" effect, which in turn facilitated a more thorough exploration and integration of divergent perspectives.

The Helios project from the onset was highly dependent upon marketing inputs as a means to determine and adjust product specifications. Helios team members were constantly making changes in the prototype. The interdisciplinary composition of the Helios team made individual team members more appreciative and aware of the interdependent nature of the problems they were working on. Gatekeeping with other labs in the division was shared by all members, rather than being invested in a single individual. As one team member put it, "We all take responsibility for initiating and following up on details with other groups."

Helios was also successful because project management was decentralized. This was a radical departure from the traditional, autocratic style that had been characteristic of the company's founder and management lineage. Reflecting on this shift, the Helios project manager noted: We have a culture that is not only top-down, but because we have a technical management, it has meant that a manager should know all the details. Now the change I see in my role is that I should know only enough details to ask the right technical questions—to give people room for influence. The message is recognizing that we shouldn't have to know the details to the degree that we sap the energy and motivation of the real problem-solvers. The Helios organization is very fluid. The Helios group is really making all the day-to-day technical decisions."

Operating as a fully self-managing group, Helios created a new paradigm for product development within the FIR division. It offered a viable alternative to the Land legacy of autocratic rule, "maestro management," and what had dubiously been referred to as the "Stalinist approach" to product development. Most Polaroid scientists and engineers were used to this management-by-fear approach. Under the old autocratic culture, knowledge workers felt like their technical competence was always on the line. As a result, they were overly cautious about publicizing their thinking and ideas in front of management. In contrast, Helios team members were never hesitant, reluctant, or fearful of challenging management's authority.

SUMMARY

Hierarchical arrangements that are not aligned with knowledge are almost always antithetical to the performance of knowledge work. When top levels intervene in knowledge work processes, the worst possible result is that those on the bottom will obey directives without question. Yet to fight against the hierarchy is often perceived as too risky. Neither side is comfortable talking directly to the other for very long. Hence, the top and the bottom struggle to understand each other from a considerable distance. The resulting communication involves a lot of shouting, but not much understanding. The old adage, "Lead, follow, or get the hell out of the way!" may need to be replaced in knowledge-work organizations with a new adage: "If you don't know what you are talking about, take the time to learn; if you can't take the time to learn, don't take the time to lead."

The democratic design principle creates structures that are temporary and malleable, allowing people's knowledge and expertise to influence the strategies, modes of operation, and decisions made within organizations. That means aligning knowledge with influence in decision making. It also means reshaping hierarchies so that positional power doesn't dominate people with critical expertise. Self-managing organizations get the people who are experts into the positions where they can influence decision making. This implies constantly shifting the way work is organized so people can enter and exit positions of decision-making responsibility as the nature of the business challenge changes. Like jazz ensembles, self-managing organizations are fluid and dynamic.

CHAPTER 5

REVOLUTIONS GONE SOUR

Learning from Evolutionary Failures

> Democracy is just stumbling along to the right
> decision instead of going straight forward to the
> wrong one.
>
> —Lawrence J. Peter

SOUTHCORP WINERY: LEARNING
THE HARD WAY[1]

Accounting for 30 percent of the country's total wine production, Southcorp is Australia's largest wine producer, employing nearly 2,500 people, with annual sales revenues of $500 million U.S. Southcorp now produces over sixteen brands and four hundred labels, and some of its well known labels include Penfolds, Lindemans, Seppelt, Leo Buring, and Matthew Lang. While the wine industry is dominated by France, Italy, and the United States, Australian wineries have sought to establish global brands with worldwide distribution and recognition. Low cost and product consistency, along with a need to improve quality and become more flexibile to market demands, have become key drivers of business success. Southcorp, like other Australian wineries, must also compete with low-cost producers in Chile and South Africa, making productivity a key requirement.

Located in the southeast Australian state of Victoria, the Karadoc winery is the largest processing plant, employing over 300 people and produc-

---

[1]Material for this account was derived from a public presentation made at "The Fifth European Ecology of Work Conference," Dublin, Ireland, May 13–16, 1997.

ing 75 million liters of wine annually. In many ways, Southcorp Wine's huge Karadoc winery was a classic failure in the way it introduced self-management into its operations the first time it tried. The Karadoc winery was organized along traditional hierarchical lines, making it rigid and inflexible in the face of demands for new product developments, higher quality standards, changing govermental regulations, and fiercer competition.

Bob Baxter, a senior manager at the Karadoc winery, was involved with that first attempt to establish self-managing work teams. Reflecting on his experience, he admits, "The way we went about it initially was a disaster and I think it highlighted all the things not to do." According to Baxter, the first attempt was a misguided effort that was forced from the top down by management with little preparation or prior communication. Utilizing an all-too-familiar totalitarian approach, top management acted quickly, imposing a team-based design on the operational level of the organization. "We did it for all the wrong reasons. We saw it as a way to reduce costs by simply cutting out the supervisors," recounts Baxter. While this slash-and-burn approach did result in an immediate 15 percent saving in direct labor costs, the sudden removal of key personnel was offset by the cumulative indirect costs caused by the ensuing confusion over roles and responsibilities, increased errors and downtime.

According to Baxter's estimates, glitches in the system resulted in a 20 percent loss in efficiency. In the end, very few people were committed to the idea of self-management, and except for senior management, nobody understood the reasons and the need for such a radical surgical strike on supervisors. Realizing they had stumbled down the wrong track, management pulled the plug on self-managing teams and reverted to the traditional structure.

THE STUCK-IN-THE-MIDDLE PHENOMENON

When companies encounter major obstacles that stall evolution toward self-management, they often get stuck in the middle between two opposing organizational paradigms. Thomas Kuhn's (1970) analysis of scientific revolutions demonstrates that fundamental change in a scientific discipline does not occur until there is a direct challenge to the existing paradigm. When anomalies arise and discrediting evidence throws a discipline into a crisis, scientists who have made professional career investments in existing theories and methods will defend and protect the dominant paradigm from outside assaults. Even in the midst of a veritable paradigm shift, there is a flurry of activity that often amounts to nothing more than extensions and modifications of the dominant paradigm.

The same is true in the case of organizations today. Managers have a great deal invested in the dominant corporate paradigm: social status and executive privilege, the need for order through layers and layers of close supervision, the illusion of unilateral control, autocratic power, the sacredness of the managerial prerogative, the view that people are dispensable, and inequitable reward systems.

Many organizations attempt to introduce revolutionary change but get sidetracked into supporting mild and incremental reforms that perpetuate the status quo. These initiatives often take one step forward—evolving toward self-management—but two steps backward as managers attempt to retain vestiges of a dominant hierarchy. These half-measures sometimes provide value and benefit, but more often than not, they do more harm than good. This is because managers and consultants alike often adapt and modify revolutionary methods to fit within their existing organizational paradigm, in effect preserving the bureaucratic design principle. In this respect, the Southcorp Winery story is not uncommon. Many companies end up stuck in the middle between a bureaucratic and a self-managing organization paradigm, adopting a patchwork quilt of programs—such as TQM, Reengineering, Socio-Technical Systems, problem-solving teams, corporate diversity programs—all stitched together rather loosely, or not at all.

The struggle to shift the existing organization paradigm from one based on a dominant hierarchy to a more participative, self-managing organization based on a democratic structure has occupied the attention of managers, consultants, and academics for the latter half of the twentieth century. Clearly, the new wave is in the direction of creating self-managing organizations, enterprises that are designed and redesigned—not by consultants, external experts, or an elite group of reengineers—but by the members themselves.

It is important not only to appreciate the magnitude of this change, but also to understand how a clash between the old and new paradigms has led to a grab bag of programs, fads, and piecemeal attempts that fall short of overturning the traditional bureaucratic paradigm. This is because the transformation of dominant bureaucratic hierarchies into democratic, self-managing work structures is truly radical, dramatic, and revolutionary. It is about changing the fundamental power relationships that have defined the status and authority of traditional management since the beginning of the Industrial Revolution. Most organizational change methods and management programs have adopted the rhetoric of revolution, but in practice the results often amount to merely extensions or add-ons that leave the core of the traditional bureaucratic paradigm intact.

Figure 5.1 illustrates how organizations remain stranded in a dominant hierarchy, or end up stuck in the middle by getting sidetracked into pseudo-empowerment or totalitarian democratic schemes. Each quadrant is defined by two dimensions representing different configurations of organizational structures with management processes.

COMPETING ORGANIZATION PARADIGMS

Autocratic Processes

1. Classic Restructuring

Form: Dominant hierarchy
Change Process: Command and control
Ideology: Efficiency
Methods: Downsizing, corporate reorganizations
Management Message: "Do it or else!"

3. Totalitarian Democracy

Form: Flat hierarchy, decentralized
Change Process: Cascade, expert-imposed designs
Ideology: Social engineering
Methods: Reengineering, STS, corporate culture programs, "self-directed teams"
Management Message: "Do as I say, not as I do"

Bureaucratic Structure ———————————————— **Democratic Structure**

2. Cooptive Participation

Form: Parallel structures
Change Process: Pseudo-empowerment
Ideology: Human Relations
Methods: Problem-solving teams, team-building, changing leadership styles
Management Message : "Can you give me any suggestions on how to improve what I want you to do?"

4. Self-Management

Form: Self-managing work teams
Change Process: Full participation
Ideology: Democracy
Methods: Participative Design, Search Conferences, town-hall meetings
Management Message : "Figure out what to do and how to do it, so long as it meets our jointly negotiated goals"

Participative Processes

Figure 5.1

The first dimension, bureaucratic versus democratic structure, pertains to the system of responsibility used to control and coordinate the work of employees, otherwise known as organizational structure. Bureaucratic structures are characterized by steep hierarchies, many levels of supervision, precise individualized job assignments and rewards; goal-setting that is unilaterally controlled by managers. In contrast, democratic structures are characterized by a flat hierarchy, few levels of supervision, flexible team-based assignments and rewards; and goal-setting is mutually negotiated between teams and managers.

The second dimension, autocratic versus participative processes, reflects the locus of authority for decision making and the extent to which information is shared in the system. Autocratic processes are apparent when managers make decisions, issue commands, and delegate orders without the direct participation of those affected. Access to information is restricted to a need-to-know basis. In contrast, participative processes place the locus of control for decision making into the hands of those who have the competence, knowledge, and expertise to make the best decision.

Successful management revolutions overturn the existing organizational paradigm, effecting a move away from the upper-left-hand quadrant of a dominant hierarchy toward the bottom right-hand quadrant of self-management. Most firms have experimented on the fringes and around the borders of self-management, experimenting with participation on the shop floor, or by reengineering business processes, but few have gone all the way to create designs that integrate democratic structures with participative processes. Pseudo-empowerment programs generate employee cynicism, while ruthless totalitarian reengineering crusades that slash and burn away jobs leave the surviving workforce depressed and drained. All of these efforts fall short of crossing the threshold into effective participation and democratic self-management. Below we elaborate on these different corporate change scenarios with respect to their phenotypical forms, modes of management, and ideologies.

1. Classic Restructuring

There has been a recent surge of "bureaucracy busting" through corporate restructuring, delayering, and downsizing. Many of these efforts, however, are simply attempts to "clean up the bureaucracy" and amount to nothing more than reshuffling the boxes on the organizational chart. Corporate reorganizations are masterminded behind closed doors by senior managers who draw up the new organizational chart and then simply present the new design to the organization as a *fait accompli.*

The reorganization may result in a "leaner and meaner" corporation—see Figure 5.1—but what remains is essentially a trimmed-down dominant hierarchy. Many bloated bureaucracies have been downsized, but failed to transform to a self-managing design principle. Slack resources and redundancies have been cut out, and survivors are asked to "do more with less." But how? The bureaucratic design principle keeps employees locked into narrow job descriptions, chain-of-command reporting relationships, and politics as usual. The steep hierarchy is flattened and layers are cut, but the organization nonetheless remains fragmented and bound to a command-and-control structure. True, there may be fewer managers in command, but the ones that remain are still calling the shots, controlling and coordinating the work of others, and issuing directives from on high. A dominant hierarchy is still alive and well, drawing on the control structure of bureaucracy and the unquestioned authority of position based on autocratic rule.

What is the lesson here? Becoming "leaner and meaner" does not develop a capacity for self-management. This is because organizational delayering—like reengineering—stops short of changing the organizational genotype. Flattening the hierarchy is merely a phenotypic change which leaves the bureaucratic design principle and meritocratic norms intact. Phenotypic change doesn't alter or redefine the structural relationship between people and functions, parts and whole. The evidence that things haven't really changed can be found in the way authority and responsibility are allocated. When employees have no authority and little responsibility, it leads to behaviors like passing the buck and just following orders.

In some corporations, massive restructuring is labeled "empowerment." Typically what happens is that a layer of supervision is eliminated, employees are suddenly informed that they are empowered to work as a team, while their jobs and support systems remain firmly entrenched in the same old rut. We call this the "dumb-sizing method," since employees are left floundering in a system that is still geared toward a machine bureaucracy while now being no longer sure where the boundaries of their responsibility really lie. Employees and middle managers alike are left in a state of confusion. Are teams now suddenly going to be held accountable? If so, why is the performance appraisal system still geared toward individual performance? Perhaps individuals will be held accountable for their contribution to the team? Or are managers still ultimately going to be held responsible for the work of individuals who report to them? In most cases, it is the latter. Employees can't control and coordinate their own work because the system hasn't been redesigned to provide them the capabilities to do so. The organization drifts into a state of laissez-faire. Unfortunately the dumb-sizing approach has been used so frequently that it has given team-based work systems a bad name.

2. Cooptive Participation

Cooptive participation—see Figure 5.1— represents an attempt to introduce participative work systems into the organization, but without fundamentally changing the bureaucratic control structure. Many organizations that set sail to the shore of self-management have found themselves shipwrecked in this quadrant. Rather than transforming the traditional hierarchy, cooptive participation schemes "fit" or "install" participation into existing bureaucratic structures.

The rhetoric of many cooptive-participation programs is that of "empowerment" or "organizational transformation," but most don't really deliver on their promise. Such programs do not offer a bona fide alternative to a dominant hierarchy because the pillars of bureaucracy are left standing. This is not to say that all cooptive-participation programs are worthless or a waste of time; some modest improvements have occurred on the operational level, but those gains are far from systemic or transformative in magnitude. The reason improvement is only modest goes back to allocation of authority and responsibility. Cooptive work systems give teams a high degree of responsibility for results without sufficient control (authority) over the situation to consistently achieve the results desired.

Parallel Structures. The phenotypical form of organization for cooptive-participation programs is "parallel structures." Parallel structures are either temporary or permanent groups that are set up to work alongside and in parallel with the formal bureaucratic organization. Some of the earliest attempts at introducing participation within the confines of the formal bureaucracy date back to early Human Relations approaches. And many popular approaches since the early 1970s—such as employee involvement and quality-of-work-life programs, TQM, and problem-solving teams—are just some examples of the use of parallel structures.

Cooptive participation programs operate in collusion with bureaucratic structures, as such programs are merely extensions of the existing paradigm. In *The Handbook for Human Resource Administrators,* Famularo (1986) reflects on Bennis' prediction of bureaucracy's demise in the 1960s: "Bureaucracy should have crashed on the rocks . . . but it did not. Many organizations are more bureaucratic rather than less. Others survived by creating new organizational structures which supplemented the bureaucracy." Famularo goes on to say that rather than date ourselves by attacking bureaucracy we ought to create interventions that accommodate its persistence into the 1980s and 1990s. Clearly, this is not a prescription for revolution. Cooptive-participation programs are mild reforms that have no intention of transforming the dominant paradigm.

Techniques that fall in this quadrant—team-building, process consultation, 360-degree and survey feedback, role negotiation—have been the mainstay of organization development consultants but they are simply attempts to put a human face on the command-and-control structure. Other cooptive-participation programs—such as job enrichment, employee suggestion systems, employee involvement and problem-solving groups, quality circles and cross-functional improvement teams—are attempts to shore up the traditional hierarchy rather than challenge it directly. Similarly, there are many examples of so-called "self-directed work teams," which is really a misnomer, since team members still report to and take their direction from supervisors who have been given new job titles as trainers, leaders, or coaches.

These cooptive schemes amount to forms of *pseudo-empowerment,* since authority and responsibility for controlling and coordinating work are still invested in a traditional hierarchical structure. Pseudo-empowerment fails to transform the structure of authority relations in the formal hierarchy. Indeed, the enormous appeal of pseudo-empowerment approaches lies in the fact that they do not require fundamental changes in the system of responsibility—in reporting relationships, coordination of assignments, and allocation of rewards. In this sense, cooptive-participation schemes are "power-friendly."

Even when exposed to a new self-managing paradigm, many managers retrofit the concept to make it conform to existing control mechanisms.

They simply can't conceive a form of organizational control without a dominant hierarchy. For many managers, an organization without traditional supervisors is seen as a formula for chaos. Instead of confronting power issues directly, most programs that work within this quadrant focus on trying to increase participation within permanent or temporary groups, within so-called teams; meanwhile the structure of authority and control between the teams, and between the teams and the rest of the organization remains fundamentally bureaucratic.

Human Relations Ideology. Interventions and work systems within the cooptive-participation quadrant subscribe—whether by conscious intent or by default—to the human relations ideology. The ideology of human relations is full of exhortations urging managers to change their behavior, to become more participative and employee-centered. Rather than changing the bureaucratic organization structure and division of labor, human relations advocates like Chris Argyris (1957, 1964) and Douglas McGregor (1960) limited their efforts to changing leadership styles and managerial philosophies. The locus of change centered on making leadership less autocratic and more "democratic," "participative," and in today's parlance we might say more "empowering."

Industrial humanists hoped that by making leadership more democratic, a change in organizational climate would result. Bureaucracy would be transformed not by flattening tall hierarchies, dismantling functional silos, redesigning fractionated work processes, or redressing the balance of power and control, but through a change in "atmosphere." Democratic leadership would lead to more employee participation (on matters defined by bosses), a more egalitarian work atmosphere, and respectful subordinate–supervisor relations. In a humanistic climate, employees could supposedly develop toward greater maturity and self-actualization. Peter Drucker, another influential voice critical of the human relations approach, noted that "Most of the recent writers on industrial psychology . . . use such terms like 'self-fulfillment,' 'creativity,' and 'the whole person.' But what they mean is control through psychological manipulation" (Drucker, 1954).

Human relationists also believe that making people feel as if they are part of a team, and substituting authoritarian practices with a "participative style" of management, will make up for the loss of dignity, meaning, and pride in work. As Eric Trist put it, "workers were to be treated better, but their jobs would remain the same" (Trist and Murray, 1993, p. 583). Rather than mounting a challenge to Taylorism and the degradation of work, human relationists took the design of jobs as a technological given. Human relationists bow down to the technological imperative, viewing the technical system of the firm as basically invariant and unalterable.

Human relationists are concerned with improving the interpersonal competence of supervisors and training in team management. It's a simple and compelling idea—that supervisors simply need good human relations skills to make work groups effective. A great deal of emphasis is devoted to training group facilitators, improving social relations, smoothing over conflict, and building up "team feelings"—all of which are typical of organization development initiatives. However, simply improving managers' social skills, no matter how well intentioned, does not transform the techno-structural blueprint of the organization.

One fallout from the human relations movement is that the concept of participation is often associated with "participative management," or a consultative style of supervision—which is actually a distortion of what effective participation means and how it really works in self-managing organizations. Instead, participation in the human relations tradition has come to be equated with a *technique of persuasion* for influencing a group to arrive at a decision that is in alignment with management's goals. Lewis Corey, a critic of the human relations movement, bluntly states that "the objectives of this use of 'group dynamics' are to get workers to accept what management wants them to accept *but* to make them feel *they* made or helped to make the decision" (cited in Baritz, 1960). Both Mussolini and Stalin controlled masses of people through cooptive participation, giving them the psychological impression of helping to make decisions affecting their lives, when in reality the content of the decisions was already decided in advance.

With cooptive participation, the main behavioral message communicated by management is "Can you give me any suggestions on how to improve what I want you to do?" In other words, supervisors trained in human relations skills learn a subtle and deceptive form of persuasiveness which is used to give workers a sense and feeling of participation, while the locus of responsibility for control and coordination remains squarely in the hands of management.

Participation in the human relations scheme doesn't really empower people; instead it relies on cooptation and manipulation. Indeed, the enormous appeal of human relations methods can be explained by the fact that they do not require fundamental changes in organizational structure or the redistribution of power. The concept of power is left completely out of the human relations equation. Instead, power struggles between managers and employees are interpreted as behavioral or communication problems. This is another signature of human relations theorists: problems in industry are seen through a psychological frame of reference—it is people's behavior that needs to change. Behavioral change—and this is the core of the ideology—is necessary for good human relations. Change behavior first, so the logic goes, and improvements in productivity will follow.

Accordingly, human relations programs focus on improving social relations, smoothing over conflict, building up "team feelings," and achieving consensus and harmony. Much effort is concentrated on attempting to change employee attitudes, supervisory leadership styles, interpersonal group relations, and managerial communications. The human relations hypothesis that making workers more happy and satisfied with their jobs would lead to productivity improvements still has wide appeal, but amounts to what Daniel Bell (1956, p. 25) derogatorily referred to as "cow sociology," reflecting the notion that contented cows give more milk.

Rather than authorizing work groups to make their own decisions (one key aspect of self-management), participative management programs are much more "informal." Work teams take their orders from an "enlightened supervisor," one trained in a participative style of management. Supervisors are trained to be informal, act friendly, show support, and solicit the work group's ideas and input, but the final say and authority for decision making still rest with the supervisor. In other words, participation at the level of work groups is not formally sanctioned or codified into the organizational structure. Instead, participation is treated as an informal option that the supervisor may elect to enact through his style of leadership. For work groups, participation in decision making is totally dependent on whether the supervisor is willing to share his decision-making authority with them. Since this form of cooptive participation is informal, supervisors are under no obligation to do so. Lamenting the weakness of the human relations approach to participation, Charles Perrow (1979) does not mince words: "One may treat slaves humanely, and even ask their opinions on matters with which they are more familiar than the master."

Organizational Schizophrenia: Turning Supervisors into Team Leaders, Facilitators, and Coaches. Rather than eliminating supervisors and layers of management as is often the case with classic restructuring efforts, in cooptive-participation programs the incumbents are simply given new titles. Supervisors become "team leaders or facilitators," while managers suddenly become "coaches." We call this the "rhetorical method." Employees are simply told that they have to work as a team, and if they need help or direction, they can consult their team leader/facilitator, who is still clearly at a higher level of a dominant hierarchy. The rhetorical method is based on the assumption that a supervisor's role can suddenly change from a police officer/boss to that of a facilitator, team leader, or coach. It is similar to the dumb-sizing method in that it is a quick fix that requires no major changes in the design of work. It is another clear example of cooptive participation.

Noting this trend, Emery points out that this approach attempts

> . . . simply to train managers in a dressed-up version of [McGregor's] Theory Y that relabels them as "coaches, facilitators, or team leaders." Management-by-intimidation is no longer acceptable to baby boomers and Generation X, but simply creating a more palatable, touchy-feely management technique isn't going to fundamentally change the DNA of the organization. It's still a bureaucracy, just a dressed-up one. And the consequences of a bureaucracy on people's initiative, entrepreneurial spirit, motivation, energy, and capacity for learning are still sadly the same. Communication patterns don't change in any fundamental way and one management fad after another will continue to distract people from making fundamental change because these methods don't change the underlying design principle. (Emery, F., 1995)

Many companies that jumped on the team bandwagon spent an enormous amount of time, money, and energy in forming employees into work groups, newly christening them a "team," providing them "team skills" training, and relabeling the title of supervisor or manager as "team leader." In reality, however, this window-dressing doesn't cover up the fact that the "team leader" is still a boss. In actuality, there is little real change in the team leader's job duties, reporting relationships, and position on the organizational chart. The fact that a supervisory position "above" the team is retained—no matter what name or title the individual holding that position is given—means that the holder of that position is still the point person and will be held responsible for the work of the team. In other words, there really isn't any substantive change in the authority structure between the so-called team leader and the so-called team.

Not surprisingly, the rhetorical method often leads to a Catch-22 situation and a laissez-faire work atmosphere. This set-up creates a great deal of confusion for both the supervisor/team leader and members of the team. It leads to what Merrelyn Emery (1993) has referred to as a "crisis of responsibility." Typically what happens is that the "team leader" either chooses to retain accountability and control (the bureaucratic design principle), or he lets go of all controls and creates a power vacuum (laissez-faire, abandoning all structure).

Simply changing the supervisor's title without changing the formal structure of the organization results in a classic double-bind situation, where mixed messages make everyone feel schizophrenic. On the one hand, team members are led to believe that they are in charge of their own work and have the authority to make their own decisions. On the other hand, the team leader is also held accountable for the work of the team. So who really is in charge? If the team leader takes charge, team members will accuse him of reverting to his old supervisory role.

Given the ambiguity of their new role, supervisors/team leaders are often afraid of exerting their authority and making decisions. To be on the safe side, they take a "hands-off" approach, which to the "team" looks like an abdication of leadership. Some supervisors never buy into the team concept and continue to behave like traditional supervisors. This also alienates team members, who have come to expect their reformed boss to be more "participative," not autocratic. In many cases, teams are afraid to take initiative or make decisions because they are not sure if they really have the authority to do so. The result is a crisis of responsibility—where nobody is sure exactly where the responsibility for control and coordination of work really lies. The team leader can never be certain whether the team *will actually take responsibility for* control and coordination of the work into their own hands. It is an uneasy alliance based on a blind leap of faith. In either case, the "team leader" is blamed for failing to make the team concept work.

The first response—a "hands-off" approach—doesn't lead to self-management but to an erosion of the traditional authority structure. The team leader allows his authority to erode to a state of permissiveness which amounts to a transition to laissez-faire. Can we then blame supervisors and managers who find themselves in such a double-bind? Moreover, what if the team *does* take charge and inadvertently oversteps its bounds or is about to make an irreversible mistake? Then what is the team leader to do? Sit quietly on the sidelines and pretend that upper management will not reprimand him for allowing the team to make a blunder? Perhaps it is even worse when the team takes charge and *is* successful, for what use is there then for such an extraneous position as that of "team leader" or "facilitator"?

There are other complications that typically occur within this crazy-making, double-bind situation. Senior and middle-level managers will usually only communicate with the ex-supervisor, not directly with the team. This sends the signal that the "team leader" is still in a position of authority, which further adds to the confusion. Team members may feel betrayed or suspicious when the team leader filters or fails to convey management's messages.

This example of pseudo-empowerment and laissez-faire is not uncommon. Indeed, our observations suggest that the majority of companies get stuck in the middle because they have little understanding of what genuine self-management really looks like in practice. Such confusion among managers and consultants alike is widespread. In light of Kuhn's criteria, one reason for such confusion is the general lack of awareness and understanding of the genotypical structural design principles that underlie bureaucracy and self-managing organizations. Cooptive-participation work systems that are based on pseudo-forms of empowerment attempt to create self-managing groups within the constraints of bureaucratic structures. These organizations will be fraught with inconsistencies, contradictions, and communicative double-binds. The design principles for bureaucracy and self-management are irreconcilable; like oil and water, they don't mix.

Participative processes are ineffective and cooptive when they operate within the bastions of bureaucracy. Cooptive-participation programs also have a dismal diffusion record, as they become encapsulated by traditional control structures. Work systems that have settled on cooptive participation are stuck between two paradigms.

3. Totalitarian Democracy

This quadrant of Figure 5.1 captures the Kuhnian observation that in times of major transition, there are often considerable overlaps between the ways problems are solved by the old and the emerging paradigms. In this quadrant, what we see are radical attempts to move toward self-managing organizations using autocratic change-management processes. The sought-after outcomes may be less bureaucracy, decentralized structures, more empowered employees, and "self-directed" work teams, but the process for getting there is anything but democratic. Indeed, the mode of change and design is still based on the domination and rule of experts.

Many organizations that have attempted to move toward self-managing work systems in this manner have done so by flattening the bureaucratic hierarchy, delayering, cutting levels of management, and eliminating supervisors. A number of these initiatives have also been equated with "empowerment," as employees are expected to do more work with fewer resources. However, simply transitioning from a centralized to a decentralized operation may result in a "leaner and meaner" structure without necessarily changing the basic design principle. The means of bringing about this so-called "transformation" depend heavily upon a top-down change process, where an elite group imposes its new design or structure on the rest of the organization. The recent flurry to reengineer the corporation and bust up the bureaucracy are notable examples.

Not only is the change process associated with these efforts highly autocratic, so is the result. Although the number of levels in the organization may be dramatically reduced, and the size and shape of the boxes on the organizational chart may be reorganized around "processes," the autocratic dimension of the management hierarchy is left untouched. The few autocratic managers remaining still have unilateral power to intervene and direct the affairs of work groups below them. Many firms implement self-directed work teams at the operational levels of a business, but senior and middle management remain firmly autocratic. In these so-called team-based organizations, managers continue to issue directives and set goals as usual—expecting teams to follow orders just as individual subordinates did in a bureaucracy. In effect, decision making is highly politicized and top-down. We call this change strategy and its resulting work system a *totalitarian democracy.*

Consider the way authority and responsibility are allocated in a totalitarian democracy. Senior and middle managers have high authority to make decisions with limited responsibility for the consequences those decisions have on the entire organization. A simple example concerns the widespread use of profit centers. Profit centers seek to minimize costs, maximize revenue, and focus on short-term results, but often at the expense of long-term gains. The result is a flat-footed organization unable to adapt and change when the marketplace delivers a curve ball.

Top-Down Culture Change. Other variants of totalitarian democracy include corporate-culture-change programs. Top-management directives to shake up the bureaucracy often result in decentralization of operations, shifting from bureaucratic control to building a strong corporate culture, or what academics have referred to as "clan-based" control. There is a great deal of emphasis placed on creating a "shared vision," "corporate values," and the like. At the same time, there is an obsession with the need for strong leadership and with having senior managers out in front to "drive" the change effort. The corporate culture program and the visioning process start at the top and are cascaded downward, or "rolled out," to the rest of the organization. Typically, senior managers hold numerous communication meetings where they "enroll" people in the vision and indoctrinate the masses into embracing and supporting the new organizational culture.

The totalitarian dimension of this indoctrination process is apparent in that it doesn't leave room for open and honest dialogue. Instead, people are expected to conform and "buy into" management's grand vision and organizational plan. With top management driving the effort, there is little opportunity for the average employee to directly influence strategy, policy, or organizational design.

Management sends the subtle message "Do as I say, not as I do." This message reinforces the autocratic force of managerial power, which also conveys the demand for obedience. The message to employees is "Don't think, don't question, don't learn, just get with the program." To ensure compliance and conformity, employees are mandated to attend numerous education and training sessions where cultural propaganda is disseminated. With this "totalizing" approach, every employee is indoctrinated to the expected cultural norms and behaviors. Autocracy is still alive and well in these organizations; it is simply camouflaged behind the dictates of the new cultural directives.

Democracy Through Domination? Pseudo forms of empowerment come in many guises, but this form relies less on cooptation than on a forcing strategy. Many organizational change and transformation efforts that claim to harbor democratic values also fall into this quadrant. These programs are usually spearheaded by organization development staff with the support of senior management. In other cases, "transformational managers" arise to lead the change effort. These change-management approaches are inherently totalitarian because they resort to the unilateral use of power.

Why are these approaches labeled "totalitarian democracy"? Because many of them promise that the change will bring about a more egalitarian and democratic work system. But can people truly embrace a more democratic work system if it is shoved down their throats and imposed upon them from above? Isn't that a contradiction in terms? And here, alas, lies the rub. The question is: Who will lead the revolution? In these cases, it is the elite who lead, the transformational leaders, and those few in the know.

While these efforts espouse democracy, empowerment, self-management, and the like, it is the elites who are in charge of introducing so-called transformation programs for the good of the employees. Empowerment is seen as a gift that can be bestowed upon employees by managers. Questioning the integrity of such schemes, William Scott (1962) raised a poignant question: "Does not this elite represent simply a different kind of hierarchical dominance?" Most of these efforts simply replace the traditional command-and-control form of domination that exists in a traditional bureaucracy with a more sophisticated and palatable form of domination—a substitute autocracy—that draw its legitimation from the rhetoric of democracy and empowerment. Political scientists have called this form of domination an "autocracy of the left," where power to rule is legitimized in the name of the people.

Self-managing organizations cannot be designed by brute force and totalitarian rule. People don't learn democracy and become empowered by obeying the commands of an autocracy. People cannot learn how or why it is necessary to work in a more collaborative, team-based work setting if such systems are imposed upon them by mandates from senior management or expert consultants. What proponents of these approaches fail to realize is that their means for designing a work system are incompatible with their espoused ends—that their totalitarian character reproduces the very social order they purport to change!

The design of self-managing organizations requires a more direct form of participation. Only if people are given the freedom and power to participate directly in the design of their work system—the product of many creative minds working together in a learning mode—can a genuine form of democratic organization emerge. It means that there is no single "right answer" or "optimum design" that can be computed from some proven formula.

Social Engineering Ideology. It is important to understand the ideology that guides the design of totalitarian change-management initiatives. Social engineering is the common underlying ideology that legitimizes the exclusion of "the managed" from participating in the design of their own work, and in the governance of their own work system. With social engineering, the dominance of hierarchy is hidden within the privilege of expertise. This is why great emphasis is placed on tools, techniques, and methods: they divert attention away from critical inquiry, dialogue, and open discourse.

Totalitarian change processes consider organization design to be the purview of technically trained experts who hold the exclusive authority for administering and implementing the proper technique. Experts know best. Technique replaces dialogue and deflects attention away from the possibility of allowing employees to directly question existing power structures. Instead, issues of power are reduced to the technical, where the focus is on following the prescribed method. Noting this trend, Alvesson and Wilmott state:

> Received management wisdom takes it for granted that the social divisions between managers and managed are either natural (e.g., based upon superior intelligence or education) and/or functionally necessary. Received wisdom then proceeds to concentrate upon refining the technocratic means of raising employee commitment and productivity. This philosophy, in our view, is symptomatic of a way of making sense of management that reduces the political to the technical, and represents the politics of management practice in terms of the development and application of formal procedures and impartial, "professional" skills and competencies. (Alvesson and Wilmott, 1996)

Social engineering worships the myth of order and rationality. Organizational design and managerial decision making are seen as purely technical matters. Social-engineering design logic is hyperrational, linear, sequential, highly structured, and of course, expert-driven. The change process is conceived as a mechanistic, Step One–Step Two–Step Three straight-line approach, bolstered by complicated analytical techniques.

Engineering and architectural metaphors are prominent in Reengineering, as there is an overemphasis on fixing things, rearranging the parts, and redrawing the blueprint of the organization. The "organizational architecture" metaphor conjures up the image of a master designer sitting behind a drafting table, drawing up the new grand design for the organization. However, unlike a house or building—which are static and inert structures—organizations are dynamic living systems capable of learning, creativity, and growth. Architects design buildings to last for several generations, but the life span of an organization's design in today's turbulent environment is probably only two to three years, if not less.

Social engineers take pride in developing a grand master plan which is heralded as a system-wide solution. One size fits all. Grand master plans usually produce ordered regimes characterized by a sterile uniformity. Like other social-engineering techniques, Reengineering is based on the machine-engineering metaphor—a view that treats people as if they were nothing more than redundant parts. With Reengineering, an elite few— often called the Business Process Redesign team—are given the authority to make sweeping changes in the organization. Reengineering efforts often stall when the BPR team attempts to impose its Reengineering blueprint on the many. Other design methods—like the classic STS approach—also rely on experts working in isolation from the rest of the organization. And it doesn't matter whether the experts are from the outside or the inside, the effect is the same. Whenever a new organization design is the product of an autocratic process drawn up by an elite group, the majority of organizational participants will resist an imposition of the master plan. Widespread employee resistance to the totalitarian mode of Socio-Technical-Systems redesign was quite evident in one organization, where employees cynically referred to the STS acronym as the "Shoot-the-Supervisor" approach.

Communicative Distortions. In a traditional machine bureaucracy, there is no question that management is invested with the ultimate power to make decisions. However, within a totalitarian democracy power is more diffused, as it is hidden behind the smokescreen of the collective and obscured by rhetoric and consulting jargon. Consultants talk a good game of getting the whole system in the room to make decisions, but in reality, "organizational goals" in totalitarian democracies do not reflect the goals of *all* individuals, but only those of the dominant hierarchy.

Consultants also proselytize about "high involvement" and "whole systems" change, but autocratic processes characterize the way organizational redesign efforts are structured and managed. For example, in the case of STS, a steering committee and design team are created to lead and manage the large-scale redesign of the organization. Reengineering does the same thing, by appointing senior-management "czars" and a Business Process Redesign team. Even the language of Reengineering has totalitarian overtones, where "czars" ruthlessly impose their power on subordinates so that they are coerced into accepting the ramifications and fallout that Reengineering leaves in its wake. Hammer and Champy (1993), the leading advocates of Reengineering, strongly assert that

> It is axiomatic that reengineering never, ever happens from the bottom up. . . . The first reason that the push for reengineering must come from the top of an organization is that people near the front lines lack the broad perspective that reengineering demands. . . . Second, any business process inevitably crosses organizational boundaries . . . some of the affected middle managers will correctly fear that dramatic changes to existing processes might diminish their own power, influence and authority. . . . If radical changes threaten to bubble up from below, they may resist it and throttle. Only strong leadership from above will induce these people to accept the transformations that reengineering brings. (Hammer and Champy, 1993)

The totalitarian character of these approaches to design and management is embedded in the view that members of the organization have no legitimate interests independent from that of the collective. But this view is of course unrealistic; individuals often do have interests of their own that may conflict with the interests of those in power. If this is the case, totalitarian democracies seek to "transform" such conflicts of interest by appealing to the common interests of the collective. This idea is similar to Rousseau's notion of a collective body, a *general will*, which supersedes the rights of individuals. Elaborating on this, Keeley points out,

> To this general will, individual rights are surrendered in the act of association. The general will aims, above all, at maintaining the well-being of the body politic: toward this end it enacts, through

wise interpreters similar to Plato's rulers, laws that compel individuals to sacrifice personal interest and perform necessary duties
for the sake of the whole. (Keeley, 1988)

The problem with this approach is that the cure may be worse than
the disease. Could not overly zealous "change agents" with their evoca-
tions of empowerment, high performance, and transformation be, as
Scott (1962) states, "open to charges of exploiting people in the name of
the people"?

Doctrinaire Mentality. One of the symptoms of totalitarian democracy is
an intolerance for critical inquiry and open discussion of alternative ideas.
As a consequence, there can be no genuine learning. There are numerous
forms that this intolerance may take. Consider the way management fads
gain legitimacy and popularity: the proponents of various methods and
techniques are ascribed "guru" status, and their way becomes the *only way*
to reach organizational salvation. Indeed, the path to salvation has already
been mapped out, and truth is to be found in chanting the mantras and
parroting the model of the new guru. When senior managers and their staff
adopt ("bless") a particular method or technique, anyone who questions
the validity of the method, or disagrees with its principles, is immediately
labeled a resister and is cast out as a heretic.

Hammer, for example, concedes that senior managers may carry
those wounded by Reengineering for a short time but they must not tolerate any form of resistance; in fact, he asserts, they must "shoot the dis-
senters!" (Hammer in Kalgaard, 1993). Disagreement is equivalent to
treason. For Hammer (1994), the ends justify the means, and leaders committed to Reengineering "have no choice in how they deal with those
attempting to impede their efforts." This doctrinaire mentality suppresses
democratic dialogue and creative inquiry, and tends to have a homogeniz-
ing effect on the process of thinking in the organization. Independent
thinking is suspect, something reserved for "eggheads" and "navel-gazers."
Action is valued for action's sake. Focus is directed to application of the
right tools, those prescribed by the expert or management guru. As Montuori (1997) points out, we are conditioned to "do it," but we are not
encouraged to "think about it." The change process becomes totalitarian
in quality, led by a flock of dogmatic followers and "true believers" who
are intent on imposing their totalizing solutions on the unwashed. There

is a strong sense that the lines have been drawn, and the corporate world is now divided into two camps: those who are with the program and those who are not.

4. Self-Management

In this last quadrant of Figure 5.1, participative processes for decision making function within democratic organizational structures, a combination that results in genuine self-management. Democratic structures provide formal mechanisms for widespread and direct participation in meaningful decisions. Self-management differs from cooptive participation in that employees are provided with decision-making rights, which are formally sanctioned by a structure of democratic authority. Self-management also departs from the heavy-handed totalitarian approaches that still rely on the rule of elite experts and the imperial power of autocracy.

Unlike programs in the adjacent quadrant, here participation in decision making is not a technique that is used to coopt employees into accepting management's goals, but a legitimate right that is protected by formal structures and rules that define the scope and boundaries of authority. Under cooptive programs work teams are often granted more opportunity to participate in decision making but not the formal authority to determine the outcomes of their decisions. In other words, employees are often granted more influence, but not actual *control* over their own work. However, participation in self-managing organizations is not dependent on the personal whims of managers who can grant or withdraw it at will, or experiment with it on an ad-hoc basis; rather, it is a built-in component of the organization's design.

Introducing participative processes into organizations is an important step toward developing and utilizing the skills, knowledge, and expertise that employees have to offer. Broader participation tills the soil for self-management, but it doesn't plant its seeds. Effective participation needs the protection of a democratic structure; otherwise the locus of control for decision making will still be invested in the authority of position. Employees may have more influence through participation, but not the responsible autonomy that allows them to make the final decisions concerning the management of their own work. Self-managing organizations are about more than simply providing employees more influence or "say" in decision making. Self-managing organizations are based on *full participation*, where employees not only can influence a decision, but have equal power to decide the outcomes as well.

The self-managing organization is based on a "nondominant hierarchy" that results in a greater equivalence of power between those entrusted to create wealth for the shareholders and those who actually do the work to create the wealth. Power is a lot like alcohol; if everybody can share it, a good time can be had by all. However, if only a few people consume the whole supply, you probably don't want to be around to be subject to their abuse. The formality of democratic structures provides an institutional check on abuses of power. Indeed, the whole character of "superior–subordinate" relationships is transformed in self-managing organizations. Relationships are based on the give and take of equals, rather than the dominance of superiors and submission of subordinates. A shift to self-management means that goals cannot be imposed by management in a unilateral fashion; they have to be negotiated.

In self-managing organizations, power is shared between and across levels of hierarchy, so that power is never concentrated in the hands of an elite group. This form of power sharing prevents any one group or level in the hierarchy from claiming a monopoly on management prerogatives. Such power-sharing arrangements require a fundamental redesign of the hierarchical system of authority for making decisions. As the hierarchy is redesigned to be more democratic, the nature of power is transformed. Authority is based less on status and hierarchical position than on mutual influence and shared expertise. No one person—no matter how smart he or she is—really understands the complexity of an entire work process or the vagaries of the market. Not even Bill Gates. Yet authority aligned with position relies on the pretense that the "boss knows best," and projects the image of the "omniscient leader." Learning and communication do not flow between levels, since superiors are "supposed to know," even if they do not. Too often we find the pretense of knowing rather than genuine knowledge. This attitude is quickly becoming a luxury that most organizations cannot afford; it is unrealistic to expect managers at all levels to know more than their subordinates.

A democratic structure, which aligns authority with expertise, reverses the bureaucratic principle built on the hierarchical distribution of tasks. In a traditional hierarchy, the higher one ascends up the ladder the greater one's authority and responsibility over others. In self-managing organizations, responsibility for the control and coordination of work is located at the same level at which the work is performed. This system of authority is based not on a traditional hierarchy but on self-managing teams. Self-managing teams have formal authority to make binding decisions within their sphere of responsibility. Self-managing teams set reasonably challenging goals and hold their members accountable. This results in a fully self-managing democratic workplace, where managers and employees mutually influence one another to achieve a shared vision.

Consider the way authority and responsibility are allocated in a self-managing organization. At every level, employees have authority to make decisions, and are highly responsible for the consequences of those decisions. This requires vertical, horizontal, and through-time compatibility of performance criteria for each unit, as well as relevant performance measures and an appropriate incentive system.

The democratization of hierarchy doesn't mean that the sovereignty of the enterprise is simply transferred to employees, nor is it a simple move toward collectivism, socialism, or an outlet for group tyranny. Rather, organizational governance is determined and clearly spelled out by the consent of the many, rather than by the arbitrary domination of the few. This is the essence of democracy. The self-managing organization is in alignment with our highest democratic ideals.

Transforming Work Through Participative Design. Participative Design is a means—a process for design, that is congruent with the ends—the creation of a high-performance, fully self-managing organization. Participative Design sessions provide individuals an opportunity not only to learn about self-management but to experience it first hand. The methodology models the outcomes it is intended to create: self-managing work teams, norms based on equality, power-sharing between levels, and an open exchange of information.

Participative Design sessions bring people who normally don't talk to each other together to co-create a new design for the organization. This method shifts the responsibility for design to the local level, tapping the creativity and wisdom of people who normally would be left out of the design equation. Participative Design sessions also require groups that are normally separated by hierarchy, status, function, or specialization to interface in ways that are fundamentally different from those taking place under traditional bureaucratic structures. By the nature of their design, bureaucratic structures inhibit spontaneous cooperation and collaborative problem solving. Participative Design sessions, by contrast, use participative processes and democratic structures, along with a common language based on the design principles, to enhance group learning across boundaries and levels. Participative Design creates a "community of inquiry," where employees are given the autonomy and structure to arrive at their own local solutions to work design.

This approach to learning and design allows face-to-face interactions between divergent coalitions, functions, and knowledge networks. Conversations in these sessions bridge the chasms between levels of hierarchy, different functional departments, and professional orientations. These sessions encourage democratic dialogue, where interdependent parties must work through difficult issues together in order to arrive at negotiated outcomes. The sessions are designed so people feel free to express competing views and divergent perspectives. Participative Design sessions are typically high spirited, as heated arguments and vigorous debates over design issues are worked out in a civil manner. These groups not only emerge with local design solutions, but walk away with a greater capacity for systemic thinking—increasing the organization's capability for synergy between units.

For executives and middle managers, these deep conversations are often enlightening because they demonstrate how people from different backgrounds, levels, and areas of expertise can be trusted to work side by side to create a new organizational design that takes everyone's interests into account. This is democracy in action.

Cooptive participation programs, on the other hand, seek harmony through consensus, which is really just a mirage since employees are not really in control of the participation agenda. Wynton Marsalis compares democracy to jazz: "Democracy is harmony through conflict." One caveat. There must be an organizing principle, shared theme, or conceptual vision that links all of the diverse perspectives in the design process together; otherwise the result will not be democratic dialogue so much as a collection of splintered interests groups and a cacophony of soloists all vying to defend their own positions. This is where the democratic design principle comes in. Participative Design sessions educate people, so that everyone who participates develops a shared understanding of the design principle. It is used as a conceptual anchor that guides the redesign effort toward the creation of local solutions. When people lack this conceptual grounding, they will either never agree on an integrative design solution for the whole organization, or they will simply flounder in chaos, producing designs that are merely extensions and modifications of the bureaucratic paradigm. We have seen this happen in several organizations that rushed into Participative Design although senior managers didn't fully understand the implications of changing the design principle. The employees derogatorily referred to the "PD" acronym as a method for "Participative Destruction."

In traditional organizations, senior-level management is expected to be responsible for the survival of the enterprise. In self-managing organizations, every employee becomes a strategic partner in the enterprise, whose knowledge and expertise are applied as a source of competitive advantage. Through Participative Design, employees at all levels are empowered to redesign and change their own workplace as a means of contributing to the survival and success of the organization.

PARTICIPATIVE DESIGN AS CO-CREATION

Participative Design is not simply a technocratic tool that will get us from point A to point B in a linear fashion. This method isn't about reengineering people into a new design; rather, it is a tool that allows people to co-create a new organization that is in alignment with the democratic design principle. The former approach takes an omniscient view of the design process, assuming that designers know in advance exactly where the organization is headed, and need only issue a clear road map for getting from the present to the desired future state. This scenario doesn't allow for creative interaction beyond the usual firefighting and minor incremental adjustments to existing schemas. There are a plethora of blueprints, maps, protocols, models, and elaborate methods out there in the marketplace which give the impression that the pathway from the old to the new paradigm can be traversed by following a well-trodden sequence of linear steps. The truth is, organization design is not as linear and rational as the engineers portray it to be—it's much more messy and fraught with complexity. The capacity for creativity, the desire for participation, and engagement in active learning cannot be "engineered" into an existing system. These capacities can only develop and evolve over time when conditions allow people to genuinely participate and have control over their own affairs.

The evolution toward self-management is a learning process which involves overcoming the passivity and lack of trust that are the legacy of traditional hierarchical structures. Participative Design stimulates learning for collective action, redesigning the work environment in a way that respects individual differences, while integrating various organizational units on the basis of shared goals for improving performance. In this sense, Participative Design is simultaneously an educative and a practical process, one which does not seek an "ultimate" design that can be imposed on the many, but mobilizes commitment to local design solutions. By starting with issues that are of interest at the local level, trust and competence can develop. It makes no sense to start a Participative Design effort unless it appeals to the real interests of a majority of employees. Employees from every level of the hierarchy are involved directly, from the early conceptual stages, through design, and all the way into implementation. Unless people are engaged directly to participate in the redesign of their own work—to substantially change it from a traditional hierarchy to a democratic structure based on full participation—self-management will also become another empty cliché, another failed evolutionary attempt to shift the management paradigm—another revolution gone sour.

SOUTHCORP WINERY REVISITED

After learning the hard way that top-down change doesn't produce self-management, Bob Baxter, the general manager at Southcorp's Karadoc winery, turned to Participative Design for help. Baxter's view is that Participative Design is "a process of empowerment. . . . teams are the means, not the end." "What is important is the accountability of our people for their actions," says Baxter. His philosophy is, "If we can manage the quality of work life issue, then the cost, quality and service issues, will, to a certain extent, manage themselves."

Baxter's vision for self-managing teams in production grew out of a need expressed by the workforce. Baxter recalls, "People were not comfortable with being told what to do, they were forever complaining about the middle management layer, the supervisory level, and the leading hand. Workers couldn't understand why some of the decisions were being made and enforced upon them. There seemed to be a lot of bias, a perception of favoritism, and a lack of objectivity. As a result, there wasn't much com-

mitment, enthusiasm or job satisfaction, and I don't believe we were performing as well as we could have been." The Karadoc winery already had
some experience using cross-functional teams for problem solving, but the
role of self-managing teams was going to be quite different. As Baxter put
it, "What I wanted were teams that would be managing their day-to-day
work, not just special projects."

The Participative Design of the Karadoc winery resulted in a new, self-
managing team-based structure. Teams are organized such that there is a
single team for each shift across the two bottling lines. Maintenance and
forklift personnel are now part of each packaging team. There is also a
quality-assurance support team, which assists operators in developing the
skills to perform their own quality assurance. Baxter notes that marketing
people now come on-site to involve the production teams in discussions
focused primarily around product development. Recruitment and induction are critical to the success of the teams. As Baxter points out, "We have
to make sure that the people we take on board are consistent. . . . the selection and recruitment process and induction programs need to take into
account what we are doing with teams. Attitude is more important than
skills, since we can train people on equipment, but we can't change their
attitude."

Teams now assess new recruits after a three-week induction period. If
a recruit doesn't fit the bill, the teams may reject that person if their levels
of interest and enthusiasm are unsatisfactory. There is a 20 percent rejection rate. Self-managed teams are integrated into Karadoc's Enterprise
Agreement (a legal Conditions of Work Agreement ratified by an Industrial Relations Court) and their goals and strategies are consistent with the
organization's strategic plan. Employees can share bonuses over and above
normal wage increases based on performance. Performance indicators and
targets in the areas of productivity, safety, and quality are set by the teams
themselves. Teams are multiskilled, and within each team there is a trainer
whose role is to ensure adequate levels of training within the team. The
trainer develops an annual training plan for each team member. Approximately 7 percent of wages are spent on training at the Karadoc winery. On
the production line, a career path progresses people through ten key skill
blocks. Pay is based on skills acquired, whether used or not, and training is
based on the perceived need for using those skills.

Self-managing production teams have resulted in a great deal more
flexibility. With the rapid introduction of new packages and products, flex-

ibility is paying off. Baxter estimates efficiency improvements on the order of 28 percent, and teams have reduced waste by 38 percent. Customer complaints have fallen by 14 percent. In addition, safety performance has been improved dramatically. Ten years ago, lost-time injuries totaled 2,000–3,000 worker hours per year. That figure has dropped to 20–30 worker hours a year, with a new target for zero hours.

PART

TWO

CHAPTER 6

DEMOCRATIZING THE STRATEGY CREATION PROCESS

How Motorola Held Strategic Conversations to Reinvent a Global Product Strategy

---

> The best way to predict the future is to create it.
> —Peter F. Drucker

It is one thing to extend greater participation in decision making to employees on shop-floor matters, but should employees also participate in the strategy-creation process? Isn't strategy development the exclusive responsibility of senior management? If this were still the industrial age, our answer to the latter question would be a definitive yes. Modern post-industrial enterprises, however, are no longer coddled in a stable and pre-dictable environment. As managers venture to lead organizations into uncharted territories, existing maps of business terrains are of little use. A rough sketch map is often the best that is available. Planning large-scale strategic change for innovation, growth, or renewal entails moving organizations along a path that cannot be charted in advance. Successful organizations will be those that learn how to maneuver in shifting terrains, rather than relying on well-worn pathways based on their past history of success. This new terrain requires a more intelligent enterprise—one capable of inventing its future in real time.

Conventional approaches to strategic planning may have sufficed when the environment was more stable, and accurate predictions and projections of the future could be made by strategy analysts and forecasters. Those days are over. Strategy making is now everybody's business, and that requires a completely different approach to strategy formulation. Moreover, if these trends continue, organizations need the capacity to change their strategy at a moment's notice. What is needed now is a new process for strategy creation—a process ideally suited to the new environment—not another quick fix.

Planning for a future state that is unknown requires a different type of organizational compass—one that helps organizations to respond proactively to environmental discontinuities and shifting circumstances. Discontinuities are unpredictable events that preclude the use of rational forecasting and planning methods. Such discontinuities might have their genesis in technological innovation, shifts in consumer attitudes or social values, changes in government regulations, or new and unconventional competitors.

If you agree that discontinuous and rapid change characterizes the foreseeable future, it won't do you much good to go looking for a one-shot magic bullet because you will never find it. And the present confusion is not a pretty sight for most. One thing is clear. The time-honored, top-down approach to planning is quickly becoming obsolete. As Liedtka and Rosenblum (1996) point out, "This new reality calls for a fundamental reconceptualization of the traditional Balkanized strategy frame that draws boundaries between organizations and their environments, senior managements and subordinates, mindsets and skillsets, and strategy content and process" (p. 141). Many executives know they are now facing a complex, dynamic, and uncertain environment, but still keep relying on planning processes suited to the era of Norman Rockwell and the *Saturday Evening Post*.

RETHINKING THE STRATEGY-CREATION PROCESS

Conventional strategic-planning processes do not foster widespread diffusion of strategy-making capabilities throughout the organization. You know the drill for the old ways. Top management figures out the strategy and the troops are given their marching orders. Strategy development is treated as a task that can be divided up into bits and pieces: intelligence gathering is assigned to different staff and functional specialists, industry analyses are outsourced to expert consultants, while an elite group at the top integrates all the information, acting as the brain of the firm. After "the plan" is developed by the upper echelon, it then has to be "rolled out" to the rest of the organization. Numerous meetings are held in each functional area and at different levels of the management hierarchy. Implementation gets under way only (if at all) after there is sufficient "buy in" to senior management's plan. Many well-laid plans like this have either been filed away in a drawer, or their implementation has floundered. Why? Because conventional strategy-development processes segment thinking from doing, and planning from implementation.

Popular thought leaders on strategy, such as Gary Hamel and C. K. Prahalad, assert that this approach to traditional strategic planning is dead. In their book *Competing for the Future,* which is now the strategy bible for managers around the world, Hamel and Prahalad (1994) write:

> Strategic planning typically fails to provoke deeper debate about who we are as a company or who we want to be in ten years' time. It seldom escapes the boundaries of existing business units. It seldom illuminates new white-space opportunities. It seldom uncovers the unarticulated needs of customers. It seldom provides any insights in how to rewrite industry rules. It seldom stretches to uncover the threat from nontraditional competitors. It seldom forces managers to confront their potentially out-of-date conventions. Strategic planning always starts with "what is." It seldom starts with what "could be."

How can management create strategies in a moving-target world? What does it take to invent new industries or turn a business on a dime? How can managers subtly change the competitive rules of the game in their industry to gain a competitive advantage? Unless a business learns to reinvent itself, much of the new wealth created by deregulation, globalization, and technological innovation will be discovered by start-ups or industry newcomers.

Hamel (1997) asks this rhetorical question: "If an innovative strategy drives wealth creation, then why isn't the pursuit of such a strategy front and center in most organizations today?"

We believe the answer is that organizations aren't pursuing wealth-creating strategies because entrenched bureaucratic planning processes are getting in the way. Old Soviet-style central planning might have sufficed when industry environments were less complex and uncertain. But in today's turbulent environment, products are evolving, markets are emerging, regulations are being torn down and built up at the same time, and technology is changing on a daily basis. Today, bold, creative, and innovative strategic thinking is not an option, it's a necessity.

Hamel (1997) states, "Strategizing isn't a 'thing,' and neither is it a process. Instead it must be a deeply embedded capability (or skill)—a way of understanding what's going on in your industry, turning it on its head, and then envisioning the new opportunities that fall out." He offers five ways to build the corporate strategy muscles:

1. Bring new voices into strategy creation to eliminate corporate blindness.
2. Hold new conversations by putting the people who hold all the resources (senior managers) alongside newcomers and young people from the field who have been left out of strategy creation in the past.
3. Change perspective, see the world and what the company does through a new lens or from a new vantage point.
4. Cut the time lag between ideas and action. Accelerate the time it takes to get employees emotionally committed to a new strategy by getting individuals throughout the organization deeply involved in the strategy-creation process.
5. Develop strategies which take you in the right direction, then progressively refine them through rapid experimentation and adjustment.

Hamel and Prahalad are quick to point out in their lectures that it's easy to see a brilliant strategy in hindsight. Most consulting firms that specialize in strategic planning produce three-ring binders, which read like doctoral dissertations, about current conditions in an industry. But little imaginative thinking comes out of such left-brain analytical exercises. This practice promotes a lot of "me-too" lackluster visions of the future.

Hamel and Prahalad (1994) also encourage managers to nurture key corporate skills or "core competencies" by creating a tangible corporate goal that represents a stretch or "strategic intent" for the organization. This implies that the enterprise has a vision of the competitive position they hope to build ten years down the road. However, Hamel and Prahalad do not explain *how* an enterprise can do this, nor do they provide a road map for getting the whole system involved in the strategy-creation process.

Liedtka and Rosenblum (1996) agree: "While willing to embrace new concepts like 'strategic intent' and 'competing on capabilities' as promising alternatives *in theory*, we have stopped far short of reexamining what these actually mean for the strategy-making process *in practice . . ."* (pp. 141–142, emphasis in original).

HOLDING STRATEGIC CONVERSATIONS: THE SEARCH CONFERENCE PROCESS

Clearly, the primary source of competitive advantage in the twenty-first century will be based on an organization's capability to tap its collective intelligence, as well as its capacity for effecting rapid strategic change. For companies seeking to improve customer loyalty and satisfaction, every employee must become an operational strategist. Hamel (1997) believes this too, as he calls for hundreds, if not thousands, of new voices to be involved in the strategy-creation process if companies are to increase their odds of securing a viable long-term future. Strategies that yield success in the future will be those that are created *by the employees, with the employees, and for the customer.*

Self-managing organizations have developed this capability by democratizing the strategy-creation process. Companies are now learning how to develop breakthrough strategies by utilizing a continuous, interactive, and participative process that empowers managers and employees from all levels to take collective responsibility for the future of the enterprise. Indeed, Microsoft's Interactive Media division doesn't just espouse the idea, it has pioneered the effort to democratize the strategy-creation process. Progressive managers at Microsoft are now using a method called the "Search Conference"—a democratic process for holding strategic conversations with hundreds of people—enhancing their capability for social creativity and rapid strategic change (see Chapter 7). In fact, Microsoft has convened over thirty Search Conferences to date, involving thousands of employees in strategy development.

Other companies—such as Hewlett-Packard, Xerox, DuPont, StorageTek, Lucent Technologies, and Procter & Gamble—have found the Search Conference to be a useful method for engendering greater levels of participation in the strategic-development and implementation process. The Search Conference operationalizes all five of Hamel's principles and applies them to reduce the time between strategy creation and execution. It's a method for stimulating and diffusing strategic conversations throughout the firm for the purpose of creating a coherent strategic intent that is linked to local action initiatives.

As we pointed out above, there is an urgent need for bringing together many different voices into the planning process. Planning in the midst of a turbulent environment requires new processes that allow people to learn and plan together in real time. Organizations must engage in rapid strategic renewal. Indeed, mobilizing large-scale strategic change requires the creativity and commitment of all of the people throughout an organization. In turbulent environments, every employee must take responsibility for the future of the enterprise.

What Is a Search Conference?

Social scientists Eric Trist and Fred Emery (1960) discovered how an open-systems approach to planning, coupled with democratic, task-oriented, self-managing groups, could be a powerful motivating force for effecting strategic change. They invented this method during a consultation project with senior executives to help with the merger of two British aircraft engine makers (which became Bristol-Siddeley, later acquired by Rolls-Royce). Emery and Trist designed a retreat where key managers and executives from each company would participate in a process that they later called a Search Conference (SC). The name came about because the primary function of the conference was to engage in a collective "search" for new trends and strategic opportunities. In searching for sudden shifts or emerging possibilities, conference participants discovered unexpected new directions and innovative ways of approaching old issues. In essence, when uncertainty is high, the primary task of strategic planning changes from incremental improvement in market share and position to searching for new strategic intent and innovative initiatives.

The Search Conference is a democratic process for creating strategic intent, which involves employees directly in the process—not as a means of soliciting their input, or getting their "buy-in" to a master plan already crafted by the those at the top, nor by "enrolling" people in a vision. Rather, Search Conferences empower the participants to actually create and implement action-based strategies. These conferences are normally two-and-a-half-day events, usually held off-site in a retreat-like setting. Ideally, twenty to fifty people are selected to participate in a Search Conference, based on such criteria as their knowledge of the system, whether they offer a diverse perspective on the strategic issue under consideration, as well as their potential for taking responsibility for implementation. In this respect, participants attend not as representatives of stakeholder groups, but because of their importance to the conference task. The idea is to *get the right system in the room*, selecting people from within the organization who have the critical knowledge, creativity, and ability to develop and implement breakthrough strategies (Emery and Purser, 1996).

Critical knowledge for active adaptive planning in any enterprise is not just in the heads of a few specialists or executives; it is widely distributed among all employees. Experts can be helpful, but in Search Conferences they play a supporting role. Furthermore, high commitment is earned through direct engagement, not analytical detachment. Participants in a Search Conference temporarily set aside their spreadsheets in order to search for possibilities that may not be contained in existing bodies of data and current assumptions of what is relevant to their future. The emphasis is on becoming more open to and aware of trends and possibilities on the horizon.

Participants in a Search Conference work on planning tasks in a mixture of large-group plenary sessions and small self-managing groups. As a whole community, participants scan their external environment, review their history, and analyze the strengths and weaknesses of their current system, which provides a shared context for their most important tasks: the development of strategic intent and implementation plans. Throughout the entire conference, strategic conversations are shaped as people identify their areas of agreement and common ground. The whole process gets mapped out as groups of people generate, analyze, and synthesize these conversations into a coherent strategic intent for their organization.

The Search Conference fosters organizational learning across vertical and horizontal boundaries, as it includes people from diverse parts of the organization who normally would be excluded from the strategy-making conversation. It provides everyone a shared context in which the strategic thinking of individuals can be articulated and shaped into a shared vision for the firm. Leidtka and Rosenblum (1996) argue that "it is through conversation that we come to co-create the shared meanings behind the strategy"; thus, excluding managers and employees from these conversations leaves them without a "context in which to understand the strategic choices made." One has to participate directly in the strategy-making process not only to have a context for thinking and action, but also to be engaged and committed to strategy implementation. Those that are left out of the strategic conversation will be confused and disconnected from the strategic-change process.

Table 6.1 illustrates how the Search Conference differs from traditional strategy-making processes. As shown in Table 6.1 below, with traditional approaches, a small elite group of senior managers craft a strategic plan and then simply tell others about it. Communication flow is one way and top down. Since there is very little commitment to "the plan," implementation usually flounders. A slightly less prescriptive approach is where senior management crafts a vision for the organization, and then tries to "sell" it to the rest of the organization. Communication of the vision occurs through a roll-out, as numerous information-giving meetings are cascaded downward in an attempt to get other managers and employees to "buy into" it. Because the rest of the organization has been left out of the strategy-creation process, senior management's vision usually sounds like a bunch of empty words or high-level abstractions that have little meaning or relevance at the operational levels. Another, more recent approach that has gained popularity is what Peter Senge (1990) calls "enrolling people" in

Table 6.1 Traditional Strategic Planning Approaches Versus the Search Conference Method

	Traditional Strategic Planning Approaches			Search Conferences
	Tell	Sell	Enroll	Co-create
Locus of planning	Senior Management	Senior management	Senior management with some input from employees	Diverse group of stakeholders from various departments and levels
Strategy-creation process	Elite, top-down, one way, forced march	Cascade, roll-out of plan to get "buy-in" to the top's plan	More interactive process to build a shared vision, usually conducted in a series of meetings	Direct, widespread participation using large group meetings for holding strategic conversations
Issues	Myopic, implementation flounders	Myopic, time consuming, causes skepticism	Not only time consuming, but fails to articulate strategic intent	Requires commitment to participation and good preparation

creating a shared vision. It involves an iterative process of soliciting ideas from various groups within the organization before senior management sits down to draft the vision. Communication is less top-down, but the locus of strategy making is still confined to senior management. The Search Conference, which is based on widespread participation and far-reaching conversations that span boundaries and levels, is about co-creation. It is a collaborative process where everyone throughout the firm creates the vision and forges a strategic intent together, as a community.

The Search Conference method has a number of benefits and advantages over traditional planning approaches. These are summarized below:

Practical Planning. The first and foremost advantage of the Search Conference is that it produces a practical plan for orchestrating the resources of the firm toward a future that builds upon its core competencies.

Active Commitment. Those who participate develop a plan based upon a deep emotional and intellectual commitment to creating a desirable future for the firm—not some cold, analytical, staff-driven exercise that nobody cares about or believes in. The Search Conference planning process is enduring because leaders of the enterprise are able to develop the organization's capacity for active adaptation that builds common ground around desired future directions. In addition, the process allows divergent views and conflict to surface, while simultaneously helping groups to identify and build upon areas of common ground, focusing on issues of mutual interest. Social creativity is unleashed in Search Conferences; this can produce a profound change in an organization's ability to change the rules within its global and industry environment. Instead of being a passive victim of fate, the enterprise can learn how to actively influence and adapt to its environment—faster than its competitors.

Magical Thinking Is Avoided. Too often executives are coerced into creating grand visions, but are unable to translate such lofty statements into concrete strategies that have meaning for operational-level people. Search Conferencing helps people to think outside the box, but it also has a convergent phase that forces people to ground their visions in specific strategies and concrete action plans, along with providing mechanisms for monitoring and coordinating the implementation process.

The Search Conference shifts planning away from tactics, operations, and short-term goals to focus on strategies and long-term purposes. Because the path to the planning solution is nonlinear, the process becomes a way to create a perceptual synthesis that overrides analytical conceptualization; it allows everyone to be an expert. The activities in the Search Conference are focused on community building and creating a basis for collaboration. They are thus very different from traditional, hierarchical planning processes. In a Search Conference, participants analyze and synthesize their own data, making sense of it in such a way that it becomes relevant to their own future. Not all participative events are Search Conferences. Some consultants favor having people write in workbooks or fill out predesigned worksheets; although participatory, such processes lead to private, abstract thought and not to bringing people together. These methods hark back to design principles where responsibility and control are located at a level above where the work is actually getting done. Search Conferences are different, in that the people doing the planning, the learning, and the work have the responsibility for the outcome of the conference.

A Search Conference is also unlike team building, which tends to force groups to reach consensus. Rather, Search Conferences help participants to focus on identifying common ground, so that groups can safely discuss their differences. It compresses the resistance to change into a well-orchestrated process where all the key players can bring forward their concerns, while at the same time moving toward action.

One word of caution: Search Conferences are not for the faint-hearted. The conference is an evolving and open-ended process; specific outcomes cannot be specified or predicted in advance. However, the pay-off is phenomenal: a committed group of knowledgeable people who have a deep understanding of the challenges confronting their organization, shared agreement around strategic intent, action plans that are in alignment with the corporate vision, and a mechanism for engaging the whole system in strategy implementation. If designed and managed properly, the learning process of a Search Conference can have a catalytic influence on people, helping them to move toward a shared future direction.

Motorola is facing pressures that are typical of the information technology industry—worldwide competition, continually changing customer requirements, and rapidly changing technology. This was certainly the case for Motorola's Mini-Chip Business Unit. Launched in 1991, this small but critical operation produces state-of-the-art microchip semiconductors that supply Motorola's wireless equipment business. In 1995, a new director of the microchip business unit was appointed. His assessment led him to believe that it was time to hold a worldwide strategic planning session. According to the new director, "We are poised to grow, but how to do it is the question we need to work out in the upcoming strategy session." Before he took charge of the Mini-Chip Business Unit, previous planning sessions had typically degenerated into discussions of tactical and day-to-day operational issues. The new director wanted to avoid this scenario. His intention was to hold a major planning session that would facilitate strategic thinking and keep the group focused on the future of the business.

MOTOROLA HOLDS A SEARCH CONFERENCE ON GLOBAL PRODUCT STRATEGY

Twenty-five key managers and technical professionals from the U.S., Europe, Japan, and Hong Kong gathered in Tokyo for three days to discuss where the industry was heading, and how they could take advantage of growth opportunities by leveraging their core competencies. More importantly, this group came together to create a set of strategies which they could all support. The expectation was that each manager would leave the planning session as part of a self-managing team responsible for involving others in the strategy-implementation process.

The Methodology of the Search Conference

The Search Conference is designed to develop a common database related to environmental trends and the need for change, a shared vision for a desirable future of the organization, and clear next steps for moving the whole system toward the desired future state. Beyond this, action groups will evolve strategies for the diffusion of the strategic change process throughout the organization. As Figure 6.1 illustrates, the design of Motorola's Search Conference consisted of three phases organized into a task sequence that follows the logic of an open-systems approach to learning and planning (Cabano and Fiero, 1995).

During the first phase of a Search Conference, participants are engaged in learning about changes in their industry and business environment.

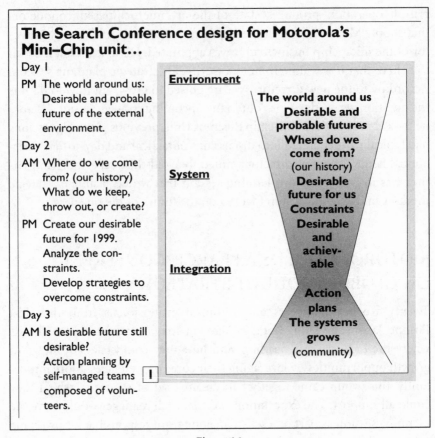

The Search Conference design for Motorola's Mini–Chip unit...

Day 1

PM The world around us: Desirable and probable future of the external environment.

Day 2

AM Where do we come from? (our history) What do we keep, throw out, or create?

PM Create our desirable future for 1999. Analyze the constraints. Develop strategies to overcome constraints.

Day 3

AM Is desirable future still desirable? Action planning by self-managed teams composed of volunteers.

Environment

System

Integration

The world around us
Desirable and probable futures
Where do we come from?
(our history)
Desirable future for us
Constraints
Desirable and achievable
Action plans
The systems grows
(community)

Figure 6.1

Conducting a broad and sweeping scan of their external environment, conference participants pool their perceptions of significant changes, emerging trends, and likely future demands; this results in a shared picture and appreciation of challenges facing their business.

The change formula popularized by Beckhard and Harris (1977)— $C = abd > R$—where C = change, a = level of dissatisfaction with the status quo, b = desired future state, d = practical first steps toward desired state, and R = costs of changing, or resistance—is built into the conference tasks. The tasks during this phase of the conference are designed to build a sense of community while at the same time jolting the system out of its complacency. Dissatisfaction with the status quo builds as participants learn about the pressures and demands on their business, and the need to respond more effectively to such demands in the probable future.

During the second phase, the focus of the conference shifts to examining the organization's capabilities and core competencies. Participants focus attention on the past, present, and future of the organization. This phase culminates in the generation of a shared agreement around strategic intent based on prior collective analysis. The process is designed to facilitate strategic conversations about the firm's future, converging on practical strategies that enhance the organization's competitive advantage.

In the final phase, conference participants work on the development of action and communication plans. This includes devising a plan for engaging the whole organization in the strategy-implementation process. This method is unique in that all of the hands-on work in a Search Conference is conducted by self-managing teams, which are responsible for the entire planning process. Even after the conference, those who created the plan are responsible for its implementation.

The Search Conference Process at Motorola: Day 1

Motorola held its Search Conference in Tokyo for three consecutive days. Participants worked on tasks alternating between large-group plenary sessions and small self-managing groups. Using this format, the conference began with informal introductions and a large-group environnmental scanning session where all twenty-five of the participants identified key trends and forces within their industry. A broad but far-reaching scan of the industry environment is part of every Search Conference, as it provides a shared context in which planning can occur. In a very short period, the Search Conference helped participants to develop a common database about their external environment. They constructed a collective map that displayed changing social values, market demands, customers' needs, competitive benchmarks, industry trends, technological innovations, and corporate pressures. This collective map of the Mini-Chip Business Unit's environment was posted across the wall at the front of the conference room.

Small groups were then instructed to analyze the implications of what these trends meant for the future of their business. The key question they addressed was, "What is the probable future environment for the Mini-Chip business if trends continue on their present course?" Their collective assessment revealed compelling business reasons to change, along with some possible strategic opportunities that could lead to a step-change in business performance.

SCANNING THE EXTERNAL ENVIRONMENT FOR TRENDS AND DISCONTINUITIES. . .

It is time to analyze the semiconductor and electronic industry environment. We ask, "What has
happened in the last 3 to 5 years that
is novel or significant?"

Participants identify a storm of
changes in their industry environment:

- Asian market is now the consumer market
- Wireless growth and acceptance by consumer
- Manufacturing in third world is increasing
- Access to Internet is increasing exponentially
- Multi-media is increasing

An assessment from one of the small groups that reported out in the plenary session on the probable future for Mini-Chip's industry reads:

- Expansion and diversification of wireless technology and markets.
- Third world economic growth will result in improved living standards and further democratization.
- Regional economic alliances will result in a shift in market shares and manufacturing bases globally.
- Wireless technology will evolve—allowing a phone number and communication tool to move with an individual.
- Higher levels of system-level integration will develop in the personal-communication arena.

The Search Conference Process at Motorola: Day 2

On the second day of the conference the focus shifts to assessing the internal organizational capabilities of the Mini-Chip Business Unit. The morning begins by having the group discuss the historical developments that have occurred in the business since its inception. We call this the "history session," and many participants have found it to be a valuable learning experience. A historical appreciation of the organization is developed as participants are asked to talk about the significant milestones, critical incidents, and turning points that have shaped their corporate culture and brought the organization to where it is today. The human side of change is brought into focus as participants are asked to identify the cultural traditions and values that they want to preserve and carry forward as the organization moves into the future.

Typically, as was the case in the Motorola conference, the history session has participants sitting together in a circle with a facilitator. Those who have the longest tenure in the company, "the elders," are asked to speak first. After they speak, others chime in with more war stories and recollections of key events. Everyone in the group listens intently to the stories people tell, bringing the group's history to life.

A pattern emerges: key events seem to be linked with the succession of different managers over the last decade. Newcomers to the business listen with rapt attention. It becomes obvious to Mini-Chip participants that the founders faced significant obstacles ten years ago on the journey toward creating this unit.

- There were many false starts; corporate management was slow in supporting the business but finally an internal customer funded the birth of the Mini-Chip business.
- The "dirty dozen" found office space and the business became a reality.
- With pride, one of the elders recalled the day when George Fisher, then CEO of Motorola, called their little division "the king's jewels" upon which the future of the whole company rested.
- There were territorial issues with other units and arguments over the merits of different technologies.

The retelling of significant historical events, recalling the details of significant turning points and their relation to how the division has evolved over time, reaffirms the strengths of the Mini-Chip culture and establishes a sense of belongingness and community. Participants gain a greater appreciation of the human dimensions of change through time. The large-circle seating arrangement during this session also contributes to a feeling of

---

MOTOROLA'S HISTORY OF SELF-RENEWAL . . .

The people at Motorola have renewed themselves over the years as they moved from car radios to semiconductors, and from there to cellular telephones. They shifted the lens and envisioned themselves as a consumer and professional electronics company. Each time they made such a significant strategic shift in their identity, they managed to do what was necessary to make that renewed direction a reality.

Today Motorola is creating a wireless world where your phone number will follow you regardless of your location; where you can stay connected no matter where you are with a portable hand-held device; and where your new communicator will allow you to merge images, data, and voice. Motorola has survived and thrived because it is willing to re-examine itself, because its employees have been empowered to challenge corporate traditions, and because it is aware of the fleeting nature of present success.

The challenges never stop. In early 1995 Motorola held a 60 percent marketshare in cellular phones and was admired by Wall Street. Then Nokia and Ericsson came along and cut its marketshare in half. Top management had ignored key customers' clamoring for digital phones; the semiconductor division, of which Microchip was a small part, didn't keep pace with change. Renewal efforts in a small business unit aren't sufficient to spark strategic renewal in its divisional parent.

---

equality, since anyone can choose to tell a story without regard for his or her status or position.

By this point in the conference, participants have discovered some areas of common ground, and a sufficient level of trust has developed to allow them to conduct a critical assessment of the operation's current strengths and weaknesses. Now participants are asked to evaluate aspects of their business system that are working well and which need to be maintained, problematic areas or outmoded procedures which needed to be changed or discontinued, as well as processes which currently do not exist but which need to be created. A quick and dirty way to do this is simply to have groups respond to three simple diagnostic questions: What parts of the business are performing and working well, that we want to keep, improve upon, or strengthen? Which parts of the business are performing poorly, are not adding value, and should be corrected, phased out, discon-

---

What does the whole-group history dialogue do for participants in open system terms?

Without an awareness of its history, the group may not manage boundaries properly and could lose track of their identity as a system. These pieces also provide a tracking process, and inform the members what could fit into *Mini–Chip*'s boundaries and what should be kept out. This is important in forming alliances, acquiring other businesses, or considering divesting a unit which may contain core competencies that would be lost or need to be rebuilt.

---

tinued? What parts of the business are missing or do not currently exist that we want to create or invent?

Motorola's Mini-Chip unit is already a well-run operation and there are many aspects of it that participants want to build upon. These include

- the small group team environment in product development
- a culture of tenacity
- benchmarking
- world-wide job rotation
- an empowered work culture and the close communication that makes it work
- strong credibility with customers
- excellent training
- a strategic ability to influence other players (offshore suppliers, contract houses, et cetera)
- project planning abilities are a strength and good support for the regions

Motorola, like any other major corporation, has its weak spots. Participants identified a number of current issues and problems that were potential barriers:

- strategic business-unit boundaries
- tariffs
- the current situation in the testing lab

- high wafer costs
- internal conflicts around products and people
- inadequate back-end reliability
- too much dependency on one internal customer
- the R&D process for a product group is in need of improvement.

The third list usually fills quickly with breakthrough ideas for improving current business processes. This diagnosis of the present system generates useful data and creative ideas for change. In the Motorola conference, participants listed such items as:

- creating centers of excellence worldwide
- generating systems solutions and defining wafer-technology platforms
- entering a new market and gaining more regional autonomy and funding
- expanding benchmarking activities
- attracting more external customers
- creating a concise packaging roadmap with modeling tools
- finding new ways to listen to customers and markets
- reducing cycle time for new product introductions and partnering with customers
- shifting the leadership to the regions in product development to eliminate redundancies across regions.

By the evening of Day 2, small groups were working to develop a shared strategic intent for the Motorola Mini-Chip business—a desirable future scenario. They were asked to create a desirable future scenario that would challenge current assumptions about the market, entertain new technological innovations and new products, explore new organizational architectures for the division—the sky was the limit. The output of all the previous tasks became inputs for this task; participants were encouraged to set existing constraints aside and to exercise their creativity and imagination and dream large.

The Search Conference builds upon Ronald Lippitt's (1983) research on strategy sessions. He found that groups which focus their attention on their preferred future are more likely to exhibit positive energy, commitment, and enthusiasm than are those which get mired in solving past or present problems. However, the goal is not so much to try to predict the future as to elicit people's ideals for the type of future they wish to create. By definition, a desirable future is based on highest aspirations; it is a stretch goal that can never be fully realized or attained. Envisioning the desired future state is also very different from conventional planning techniques, which simply extrapolate current trends into the future. Instead, participants in the Search Conference are engaged in ideal-seeking behavior, collectively imagining the type of future they are intrinsically motivated to help create, and then barn-raising their plans together as a learning community.

A lofty image of a desirable future for Motorola's Mini-Chip business is thus backed up with a concrete and coherent set of strategic goals, long-range targets, and descriptions of desired end points. Specifying these long-term objectives provides a pragmatic basis for translating their desirable future into a clear set of action and implementation plans. Working in small groups, participants in the Motorola Search Conference generated a list of ten strategic goals. Then, in the plenary session, facilitators helped the large group to integrate and prioritize the list. This was done by merg-

What happens when too many goals are identified?

In cases where there are more goals for the desirable future than can be comfortably managed by the community, then the number must be reduced by integrating those which have strong interrelationships and/or by using a prioritization process.

Shall we vote? The group may slip out of self-management by mistakenly taking a vote. An aggregate of individual votes will give an entirely different result than a careful considered community process. Such an important task requires serious reflection and discussion.

To achieve this the community goes back to their previous groups and chooses the three or four most relevant criteria for deciding on priorities.

Based on this criteria the number of priorities is reduced to six or seven goals. Reports can then be taken in the normal manner followed by community discussion and negotiation of the final set.

ing items that were similar across small-group reports, separating unique and stand-alone items and identifying conflicting items between different group reports.

For goals in conflict, facilitators placed these items on the "disagree list." By the end of the evening, all twenty-five of the Motorola participants had come to publicly agree upon six combined stretch goals for the Mini-Chip business:

1. We will have the largest portion of the worldwide market, which means we must grow faster than the market. We will invest in at least one emerging market/application.
2. Worldwide centers of excellence will exist for marketing applications, design, development, manufacturing, and global teamwork.
3. We will drive the semiconductor, packaging, and assembly/test technology platforms and have guaranteed access to them.
4. A systems solution approach and key customer partnerships will be in place by 1999.
5. Development and manufacturing cycle time will be reduced and give us a key competitive edge—seven days from order to customer's dock.
6. Quality and reliability will be greater than Six Sigma and qualification cycles will disappear.

The Search Conference Process at Motorola: Day 3

The next morning, Motorola participants turn their attention to dealing with constraints, action planning, and implementation issues. One third of a Search Conference is allocated to developing plans for implementation. Participants self-selected themselves into implementation planning teams which coalesced around each of the six strategic intent areas. Before plunging directly into implementation planning, these groups spent several hours developing specific strategies that outlined how existing and probable constraints to achieving their strategic objectives could be overcome.

Constraints are challenging and difficult to deal with, which is why they are addressed toward the end of the Search Conference. Many conventional approaches to planning attempt to deal with constraints head-on. Converging upon constraints early in the conference would inhibit

Integrating the results of small group scenarios...

Whenever several groups go off to do work the results must be integrated together when they return. This creates one shared community perspective but not without conflict. The two questions noted help rationalize, not resolve, conflict between groups so they can recognize and build on common ground. If they failed to ask these questions the groups would focus on what was different in their perspectives rather than what is common or similar. Once such conflict is rationalized, the leadership group is ready and committed to act in concert toward creating an active, adaptive relationship between it and its environment.

There are two questions that are asked after each sub-group presents:

1. Do you have any questions for clarification? As each group presents there are a number of terms and wording that are discussed to avoid confusion and make their meaning plainly evident. Once everyone is clear we can go on.

2. Is there anything up there in that desirable future of your unit that you could not live with or are not prepared to make happen?

creative thinking, narrowing the focus to solving current problems rather than opening up the search for fruitful and innovative possibilities for the future. Interim reports from each of the six implementation teams were taken before lunch. Since the Mini-Chip Business Unit is a relatively small division within Motorola, it is not surprising that participants identified a significant portion of its constraints as being internal to the corporation.

The final integrated list revealed two sets of constraints. External constraints included defense spending cuts, competitors' strategies and Motorola's equipment-market share, the degree of acceptance both of their products and the wireless system by customers, political situations, trade barriers, tariffs, and the situation in Asia. Internal constraints included organizational structure issues that limit their ability to provide system solutions, technology availability from R&D, capital-funding and human-resource issues, and a reluctance on the part of internal customers to allow them to support external customers with advanced technologies.

As is usually the case, this was a low point in the Search Conference: participants were overwhelmed by the magnitude of the constraints and a sense of powerlessness set in. But the Motorola group got through it as they developed some very creative strategies to deal with their difficulties. Creative strategies for overcoming the constraints arising from a competitor's strategy included these:

- Motorola could hire some of the competitor's key people, duplicate its technology, buy the competitor, or form a joint venture or alliance with it.
- Motorola could thoroughly learn its competitor's internal structure and create a history map of its evolution, understand its customer focus, benchmark its products for strategic vulnerabilities, and ascertain its research-and-development expenditures.
- Motorola could also ignore the competitor's strategy, go its own way, pull out of that market, or invest elsewhere.

Before moving into implementation planning teams, conference participants decided to reduce the six richly detailed strategic intent goals into three clusters. They categorized these clusters as technology, marketing, and organizational structure. Participants then self-selected to join one of the three self-managing implementation teams. Each team then developed action plans (strategies and tactics) for each area of strategic intent. Each team had responsibility for clarifying and deciding upon:

- time parameters for each team;
- criteria for monitoring progress;
- when each team would meet again;
- how they would proceed to manage themselves;
- how to bring other Motorola players into the implementation phase.

At this point in the conference, the implementation planning teams are now on their own, fully responsible, and will not appreciate a manager telling them what to do. Collaboration has by now become an expected behavior.

After a Search Conference, participants have the empowerment and momentum to take action plans forward. Effort must be made, however, to ensure the continuity of self-managing teams once they return to their organization. Organizational reentry of implementation teams requires careful planning, ensuring that they have the authority and legitimacy to implement the strategy. Implementation teams need sanctioning from sponsors; they need access to resources, information, and time for meetings.

A BRIEF ASSESSMENT

Six months later, the general manager of the Mini-Chip Business Unit summarized his assessment of the results that were spin-offs from the Search Conference:

> The three implementation teams are all doing well: The technology implementation team has built upon our strengths and is beginning key programs to fill our technology voids. The marketing team has made significant progress expanding our markets and beginning a systems-solution approach to our customers. The implementation team working on the Centers of Excellence has initiated a critical shift. The design of new products will no longer be centered in the United States; instead it will be dispersed into the regions. This allows us to respond more quickly to customer needs and eliminates redundancy by having expertise in one center available to other regions. Critical resources have been made available to the regional centers in support of the goals developed during the Search Conference. For example, there is now a design engineer in Japan, an applications engineer in Europe, and a new-product-development champion in the United States.

The Search Conference at Motorola was a frame-breaking experience for managers. The emphasis on developing shared agreements around strategic intent has brought discipline and focus to the managers in this extended global business. The general manager of Mini-Chip remarked:

> I am delighted with the leadership emerging from our Japanese operations. We shared the essence of the future we wanted to create with the entire organization through staff meetings and communication meetings. We are maintaining the focus on the strategic goals rather than just the action plans. Organizational members are clear about our desirable future and can align their

activities accordingly (even if they are not directly involved in implementation). Commitment to our desirable strategic intent for the business is high and we now work as a global team, rather than as separate players taking orders from headquarters in the United States. This will pay dividends for us over the long term.

CHAPTER 7

THE SEARCH CONFERENCE

Engine for Rapid Strategy Creation at Microsoft and Charles Schwab

Democracy is the art of thinking independently together.

—Alexander Meiklejohn

Microsoft's strategic recipe for success—control of the operating system for personal computers—has made Bill Gates the richest man in the world. Since 1980, Microsoft has provided the majority of the software that controls the way users interact with their personal computers. Microsoft's stranglehold on PC operating systems has evolved from DOS, to MS-DOS, Windows, Windows NT, Windows 95, and Windows 98. Virtually all PC users in more than fifty countries, speaking thirty languages, punch up Microsoft logos when they run an operating system or an application program.

Like Microsoft, Digital Equipment Corporation had great success in the 1980s. Under CEO Ken Olsen's leadership, DEC's proprietary systems strategy raked in the cash. However, when the new paradigm of open systems came along, Olsen didn't realize its strategic importance. He resisted it and was later caught flat-footed. Digital was broadsided by a sea change in the industry that turned its successful business strategy into a competitive liability. In 1997, the once proud company was at the bottom of *Business Week*'s list of strategic performers.

When IBM failed to grasp the importance of the microprocessor and the PC, it too struggled for years. The company is now more a follower than a leader. Like open systems for DEC, the Internet is a technology tidal wave with the potential to upset Microsoft's dominance of the software industry. The Internet is to Microsoft what the microprocessor was to IBM—both a threat and a potential opportunity. The Internet is a threat because, by design, it has no central operating system that Microsoft or anyone else could patent, license, or otherwise control. It takes microcomputers out of their isolation and links them in networks. The larger the net-

How did the Internet produce a sea change in the world of computing? Tim Berners Lee, an innovative researcher in Geneva, Switzerland, found a way to let an author easily link words and pictures in one document to other documents, which could be stored anywhere on the Net. Within months, computer hacks built millions of linked documents. Users could access information by clicking on a phrase or icon in the first document to access the related document. This section of the Internet became known as the World Wide Web.

Despite this accomplishment, there was no simple way to find and view these documents. In 1993 Marc Andreessen and his associates created Mosaic, the first Web browser, for Apple computers and Windows PCs. The Web itself became a computing platform for new kinds of applications and publishing. Andreessen recognized that the net could make the PC as indispensable to everyday life as the telephone, and in 1994 went on to cofound Netscape, located in Mountain View, California. Netscape's "free" Navigator browser delighted its forty million users and had the potential to replace Windows by calling up information from the Internet, corporate Intranets, and even users' PCs. In other words, a browser can also be a vehicle for high-dollar business-applications software.

Even with a browser it was easy to get lost in the Net. Web pages sat there as static displays. Sun Microsystems solved the second problem when it introduced Java, with its compact application programs, which made Web pages come alive so people could get real-time sports scores, news, and stock prices—or even manipulate numbers to test assumptions on statistical tables. With Java interpreters on all the major computers everybody could have applications that were hardware and software independent. People could share and distribute information more readily. Java could become an alternative platform for running network-based computers and end Microsoft's reign as the king of the operating-system world. Java, says Microsoft's executive VP of sales and support Steve Ballmer, has made Sun the number one competitor in Microsoft's crosshairs.

work a computer is linked to, the more useful it can become. For example, spending just on Intranets—private networks within businesses—will reach $13 billion by 1999. Intranets can tap into the Internet to link teams together across time and space, offering more power than Windows ever could. With the prospects of the Internet looming over Microsoft, the Windows operating system could become a much smaller player in a networked world.

BILL GATES SHIFTS MICROSOFT'S STRATEGIC DIRECTION

Microsoft was almost too late in recognizing and responding to the Internet. In October 1994 Gates issued a memo to the leaders of each of Microsoft's four product groups—personal and business operating systems, desktop applications, and consumer software—to start adding features that would take advantage of the Internet's communication and information retrieval capabilities. On Pearl Harbor Day, December 7, 1995—the fifty-fourth anniversary of the day Japan's Admiral Yamamoto feared he had awakened a sleeping giant—Gates retargeted a large portion of Microsoft's gargantuan $1.4 billion R&D budget. Thousands of programmers had their projects terminated and were set to work developing a major presence in Internet software products. In just six months, the company turned on a dime to focus on the Internet's fifty million users. Gates initiated a warp-speed transformation that set a standard for corporate nimbleness and reinvention in the highly uncertain terrain of the digital age. Microsoft's developers embraced current Internet standards, sought to shape key standards on the Net to the company's liking, and worked relentlessly to add extra functions to give Microsoft the edge. The idea was to create software that could help people find, create, and use information on the Internet while subtly changing the rules to Microsoft's advantage.

With its strategic intent reset, Microsoft's fast-paced product development cycle tapped the company's years of consumer-product research to improve its mediocre Internet Explorer browser. It soon became a technically advanced product, competing head-to-head with Netscape's flagship Navigator browser. In a very short period of time, Microsoft reinvented itself to become a competitive provider of Internet access. The company's collections of word-processing and spreadsheet tools were reworked to allow a browser to retrieve data stored on corporate networks or on the Internet. Users were enabled to see and partially manipulate Word and Excel files on the Internet even if they didn't have the programs in their PC. A new version of the Windows NT network software was released to run the heavy-duty servers (to compete with Sun's servers) that act as traffic cops on the network. All this was just the beginning of the actions of a sleeping giant that had found a renewed focus.

RAPID STRATEGY CREATION AT MICROSOFT'S CONSUMER PRODUCTS DIVISION[1]

In the midst of the sea change within the industry, the Consumer Products Division at Microsoft was faced with the challenge of rapidly developing a product strategy for the entire division. It was a pivotal point for the division as millions of people were subscribing to on-line services, and it was clear to Bill Gates that the Internet was going to open up huge opportunities for marketing and selling consumer products. The window of opportunity wouldn't last long, so the Consumer Products Division had to act quickly. But senior management had a difficult time getting its act together to formulate a strategy that the business units would support and buy into. "There had been a chance to reformulate Consumer Products strategy through the previous winter. People had a lot of good intentions and a fair amount of frustration by the time I walked in to help out," Liz Dunn recalled at the Large Group Intervention Conference. Dunn, former director of product planning for Microsoft's Consumer Products Division, is currently the executive producer of Dreamworks Interactive. In 1995 Dunn was called in to work with the senior vice president of the Consumer Products Division and the senior managers of each of the businesses. Consumer Products is now called the Interactive Media Division, which is partly the result of the work that Dunn and her colleague Kevin Purcell did over an eight-month period—orchestrating a series of eight Search Conferences that involved over eight hundred of their knowledge workers in the strategy-creation process.

---

[1]Material for this account was derived from a public presentation made at the "Organization Development Network Large Group Intervention Conference," Dallas, TX, March 17–20, 1996.

The Interactive Media Division (IMD) is expected to blossom into a profit engine after the millennium. The reason is that over 40 percent of households now have personal computers—a number that will continue to grow. Personal computers in homes with kids are at an even higher percentage. Patty Stonesifer, the highest-ranking woman executive at Microsoft, now heads IMD. IMD has an R&D budget of approximately $500 million and is supported by 1,800 technical professionals who develop CD-ROM games, reference works, and on-line content. IMD competes with America Online, Broderbund, CNN, and Disney. It is involved in developing MS-NBC, in rethinking the Microsoft Network, and now it works with Dreamworks SKG to develop interactive software games that have the Spielberg magic built into them.

Before IMD was created, the Consumer Division made all of the products that are aimed at the home rather than the office; these include children's software, games like Flight Simulator and Golf, productivity products like Microsoft Bob, Publisher, and Money, and information CD-ROM products like the *Encarta* multimedia encyclopedia. Some of these products were very successful and others had stumbled in the marketplace because of strategic miscues. Dunn told the audience at the Dallas conference that it was her job to define the strategic problem and come up with a process to solve it. Moreover, Consumer Products was lacking clear strategic goals and product plans for each business. While each business was responsible for its own profit and loss and had its own list of customers, all of these businesses needed to fit together in a way that made sense at the division level.

Microsoft's corporate assets—creative people, production facilities, the marketing division, and lots of high-powered technology—needed to be leveraged across all the products. More important, whatever strategy was developed had to take advantage of the company's core competencies. The customer segmentation for this business was complex because this division sells its products to both homes and families. Within those families are different markets: children, adults who are game enthusiasts, and productivity customers. One of the challenges this division faced was to develop a brand strategy specific enough to help business customers understand what products they were buying and why, yet not so specific that home consumers would feel excluded from the target audience. In other words, the brand had to address all of a family's needs in the home. Crafting a division-wide strategy that satisfied the diverse interests of each of the business groups would be an intense challenge in Microsoft's in-your-face confrontational culture.

Dunn had a formidable task ahead of her. She needed to create a strategic pathway that would bring everyone onto the same page fast. She explored several alternatives for doing this. The first and obvious approach she considered was one Hamel and Prahalad (1994) frown upon—a classic top-down cascading process. First, division-wide goals would be developed that would guide business-unit strategies. Business-unit strategies would in turn guide the development of operational tactics for each function. In other words, the vice president and senior-level business-unit managers would get together behind closed doors, pow-wow until they came up with a strategy, and then communicate it to the rest of the division. As Dunn pointed out at the conference, the senior group had tried doing this for the previous six months and it hadn't worked particularly well. These were very talented senior managers; each had shipped lots of successful products; yet they just couldn't come to an agreement on how to develop a division-wide strategy.

In times of uncertainty and change, when a new technology like the Internet comes along people often desperately want to believe that senior management has all the answers. And top management, in most companies, are hesitant to admit that they aren't sure what to do for fear of demoralizing the rest of the organization.

Microsoft is by nature a fast company. As a norm, things happen quickly and employees want to gallop toward the next competitive challenge—they just want to know where to gallop to. The old Soviet-style planning alternative hadn't yielded particularly good results at Microsoft. Employees were perched on the edges of their seats waiting for something to happen, and another alternative had to be found quickly.

Dunn recalled having talked to several highly regarded strategy-consulting firms. She felt they had some valuable things to offer in terms of an objective industry analysis, but Microsoft had that data already. Dunn soon realized that she needed a *process* that could stand the shock waves of putting a bunch of ego-strong geniuses together in one room for a few days and have them come out with a plan that everyone could buy into. She needed a strategy-creation solution specific to Microsoft's quirky culture, one that would tap the energy and creative assets of the company.

Dunn got lucky. She bumped into Kevin Purcell, an energetic internal consultant at Microsoft who had experience in applying the Search Conference method. Dunn was relieved when she learned that the Search Conference was a rapid process which could be used for holding strategic conversations with hundreds of people in the division—not only to get their buy-in and commitment but to engage them actively in the strategy-creation process. She became an advocate for the method. However, Dunn and Purcell had to convince the vice president and the three business-unit managers to support the process.

Dunn and Purcell scheduled a meeting with the senior management group to make their proposal for convening a division-wide Search Conference. At the Dallas conference, Purcell tells the story of how he gave his standard pitch and was instantly attacked by one of the managers. Based on Purcell's recollection, the meeting went something like this. "Are you out of your mind, Purcell?" the manager snapped. "This is a formula for complete chaos and anarchy!" Dunn intervened, trying to smooth his ruffled feathers. "This is really a well-thought-out method, it has worked great at other companies like Hewlett-Packard, Motorola, and Xerox. If we really want to tap the talents of our people, and have them get behind the strategy, I think we should consider this approach." By the look on their faces, the other managers in the room were also uneasy. A heated argument erupted among them. "This Search Conference thing is simply not going to work!" shouted one of the managers. They kept arguing and yelling: "This is a crazy idea, and it can't work here!" "Then, it was as if the ceiling parted and a light shone down from above," Purcell recalls, chuckling. "And I wasn't sure if that light was coming from God or from Bill." One of the three business-unit managers, who had just joined the division and who wasn't as polarized in the battle over strategy, literally jumped to her feet, rushed to the whiteboard, grabbed the marker out of Purcell's hand, and said, "Wait! This is how we can do it!" She furiously started drawing pictures, diagrams, erasing items Purcell had written, and outlining a way of orchestrating the whole Search Conference process. The arguments continued among the three business unit managers for another half-hour. Then, after much debate, the senior managers turned to Purcell and asked, "Well, when are we going to do these Search Conferences?" The senior managers had arrived at a much more sophisticated plan for holding a series of Search Conferences, one that made Purcell's original proposal look like kid stuff. Purcell wasn't at all surprised. He explained, "The way people build products around here is they yell and scream, fight it out, and then, after they clean up all the blood off the floor, they come to agreement. This process was no different."

This is how good ideas are born at Microsoft—through intense delibera-tions where people mix it up until they come up with something that exceeds everyone's individual expectations.

Consumer Products Division Search Conferences

The senior management devised a plan for convening a series of Search Conferences in the Consumer Division. What happened? First, a series of Search Conferences were convened for each of the four business units. Each business unit used the Search Conference to develop its own strategy. Each of the four business unit conferences involved approximately thirty participants.

Each business unit conducted its own follow-up sessions after the con-ference to diffuse the strategies to the rest of the unit. For example, one senior manager assembled her whole business unit in the room, several hundred people, and walked through the strategy. She began by explaining the overarching strategy; then individual contributors—the people that build the products—presented various parts of the strategy. Individual contributors who had committed to particular strategic initiatives coming out of the Search Conference enlisted people in the cause. Having people own leadership of action-planning initiatives was a really important part of getting the whole division energized and moving forward.

Since everything at Microsoft works by e-mail, business-unit managers sent out detailed messages to the whole business unit right after a confer-ence. Their e-mail explained the strategies, and provided a list of contacts for people who wanted to talk further about the strategy. Senior business-unit managers realized the importance and urgency of communicating the strategy to those who hadn't participated directly in the Search Confer-ences. Unless they acted fast, the rest of the organization probably wouldn't understand the strategy. They went to such great lengths to communicate the strategy that people got sick of hearing about it.

After the four business units had completed their Search Conferences, six representatives from each business-unit conference were selected to participate in a cross-division strategy-integration meeting. In one day this group met to mesh their business-unit product strategies into an inte-grated, overarching division strategy. Representatives from each of the four business units informally presented their product strategies for about ten minutes each. All of the product-strategy presentations were posted on flip charts all around the room for everyone to see. It was like a science fair or a poster session—participants spent the next several hours walking around the room, reviewing the product strategy presentations and posting their feedback and comments on the flip charts. The dialogue among participants was intense and high spirited. The atmosphere was festive, like a huge carnival. After the feedback session, representatives from each of the business units huddled together to synthesize the information and to summarize what they had learned.

While the representative groups were meeting, the senior management team also met to integrate the key strategic ideas they had gathered from the four previous business-unit Search Conferences. Based on their discussions, the senior management team drafted a Consumer Division mission statement. It was three paragraphs long and it took them forty minutes to do it. Both of the groups reconvened in a plenary session, and the senior management team presented it. They received applause. Purcell reflected on this moment: "I've never seen anything get applause at Microsoft. I remember the vice president turned bright red when people applauded. I think she was shocked and surprised."

How many executives would like to have this kind of pleasant surprise? Wholehearted commitment to a business strategy isn't the normal course of affairs with traditional top-down planning. In most organizations, the top dog stands up at the podium and hands down the vision (which has been developed exclusively by senior management) to the assembled masses. Usually the rank-and-file are thinking, "I don't agree with all of that. I am not going to try to make that part of the strategy come true." Taken aback by the positive and unexpected response, Microsoft managers asked employees why they applauded. Employees said they were inspired that managers had really listened to them and incorporated their ideas into the mission statement, and that it made sense.

Now there was agreement on the strategy across the boundaries of the division. Following the cross-division integration meeting, each business unit held another one-day session to start building action plans. Employees who had not participated in the previous Search Conferences were enrolled in these action-planning sessions, increasing the critical mass. These sessions were held for the purpose of crafting more specific action plans, incorporating the feedback from the other units, and clarifying implementation strategy. In less than four weeks, this rapid strategy-creation process removed the functional blinders from everyone's eyes.

The four series of Search Conferences—which culminated in a one-day cross-divisional integration meeting—produced a shared strategic intent for the Consumer Products Division. But the process didn't end there. The Consumer Products Division strategy was rolled into four more Search Conferences to enhance division-level synergies and product integration (see Figure 7.1). This approach was used to leverage Microsoft's resources and core competencies across division boundaries.

Four cross-divisional Search Conferences were convened around strategic-product themes. For example, one conference convened participants from different business units to focus on long-range plans for developing tools and technologies for the Internet. A second conference focused on strategies for developing creative content, while a third conference focused on marketing. Forty participants—representing various levels, technical competencies, functions, business units, and countries—attended each conference.

MICROSOFT'S CONSUMER PRODUCT DIVISION RAPID STRATEGY-CREATION PROCESS

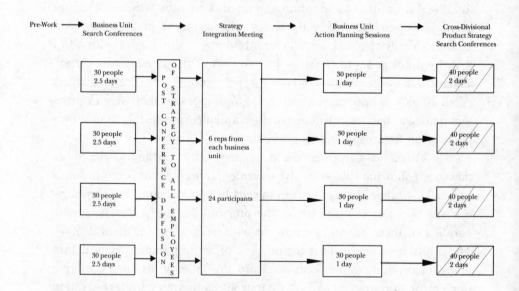

Figure 7.1

Results, Outcomes, and Key Discoveries

Through Search Conferences, integration events, and action-planning meetings, nearly 800 of Microsoft's knowledge workers in what is now the Interactive Media Division have been involved in the rapid-strategy-creation process. The results were significant. Many of Microsoft's key assets were realigned around strategic opportunities that were identified by participants in the Search Conferences. Many key strategic decisions were made as a result. It became clear to participants that the Consumer Products Division couldn't be all things to all people, and that it didn't need to develop products for every last consumer category. Instead, the Search Conference process redirected the division's focus to product areas that could build on Microsoft's core competencies. The overarching strategy for the division focused on pursuing strategic opportunities that required a significant amount of R&D investment (a Microsoft advantage), that leveraged existing technologies, that required an infrastructure, and that needed a long-term view. Given this clear focus, it soon became apparent that a number of products then under development didn't make strategic sense. As a result, senior management made a very difficult decision to cancel a number of products. Yet the people working on these products understood the reasons behind the decision because they had participated directly in developing the business strategy. They moved quickly on to developing the next wave of innovative products—products that were in alignment with the division's new overarching strategy.

Looking back on the rapid-strategy-creation process, Dunn remarked at the conference, "This is the first time we've had something we could call a strategy versus a collection of tactics in different product areas." A senior manager in the division agreed. "Prior to this process, the way strategy was developed here at Microsoft in a product group was to get a group of smart people in the room and see which one came up with an idea for a product first, and then fund it. That's how competitive and formal it was. It gave us a lot of tactical plans but very little collective focus." Dunn also felt that people had learned that strategy creation in the software industry is a never-ending dynamic process. As Dunn pointed out, "People so desperately want to know what their marching orders are going to be for the next three to five years, but now they understand that's not how it's going to work. . . . they now realize this is an ongoing process, not something you do once."

Would they do it all over again? According to Dunn, senior business-unit managers are planning to do yet another round of Search Conferences. Search Conferences have now become the modus operandi for their annual planning process. However, Dunn says, "It is a pretty exhausting process. If you told some of the people involved that they had to do it over again, they'd probably jump off a cliff. It is a very draining process because it forces you to use all of your energy and brainpower while you are there."

Microsoft followed three simple but powerful principles when designing Search Conferences to create a winning strategy—what they refer to as defining the three P's: Purpose, Pre-work, and Participants.

Purpose: Getting a Clear Focus. Much time was spent up front defining a clear purpose for each of the conferences. Dunn and Purcell worked with senior managers to help them reach agreement on the purpose of the process. They went to great lengths to ensure that the purpose was crystal clear—so clear that every person involved in the strategy-creation process could eat, drink, live, and breathe that purpose *before* they attended the Search Conference.

The purpose was crystallized two to three weeks before the Search Conference. Not only was there absolute clarity about the purpose, but everyone had to agree that it was useful to take two and a half days out of work to participate in the conferences. This is an interminably long time at Microsoft. Two and a half days in a fast-moving, high-tech industry was a very big time commitment, signaling that something meaningful was on the line. For example, the cross-division "Tools and Technologies for the Internet" Search Conference convened 29 of their best software developers in a room on one week's notice, starting on a Sunday morning. All the software developers knew that Bill Gates was committed to meeting the challenge of the Internet, and they were the ones selected to do the work to create breakthrough strategies. That was a clear and compelling purpose. The best and brightest software developers would not have shown up at nine o'clock on a Sunday morning unless they knew it was intensely important.

Participants. Once the conference purpose is clarified, then it is necessary to select the right participants—those who have critical knowledge and who are willing and able to take part in the implementation. With those criteria in mind, the senior manager for each business unit created an initial short list of participants. Those people on the short list were invited to a kickoff orientation meeting that went over the purpose, reviewed the criteria for deciding who else ought to participate in the Search Conference, and began to outline some conference pre-work tasks that needed to be done. At this meeting, the list of participants was expanded, as names of people went up on a whiteboard. Reviewing the list, the senior manager asked, "Is this the right group for the conference? Are we leaving anyone out? Is there anyone we are inviting who doesn't meet the criteria?" Dunn points out that because Microsoft is a brutally honest culture, people had no problem identifying which names should be removed from the list, even if the names they identified were their best friends. "It's a very confrontational culture," remarks Dunn. "You never have to guess about how anybody feels about anything. It's always right out there, in your face."

In these orientation sessions, the senior manager would provide an overview of the agenda and conference logistics. For example, a conference might begin in the early evening with dinner on a Wednesday and continue on through about ten at night. On Thursday the group would work all day and through the evening. The conference would end around mid-afternoon on Friday. The conference would be held off-site to avoid distractions. Some participants would say, "Gee, I have to miss two hours." The senior manager would look at them and reply: "Well, what are you going to do about that? You know, it's important, you are either there or you are not." It is also important to point out that people from Europe and Australia traveled to Redmond, Washington, to participate in a number of the conferences.

Microsoft discovered that those who participate in the Search Conference also have to be directly involved in the implementation process. Otherwise, people begin to think they have a license to develop plans and directives for others to implement. When planning is divorced from implementation, the mentality becomes, "Well, here's what you guys should do about that. Here's what you guys should do about this . . . and so on."

Pre-work. Homework always pays off. Conventional sources of data deemed important to the conference ought to be made available to participants before they show up for the two-and-a-half-day effort. While this information is important, rapid strategy creation relies most heavily on the tacit practical knowledge that is inside people's heads. Some individuals may have critical knowledge but are not on the Search Conference participant list because they are not considered potential implementers of the strategy. Their knowledge should still be factored into the strategic formula, so part of pre-work involves identifying key stakeholders, interviewing them, and gathering this information as input to the conference. At Microsoft, participants created a stakeholder interview list, gathered the data from the interviews, and placed all the relevant information on an Intranet "share file." For example, the Search Conference pre-work conducted by participants in the Games business-unit group involved first brainstorming a set of interview questions; then each participant typically volunteered to interview three or four people from the key stakeholder list. They customized the list of questions for the people they were interviewing. Stakeholder interviewees included people from top management, international and domestic marketing departments, and product support, as well as numerous retailers and customers. Those that would be attending the Search Conference interviewed all these people, conducted their own market analysis, and then uploaded all the information they had gathered on a central Intranet file. Every time someone finished an interview, he or she made sure that it was available on the "share file."

By the time participants arrived at the Search Conference, they already had the benefit of having reviewed the data gathered from the stakeholder interviews. In some cases, additional customer research was conducted when there was a need for more specific data. All this pre-work activity allowed participants to fill the critical knowledge gaps before jumping into the planning session.

RAPID STRATEGY CREATION AT CHARLES SCHWAB'S INFORMATION TECHNOLOGY (IT) DIVISION[2]

Charles Schwab is a retailer of financial services and products that has experienced burgeoning growth. The former securities-industry upstart has continued to reinvent itself as a financial-services powerhouse. Schwab has moved away from its discount-brokerage base to focus on new value and service propositions. Continuous growth depends on a large transaction-

[2]We are deeply grateful to Dr. Cynthia Scott of ChangeWorks for providing us with case material on the Charles Schwab IT Search Conference.

processing and record-keeping engine tied to state-of-the art remote service centers. Schwab is also known for its very efficient front-end marketing.

Schwab is now in the midst of reinventing the industry paradigm for financial services and what it means to provide professional financial "advice." Drawing upon its entrepreneurial culture, management talent and depth, sense of mission, brand name, capital resources, and experience in managing remote-call-center sales and support, Schwab's overall strategy is to be in the top 10 percent of public companies with over $5 billion in market value. Schwab's vision is to be the most useful and ethical provider of financial services in the world. The Search Conference was based on upholding these values and driving them deeper into the strategy.

Business Challenges and the IT Organization

One of the main cornerstones of Schwab's success has been its information technology, or IT. The IT organization—known as "SITE" within Schwab—faced the challenge of supporting the firm's phenomenal growth. Dawn Lepore, Executive Vice President and Chief Information Officer for Schwab, realized that a faster, more effective approach to strategic planning was needed if Schwab was to meet the challenge of doubling its rate of growth over the next two years. In addition, a tidal wave of new hires was flooding the Schwab organization. Lepore led the crusade for getting more voices involved in the strategy-creation process. Martha Deevy, Senior Vice President of Technology, Finance and Planning, joined Lepore in building a strong guiding coalition that would lead strategic change throughout the IT organization. Formerly the head of business development at Apple Computer, Deevy was a relative newcomer to Schwab. After one year on the job, Deevy had gone through one round of an annual planning cycle; she agreed with Lepore's assessment that a more innovative approach to planning was needed to meet the demands for double-digit growth and the influx of so many new people. The SITE organization faced a number of key challenges:

1. the need to align IT with business goals;
2. the need to utilize IT for competitive breakthroughs;
3. the need to integrate the IT architecture and the strategic plan;
4. the need to employ organizational strategies, using sophisticated measurement and performance metrics.

Lepore was particularly concerned that the newly formed Senior Leadership Team (SLT), which consisted of some forty vice presidents in the SITE organization, needed to share a strategic direction if they were to meet future business challenges. Most of the members of the SLT had technical backgrounds and had been with the company less than six months. In early winter of 1997, Lepore and Deevy teamed up to begin the strategic task of reinventing the IT organization. Lepore and Deevy both agreed that the SITE organization needed a more strategic focus to meet the demands of business growth. In addition, high-level strategic conversations within Schwab were already happening at the corporate level, and Lepore knew that the SITE organization needed to be part of that conversation. After numerous meetings, Lepore and Deevy were convinced they needed to sponsor a planning process that would make the SITE organization less reactive and more strategic. They were also convinced that the newly formed Senior Leadership Team needed to be part of the strategic conversation, since many of them were new and not accustomed to thinking strategically about IT issues.

The Senior Management Team (SMT), which was composed of eight senior executives (including Lepore), also needed to be involved in the strategy-creation process for SITE. In years past, the SITE organization had been seen as out of touch with the operational side of the business. Lepore was intent on repositioning the IT organization so that it would provide more leverage for Schwab's overall business strategy.

Organizational Design and Leadership Challenges

Faced with rapid growth, the centralized structure for the IT organization was decentralized, creating the need for a broader base of people involved in decision making. Part of the strategic initiative was to quickly get the newly formed SLT up to speed and enable them to make a strategic contribution to an increasingly complex environment. Because this SLT was composed entirely of knowledge workers, and issues surrounding technology are hotly debated, Lepore and Deevy wanted to utilize an approach that would not create resistance and divisiveness. They were clear that whatever process was used, it had to build a shared context from which to shape strategic conversations.

Preparing for the Search Conference at Schwab

Lepore and Deevy sought outside consulting expertise to help plan and guide the strategy-creation process for the SITE organization. Lepore was already working with Dr. Cynthia Scott, an external consultant on other leadership issues; Scott informed them that the Search Conference methodology might be appropriate for their needs. Deevy had heard of "scenario planning," another strategic-planning tool that she thought might be useful for their purpose. Scott recommended that Deevy talk to one of her colleagues, Dr. Steve Rosell, another consultant well versed in both scenario planning and Search Conference methodologies. Based on the business challenges and the objectives Lepore and Deevy were trying to achieve, Rosell recommended that they indeed consider convening a Search Conference for both the SLT and SMT members. After learning more about the Search Conference process, Lepore and Deevy agreed it was a good fit for for what they were trying to do. Lepore and Deevy agreed to sponsor and support the process.

Scott and Rosell teamed up as outside consultants to guide Lepore and her team through the Search Conference process. A planning committee composed of seven SLT members was formed to start planning the Search Conference. They picked a date several months ahead and started working backward on the tasks that they needed to accomplish. The planning committee recognized that many SLT members lacked a shared context for the financial-services industry, were not aware of Schwab's competitive position in the market, and didn't understand the operational realities that were driving Schwab's strategic goals. Most members could recite what Schwab's strategy was, but they lacked an understanding of either why it was important or how it could be achieved.

To fill these knowledge gaps, the planning committee began gathering data and information, hosting a series of educational meetings prior to the actual Search Conference. An outside consulting firm specializing in IT for the financial-services industry was contracted to do an industry briefing. This briefing included their analysis of the business drivers for IT, key technology, vendor trends, as well as IT governance and management issues. The entire SLT was invited to a half-day briefing. The planning committee also began meeting with internal customers within Schwab to learn more about their own strategic plans, and to better understand how the SITE organization could fulfill their IT needs in the future. Enterprise round-table meetings were held for two consecutive months, during which representatives from various business units shared their strategic insights about new business initiatives, changing external factors, and how technology could play a strategic role in growing these businesses in the future. Brown-bag lunch meetings were held every week with SITE members to bring people up-to-date on what was being learned.

In addition, Dan Leemon, Schwab's Executive Vice President and Chief Strategy Officer, met with SITE members to share what was simultaneously being discussed by Schwab's Management Committee in terms of Schwab's corporate strategy. Leemon provided a very clear picture of the strategic conversations that were happening at the senior levels. All of the data collected through interviews with internal customers, along with industry analyses, were published in a several-hundred-page "briefing book" prior to the Search Conference. All these events were primers for, and used as inputs to, the actual Search Conference.

With so many new members in the SITE management organization, these information-gathering activities and the Search Conference itself provided a perfect vehicle to increase the alignment of SITE within the larger organization. The preparation and design of the Search Conference was focused on creating financial targets for 1998 that could be broken down into cost-center details to structure the 1998 budget.

Senior Executives Meet to Recollect the History of Schwab

Prior to the Search Conference event, the SMT met off-site as part of a pre-strategy session and team-building effort. Many of the members of the SMT were also new to Schwab, and Lepore felt it was important to provide this group an opportunity to come together as a team. One of the highlights of this off-site meeting was a period where the group "painted a picture" of the history and evolution of the Charles Schwab organization, and how key historic events and turning points had shaped the character of the SITE organization. Since many of the SMT members were new, those that had been around longer provided an oral history of past leaders' contributions, sharing and passing down the organizational folklore to the new initiates. This conversation about the history of Schwab during the off-site meeting was captured through "strategic illustration," a new and powerful technique for creating a graphic representation of a group's shared understanding. An illustrator drew colorful graphic images, translating the stories people told of Schwab's history onto a 21-foot-long piece of paper posted across the wall. This session provided an opportunity for all the new team members in the SMT to share their views and appreciate those of their peers.

This strategic illustration of Schwab's history was used in the Search Conference to give the entire SLT an opportunity to understand the historical context in which SITE is operating.

The IT Search Conference

This three-day Search Conference brought together the right information and the right people, at one time, to address and resolve the key strategic issues facing the IT organization. The conference drew upon data and information from three areas: the industry, the company, and the IT organization itself.

During the history session, the conference community participated in adding their own recollections of the history to create an embellished graphic illustration. One new member of the group remarked that this session on the history was like being "taken to the campfire and to be told all the stories of the tribe." This person remarked how he now "felt really part of the organization and ever more involved in creating a shared future."

After many heated and high-spirited conversations, participants came to an agreement on five key strategic goals. For obvious proprietary reasons, the nature and content of these strategies cannot be revealed. But suffice it to say that the level of excitement, energy, and commitment was such that the SITE organization had developed a shared strategic intent and collective point of view about how IT would play a distinctive role in reinventing Schwab's future.

Toward the end of the conference, there was general agreement that further work needed to be done to develop complete action plans supporting the initiatives. Participants also acknowledged that certain initiatives needed very quick action in order to ensure that funding requirements were included in the annual plan. Each group was given the responsibility of developing and presenting a completed action plan that would provide specific actions and milestones for 1998. Each action planning group was "chaired" by a vice president and "sponsored" by a senior vice president. This structure was intentionally put into place to help drive decision making down the hierarchy. The chair was responsible for driving the process

THE SCHWAB IT SEARCH CONFERENCE:
THREE-DAY AGENDA

Day 1:   2:00–6:00 P.M.
- Introduction to the Search Conference
- Expectations
- Introduction of new SLT members
- Broad environmental scan
- Groups identify three to five major global issues
- Examine and analyze desirable and probable futures
- Establish a common and shared context for the environment

Day 2:   8:30 A.M.–8:30 P.M.
- Review and reflections
- Scan of SITE business environment
- Key trends affecting the future of SITE; probable future if present trends continue and nothing is done
- Small-groups reports and discussion
- History of SITE; add to previous graphic illustration
- Present system analysis: keep, drop, create in the present SITE
- Desirable future for SITE
- Small-group reports
- Criteria for prioritizing strategic goals
- Reception and dinner
- Prioritize and integrate strategic goals
- Meeting of SLT planning group

Day 3:   8:30 A.M.–5:00 P.M.
- Review and reflections
- Form groups around each strategic goal
- Small groups develop strategy and action plans to achieve their strategic goal by the year 2000
- Interim reports by small groups
- Groups continue
- Report of small groups and discussion of action plans
- Next steps and follow-up

and working with the team to develop the action plan. The sponsor was there to provide advice and direction and to "block and tackle" between organizations if necessary. Conference participants agreed to meet periodically throughout the year to evaluate how well SITE was moving to implement its strategic initiatives.

All participants at the conference knew that, without a clear understanding of how the group would take the learnings from the conference and implement them, this effort would run the risk of simply being another "off-site." Even before the conference adjourned, several actions were agreed to, to ensure adequate follow up:

- The Planning Committee would have near-term responsibility for planning follow-up steps and meetings.
- The break-out groups formed during the conference would have ongoing responsibility and accountability.
- Dates for report-backs and follow-up were established.
- Agreements were made to incorporate the strategic framework developed at the conference into the annual planning process, which was just about to kick off.

The committee, rechristened the SLT Steering Committee, became responsibile for mapping out the follow-up steps and action plans. They used the annual planning process and the monthly SLT luncheons as communication vehicles, and articulated expectations for each action-planning group initiative.

Follow-up Reflections

There were changes resulting from the Search Conference that had very positive impacts on the Planning Process and the organization.

1. The direction-setting work and the strategic conversations that resulted in a shared set of strategic initiatives resulted in a greater sense of "ownership" by the officers in SITE. This shared understanding of how the direction was developed and how priorities were set carried over into the annual planning process. When it came to making hard budget-allocation decisions, there was less internal conflict and poli-

tics, since everyone was more aware of the business context and under-stood the necessity for the trade-offs that needed to be made.

2. The Search Conference identified the need for SITE to "integrate" more tightly than they had in the past—which meant integration of systems and decision making. One outcome of the Search Conference was the agreement to put into place a Project Office to manage the integration, and to develop other processes and review boards to facilitate system-wide integration. Since these actions have been put into place, the SLT is beginning to behave differently. SLT members now have greater awareness of how their IT projects impact the entire systems plan. SLT project managers display a growing willingness to signal problems early in the process in order to avoid problems later down the line.

Perhaps the biggest win coming out of the Search Conference was developing a greater sense of urgency among the senior management of SITE, and a shared sense of ownership of the problems. The Search Con-ference, however, was only the beginning; the hardest work comes in the implementation. As a positive spin-off, Dan Leemon, the Chief Strategy Officer for Schwab, was so taken by the positive energy and results of the Search Conference that he became interested in launching similar efforts in other parts of Schwab.

COLLABORATIVE CHANGE PROCESS WITH KNOWLEDGE WORKERS

Microsoft and Schwab have taught us some significant lessons about what happens when the task involves attempting to change the way knowledge workers go about their business. Clearly, one of the most significant chal-lenges for the next century lies in designing organizations to effectively manage and organize knowledge-based work. Quality and productivity improvements in knowledge-based work are not derived solely from installations of new technology, but also require substantial changes in business processes and organizational arrangements. Further, as work cen-tered around production processes continues to shift to work that is dependent on people to generate ideas, as well as to think systemically about the design and delivery of products and services, new methods are needed for unleashing and tapping this creative potential.

We have learned that the effectiveness of knowledge work can be enhanced through such methods as Search Conferences and Participative Design, but the process requires careful thought, a lot more customization (off-the-shelf techniques won't work), and some translation. Methods introduced into knowledge-based organizations—like Microsoft—are extremely sensitive to the reactions of knowledge workers. When we attempt to intervene in knowledge-work systems, we are confronting people with the way they think, and the processes applied often identify imperfections in human dynamics that limit the rate or quality of knowledge production. Strong egos are involved here, and feelings are easily hurt.

In contrast, when manufacturing facilities are redesigned, the changes are more depersonalized; it is not the individual worker but rather the "system" of technology, work design, and social relations that is to blame for whatever problems exist. Changes in the work are focused primarily on these systems, although individuals are also asked to change their behaviors to fit the new way of working. Technical and interpersonal training may accompany this request, but this training is presented as something that the organization should have provided all along and as something that will empower the individual to contribute his or her previously constrained full potential to the success of the enterprise.

In knowledge-based change efforts, the finger seems to be pointed more directly at the knowledge worker; as a professional, the knowledge worker is already supposed to know what it takes to think effectively, and is supposed to be able to rise above the dynamics created by the organization or situation to get the job done. Changes in systems and training accompanying interventions may appear more remedial in knowledge-work settings, in that autonomous professionals are being told that their ability to think must be examined and improved. The "system" may be at fault, but to accept this is to admit that the system influences one's ability to think in the first place, which is a difficult admission for some autonomous professionals to make (Purser and Pasmore, 1992).

Given the difficulties inherent in influencing knowledge work directly and in confronting the behavior of highly autonomous knowledge workers, intervention into knowledge work must be undertaken with care and sensitivity. We have found that in order to initiate a rapid-strategy-creation process in knowledge-work organizations, the Search Conference method needs to involve knowledge workers more directly in the pre-work and planning activities. In addition, greater emphasis needs to be placed on recognizing what is "good" about the current system, in order to reduce defensiveness and build trust prior to engaging in future-oriented strategy work.

In knowledge-work systems, it is imperative that the design and implementation of the strategy-creation process be developed with the collaboration of the knowledge workers. The admonition to "get the whole system in the room" is especially good advice in the knowledge-work arena. Knowledge workers are highly sensitive to top-down change processes that threaten to impose methods of working upon them. The first rule of thumb for conducting this process is, "Don't ever *tell* a knowledge worker what to do or how to do it." Knowledge workers need to think things through for themselves.

The approach we favor is much more participative than consultant-centered interventions have tended to be in the past. Knowledge workers can and must design their own active learning experiences, to which we contribute helpful suggestions, methods, and insights. With this approach to strategic change, the consultant is an equal partner in—rather than a director of—the intervention. With this form of collaborative consultation, the goal is to use participation to reshape the distribution of power in the system in order to enable the organization to function in a more effective and equitable fashion.

In addition to abandoning the "director role," the consultant must also fight the temptation to outline what is potentially wrong with the system—what needs to be "fixed." Most other strategic-change processes have been based on an implicit assumption that the current system is operating suboptimally and is therefore deficient. Given the personal sensitivity to criticism prevalent in knowledge-work systems, it is much more effective to start with an "appreciative" focus—that is, to pay attention to the positive and creative aspects of the current system, and to try to understand what it is about the system and their way of working in it that people value. Eliciting desirable futures for the system helps organizations focus on what their people find good, energizing, and meaningful. Translated into the knowledge-work arena, we could say that knowledge workers will engage in activities that they believe will make their work better for them—and they will passively or actively resist everything else. We need to help knowledge workers appreciate the "light"—what they really value in their work—and use this as the basis for energizing them to change their behavior and the system.

CHAPTER 8

DEMOCRATIZING WORK

The Participative Design Method

The great leader is he who the people say, "We did it ourselves."

—Lao-Tzu

Does your organization have a clear purpose and a compelling business strategy? Are its work arrangements and business processes aligned to make that strategy a reality? Are the skills, knowledge, and competencies of its people adequate to do the work? Has your organization transformed its strategic imperatives into an effective organizational design that captures the hearts and minds of people throughout the organization? These are the sort of questions managers will face as they attempt to design self-managing organizations.

Many managers will also inevitably have to face the fact that their existing bureaucratic structures have been unable to systematically provide the capabilities for learning and development of their members. This is particularly true of the people at the bottom of the organizational pyramid. Work in traditional hierarchical organizations has been downgraded, deskilled, and simplified. The traditional role of management—with its emphasis on controlling, directing, planning, and coordinating the work of those below them—has actually worked against providing the conditions for learning, self-direction, and responsible autonomy.

Organization design is a tool. As a tool, it enables managers to match strategic demands with the right organizational architecture to bring about continuous high performance. This matching process is ongoing, requiring a dynamic organizing capability that can make the best and most efficient use of the organization's core competencies to respond effectively to changes in the global competitive environment. Organization design is a management tool for building organizational capabilities that align internal components—structures, processes, reward systems, and people—to support the business strategy.

As Figure 8.1 shows, when these components are aligned, the organization will be more effective, flexible, and adaptive. When these components are misaligned or ignored, the organization will likely suffer from strategic drift and performance problems, such as a decrease in productivity, customer complaints, and a lack of employee commitment.

THE DESIGN PATHWAY

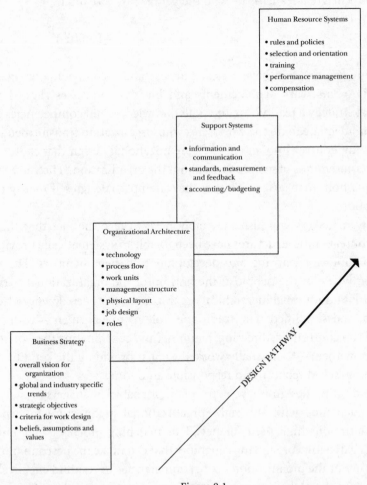

Figure 8.1

Every CEO's ongoing challenge is to develop and institutionalize an organizational capacity to learn and continuously adapt to today's fast-paced business environment. Therefore each of the organization's interrelated component parts will need to be fundamentally changed in order for all of them to become mutually reinforcing and aligned with the business strategy. A self-managing organization is able to continuously redesign work since people are able to keep discovering new and better ways of working together.

Steps Along the Participative Design Pathway

As with any other venture, the project of designing the self-managing organization will be only as successful as the quality of its planning. There are a number of essential steps that need to be taken to lay the groundwork for a successful Participative Design effort. These steps are described briefly below:

1. Get Your Strategic Act Together First. Several key questions need to be addressed: Do we have a business strategy that can guide the redesign effort? Do we have the capability of reinventing our strategy as business and market demands change, as they inevitably will? As we have shown in the previous chapters, organizations now require a capability for rapid strategy creation. An effective strategy and a widely shared vision of the organization's future are necessary precursors to a large-scale redesign effort.

2. The Vision Prerequisite. Senior management is responsible for building a coalition of people with relevant knowledge to create, clarify, and communicate the vision, and they must develop an action plan to achieve it. Senior executives will need to define a clear, compelling business case for change. Along with a clear and compelling vision, senior management must also create a sense of urgency, clarifying the strategic challenges that confront the organization and communicating the strategic imperatives for change throughout the organization. Some typical challenges might include:

- changing customer requirements
- competitive threats
- sustaining or increasing market share
- re-creating product interest in mature markets

The design pathway suggests that organization design always occurs within the context of its environment, particularly when new designs are generated in anticipation of future changes. Figure 8.2 shows that there is often a mismatch between the sharply increased rate of the change confronting corporations and the anemic rate of organizational learning found within conventional command-and-control organizations.

3. Accelerating the Rate of Organizational Learning. The Rapid Strategy Creation (Search Conference) and Participative Design approaches are geared toward accelerating the organizational learning curve. Search Conferences are used to invent the future in collectively desirable ways. These future-focused conferences help to elicit strategic conversations among hundreds if not thousands of people in the enterprise. Search Conferences help to build coalitions and a network of people who have a shared appreciation for the strategic business environment; this provides a strong foundation for creating a shared strategic intent. Search Conferences are used to mobilize large groups of people within the organization by getting them involved as co-creators of the strategic direction for the firm.

THE LEARNING AND CHANGE CURVES

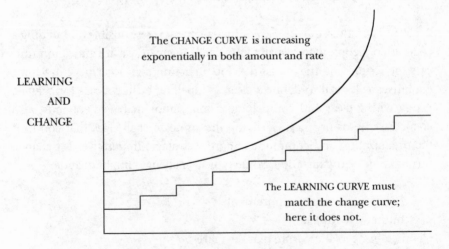

Figure 8.2

The Microsoft and Schwab cases presented in Chapter 7 illustrate how the Search Conference can be used to rapidly create a strategy that is widely shared by members, mobilizing the organization to change. The Search Conference is often staged as a kickoff event, which usually precedes a major organizational change or design effort. The Search Conference is thus useful for establishing the strategic intent that should drive changes in organizational architecture. Search Conferences also provide participants with their first experience of working in groups that can take responsibility for coordinating and controlling their own work—in other words, a test drive of the self-management paradigm. The dialogue experienced in Search Conferences creates a "community of commitment," where participants rise to the occasion and begin to take collective responsibility for the future of the enterprise. Participants are often directly involved in the implementation of strategic goals following the conference itself.

Search Conferences are then followed up by Participative Design (PD) sessions, which utilize an action-learning process to proactively design and change the organizational architecture to support the business strategy. A typical PD session is a forum where appropriate people come together to examine the structural relationships between themselves, their work, and the business strategy. The general purpose of a particular PD session is to engage those affected in determining more effective and meaningful ways to get their work done. Every PD session entails having participants develop concrete plans for how they would effect a transition of their work group from a traditional bureaucratic structure to a more flexible and self-managing form of organization—including the nuts and bolts of how it will be done. The work group's proposals for change, and the associated implementation plans, are input into an ongoing process of dialogue, which may include numerous design sessions, until the requisite changes and plans are evident to everyone, and implementation can proceed smoothly.

4. Prepare to Make an Organizational Choice to Democratize. Once a viable and widely shared strategy is in place, the CEO, along with the senior management team, needs to make a conscious and informed choice of how their organization in the future will be designed, structured, and managed. This choice is really quite simple, but fundamental in terms of the implications and magnitude of the change and resources that will be required. A decision must be made whether the firm will restructure itself to be a flexible, self-managing enterprise—a choice to support and implement the democratic design principle. The only other choice is to stick with a traditional command-and-control hierarchical organization, with all its bureaucratic variants.

Some people tend to think the need to choose between two fundamentally different design principles is polarizing the issue too much, that it relects a simplistic "either/or" logic. Such reactions are often voiced by managers who stand to lose the most in making a shift to self-management. The fact is, bureaucratic command-and-control organizations are designed according to a fundamentally different logic from self-managing organizations. A good analogy is to consider just how different democracy and capitalism are from communism and centrally planned economies. There may be many variants of democratic government from country to country, but certain principles distinguish democracies from totalitarian and communist-run societies. Similarly, there may be many variants of the self-managing organization from company to company, but all these phenotypical differences are rooted in a common democratic design principle that makes these firms fundamentally different from traditional command-and-control organizations.

Tinkering around the edges or making piecemeal changes in the organization always leads to disappointing results. To reap the economic and social benefits of self-management, senior management needs to have a wholehearted commitment to go forward and a clear understanding of the consequences of that choice. Making an organizational choice to democratize the enterprise means establishing reciprocal power relationships, where one level does not have unilateral power over another level. In other words, senior, middle, and operational-level managers will become part of a 360-degree governance system, where each level of management will be held accountable for their actions by all other levels. Senior management will need to support and fully understand the move to an organization where empowerment backed up by accountability is the norm throughout the enterprise. They will need to commit themselves to shifting decision making to the lowest effective level. Obviously this will lead to a team-based organization with fewer management levels, one where control and coordination of work will be done by those closest to the customer.

The role of a consultant in this phase is to help senior leaders understand the new organizational paradigm and recognize the need for change. Before introducing Participative Design, consultants need to make a reasonable effort to ensure that there are opportunities for significant benefits to the client. This requires spending a lot of time on the front end before any PD sessions are conducted. In addition, consultants need to spend their time helping all levels of management see the magnitude of the change they are approaching: the powerful consequences of shifting from a traditional command-and-control structure to a self-managing democratic organization. This will involve clarifying the type of enterprise-wide improvements that need to be made; assessing the leadership's willingness to make the needed changes as individuals and as an executive team; assessing the organization's capabilities to make the needed changes, the obstacles that presently exist, and the likelihood of success given the current state of affairs; and gauging how urgent it is to proceed with and follow through on the needed changes.

In other words, consultants need to work as closely as possible with senior management to clarify the goals, expectations, and impact that they hope to achieve with Participative Design. Consultants must also work to build consensus at all levels on the importance of the redesign effort, the rationale for using Participative Design, and the pace at which the agreed-upon changes should be made. This consensus-building approach provides natural opportunities to build understanding, acceptance, and support for the Participative Design process.

A great deal of learning, exploration, and education often needs to occur before senior management can make an informed choice to go full speed ahead with a design process. This education and learning process must start at the top of the organization. These executives will be looking at the design principles and case illustrations we have articulated in this book and seeking out further opportunities to broaden their understanding. They might choose to attend briefings on the design pathway with competent professionals, visit leading companies in their industry, attend conferences on best practices, or they might be fortunate enough to have internal efforts already under way on the periphery of their own business, which they can benchmark.

5. Leading the Participative Design Process. Once the commitment to self-management has been made, the CEO, along with a guiding coalition of formal and informal leaders throughout the corporation, must monitor and lead the process. They cannot simply leave it in the hands of their organizational-change specialists. In cases where top management lets go of the reins, participants in PD sessions will inevitably ask, "What's the answer we are supposed to come up with?" In the context of self-management, it is quite appropriate for senior management to provide a clear directional statement about the boundary conditions for the design. A clear directional statement will free up a lot of energy, increase trust, and let people settle into a more "task-oriented" style of fleshing out the details in support of the strategic direction.

In order for people to commit themselves to change to more self-managing work structures, they need to know, "What is in this for me?" Change leaders will also need to examine "win/lose scenarios" to make sure everyone can buy into the democratization process. Who is going to win and who is going to lose in a shift to a self-managing organization? The reality is that there will be real and/or perceived winners and losers. Supervisors and middle managers may be concerned that they might be losers coming out of this process—particularly in the wake of methods like Reengineering. Top management must address this issue in a meaningful and honest way. They must figure out how to create a situation where managers can clearly perceive that their future will be as desirable coming out of the process as it was going in. And this is often not an easy task.

6. Building Internal Change-Management Capabilities. Management of the design process requires building a cadre of internal change leaders who can move the whole organization along the path of self-management. Internal consultants should be developed who can present new paradigm ideas throughout the organization and manage high-involvement learning processes such as Search Conferences and Participative Design sessions. Preferably these internal consultants should be line managers who are given special assignments to lead the change effort within their divisions or departments. We have found that organizations that have succeeded in making the fundamental change to self-management employed this strategy, rather than relying exclusively on organization development and training staff. These organizations recognized the need to build critical mass and made a significant investment in building internal change-management capability.

Internal change agents are trained to design and manage Participative Design sessions and Search Conferences. In some cases, internal consultants may retain their regular jobs while devoting about a third of their time to the change effort. A significant number of managers may also cycle through these roles. We suggest that a ratio of one internal change agent per hundred employees is a good rough guide to make the shift to self-management viable.

Internal change agents work to help the workforce to (1) become cognizant of the competitive environment and the business case for change; (2) recognize the need for radical change in systems, structures, and work processes; (3) make a free and informed choice to adopt self-managing design principles; and (4) infuse energy, commitment, and enthusiasm to support and spread self-management throughout the enterprise.

Before Participative Design sessions can get off the ground, a critical mass of commitment is required. Internal consultants can be helpful by staging events to help create a sense of urgency and to nurture the process along. Developing a critical mass of support often involves holding information sessions, convening workshops led by formal and informal leaders, and arranging visits to other self-managing organizations. Ideally, a third to half of the workforce should understand and be committed to the new organizational paradigm. Critical mass is needed before proceeding forward deep into the actual design process. This doesn't mean that further learning and exploration won't be required. Indeed, for self-management to really take hold throughout the enterprise, people at all levels and in every part of the business need to embrace the new design principles, and to understand what they are getting into on a very practical and concrete level.

Both internal change agents and external consultants work closely with groups within the organization in a collaborative way, leveraging the knowledge and expertise that are already available among employees so they can engage in the participate design of their own work.

7. Setting Expectations and Design Goals. Senior management needs to specify broad parameters, establish clear boundaries, and clarify their expectations for the design process. They should provide an umbrella framework that communicates the scope and magnitude of the transformation effort. The project schedule for the redesign effort will depend on many factors such as:

- the degree of commitment and readiness demonstrated by senior and middle management in both word and deed;
- how quickly the leadership group learns to work together, and the degree to which it is willing to be mutually accountable for specific results which cross business-unit boundaries;

- the size of the organization being redesigned;
- the extent to which the organization has utilized participative processes in the past and has clearly begun to move outside of the control paradigm;
- the sequencing and coordination of numerous PD sessions and large-group events;
- technical and team training required.

Throughout the process, informal and formal progress reviews are held with key executives. Participative Design is not completed until the organization has taken the necessary and cost-effective steps to secure real change and impact. Normally this means that participants themselves will be directly involved in implementing their team's recommendations. It helps to have a detailed project plan and timetable for managing the entire Participative Design process from beginning to end. Beyond that, the people themselves will take responsibility for implementation and making it work. Consultants may be helpful during the implementation phase, if only to monitor the progress and the results achieved by grassroots implementation teams. More extensive involvement on the part of consultants may be appropriate in some cases to help coach managers who are having a difficult time making the transition to self-management, or in helping to form and assist Participative Design implementation teams.

THE PARTICIPATIVE DESIGN WORKSHOP[1]

If groups of people are to be expected to take responsibility and become self-managing, they have to be active co-creators, not passive recipients of the design process. In other words, people have to be provided the opportunity and tools to design their own section of the organization. For many years, STS and other large-scale change methods have used elite design teams and representatives to conduct the major design work. As we discussed in Chapter 3, these approaches, which rely on elite representatives, create an unhealthy reliance on experts—whether they be internal design

---

[1]Much of the discussion that follows was adapted from Merrelyn Emery's *Participative Design for Participative Democracy* (1993). We are greatly indebted to Dr. Emery for allowing us to incorporate her seminal work into this chapter.

teams or external consultants—which in turn hinders the emergence of a self-sustaining organizational learning process. Merrelyn and Fred Emery—co-inventors of the Participative Design method—found that the most effective way to transform an entire enterprise to self-management is to involve employees and managers in Participative Design Workshops (PDWs).

The PDW is the basic building block for creating the self-managing organization. The mortar, if you will, that binds these blocks together is that people learn (during the workshop) how to use simple tools for analyzing and redesigning their current work structure. Participative Design sessions rely on people to use their collective knowledge, skill, judgment, and creativity to build greater autonomy into every level of the organization. Organization members have by far the most detailed knowledge of their own departments, and they require simple concepts and tools in order to redesign them. Participative Design creates momentum for radical change because the process is simple, direct, and straightforward. People who go through the workshops diffuse what they learn to others. Participative Design grows out of years of experience-based action research that has produced a method that maximizes organizational learning and diffusion.

The most basic assumption underlying Participative Design is that the most adequate and effective designs come from those whose jobs are under review. The Participative Design process allows people to pool their various perspectives and detailed knowledge into a collective and comprehensive design. Moreover, this process allows people to become directly involved in working and hashing out their own designs, a requirement for ensuring the necessary level of motivation, responsibility, and commitment to effective implementation. Participative Design avoids the problems that typically occur during the implementation phase of most redesign processes—problems that can usually be traced to the fact that the new designs were imposed from above or by external agents such as consultants or design teams.

The Basic Outline of a Participative Design Session

The basic Participative Design Session usually involves 24–32 people from the organization, and is typically conducted in a two-day session. The

Participative Design process consists of three phases: analysis, redesign, and implementation (see Figure 8.3 below).

In the first phase, the design session begins with general introductions and a run-through of the agenda, explaining the purpose and process of each activity. This is important even when teams have had prior briefings because it provides an ongoing context—the agenda and explanations are posted and remain so throughout the session—and also serves as a reminder of how the work is progressing in reference to the agreed-upon time constraints. Before the analytical work begins, the facilitator introduces the organization design principles. The facilitator also presents the

A DETAILED LOOK AT THE PHASES OF A PARTICIPATIVE DESIGN SESSION

Phase one: analysis	Phase two: redesign	Phase three: implementation plan
Top management visits briefly to share organizational purposes.	Facilitator introduces the democratic design principle.	Groups develop a comprehensive and measurable set of goals and targets for the unit.
Facilitator introduces the six critical human requirements, then provides a briefing on the bureaucratic design principle.	Facilitator explains the impact of the new design principle on improving the six critical human requirements and skill levels.	Groups spell out their requirements for training, equipment, internal coordination, and external relations.
Facilitator introduces the matrix for mapping the skills currently held.	Groups draw up their existing workflow and organizational structure.	Groups review how to phase in career paths based on payment for proven skills held.
Facilitator explains the inverse relationship between the old design principle and critical requirements and skills.	Groups redesign their own structure to produce the best possible design for everyone.	Groups test their new work design against the six critical human requirements and explain how their scores will improve.
All groups create and complete the two matrices for human requirements and skills.	Facilitator holds interim plenary so that groups can learn from each other's efforts, challenge one another's assumptions, and create a truly systemic design.	
Groups report findings and use their patterns as diagnostic tools.		Groups finalize their design. Management returns to listen, negotiate, discuss, and understand as groups present final reports and implementation plan.

Length of Participative Design session: one to two days

Figure 8.3

Adapted from Cabana, 1995. "Can people restructure their own work?" *Target* 11(6), 16–30.

six critical requirements for motivating work, and explains how the designs of traditional work systems usually fail to satisfy these requirements. Groups then move quickly into analyzing their own work system using the matrices. During the second phase, groups are exposed in more depth to the self-managing democratic design principle. The facilitator explains how self-managing work systems are designed to satisfy the six critical requirements for motivating work. During this phase, participants analyze their technical system, business process and workflow, variances and bottlenecks, and the existing organizational structure. After conducting this analysis, groups move quickly into redesigning their entire unit to be self-managing. In the last phase, participants work on final design tasks, setting measurable goals and assessing their needs for training, changes in career paths, rewards and performance management systems, and so on. Groups make proposals, and finalize their new design.

Introducing the Design Principles. Early in the workshop, participants are introduced to the nature and importance of organization-design principles. According to Emery's theory, redundancy is the key to system reliabil-

---

Table 8.1 Basic Outline of a Participative Design Session

Purpose, Rationale for Change

Introductions and Overview

Education and Explanation of the Design Principles

Work System Analysis

    Groups fill in matrix for six psychological criteria for motivating work

    Groups fill in essential skills matrix

Report Outs and Diagnostics

Work Flow Analysis

    Groups map the work process, identify key variances

    Groups draw up existing organizational structure

Report Outs and Diagnostics

Redesign

Interim Plenary

Final Design Tasks

Final Reports

ity. For example, high-reliability systems—such as strategic air defense, airliner design, and nuclear-power plants—utilize backup components and are designed with redundancy in mind. The same requirement is true for organizations. The more redundancy an organization can build into its system, the greater its capacity for adaptiveness. Emery distinguishes between two basic ways of building redundancy into a system: either (1) by adding redundant parts to the system; or (2) by adding redundant functions to the parts. The distinction is fundamental to the principle by which organizations are designed, resulting in two fundamentally different design principles, often referred to as Design Principle 1 (DP1) and Design Principle 2 (DP2).

Design Principle 1 builds in redundancy by designing into the system a multiplicity of identical and replaceable parts. For example, the presence of four backup systems in the Russian space station *Mir* is supposed to guarantee a reliable source of oxygen for *Mir*'s astronauts. A good example of a social system that relies on redundant parts is the large army. Large armies derive a measure of flexibility by building in more parts than are required at any given moment. No one part is indispensable. This approach—which treats those who perform jobs as interchangeable parts—protects the organization from damage due to the failure of any given part; if one part (soldier, tank, battalion) fails, another can easily take over. Supposedly unreliable people need supervision to make them reliable. The boss attempts to make employees more reliable by telling them how they will do their jobs, which people they will work with, and whether they can make changes or improvements. Sanctions, punishments, and rewards are also used to elicit compliant behavior from the troops. The boss is responsible for results, not the people actually doing the work.

Design Principle 1 (DP1) is the DNA that underlies all dominant hierarchies. With DP1, responsibility for control and coordination of work tasks is located *not at the level at which the work is actually performed, but one level above* (see Figure 8.4). This comes straight out of scientific management. Control and coordination, the two key dimensions of human organization, are vested in the supervisor. The supervisor/manager controls subordinates by specifying each individual's jobs, tasks, and assignments. Coordination of efforts between individuals and jobs is also supervised from above.

Making an organizational choice to democratize requires changing the

TWO FUNDAMENTAL CHOICES OF ORGANIZATIONAL DESIGN

Bureaucratic Structure

Coordination and control of work tasks is done by a supervisor.

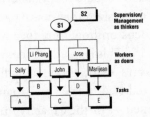

Democratic Structure

Coordination and control of work tasks is done by those doing the work.

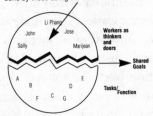

Mind Set...

- People have specialized skills and are easily replaced.
- The work (technical system) is designed first. The people (social system) must adapt and fit in.
- Workers are cogs in the machine of the enterprise, a commodity.

- Total specification of everything.
- Within a complex organization, simple jobs are created.
- The building block of the organization is one person-one task.
- Competitive structures, processses and reward systems are the best way to produce high performance.

People Act As If...

- The environment our enterprise exists in is stable and unchanging.
- There is little to learn at work.

- Success comes from reacting resourcefully to problems.
- Procedures are sufficient to guide behavior. Change interferes with productivity and can often be postponed.
- Responsibility and blame can be shifted to others.
- We are separate and therefore I can win at your expense.
- We don't need to coordinate work closely with other functions. Their problems are their problems.
- Unspoken assumptions need not be explored. Simple solutions to problems are adequate.

Mind Set...

- People possess many skill sets and can do many jobs/functions.
- The needs of the work (technical system) are balanced with the needs of the doers of the work (social system).
- People are learners. Machines and information systems can extend the skill set of employees to many functions.
- As little as possible is specified, leaving the rest to the skill and discretion of the workers.
- Complex jobs are created within a simple organizational structure.
- The building block of organization is the self-managed work team.
- Cooperative structures and reward systems are the best way to produce high performance.

People Act As If...

- The environment our enterprise exists in is constantly changing.
- Skepticism and doubt are valuable and enable continuous learning.
- Success comes from sensing trends and initiating change.
- Outcomes are best reached with flexibility built into the approach.
- I am fully responsible for any work I agree to perform.
- Every task is part of some larger whole. I can't win at your expense.
- Everyone's ideas are taken seriously. Cooperation is essential for our mutual survival.
- Making our assumptions explicit and exploring them is worth the temporary discomfort.

Figure 8.4

design principle. The second organization design principle (Design Principle 2) provides flexibility by building redundancy or excess capacity into the system. Redundancy, or excess capacity, is commonly referred to as "having enough slack in the system." This notion of redundancy runs counter to conventional wisdom. We usually equate redundancy, or slack, with inefficiency, waste, or anything in the system that doesn't add value. Indeed, many improvement methods focus on how to reduce waste, cut slack, and eliminate non-value-added work. This is not the issue. We are all for eliminating bureaucratic red tape and work process inefficiencies. However, problems arise when slack is reduced to such an extent that an organization no longer has room to maneuver or the capacity to redesign itself. The organization has become "lean and mean" without becoming any smarter. What remains is a streamlined core work process—minus the capability to adapt and change that work process in response to new demands. A system that is over-designed—one where each person is narrowly confined to his or her job, where the work is prescribed to exact specifications—allows little opportunity for learning. Flexibility is reduced; the system simply does not have the capacity to innovate or to respond quickly to problems and challenges.

Redundancy and system reliability can also be achieved by building more functional capabilities into the parts. In other words, rather than building redundancy by designing specialized parts, the functions and capabilities of the parts are extended, in what Emery refers to as "redundancy of functions." This design principle increases the capacity and range of the functions that each part or person can perform. Self-managing organizations have a superior competitive advantage because they build redundancy by extending the skills and functions of their people and because they relocate responsibility for the control and coordination of work at the level at which the work is actually performed.

Design Principle 2 (DP2) is the underlying DNA of self-managing organizations. The basic module is a self-managing team that takes responsibility for its own control and coordination. It is democratic because the members of the work team can decide among themselves how they want to share and allocate the requirements for the control and coordination of task-related activities. The range of responsibilities and the degree of self-management will differ for different organizations and groups. At the lowest level of self-management, teams may simply have the right to decide on working methods and allocation of work among them-

CHARACTERISTICS OF
THE BUREAUCRATIC ORGANIZATION

A discussion of the characteristics of the bureaucratic organization points out the easy familiarity people already have with its built-in shortcomings:

- Bureaucracy fails to satisfy people's critical requirements for work, which results in lower work quality and productivity. The job erosion caused by treating people as narrow parts of the machine inevitably leads, over time, to alienation and low commitment.
- Bureaucracy confines coordination and control of interdependent tasks to the supervisor's role.
- Subordinates (both exempt and nonexempt) selectively communicate what makes them look good and listen only to the upward or downward communications that suit them.
- Competitive structures pit person against person, group against group—each person vying for promotion or security.
- People create a shadow or informal organization (e.g., cliques and rumor mills) and seek to turn the requirements of coordination to their advantage, such as by creating informal production norms.
- Programs such as TQM, empowerment, and Reengineering are not sustainable, as they usually retain centralized decision making and do little to alter an organization's power structure. In other words, these programs adapt to the existing hierarchy, and this places an inherent limit on the degree to which employees can be empowered without risking the loss of managerial control.

selves. At a somewhat higher level, they may select, hire, and train their own members; do their own maintenance; and check their own quality. At an even higher level, self-managing teams may be involved in redefining their own goals and reviewing and evaluating the performance of their peers. More mature teams may proceed to a higher level of self-management, which involves them more deeply in long-range planning, strategy creation, and development of new products and work practices.

Design Principle 1. The bureaucratic design principle is explained, noting its inverse relation to the six psychological requirements of productive work (see page 224), and to the notion of skills. During the workshop, participants find out how the design principles structure the way work is organized and their effects on organizational behavior.

Design Principle 2. In contrast, the traits and characteristics of an "ideal" self-managing organization, based on Design Principle 2, are discussed. The structure of a participatively designed organization reflects the following principles:

- By adding redundant functions (sets of skills) to the parts (people), each person is able to perform multiple functions and tasks, and therefore has more value to the enterprise.
- Each person has the ability to perform functions not called for at the moment and can jump in with them when needed.
- Redundancy of function means that people are skilled in a wide variety of social, business, and technical tasks and functions. In situations which require specialized expertise, such as doctors, lawyers, R&D professionals, and management teams, the group design may have individuals with specialized roles. Even within this design there will be some overlapping skill sets and joint coordination of performance goals.
- People work in self-managing teams that share responsibility for monitoring and controlling the contributions of their members. Teams secure the training they need to become self-regulating. They also get up to speed on the business's broad strategic direction, key objectives, and overall products and services.
- Self-managing teams will also build very strong links with other teams (their internal customers and suppliers), support groups, and management. Self-management means implementing teamwork and cooperation so that agreed-upon goals can be met.
- Self-managing teams will have regular contact with customers, suppliers and strategic partners. They will have mechanisms for regularly scanning and learning from their environment so they are aware of what is happening around them.
- Just as self-managing teams are the basic building block of a self-managing organization, team processes and responsibilities become the basic building block of a boundary management role. These middle managers assist teams in their efforts to become increasingly proficient in self-management.

People cannot be expected to accept responsibility as a group unless a number of conditions are met. The psychological requirements that individual workers have of their jobs are just about equally relevant for a face-to-face group of workers. Such a group must know that they can aim at targets that are explicit, realistic, and challenging to them; and they must have feedback on their group performance. Self-managing teams must have a comprehensive set of goals, including human, social, and environmental, in addition to the purely economic and technical ones. Self-managing teams must be involved in setting their own goals too, but these must be negotiated with management. In addition to these requirements, self-managing teams must feel that the membership of their team is to some degree under their own control. They must also be free to organize their own liaisons and to choose their informal leaders. Leadership is usually a shared and rotating function, which changes according to the demands and circumstances of the task environment.

Cohesive teamwork requires sufficient multiskilling to allow for flexible allocation of work within the group, to both individuals and subgroups. The allocation of work is determined by team members themselves, with explicit boundaries and rules to ensure high quality, safety, reliability, and so on. There is often a fair amount of on-the-job training that goes on; team members will work to increase the extent and level of skill in the group to improve their performance, adaptiveness, and cohesion. All of this effort requires more explication of goals, methods, and responsibilities than is normally the case in traditional organizations. Clear responsibilities and goals are a requirement, otherwise there is a danger of drifting into a laissez-faire atmosphere, where people begin to believe "empowerment" means that people are free to do whatever they want. Groups must articulate and agree on mechanisms for decision making and on methods for controlling and coordinating their own work.

It is absolutely critical for the continued development of self-managing organizations that group members have conceptual knowledge of Participative Design principles. With this knowledge, people can deliberately evolve their design toward greater group responsibility and effectiveness. Without this knowledge, the design may erode and regress back to Design Principle 1. Simply setting up teams and telling them they are self-managing —without a deep appreciation of what is entailed in responsibility for control and coordination, without a knowledge of the design principles, and without an opportunity to agree as a group on their own design—will leave teams floundering, frustrated, and fragmented.

The Six Critical Human Requirements for Motivating Work

The PD session begins with an activity that provides participants with detailed instructions for creating and completing the critical human-requirements matrix. Cumulative investigations in Europe, Scandinavia, Australia, India, and North America have enabled social scientists to identify a number of important determinants of the psychological requirements of productive work, located in both the interface of the social and technical systems and the social climate of the work situation. There is a core of six such requirements for motivating work. Merrelyn and Fred Emery discovered that these requirements must be designed into the work structure in order for people to be fully responsible and committed to their work.

The six critical requirements are the core elements for building satisfying jobs and empowering people. While additional elements can be added to these critical requirements, the core six are the building blocks for designing any effective organization and therefore are at the heart of Participative Design.

The first three critical requirements—*autonomy, opportunity for learning,* and *variety*—refer to the content of the job and need to be optimal for any given individual. In other words, each person's need for autonomy, learning, and variety is different. Different people doing the same job may experience the first three work dimensions as being present either too much or not enough. On the matrix, autonomy, learning, and variety are rated from −5 (too little) to +5 (too much), with 0 (zero) being optimal. The last three requirements—*mutual support, meaningfulness,* and a sense of a *desirable future*—are dimensions that one would seek to maximize, and are scored from 0 (none) to 10 (maximum). The final matrix is a group product that expresses the relative distribution of scores within the work unit, department, or section.

1. Sufficient Elbow Room (Autonomy). This is the sense that people feel they are their own bosses and that, except in certain circumstances, they don't need a boss breathing down their necks. The need for elbow room varies tremendously among individuals. People need to feel they are free to make decisions about how they do their work. However, we must also be careful to see that people have enough structure so that they know what to do.

2. Opportunity to Learn on the Job and Keep on Learning. Learning is possible only when people (a) *can set goals* that are reasonable challenges for them, and (b) *get feedback* on their performance in time for them to correct their behavior. That is, each individual must be able to set challenging goals for himself or herself, rather than having someone set their goals for them. A good job challenges you. If a supervisor says: "Have this work finished and on my desk by next Monday," and you feel it could be completed much earlier, that will not provide an optimal level of challenge. Moreover, accurate feedback about performance has to be there when workers need it so they can learn from and correct their mistakes. On-time feedback provides opportunities for experimentation to find better ways of working. Without on-time feedback an individual will not know if he or she is doing things correctly, and goal achievement becomes simply a matter of luck.

3. Variety. Some people like to have a lot of variety whereas others prefer to do routine work. People need to be able to vary their work so as to avoid boredom and fatigue, and to work at their best by settling into a satisfying rhythm of work. Individuals need to be able to plan their work so no one gets too much of the routine work and no one is stressed by performing too many demanding tasks.

The next three critical human requirements relate to the social climate of the workplace—the workplace's atmosphere. People can never get too much of them. In the redesign effort, each participant will assess whether the workplace provides a high degree of mutual support and respect, meaningful work that is socially useful where they can see the whole product, and a desirable future. These three are scored from 0 to 10, the highest score being optimal.

4. Mutual support and respect. Conditions must be such that individuals can and do get respect and support from their coworkers. Conditions must be avoided where it is in no one's interest to help another; where people are pitted against each other so that "one person's loss is another's gain," or where the group interest suppresses the individual's capabilities. When the workplace system is designed effectively it results in cooperative efforts, not competing work goals.

5. Meaningfulness and pride of ownership. A sense that one's own work meaningfully contributes to the general social welfare. This includes both the quality and the worth to society of the product or service, as well as the participant's knowledge and understanding of the end use or purpose of the whole product or service. If people believe the product they are producing or the work they are doing is shoddy or is not valued by the community, they will not believe they have a meaningful job. Moreover, people need to see how their job contributes to the whole product and to be proud of the quality of their work. When the workplace system is designed effectively people know how their work fits into the bigger picture—and feel pride and ownership about what they do.

6. A desirable future. Put simply, this is a career path that will continue to allow for personal growth and development of knowledge and skills. When people master new skills and contribute to the management of their group, their aspirations will grow.

Experience has shown that these psychological requirements cannot be better fulfilled by simply rearranging or enlarging individual jobs. Many attempts at empowerment simply result in delegating more work to individuals, without giving them real authority to make their own decisions. Genuine empowerment is best achieved by relocating responsibility, for *control* over effort and quality of the work process, as well as for *coordination* with the people who are actually doing the job.

During the PD session, participants work in groups to analyze their jobs as they currently exist. Participants are asked to evaluate their existing tasks and work environment in terms of the six psychological requirements for motivating work. The pattern in the matrix usually reflects the psychological effects of a Design Principle 1–type bureaucratic organization. Departments or sections typically show a majority of low scores on the first three requirements. Scores on the second three are less predictable. From the pattern in Table 8.2, we can deduce that Jim is the supervisor; he is very happy with his autonomy, but has to look after too many things (variety and setting goals). Because he is a supervisor, nobody gives him much feedback and he doesn't feel that he receives much respect or support. He does, however, tend to foresee a desirable future for himself in the organization.

You might also be able to guess that John is probably Jim's favorite.

Table 8.2 Matrix of the Six Psychological Requirements for Motivating Work

		Names of Participants			
Psychological Criteria	Mary	Jim	John	Alice	Joe
1. Autonomy/Elbow room for decision making	−2	0	−1	−3	−2
2. Learning					
(a) setting goals	−4	+3	−2	−3	−3
(b) getting feedback	−3	−4	0	−4	−4
3. Variety	−3	+5	0	+4	−3
4. Mutual Support	8	4	2	8	8
5. Meaningfulness					
(a) socially useful	9	9	9	9	9
(b) seeing whole product	4	10	7	3	4
6. Desirable Future	3	7	6	2	2

John's scores also show that he receives low levels of social support and respect from his peers. As Jim may be grooming him to take over, John also seems to feel that he has a desirable future ahead of him. Mary and Joe, on the other hand, have simple and fractionated jobs. And Alice scores even worse. She comes across as the low person on the totem pole, doing most of the grunt work of the department. All three are aware that they see little by way of a career path or a way to improve their chances on the job market. However, to put up with this impoverished work setting, Mary, Joe, and Alice stick together and look after each other. They have created an informal subsystem, and give each other mutual support to fight against the bureaucracy. They all recognize that the work of their department is socially useful, but only Jim and John seem to be in a position to really see how their jobs contribute to the whole.

This is only one example of what can be deduced from such a matrix. In a real PD session, much of this is already known by participants and the diagnostic use of the matrices in the report session is confined to noting the major problem areas that need rectification in the redesign.

The higher the quality of the work life the producers of products or services enjoy, the higher the quality of the products or services they produce. Put another way, those who do not enjoy a high quality-of-work-life convert their dissatisfaction with their jobs into poor-quality products and services. Meeting the needs of the six critical requirements means restructuring the workplace. Again, this means that responsibility for control and coordination over the work process must be reallocated with the people who are actually doing the work.

Conducting an Essential Skills Audit

The next task during the PD session is for groups to draw and fill in a matrix of skills currently held. These skills should be the essential ones that are required of the work unit to transform inputs into quality outputs. After the participants identify their skill sets, they indicate the level of competence and expertise they possess relative to each skill set. A simple skill matrix can be constructed by marking a zero to indicate a complete lack of knowledge or competence; a checkmark to indicate a sufficient level of skill so that you can back up someone who regularly performs the job; and two checks to indicate a high level of skill where you are proficient enough to teach someone else how to perform the activity.

It is clear from Table 8.3 that only Skills C and D are covered within the department for a high level of skill. If Mary happens to be sick, only Jim can cover for Skill A, and at a lower level of skill. As one can see from the matrix, Jim already has too much to do. This department may be able to muddle through in the short term on skills B and E. However, the basic rule for a multiskilled work team is that there must be at least two people with a high level of competency in a particular skill, with several additional people to serve as backups. Of course, the larger the team, the more skills will have to be distributed across various team members.

Table 8.3 Essential Skills Matrix

Essential Skills	Mary	Jim	John	Alice	Joe
A	√√	√	0	0	0
B	√	√	√	√	√√
C	0	√√	√√	0	√
D	√	√√	√√	0	0
E	√	√√	√	0	√

Within self-managing teams, the essential skills matrix chart is a guide to learning on the job, and can be used for assessing training needs. These needs will have to be met for any collection of people to be able to transform themselves into a self-managing, multiskilled team. Based on the simple matrix of Table 8.3 above, the group would identify skills A, B, and E as requiring further training. In the final session, they would return to this analysis and use it to determine who should receive what training on which skills; whether such training can be done on the job or not; the time required for gaining mastery of a skill block; and so on. In the above example, it is also easy to see why Mary, Joe, and Alice rate their desirable futures low. Mary and Joe are stuck with basically simple dead-end jobs, while Alice has few skills at all, and little opportunity to learn. With the change to a self-managing, democratic structure, the department has the chance to redesign career paths based on payment for skills held. Using the same skills matrix, departments going through Participative Design will generate design proposals that have new career paths built into them. Such a career path is democratic, since movement and progression are determined by the individual, rather than by the imposed structure of the organization.

These two matrices, Tables 8.2 and 8.3, show where the gaps exist in both critical human requirements and job skills. These matrices also indicate how work can be redesigned to create a self-managing work system.

Analyzing the Technical System and the Work Flow

After participants have analyzed the motivating potential of their work and skill sets, they turn their attention to the technical system and current flow of work—mapping out the inputs, the transformation processes, and the outputs, and indicating where key decisions are made and all the steps involved in the process. To further refine their diagnosis, participants identify key issues, bottlenecks, or glitches in the technical system—where errors or problems typically occur. Following the technical analysis, participants draw the existing organizational structure as it is today, noting the occupants of current positions.

Generating Redesign Proposals

After the participants have diagnosed their current work system using the matrices and the work-flow analysis, they are ready to consider options for redesign. Groups must have sufficient time during this phase to review their data and refine their diagnoses. Participants continue to work in groups to generate new designs for their organizational units. Their new design proposals will be measured against whether they enhance people's critical psychological requirements, build flexibility through skill redundancy, and reduce bottlenecks in the technical system. An interim plenary session is essential, in which groups present their design options, compare notes, and receive feedback and criticism from other groups that have to interact with the section or business being redesigned. Once the options have been thoroughly discussed and understood, the facilitator provides a set of design implementation issues that need to be taken into account when groups finalize their design.

Final Design Tasks

PD session participants are briefed on the final design tasks that need to be achieved to ensure the successful implementation of their new design. Since groups manage their own implementation, the cycle time from design to actually working under the new arrangements is dramatically reduced.

Establishing Clear and Measurable Goals. Participants will establish a comprehensive and measurable set of goals for each team. Goals might include: cycle time reduction, metrics, rewards, process improvement, quality, problem-solving capacity, documentation, personal development, and customer response time. The team must set its own full range of goals: operational, business, human, and technical (see Figure 8.5). If we focus only on production or service goals, the faster workers will set a pace that exceeds some people's capacities, and overall team performance will fall.

As we stated earlier, people can't be expected to work as a team unless they know they can aim at goals that are explicit, realistic, and challenging for them. After the first crack at their goals, teams will still need to negotiate with middle management. Self-managing teams are not free simply to decide their own goals independent of the needs of the business. Middle managers are the system integrators that link operational requirements to strategic business goals. A key role for middle managers in self-managing organizations is to negotiate goals and targets with self-managing teams. Managers ensure that mechanisms are in place which clarify the mission

A TEAM'S GOALS AFTER A PD SESSION

Industry: Computer

Products: Electronic Pens

Unit: Testing and Technology

Failure Analysis Group—Goals

- Identify six common variances of incoming pens by 11/95.
- Reduce customer complaints to one per month by 11/95.
- Implement digital technology via computer network to customers by 2/96.
- Institute personnel development system by 10/95.
- Create documentation database for all processes for multi-access by 9/95.
- Complete negotiation and design of skill-based pay system by 2/96.

Adapted from Cabana, S. 1995. "Can people restructure their own work," *Target*, 11(6), 16–30.

Figure 8.5

and the goals which enable them to monitor and provide feedback to teams on their performance. This requires middle managers to work together by sharing information and coordinating work across unit boundaries.

Defining Training Requirements. Teams will also determine their training requirements from a careful examination of their skills matrices. Training requirements are not imposed on teams from above. That would violate the spirit and values of a self-managing workplace. Instead, participants identify the training they will need that will help them to function as a self-managing multiskilled team. The skills matrix from the analysis phase helps them to identify the appropriate backup skills, so that at least two people on each team hold important or essential skills. Teams will also need to identify additional organizational arrangements required to make them self-managing, such as feedback mechanisms, processes to ensure job rotation, equipment and other resources, regular meeting times, and procedures for coordinating relations with external groups.

Designing New Career Paths. A new career path based on payment for competency and mastery of skills held often accompanies self-managing team designs. Economic gains must be shared in an equitable manner with those who are responsible for the performance improvements. Because self-management is based on democratic principles, the pay schemes will have to be revamped to become a congruent component of the system. A genuine self-managing team will move heaven and earth to meet its goals. And its members will expect their achievement to be compensated. One form this might take is a pay-forskills compensation system; skills are assessed on a point system; when people reach a certain number of points (which correspond to the number of skills they possess) they move up a band. In some self-managing organizations, all members receive an annualized salary. Subsequently, there is no overtime pay and no shift differentials.

In executive teams and specialized groups of professionals, the typical DP1 pay system rewards individual contributors for their functional expertise. This does not support joint coordination of common business goals that cross functional boundaries. In a self-managing organization, the compensation system may be adjusted to support group accountability for performance goals that cut across the white spaces of SBUs and functions such as marketing, product development, and manufacturing. Gain-sharing plans can also be used to reward group performance.

Explanation of How the New Design Will Improve the Quality of Work Life

At this point it is essential that participants provide a statement on how the new design will improve the quality of working life on the unit by its positive impact on the six critical psychological requirements. People will not adopt the new way of working if they do not believe it is going to make their jobs more interesting and rewarding. If the scores on the six critical requirements do not improve, then neither will productivity, quality, and cost effectiveness when the design is completed.

Groups Finalize Their Designs

Typically a design emerges that places people in self-managing teams, meets the six requirements for work, has a very positive impact on quality and productivity, and also clearly specifies reporting relationships. Toward the end of the session, teams spend time finalizing their redesign and get as far as they can with the additional tasks. Completing these in the PD session is not essential. However, it is important that the teams which participate understand enough of its detail so that the redesign can be finalized at a later meeting, and then negotiated with management.

Final reports are made; it is useful if management is present to hear these. This is particularly the case if the new designs call for significant

A PARTICIPATIVE DESIGN SESSION OF A CORPORATE TRAINING FACILITY

At one of the Big Six consulting firms, most new recruits are put through a rigorous "boot camp" training program at a state-of-the-art facility that resembles a college campus. Throughout their careers, consultants return to this training facility to hone their skills and learn new methods. Executives also attend continuing-education courses that focus on business perspectives, leadership, core skills, industry expertise, and understanding clients' global objectives.

The management of the corporate training facility was complex, involving such tasks as course development, faculty and materials procurement, classroom set-up, scheduling and logistics, transportation of trainees, course maintenance, quality assurance, and day-to-day support. The responsibility for controlling and coordinating the myriad of tasks fell to the Training Delivery Support group. As the course offerings and the number of trainees increased, the Training Delivery Support group was finding it exceedingly difficult to provide seamless service with its limited resources. In addition, varying workloads among specialists were often unevenly distributed. During some weeks, some specialists would be swamped with work requests while others sat idle with little to do. Some specialists performed routine and repetitive tasks and were very dissatisfied with their jobs. The functional structure had impeded cooperation between specialists, and the quality of their service had begun to deteriorate.

The manager of Training Delivery Support services decided to redesign the entire group to be self-managing, using the Participative Design methodology. The new design eliminated supervisors and regrouped specialized functions into five overlapping support teams.

The new design enhanced the quality of the work environment for team members, as evidenced by the change in scores on the six psychological criteria matrix. Performance improved dramatically after the redesign.

changes to existing goals and policies, or proposals for merging or eliminating various departments. Management's role is to specify the mimimum critical specifications for the design, let groups have the freedom to be creative within those design constraints, and then review and approve designs that meet the criteria. Senior leaders are responsible for articulating the business case for change and providing clear measures of what success looks like to the designers. This grounds the design in business reasoning and provides a means for dispassionate discussion of design merits without lengthy talks based on personal preferences.

SELECTING PARTICIPANTS FOR PD SESSIONS

Generally, the size of the unit or operation that is the target of the redesign will determine how employees should be involved in PD sessions. If the target unit is small, everyone should be involved in the same PD session. In large organizations, it may be necessary to select a cross-section, or "deep slice," of employees from each department, including people from various levels. It is obviously not feasible to have employees redesigning a department or unit of which they have no knowledge. However, even in large organizations there are numerous ways of getting broad participation through careful selection of participants for the sessions. For example, mixed groups from the same department can work in parallel in the same session on an overall design which can then be integrated at the end. Or, alternatively, different groups can work on designs for the whole department in a series of different workshops that can then be compared, synthesized, and integrated at a later time. The basic rule of PD still applies: *No designs can be imposed.* Even if circumstances dictate that only one "deep-slice" group can attend a workshop, this group then has the responsibility of educating and reviewing the concepts and process with their peers. Peer input is reviewed and studied before producing a final design for the whole unit.

The criteria for choosing people to attend a "deep-slice" PD session must include representation from as many functions and occupations as exist within a department or division. But the actual choice of individuals according to these selection criteria must be done by the members of the department. They must not be hand-picked by managers. It is also critical that the ratio of employees to supervisors and middle managers match the actual ratio that exists within the organization. If PD sessions are too top-heavy with supervisors and managers, it is possible that the needs, ideas, and efficient designs from the employee level won't be given a fair review.

In large organizations with multiple levels of management, many PD sessions will be required, which have overlapping membership between the middle ranks. This increases the options for middle management, and also ensures greater coherence of design and learning up and down the old hierarchy.

Putting together and orchestrating PD sessions is an art in itself, since there are many options and possible variations: using parallel teams, mirror groups, deep-slice representatives, or large-group approaches.

The Use of Mirror Groups

Some PD sessions use a "mirror group" approach, where two disparate groups work together to analyze and redesign each other's organizations. The use of mirror groups is invaluable, since often natural groups working on their own fail to question their assumptions or "the way we have always done it." Natural groups tend to be comfortable with the status quo, and their members harbor unwritten rules, norms, and conventions, along with entrenched patterns of interpersonal behavior, all of which may range from highly conscious to quite unconscious. A mirror group can ask hard questions, challenge cherished beliefs and assumptions, and push natural groups out of their complacency. The designs that result can be much stronger, more robust, and more innovative as a result of this questioning and debate.

Mirror groups help to broaden organizational learning and can be used to generate designs that foster better integration between functional departments. For example, employees working in functional stovepipes within command-and-control organizations cannot learn very effectively. However, when internal customers and suppliers are part of the design process, significant "unlearning" can occur. This may have to do with "unlearning" fundamental beliefs, assumptions, attitudes, and values related to strategy or work organization. In a PD session, mirror groups can help the members of the unit that is being designed to climb outside the box of their own limiting assumptions. Participants describe this process, months later, as extremely painful but ultimately well worth the effort involved.

REDESIGNING COMPLEX KNOWLEDGE WORK USING PARTICIPATIVE DESIGN: THE STORAGETEK EXPERIENCE

StorageTek has been a pioneer in using the Participative Design method in highly complex knowledge-based product development and manufacturing operations. Founded in 1969, StorageTek pioneered the creation of solid-state disk storage, and has grown to become a major supplier of advanced storage solutions for many Fortune 1000 companies and governments worldwide. StorageTek now serves more than 22,000 customers in forty countries spanning six continents with a global workforce of 8,000-plus employees.

The Library Advanced Manufacturing Engineering (AME) and Volume Manufacturing business groups decided to go forward with Participative Design for redesigning their operations to a self-managing work system. A vertical slice of employees representing the Library AME and Volume Manufacturing organizations were selected to be involved in Participative Designs sessions for their units. Over the course of one month, six Participative Design sessions were convened. About 21 or 22 participants attended each design session, bringing the total number of employees who participated directly in the process to 130. After all the design sessions were conducted, nineteen redesign proposals emerged. An integration team was then formed to analyze and synthesize the various design options into a more manageable set of prototypes. The integration team converged on five key design prototypes, all of which proposed combining the AME and Volume Manufacturing organizations. Employees who had partici-pated in the previous Participative Design sessions were educated and informed on how the integration team had settled on five prototype designs for their organizations. These information sessions were crucial to ensuring that everyone had enough detailed information to judge the merits of the five design proposals. Once employees understood the details of the various proposals and design options, a town-hall meeting was held off-site for all 130 of the original participants for the purpose of making a collective decision on the final design. A choice was made, the integration team disbanded, and a new implementation was formed to scope out the details for operationalizing the new design for the Library AME and Volume Manufacturing organizations.

There would be significantly fewer managers in the new organization. The new design called for self-managing teams that crossed product lines. A core group consisting of five people—called the Advanced Manufacturing

Technology (AMT) team—would borrow personnel from the Library organization to do its work, and this team would also work to improve the process of new product introductions. The AMT would bridge the boundary between product development and manufacturing. The new design also created cross-functional teams (Continuous Improvement Work Teams— CIWTs) of both a temporary and a permanent nature, that cut across product lines both to reduce redundancies and to tackle system-wide problems. In addition, another group was created, the Cross Communication Team, whose sole purpose would be to improve the flow of information and knowledge within the new organization.

Designing for Customer or Product Focus

In some cases it is simply more effective to combine two or more groups from work units into a single workshop, where they work in parallel on the design for the whole department. For example, three different groups— each of which is a vertical slice containing a mixture of people from different functions with different skills—analyzes and redesigns the whole department. They follow the same process as described above and report to each other after every task. Consolidation and sorting out of discrepancies can be done at each stage so that an accurate and clearly defined design gradually comes into being.

This approach is appropriate when a particular department or set of functions needs to redesign itself around the customer or product, and where the size of the department or division makes it inefficient to use mirror groups. For example, Mike Rogers, the area supervisor for the operations laboratory at Syncrude Canada, asked his internal customers from Upgrading, Extraction, and the Environmental Safety group to join his forty-eight employees and half-dozen contract workers in four sequential PD sessions. Everybody got to hear everyone else and participate in an open dialogue. Four alternative designs were generated; then thirty-eight employees used a Kepner-Tregoe (1965) decision-analysis process to identify the superior design. Two months later, the new design was in place. By involving other departments, the operations labs' scientists, chemists, and technicians learned that doing work to suit their three-shift schedule was simply not meeting their customers' needs for timely, accurate information.

MIRROR GROUPS

In order to maximize the effectiveness of each PD session, the Research and Development function at a division of a large pharmaceutical business used mirror groups in its redesign process. Each PD session included employees from these functions: Marketing, R&D (physicians, scientists, etc.), and Sales. They also included one or two representatives from Operations, Engineering and Administration, and HR.

Employees were assigned to mirror design groups. An effort was made to have people from different product areas and levels. Two disparate groups would work together. Initially R&D and Sales analyzed R&D's organization to develop a more effective and efficient way of working. At another table, one group from Marketing and another group from the R&D unit also looked at R&D's organization. Then they switched roles. At one table R&D helped Sales look at its organization and at another, a different group of R&D professionals helped Marketing examine itself.

Mirror groups are formed because too often when homogeneous groups, like R&D alone, work entirely on their own, they fail to question their assumptions and the way they have always done things. As a result, static designs emerge and innovative thinking does not surface.

"Because everyone was involved in the process, we owned it, so implementation was easy," says Rogers. "It took us about a year and a half to transfer all the managerial decisions into the five teams we established. There are no supervisors here any more besides me—and I am involved in long-range planning and keep out of the day-to-day work." Two supervisors went to other parts of the business where their expertise was more valuable, and another is happy being a chemist again.

Replication and Integration

In large companies there will often be a need for a series of PD sessions. Replications may occur across shifts, or across mixed groups within departments. A series of PD sessions held throughout a department, or across departments, requires a means of integrating the various design proposals at the end. Special integration events are required to discuss and evaluate the merits of various design proposals, to synthesize and integrate common features, and eventually to make a collective choice on a final design. "Town meetings" and large group conferences that include as many people as possible in the integration activities can be organized. The designs can be presented by the workshop teams, compared and contrasted, and the merits of each can be discussed. Large group meetings are not effective for doing detailed design work, but they are an excellent forum for fostering democratic dialogue, raising and debating issues, and building consensus around designs.

SUMMARY

Participative Design is a unique method which assumes that the most effective designs are more likely to come from those closest to the work process. Fundamental change to self-management not only requires that people redesign their own work, but that they do so with conscious knowledge of the design principles. When conscious knowledge of design principles is lacking, there is the danger of implementing pseudo-empowerment solutions, such as those we discussed in Chapter 5. The main thrust of Participative Design is to genetically reengineer the organization's design principle, reallocating responsibility for control and coordination in democratic structures, in genuine self-managing teams. Such a change is both deep and systemic, affecting all levels of organization. Participative Design sessions provide the ideal conditions for organizational learning, allowing people to design democratic structures to become self-managing.

CHAPTER 9

PARTICIPATIVE DESIGN OF BUSINESS PROCESSES AT SEQUA CHEMICALS[1]

> I have now spoken of three things which will help to
> unify a business—an understanding of integration as a
> method of settling differences, some system of cross-
> functioning, and a sense of collective responsibility.
> —Mary Parker Follett

Located in the heart of the textile industry in Chester, South Carolina, Sequa Chemicals employs some two hundred and fifty people. Sequa Chemicals has a long history of innovation in product development, having held the original patent for the chemical that created "Permanent Press." However, by the 1990s Sequa found itself frozen in a no-growth mode. Sequa's primary chemical-supply businesses—textiles, graphics, paper, and water-based polymers—were mature and declining. Growth could come only by grabbing market share from larger and more resource-rich competitors. It was David against Goliath—and David needed an edge.

Individual accountability, the mantra of bureaucracy, was the name of the game for every Sequa manager. Functional chiefs were able to get work done through the people who reported directly to them, but collaboration between units was dismal. Managers simply didn't know how to work together to face the tougher challenges, which crossed departmental bound-

---

[1]The authors are indebted to John Duncan for helping us to gain access to Sequa Chemicals, and for his assistance with the development of this case study. This chapter could not have been written without his generous support and advice.

aries. Similarly, the performance of senior managers was measured in terms of their meeting functional business goals, but they, too, lacked a shared purpose and a collective set of performance criteria. As one might expect, the top group paid attention only to their individual performance objectives.

Like the rest of the senior management team, Hugh Smith, Sequa Chemicals' sales director, felt that they had an intense performance challenge facing the business. "We had a lack of product development," says Smith, "and some of our products weren't being made properly." The way product development occurred within Sequa inhibited its chemists, its engineers, its marketing and sales people from developing new skills, knowledge, and systems to help the company maintain a leadership position. As with many bureaucratic organizations, there was a lot of political infighting at Sequa. The head of Marketing protected Marketing's turf, the head of Manufacturing looked out for manufacturing interests, the head of Sales worried only about sales, and the head of Research concerned himself mainly with esoteric technical problems within the laboratory. Each functional head had a litany of reasons why the other functional heads were screwing things up, but none of them had any constructive advice or any motivation to improve their collective performance. For example, one functional head felt the R&D director wasn't decisive enough, but acted as a glorified administrator. Someone else felt the Marketing director envisioned himself as a sales whiz when he didn't really understand the industry. Another director told anyone in his vicinity that Sales was inept.

Jack Cabrey, a vice president in the parent organization and Sequa Chemicals' general manager, was tired of mediating disputes between the Sales, Marketing, Manufacturing, and R&D departments. The lack of cooperation and the inability of the senior management team to coordinate projects across functional boundaries to improve the whole business frustrated him. He also felt that Sequa needed to rethink its business strategy and organizational architecture. Cabrey was convinced that Sequa needed to blow away their functional barriers, organize around business processes, and democratize the organizational structure.

For a number of years Sequa was stuck in a performance rut. Discrete parts of the business were managing to thwart each other's performance goals. Cabrey wanted to shake Sequa's managers out of their complacency and redesign the entire enterprise to improve business performance. He decided to push for a bold new vision for growth. Sequa would expand its existing business, enter new markets, develop new products, and acquire new technologies.

Venturing Down the Design Pathway

Jack Cabrey, like every CEO, had to face the first question on the design pathway: Does my organization have a compelling purpose and business strategy? Cabrey had been sketching out a rough strategy, outlining a number of broad goals for the next two fiscal years. For Cabrey, the next challenge was for the Sequa Chemicals organization to develop the capability to implement such a bold strategy, which required breaking down the functional silos of the departments and dismantling the dominant management hierarchy. Cabrey was determined to lead the change.

Part of Cabrey's vision called for Sequa Chemicals to grow to be a $200-million company. Cabrey and his direct reports agreed that an innovative organizational design, coupled with new systems and capabilities, was needed to gain a competitive advantage in the industry. Unless product development was redesigned so that Marketing, R&D, Sales, and Manufacturing worked together, Sequa risked falling behind its competitors.

No amount of tinkering would help the old work system achieve Cabrey's vision for growing the business. The business challenge was clear: Sequa Chemicals needed to grow, but such growth required that everyone share and understand the vision. The bureaucratic structure with its traditional functional architecture needed to go, along with the political infighting among its senior managers.

Busting the Old Paradigm by Shaking Things Up

The next question Cabrey asked himself was: Am I comfortable with the limitations of a command-and-control organizational structure? Cabrey's answer was an emphatic No. Was he willing to embrace the design principle that leads to a new structure for self-management? Yes. Cabrey understood the design principle, and believed broad participation was the best way to build organizational capabilities. But what about his direct reports and Sequa's middle managers? How could Cabrey unfreeze the people below him? Command-and-control management was all that they knew; they didn't know anything else.

If Sequa tried to move forward into self-management cold turkey, the long legacy of its traditional functional design, which had bred its autocratic managers, would have strangled their efforts. Just like a long-time smoker trying to quit, for Sequa to give up the bureaucracy addiction wouldn't be easy. Jack Cabrey knew his direct reports could talk a good game about teams and pretend to work together in the privacy of senior management meetings. Nevertheless, all the classic negative behaviors we find in dominant hierarchies showed up when they went back each to his own functional silo.

"The only way to change the mindset of my leadership group was to sandwich them between my commitment to self-management and the high expectations I had built up in their subordinates for greater autonomy, cooperation, and responsibility," says Cabrey. He put the pressure on from above and from below. Cabrey established a sense of urgency by assigning his direct reports to work together on high-profile improvement projects. Cabrey identified several projects that crossed functional lines, and told each of the functional heads that they would all be held mutually accountable for results.

The idea was to expose senior managers' dysfunctional behavior to public scrutiny, even as they worked on projects to improve the business. Cabrey was a committed executive who saw his task as being to light the first fire on the path toward self-management. He would keep walking forward lighting fires until there was nowhere anyone could hide. Cabrey decided that each of the middle managers would get his feet wet in this way of working—by being part of an ad hoc self-managing group that would work together to solve complex problems.

For example, Cabrey asked a team of twelve people from Marketing, Research, Manufacturing, and Engineering to use their creativity and initiative to fix the longstanding problem of substandard materials. This team conferred with ninety people who had knowledge or resources that might be needed to solve the problem. Eight months later their efforts paid off. The reserve fund for products that didn't work was cut from $750,000 down to $350,000. And while they were doing this work together, their external consultant, John Duncan, coached them about the democratic design principles that they were using to be successful.

Jack Cabrey also looked for opportunities to give people greater autonomy, so that they could teach themselves about the business. For example, a new technology was acquired and brought into the company. It was initially kept separate from the departmental silos. Cabrey formed a team from Sales, Marketing, and Research to run this new business and said: "Figure out how to work together on incorporating this new technology into the business using the team concept." And they did.

Twice a month, Sequa's senior leadership group saw their consultant, John Duncan, in meetings where they continued to work together on projects that cut across functional boundaries. This hands-on, cross-functional project work provided the opportunity for transforming the leadership group into a genuine team. After the leadership team got its act together, Sequa's thirty-five middle managers were asked to join them in the process to open up information flows, engage in democratic dialogue, and begin to build a foundation of trust so that people across all the functions could work together.

In the beginning it was a breakthrough for middle managers just to be able to stay in the same room with their peers and work on common issues and problems in the plant. Middle managers questioned the effort. Why are we here? What's wrong with the way we have managed things? What is the purpose of this team stuff? Why is Sequa going to a team-based organization and how does it work? If I can't climb the management hierarchy any more, what is my future for advancement? After a lot of discussion, middle managers eventually came to let go of their attachment to the past, and started to work across boundaries.

For example, the Manufacturing manager was put in charge of waste minimization. He chartered a group of operators and plant personnel to meet ambitious goals to cut waste. When the team achieved its goals, the Manufacturing manager became a believer in the power of participation to improve the business. After a dozen more success stories using special project teams, Sequa's senior managers became convinced that self-management could work at an enterprise-wide level. Especially in Manufacturing, many managers became very interested in learning more, especially when, as a result of their success in reducing waste, they each earned a $1,000 net bonus, which was distributed just before Christmas.

At this point Sequa's change strategy delivered on its first objective: to gain the understanding and commitment of the senior management team and middle managers to growth goals and the value of designing a self-managing organization to achieve them. Cabrey was astute enough to avoid using a heavy-handed reengineering approach, which typically makes middle managers into whipping boys. Instead, he motivated them to put new technology and process-based designs in place.

Participative Design of R&D: The First Self-Managing Team at Sequa Chemicals

During the change effort, an unexpected turn of events arose. The director of R&D suddenly announced he would be leaving the company in seven months and suggested that R&D be used as a test site for self-management. Cabrey and the senior management team seized this opportunity, turning R&D into a test site for self-management. Instead of immediately replacing the director, chemists and key lab supervisors would be in charge of managing R&D, making them the first permanent self-managing team in Sequa Chemicals. Until then the R&D department had been organized as a typical bureaucracy, with a pecking order based on where people had earned their Ph.D.

To begin the redesign process, senior management selected twenty-five people—chemists and a number of representatives from functions that were internal suppliers and customers of R&D. These were the first people to go through the Participative Design process. Participants included all the chemists, some professionals from the analytical and application labs, representatives from Sales, Marketing, and Manufacturing, as well as all of the senior managers. They met in a two-day Participative Design session to redesign the structure and management of R&D.

"We mapped out the functions of technical leadership and decided six chemists and two lab supervisors would handle the management of R&D, as well as creating several liaison roles with the parent organization," says chief chemist Bernie North. The new design for R&D focused on two essential responsibilities. One area was concerned with administrative duties, while the other focused on the day-to-day technical work. A group of twelve chemists created and analyzed a detailed list of R&D tasks that needed to be performed routinely in the department, decided who would work on which things, and then split up the liaison roles. Individuals took on responsibilities based on their capabilities and interests. In less than six weeks, a team of eight people was managing R&D.

The entire management team was impressed with the quality of work and degree of cooperation demonstrated by the chemists both during and after the Participative Design session. As a specialty-chemical producer, Sequa was a chemist-oriented culture. It turned out that within the democratic learning environment of a Participative Design session, Sequa's knowledge workers were quite competent to make fact-based decisions.

However, political infighting had historically impeded their progress. Moving to self-management helped to reduce the power struggles within the unit, which led to better decisions for the whole business.

The entire senior management team enthusiastically sanctioned the self-managing work structure in R&D. They found that the Participative Design method got R&D's stakeholders to start rethinking how they would interface with R&D. Everyone who went through the process admits that the self-examination was painful, but well worth it. It resulted in the first truly self-managing work team at Sequa Chemicals. And the speed with which R&D went through the process embarrassed the top group, which had been struggling for over eighteen months to develop their own team.

With this taste of success and short-term win in place, Cabrey's vision for a democratic team-based organization became contagious and spread to other managers. The vast majority of Sequa's senior and middle managers became converts and advocates for the vision of operating Sequa as a self-managing enterprise. A clear choice had been made to transfer decision-making responsibility and authority from supervisors to teams of people performing the work.

Formulating the Participative Design Change Strategy

There were several design options for a change strategy that Cabrey and his management team considered. One option was to keep the functional organization intact. A Search Conference could be used to channel Cabrey's strategy into a business plan with a concrete set of goals and targets for each function. Following this, Participative Design sessions could then be used to build a team-based structure within the functions, with innovative linking mechanisms (run by groups of middle managers) to coordinate work across team and departmental boundaries. With this approach, mirror groups would be used in the PD sessions to generate more innovative designs to break functional mindsets.

The way mirror groups work is that homogeneous teams from one department come up with a best design for their own work. Then they switch design roles with a group from another department. The other department critiques their design and helps them improve it. This way, external feedback can help the people in the function that is being redesigned to question their assumptions and mental models and to consider options that they normally might not entertain because of functional biases. Designs can vary considerably from department to department within the same organization.

Another option that was considered was to move toward a process-based design, organized around self-managing teams. Instead of using a heavy-handed top-down approach with all the apparatus of employing steering committees and a single design team, consultant John Duncan helped senior executives and technical leaders to consider setting broad design parameters and orchestrating a highly Participative Design process of organizational learning. They wouldn't tell the employees what to do, but they would establish a set of minimal specifications—the big-picture design—within which employees could use their wisdom and creativity to come up with the most effective local designs. And teams would be free to keep tweaking their designs after they were up and running.

Sequa's managers had a lot of give-and-take dialogue, and decided on the latter option. All of Sequa's functions would be redesigned around business processes. First, Sequa's senior management team needed to do some high-level thinking and craft a clear strategic intent for the business. Then they could use a Search Conference to create a shared vision for the redesign effort. The management of those business processes would be put in the hands of self-managing teams composed of highly motivated, minimally supervised knowledge workers. Sequa managers chose a business-process orientation because they believed it would reinvigorate product development and make it possible to grow the business rapidly. Based on their prior personal experiences with self-management during the early stages of the change initiative, they were convinced and committed to redesign the entire enterprise to self-management.

Managing the Scope of the Participative Design Effort

Sequa's senior and middle managers were ready for Search Conferences and Participative Design because of their experience of practicing collective responsibility. Unfortunately, reality delayed the senior managers' ambitious goals for comprehensive whole-system change to self-management. Marketing, Sales, Purchasing, Finance, MIS, and other administrative functions were all moving to a new site. In addition, a number of managers were preoccupied with a large acquisition deal that was in the making. At the same time, raw-material prices began to skyrocket. In this context, redesigning the whole business all at once just didn't make sense. Senior managers decided to start with the most critical business process as the first area for redesign.

If only one business process were redesigned, Sequa's senior managers understood, financial results might be minimal compared to their vision. Why? If the business process team's internal customers and suppliers remained in a traditional hierarchy, it would create a confusing blend of bureaucracy and self-management. Bureaucracy would win in the end, sucking people back into dependency on management and killing the passion people had for their work. This scenario would cut into expected performance improvements and undermine the benefits of a process orientation.

The self-management concept gave Sequa a way to enlist everyone in understanding and being committed to an ambitious agenda for growing the business. In a self-managing organization people see themselves as business partners. "It made sense. I believed we could energize people by moving into complete business processes managed by empowered teams," says Cabrey, "and that it would make us more profitable."

Crafting a Strategic Intent

A critical mass of commitment and support for the self-management paradigm had now been obtained within Sequa's senior and middle management ranks. The next task was to scrutinize its business vision and develop a shared strategic intent. In this case, the Search Conference was used to translate Sequa's strategic intent into a plan for the Participative Design of its business processes.

Top-level managers began asking strategic questions about Sequa's businesses. They worked on forging a strategic-level design for gaining a significant competitive advantage, one that also provided the architecture within which the business processes would be redesigned. During several intensive sessions, managers began holding strategic conversations, asking hard questions like: What is the right business focus? Should we focus on customers, technology, products, or producing the product at a high volume? The department heads on Sequa's redesign team (all of its senior managers plus two facilitators from the cultural-change support group) struggled with whether to be technology-focused or customer-focused, finally deciding that being customer-focused was best for the business.

Sequa's challenge was to define the customers it intended to serve, the products to be delivered to each customer, and the processes that would optimize their ability to serve those customers. They asked: Are we currently serving the right customers? Delivering the right products? What are our customers' priorities? Is Sequa implementing the right business processes? Which processes are the critical ones?

Every business needs to be good at speed, service, quality, and providing customer value, but companies usually choose to place a stronger emphasis on one or two areas. Sequa's redesign team chose to emphasize customer service and superior research as its competitive anchors. Emphasizing superior research meant that product development was the most critical business process. Sequa's entire product development process—from front to back—would be the first target for redesign.

Given this choice, they began to ask questions about their source of competitive advantage. What makes us distinctive? What businesses are we in? What part of the past can be used as a pivot point to get to the future and what is just excess baggage? Where are the opportunities to redefine our market? Sequa's senior leaders spent several days discussing their mission. Who are we? What are the five or six fundamental trends in our industry that will help us find a strategic direction for the business?

Competitive advantage comes from those things that create distinctiveness within an established strategic direction. As Figure 9.1 shows,

THE FOUR CATEGORIES—"BUCKETS"—OF WORK

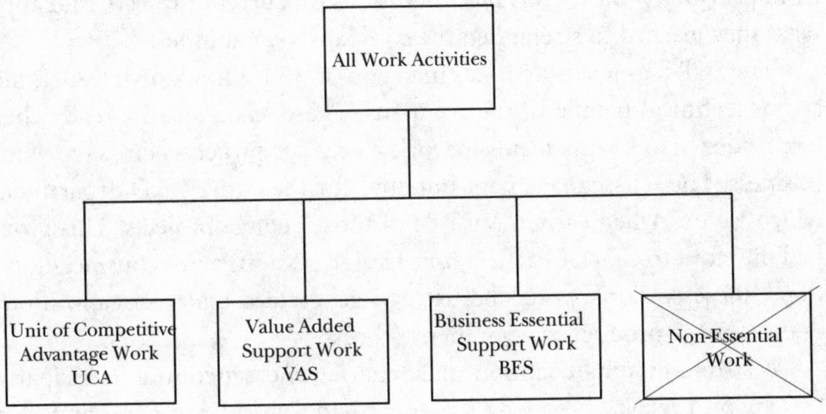

Figure 9.1

organizational capabilities can be put into four work buckets: (1) the work that creates a distinctive competitive advantage; (2) the work that supports and facilitates the business's competitive advantage activities; (3) the work that has to be done if the business is to continue to operate (much of which ends up outsourced); and (4) the work the business still does that used to be important but isn't anymore.

After a great deal of questioning and analysis, a high-level picture emerged and Sequa's source of competitive advantage became clear. Competitive advantage would come from focusing on a group of customers—monitoring their needs, developing products that satisfied those needs, and making sure customer loyalty and satisfaction were high. The support activities that were essential to achieve the competitive-advantage work were engineering development to improve production processes, manufacturing, product delivery, and service. The redesign of these activities to move from a bureaucratic functional structure to a self-managing organization would come after the competitive-advantage work was optimized.

The Search Conference and Participative Design Phase

A guiding coalition of twelve people was formed—the Sequa Chemicals Redesign Team (SCRT)—whose mission was first to orchestrate the redesign of product development. As we pointed out above, Sequa managers viewed product development as a leverage point to create new products, new processes, and new capabilities. They wanted to create a learning environment where people from many areas of the company could learn from previous projects, advance their skills on current projects, and apply what they learned to strengthen the company's capabilities.

The SCRT, as just noted, was made up of twelve functional leaders and senior technical people in the company. These leaders had already chartered a dozen or so task teams to work on change projects across the whole business. The self-management initiative for the entire R&D department, which we described earlier, was one of those change projects. This group had the clout to charter Participative Design sessions across business functions; these sessions would be used to generate a macro-organizational design for the product-development process.

A strong guiding coalition must charter and sanction a Participative Design process; its broad role is to provide vision, support, and clear boundaries for the change effort. Their role is not to impose a new design on the organization, as has been customary in Reengineering and STS efforts, but to establish the conditions within which redesign will occur. The SCRT's chartering process for the Participative Design effort is described below. In other words, SCRT's role at Sequa was to help orchestrate Participative Design sessions and Search Conferences within the company as a means of engaging participants in the redesign process.

Using Strategic Conversations to Create Management Alignment

No vision for change can succeed unless managers throughout the affected business fully understand and support the strategic thinking behind the redesign. Prior to the Search Conference, many of Sequa's managers didn't buy into the idea of fundamental structural change. Several were playing political games behind the scenes to prevent any dramatic changes in their own roles and responsibilities.

The redesign team decided to convene a Search Conference to create a vision for the future state of product development. Senior and middle managers would attend the conference to develop a new organizational architecture for conducting product development that would support their strategic objectives. Kirils Michailovs, the Manufacturing manager, saw a clear need for a product-development Search Conference. He states, "We needed to get out of these taller and taller, fatter and fatter silos where there was resistance to growth."

"All the key managers would be involved in crafting the high-level design," recalls Glen Pellet, director of environmental health and safety, "which means it stood a strong chance of succeeding." Wes Reid, the engineering manager, points out they didn't want to keep the functional orientation intact, as R&D had, because that would simply make the existing silos more rigid at a subsequent development process. "Our role was to figure out the blueprint or framework for invigorating new product development, which would become a model for what self-management was all about," says Reid.

Strategic thinkers from across the company were involved in the product development Search Conference. This included senior and middle-level managers from Accounting, Marketing, Sales, Information Systems, the business units, Environmental Health and Safety, Process Engineering, R&D, and Manufacturing. Their goal was to develop a plan for determining what product development ought to look like to be competitive in

OVERVIEW OF SCRT'S CHARTER FOR PARTICIPATIVE DESIGN OF PRODUCT DEVELOPMENT

Mission Statement

Redesign and implement an improved product-development process that will speed up the pace with which new products are developed at Sequa.

Goals

- Accelerate new product introductions.
- Create more employee ownership of product development.
- Create a development process which is more fluid, cooperative, and sane.
- Efficiently use the skills and talents of the workforce.

Scope

All employees involved in product development will participate. Customers should be consulted and involved as well. The president of the parent company will evaluate the results coming out of the redesign work and consider whether to encourage other parts of the company to explore this approach.

Constraints

The redesign effort cannot disrupt financial performance and existing operations. No new capital investments in new production capacity can be made until existing capacity is optimized.

Change Process Parameters

- No one will be laid off as a result of this process.
- Assume that your job is going to change and that it will change in a way that makes the best sense for the business.
- If you choose not to participate, then you've chosen to live with what everyone decides for you.
- The size and scope of participation in this project will be managed so that lab technicians can complete their work, people from manufacturing can de-bottleneck processes, and engineers can keep the plant up and running.
- Changes in the development process will be tested by continuous discussion with interdependent groups and our outside suppliers.
- Each of our overworked technical experts will be paired with someone to whom they can transfer their skills.
- We will use our new relational agreements to manage tension and rationalize conflict before it erupts into blame and recrimination.

the future and to outline broad parameters for the Participative Design process.

In the Search Conference, a dramatic turnabout occurred; twenty-nine key managers accepted responsibility for leading strategic change at Sequa. They were able to articulate an overall vision for product development and to develop and communicate to the employees a clear strategy for its redesign; they walked out of the conference with a shared set of strategic objectives (see sidebar below).

STRATEGIC GOALS FROM THE SEARCH CONFERENCE FOR REDESIGNING PRODUCT DEVELOPMENT

- Design an organizational structure that supports our market focus, and that places authority and responsibility at the lowest possible level. We will build a new way of working together, determine its overall goals and dimensions, and then let our people design how the parts will actually fit together.
- Accelerate new product introductions. Do that by generating 20 percent of our annual sales from new products or new markets developed in the last three years. Also by freeing up information flows around new product development.
- Achieve 10–15 percent annual sales growth with 25 percent gross profit, 8–10 percent pretax profit, and 25 percent return on net assets. We will increase our global presence, initiate two or more acquisitions, operate in multiple locations, and continue to pursue current projects.
- Make employees owners of the product-development process and involve everyone who will be in the new process in both the design of the process and the management of the process.
- Ensure regulatory compliance by employees in terms of permits, emission standards, and so on. Make safety a high priority, focus on waste minimization, and obtain ISO 9000 and 14000 certification.
- Create a compensation system that supports a team design by recognizing and rewarding all levels of performance.
- Vest authority and responsibility in separate business units instead of one functional organization. Encourage idea sharing and create conditions for entrepreneurship in the work environment.
- Optimize plant capacity by securing business that yields 10 percent margin over variable cost in underutilized manufacturing units.

Search Conference participants thought it was critical to achieve Sequa's growth objectives both with acquisitions and by strengthening product-development capabilities. They had a meaningful dialogue about what Sequa aspired to be—to both its customers and its employees. This high-involvement process produced a set of stretch goals that required fundamental structural change.

"The planning process gelled us into a real community, and enabled us to let go of our personal agendas in the interests of the whole business," recalls Wes Reid. Participants in the Search Conference realized that if they didn't act quickly, Sequa was going to fall behind its competitors. "The laggards among our managers became believers in the need for change," notes James Craig, the manufacturing engineer. "We don't have diametrically opposed goals anymore," he added, "where if this function wins, then mine will have to lose. Now we have goals we all support which are cross-functional and directed toward growth."

After the Search Conference, those who participated, as well as those whose roles would change as a result of the redesign, would be involved in Participative Design sessions. This amounted to over a hundred people. Participative Design sessions were then conducted with these people to do the micro-level design work. They would apply their more detailed personal knowledge of the product-development process to improve the work flow, cut cycle time, and enhance teamwork.

Preparing the Organization for Redesign

The redesign team prepared a fact sheet to give the employee community an overview of what was about to take place. It set forth:

1. why Sequa Chemicals needed to redesign product development.
2. who was on the redesign team and the team's mission.
3. Sequa Chemicals' newly established strategic intent.
4. the major objectives senior management hoped to achieve by redesigning product development.
5. an overview of the Search Conference and Participative Design approaches.

In the Search Conference, Sequa's senior managers learned how to cooperate across the white spaces. They learned from first-hand experience what it really meant to become a high-performance self-managing team, where each member was deeply committed to the success of the whole. Senior managers now knew that they needed to be mutually accountable to each other in order to achieve dramatic results that crossed business-unit boundaries.

"There is a sense of great joy and pride. We are now able to work together," says Jack Cabrey, "and we amazed ourselves with the clarity of our goals for improving product development and the broad commitment we have to achieve them." Indeed, Sequa's managers felt that a major bene-fit coming out of the Search Conference was that it enabled them to tran-scend their egos, political agendas, and ladder-climbing ambitions. The intensity and seriousness of the event provided the alchemy for them to become a high-performance team. "The search process allowed the silos to fall apart," says senior chemist Larry Boss. Jim Craig stressed that they had finally developed a community when people saw they all had the same fears about survival. It allowed them to set their self-interests and compet-itive strivings aside in order to work for the common good of the company.

During this series of strategic conversations, managers learned several important lessons: One, they didn't have to rely exclusively on Jack Cabrey for their marching orders. Two, they could set collective performance goals and then roll up their sleeves to do the work to achieve them. Managers didn't need to work on all the strategic initiatives together, as one big group. Various sub-teams were formed, where the best mix of skills and competencies determined membership—not one's position in the hierar-chy. They also learned to rely on their collective wisdom and expertise, and not just the thoughts of the influential high flyers and internal experts.

Translating Strategic Design into a Business Process Design

Following the Search Conference, a series of six consecutive Participative Design sessions were held to develop a comprehensive redesign of product development. Over a hundred people participated in the process. Kim Deacon, the graphics business unit manager, had this to say about the Participative Design process: "I was initially very skeptical that the self-management concept would fly. I didn't trust that chemists, engineers, and business people would be able to see eye to eye, and thought people would still cling to their own separate agendas." Deacon went on to add, "I became convinced this was going to work during the Search Conference and Participative Design sessions. The quality of effort and thought everyone was putting into that exercise showed me their concerns and desires were congruent with mine. I'm not sure I could ever trust the chemists to have the perspective to look at the broad marketplace for our products and figure out the market niche to go after. But in the context of designing their own work, they sure as hell knew what to do. People really can be trusted to contribute to the redesign of the product development process as long as all the relevant parties are also included in the design effort."

It turns out that Deacon was one of the winners, as he became a manager of the graphics business unit. Deacon says a change of this magnitude usually presents problems during implementation. However, with this effort, Deacon felt people were very accepting of the collective decision-making process, as everyone moved into the new design in a matter of weeks, with very little resistance. Deacon argues, "If the Senior Management Team or Jack Cabrey had imposed the same exact design, we would all be carping about gaps and having turf battles and things wouldn't be working so incredibly well." Reflecting on his own learning as a result of the experience, Deacon said, "Maybe it seems simple to say this, but it was really profound learning for me as a manager. Involve everyone, give them an honest say, incorporate their ideas in the design, and you will always get better buy-in. Before I would have said: Save yourself some time and tell them what to do. The nice thing about Participative Design is it allows you to rapidly create effective designs so we can keep changing to make sure the organization is aligned with the business strategy."

It was very powerful for Sequa's managers to witness over a hundred people from all over the business working together on a new design for product development. A new organizational structure was developed that resulted in an effort more focused on the needs of the industries they serve. Product development was redesigned into paper, graphics, textiles, export and specialty polymer business units. Each business unit would draw upon various support groups—R&D, Engineering, HR, Information Systems, Manufacturing, Purchasing, Environmental, and Accounting. Each business unit also identified the skill sets Sequa needed, and project leadership, marketing, chemistry, and sales roles were defined. The new design organized groups into teams, eliminating the dominant hierarchy and the traditional role of management.

The Sequa Chemicals Redesign Team took this basic structure and chose managers and core team members for each business unit. Core team members were selected according to their level of demonstrated skills and knowledge as identified in the Participative Design sessions, as well as by senior management's assessments of an individual's capabilities. In addition, the SCRT also required that core team members possess the following competencies:

1. a results orientation.
2. orientation toward teamwork and cooperation.
3. experience managing resources—money, people, technology.
4. interpersonal communication skills.
5. attitude that seeks to understand others.
6. analytical and conceptual thinking.
7. capacity for innovation.

Once they had selected the Business Unit Directors and core team members for each business unit, the SCRT sent them off to further develop their charter, team structure, workflow, resource needs, membership requirements, and work plan. Following this, the core teams met with the SCRT two months later to negotiate their final structure and membership. The SCRT also created a new position, the product-development business coordinator, who was accountable for the front-to-back performance of the entire product development process.

On the surface, the design Sequa implemented looks similar to a Michael Hammer–inspired process-based design, but looks can be deceiving. Most process-based designs that result from Reengineering efforts still retain the infrastructure of a dominant hierarchy. There is no trace of a dominant hierarchy to be found in Sequa Chemicals' process-based design: the Sales, Marketing, and R&D departments were dissolved. This is the beauty of Participative Design: it lays out a clear organizational choice between either sticking with Design Principle 1 and the dominant hierarchy that comes with it, or choosing to implement Design Principle 2, fundamentally restructuring to become self-managing.

Reflecting back on the transformation process to self-management, Jack Cabrey notes, "As a result of the organizational changes we've made, people have more enthusiasm, ownership, and have accomplished the goals of more rapid product development and customer service. These are the goals we needed to achieve to be more successful. This is a never-ending process. Constant change in our competitive environment will cause us to modify our strategic objectives every year; consequently, design, too, will have to change so it can remain aligned with the strategy. With these approaches we have learned how to do that in a way that minimizes disruptions to the business and still achieves breakthrough thinking."

The Chartering Process

The chartering process is where the redistribution of responsibility for control and coordination actually occurs. In other words, here managerial power is transferred from traditional supervisors to self-managing teams. This is where the rubber meets the road, enabling self-management to take root. In this case the chartering process was used to set the context for redesign. It also was used to make sure teams were set up so they could succeed.

The result of Participative Design sessions is a new organization design, usually one that calls for the implementation of self-managing, team-based structures. Transitioning the organization into a self-managing structure is the most critical step in the Participative Design process. The chartering process formalizes the shift to a self-managing structure. Through the chartering process, core teams are assured the authority to make the changes necessary to bring about genuine self-management. The core teams are made of up middle managers who function as implementing sponsors.

The chartering process is used with all formal teams. The role of the implementing sponsors is to generate a charge for the new team which is treated as a draft to start the chartering process. The charge usually includes the team mission, goals, scope and constraints, core roles, and target date to complete the charter. The outline of the charter serves as their agenda for the first twenty-four hours of their time together. The detailed design of workflows and task details happens immediately after the implementing sponsor approves the charter. There are ten contractual agreements that the team will form in negotiation with the implementing sponsors.

The chartering tasks used at Sequa Chemicals are described in more detail below.

Mission. The mission describes the unique contribution the team will make to the whole business that no other group will provide. It usually is described in a brief sentence. If desired, the team may also add a sentence or two that captures how they intend to operate. It is best, however, to keep

CHARTERING PROCESS TASKS

- MISSION
- EXPECTED OUTPUTS DELIVERED TO INTERNAL AND EXTERNAL CUSTOMERS
- GOALS, AND MEASURABLE OBJECTIVES FOR EACH
- SCOPE, BOUNDARIES, AND CONSTRAINTS
- RELATIONAL AGREEMENTS
- ROLES
- REPORTING RELATIONSHIPS AND STRUCTURE
- OPEN ISSUES AND THEIR PRIORITIES
- WORKPLAN AND SCHEDULE
- PERFORMANCE MANAGEMENT PROCESS

the mission to one sentence for clarity. The remainder of the charter will describe in more detail how the team intends to operate.

Expected Outputs Delivered to Internal and External Customers. Based on process maps of the primary and secondary business processes that the team will control, a list of the expected outputs from the team are described and defined. This list describes the normal expected outputs that will be delivered on a routine basis. Some of these will be only for the team's internal use, others will be delivered downstream to internal customer teams or groups, while the remaining outputs will be delivered to external customers of the business. Teams will also develop outputs that deliver feedback to their suppliers.

Goals and Measurable Objectives. Goals are stretch statements related to the team's expected outputs. They are statements of the special attention the team will give to improving its performance in select output areas. Not all outputs will have goals. Only those areas where improvements are needed or desired should be addressed. Teams usually have limited resources, which means they must be focused on delivering all their expected outputs, while devoting special attention to areas that are in need of continuous or exceptional improvement. Too often teams are expected to generally improve everything, and then nothing receives exceptional attention, which is why significant step changes never occur.

High-performance teams focus on a few outputs to produce exceptional results. Each goal should be stated in an output form: the deliverable that will occur as a result of the team's exceptional attention. Each goal will have one or more measurable objectives, breaking the overall goal down into interim milestones. Some goals may have a target date of completion of three months, while others will be of longer range. Objectives are milestone deliverables that are achievable in three months or less. This allows the team to be clear about the parts of the goal that are useful so they can closely monitor their progress.

Scope, Boundaries, and Constraints. "Scope" describes the span of control that the team is empowered to manage. Within the scope, the team is authorized to control and coordinate their designated resources as they choose. "Boundaries" are additional statements describing the team's overlaps with other teams or working groups, and where its authority ends as another team's begins. "Constraints" are those things the team must live with, and which they cannot change unless approved by their implementing sponsors.

Relational Agreements. Relational agreements are statements about the way each team member expects to be treated by his or her peers. They are positive descriptions of the behavior desired from team members to keep them from falling into any of the relationship traps that can occur in teams. This section addresses the way this group of people will behave in order to be an effective task community. When creating this list of agreements, it is good to start by listing all the possible areas where the team could underperform. Then a positive statement is drafted of the behaviors that will enable the team to avoid these traps.

Roles. *Common roles* cover what all the team members will do together, listing the kind of decisions they will make primarily through consensus. *General roles* are those that two or more, but not all, of the members will be accountable for delivering to the team. *Specific roles* are those deliverables to be provided to the team by individuals. Role statements should be in the form of deliverables, or outputs, that leave the hands of one team member and go into the hands of others, either inside or outside the team. It is not enough to merely list activities or groups to which the member belongs, because such a list lacks the clarity of deliverables which will allow the team to manage their performance well.

Reporting Relationships and Structure. The reporting relationship and structure clearly delineates where the control and coordination of the individual and collective work is to be done. There will be a distribution of responsibility within and between teams, working groups, and individuals. It is important to have a picture of what this looks like, as well as statements about who does whose performance appraisal, who does the hiring and firing for the team, and who controls budget-line items. These tasks determine the scope and boundaries of authority, and thus these statements should be made very clear and available to the team and its other key stakeholders. This allows the team to be clearly empowered by its implementing sponsor.

Open Issues and Priorities. From the beginning of the chartering process, a list of open issues is generated. This is where the team learns the skills for determining the most important things to work on. Issues that arise in conversation which are not immediately relevant to the current topic, or that are contentious and cannot be resolved, are captured on a common, cumulative list of open issues. In addition, after the roles and reporting relationships have been agreed upon, then work activities are prioritized and assignments are made. Anything that is not directly related to a goal or an output is probably nonessential work and is eliminated. The items remaining have to be prioritized in terms of resources available. The criteria for high-priority items are derived directly from the team's mission, goals, and outputs. Other criteria such as a sense of urgency, team capabilities, and willingness to work on items also come into play here.

Workplan and Schedule. Each objective is a section in the workplan. Each top priority issue is broken down into its key tasks or major events, the primary leader responsible, the other people that need to be involved, the target date for completion of the task or event, and the measures of its completion. A schedule of the team's resources, which they control, is then added. Two key elements are rationalized: the critical path of tasks and the availability of scarce resources—people, equipment, or facilities.

Performance Management Process. This consists of targets and measures for each objective and output: who does what, when it will be achieved, and the performance standards expected. There are also descriptions of how interventions to correct poor performance conditions will be made. This section also describes how people will be recognized and rewarded.

The chartering process assures senior and middle management that a laissez-faire mode can be avoided when they transfer control to self-managed teams. The appropriate level of responsibility and accountability is relocated within teams so that control is maintained in the system.

Following the Participative Design sessions, this was a relatively straightforward process at Sequa. It took only twenty-four hours for participants to go through the entire chartering process. If there is management resistance to broad-based empowerment at this point, it is usually because a crucial step on the design pathway may have been excluded or poorly handled. On occasion we have seen management cycle back to a previous step in the design pathway to work through issues, usually emotional ones having to do with their perceived loss of authority.

PREPARING MANAGERS EMOTIONALLY FOR PARTICIPATIVE DESIGN

As we described in Chapter 7, the challenge of Microsoft's rapid-strategy-creation process was to develop a five-year plan for the Consumer Products Division in order to stay ahead of changes in the business environment. Unlike Sequa, Microsoft had less need to redistribute decision-making authority because it had already empowered its employees to be full participants in project-oriented work. Yet some managers at Microsoft needed coaching in the early stages of the strategy-creation process, because they could foresee that a radical shift in strategy was going to create a need for an entirely different organization. Despite its culture of participation, Microsoft's senior product managers were initially uneasy about involving so many people in developing a strategy, and had to be reassured that things would not get out of control. Sequa's "Cultural Change Support Team" acted as an internal support group for managers and employees who needed help in making the emotional shift to a self-managing organization. They used a "stages of change" model to identify which managers would need this kind of one-on-one support.

Some people will need assistance to move out of negative perceptions (denial, anger, bargaining, and depression) into more positive perceptions (doubt, anxiety, renewed hope, and acceptance). When people are both aware of a change and can accept it, they are able to prepare for it. On the other hand, if people stay frozen in negative perceptions, they aren't ready to participate in the organizational learning that transpires in Participative Design sessions and Search Conferences.

Remember our earlier point on the importance of unlearning. It is very, very difficult for certain individuals to let go of their fundamental beliefs about how organizations should be designed and managed—especially if they are supervisors or middle managers. It's really hard not to be thinking: "Oh my God, what does this mean for me in my organization and for my position?" It isn't easy to say to a supervisor or manager, "You are justifiably going to feel nervousness, but you've got to believe what is going to come out of this is going to be really positive." Some managers need help to see that they won't get a great result unless they let go of all their notions about how it "should be."

When self-management is a foreign concept, management preparation becomes even more mission critical. Sequa Chemicals' change process was a much greater assault on management sensibilities than Microsoft's. Participative Design at Sequa would require a great deal of structural change, moving away from a traditional dominant hierarchy and functional hands-off approach toward a self-managing, process-based organization. Sequa's strategic design called explicitly for a process-based organization, intended to catalyze the democratization of their entire enterprise.

There were powerful people in both the senior and middle management ranks at Sequa who had strong personal and political stakes in keeping the existing organizational structure intact. Without a considerable amount of pre-work toward changing management beliefs, Sequa's efforts to redesign product development would have had little chance of success. That's why Sequa spent over a year helping its managers practice self-management and mutual accountability by having them work on ad-hoc improvement projects. This prepared them to grapple with radical changes in the design of work and the distribution of authority. Other organizations will be at different stages of experience and readiness for self-management.

The awareness stage of a change is primarily an emotional one, which is often ignored or poorly managed in change projects. If most managers are in the awareness stage of change, that is *not* a time to provide rational information and knowledge. If the awareness stage is mismanaged, many people will continue to have negative energy concerning the change. This is the time for them to speak their minds publicly, rather than choosing private withdrawal into resistance and possible sabotage.

For example, early on, Sequa held dialogue meetings, which created an organizational learning community, for the four levels of management in the traditional hierarchy. Some forty-seven managers engaged in dialogue; any managers who felt compelled to speak could join in the conversation and share their perspective with the senior management team. This process reduced resistance to the change.

Once Sequa's people were clearly in the acceptance stage about the move toward self-management, they were ready for more detailed education and emotionally prepared for what would be required for it to succeed. Wayne Byers, a shift supervisor at Sequa, commented on his surprise when he saw department heads going through the same unlearning struggle as everyone else: "Just like a supervisor tries to hold on to the supervisor role, department heads try to hang on to their department. Nothing builds greater trust and support more than seeing a highly respected person like Jack Cabrey or Mike Yanutola going through the same pain you are going through."

PARTICIPATIVE DESIGN COMBINES TOP-DOWN AND BOTTOM-UP APPROACHES

Crafting strategy and redesigning work have been thought of as either top down or bottom up in their approach. However, Microsoft and Sequa demonstrate the importance of combining both top-down and bottom-up approaches into highly participatory frameworks that get the best thinking from each level of management and all the employees throughout the organization. The top and middle management at Sequa unleashed their creativity in the strategic-design process by blowing apart the way they had previously thought about product development. They were able to see eye-to-eye and reach a collective strategic vision. With the strategic considerations in place, operational design could flow directly from the bottom up, by tapping into the more detailed knowledge of people who were directly involved in product development.

In 1996, shortly after the product development redesign, Sequa Chemicals had its most profitable year on record. This was primarily due to the redesign effort, which allowed closer scrutiny by those closest to the work process to ensure that the product-mix changes made were those that led to higher profit margins. Raw-materials choices were also key decisions that involved keeping abreast of timely price changes. Empowered teams were able to make diligent purchasing decisions that reduced the raw-materials costs.

Glen Pellet, a member of Sequa's senior management team, discovered an important point about timing when contemplating a move toward self-management. "A year ago, the Search Conference and Participative Design sessions would have been a complete failure. We needed time to develop trust. The struggles the senior management team went through, and then all the managers, were important learning stages on our road away from command and control. Those efforts built a sense of community and a belief in the power of democratic principles. If you want to do this work, look around and find some business challenges to tackle. Involve a lot of people in tackling them. You'll discover an order of magnitude of result that is better than simply trying to manage by issuing edicts and directives. Coming to that realization takes a lot of time. Once you've reached it, then Participative Design will be effective for you. Otherwise, expect to be disappointed."

In the past, operational design was primarily focused on exerting tight managerial control by breaking tasks into their component parts and defining jobs as narrowly as possible. More recently, the design of work processes has placed a greater emphasis on sequences of activities that, taken together, create a customer-focused product or service, rather than a functional orientation. At the level where the work actually takes place, these new operational designs organize around complete business processes. The goal is to shift all the value-adding work toward a process orientation.

Sequa Chemicals' operational design goes beyond this to incorporate self-managing teams at every level. What can we learn by reflecting back on Sequa's efforts to democratize the organizational structure? Shifting from a dominant hierarchy to a self-managing structure is like trying to solve a jigsaw puzzle without ever having seen the picture on the puzzle box. Sequa's first initiative was to create a compelling business vision and collectively realize that it couldn't be achieved with the existing traditional bureaucratic hierarchy, functional design, and autocratic management practices in place.

In the beginning, the focus was on democratizing the senior management team. The key was to shift managers' roles away from individual accountability for their departments to collective accountability for common business goals. There were no team-building sessions, outdoor adventure courses, or any sort of touchy-feely sessions. Instead, John Duncan, Sequa's external consultant, recommended the use of project teams, task forces, and other ad-hoc groups to give senior and middle management some *real work* where they could practice collective accountability. Duncan provided just-in-time education at the point in a collective task when these managers were struggling and most open to change. The moment of truth occurred when the R&D department was redesigned to be completely self-managing, without a technical director. This demonstrated the power of a high-involvement process like Participative Design.

The product development Search Conference provided a strategic context, the border of Sequa Chemicals' picture frame. Product development was the first of ten business processes to be redesigned. The strategic goals that were established in the Search Conference gave them a clear direction. Sequa wanted to be a market-focused organization, one where authority and responsibility would be put in the hands of people with critical expertise. In the Search Conference, Sequa's senior management team learned firsthand how to work as a self-managing team. As a result, Sequa Chemicals is in the process of transforming its entire management structure and workforce to operate in a self-managing mode.

The Evolution Toward Self-Management Continues

A year later, a second Search Conference was convened to identify and plan the future state of the other business processes within the company. During that Search Conference, participants realized they needed more detailed analysis of existing workflows, and more time to redesign business processes to produce the best possible designs. Small groups of five to twenty-five people were chartered to create process maps that described whole pieces of work (defined by time, territory, or technical boundaries). Each design group looked at its own work and the outputs they needed to achieve. The goal was to integrate the work of all these separate groups into a detailed process map for the whole business.

Later that year town-hall meetings were held every six weeks for two to four hours with the entire employee population. Emerging process maps from all of the various design groups were discussed, tweaked, massaged, and validated through intensive dialogue. Eventually an integrated process map was created, the "Desired Business Process Accomplishments," for the

Units of Competitive Advantage and Value Added work. Focusing on business accomplishments for the whole system generated the workflows to achieve them. This essentially prepared participants to do more detailed structural redesign work in the upcoming Participative Design sessions.

In February of 1998, Sequa Chemicals held two Participative Design sessions to redesign the whole business. In order to keep the plant up and running, half of the employees in the plant would attend the first session, and then the other half would attend the second session. The first two-day Participative Design session involved 120 people and the second involved 110 people. Participants were captivated by the design process. Hourly workers were engaged in vigorous debate with engineers concerning issues that had been the engineers' sacred domain for years. Now everyone's voice mattered. Tables were arranged seating ten or eleven people, to maximize diversity and stimulate organizational learning. At any given table, people from all departments and functions—senior managers, first-line supervisors, staff professionals, clerks, and hourly workers—sat together to discuss substantive design issues.

The theme of the first day was "What's in it for me? Why should I participate in this change?" Here's where people took their blinders off and started to see beyond their roles into the inner workings of the whole business. One participant described the experience as just-in-time training in business literacy, commenting, "I am beginning to understand how this place really works." This experience made it possible for people who had been resisters to be willing to view the business as a whole. At their small tables, people analyzed the detailed process map and began grouping together whole pieces of work, combining tasks that were interdependent into structural work units.

During the first day of the session, the room itself was configured and arranged as a mirror of the process map for Business Essential work. People whose roles were to perform Business Essential work met in small groups to identify and define process accomplishments for their work. These groups identified how tasks would need to be redesigned to provide whole jobs for people, identified key interdependent work flows, and then designed structural units around business processes.

By the end of the Participative Design session, groups had to agree to one design for all of the business processes. For example, various small groups met together to combine and integrate their design ideas. These integrative designs were posted on walls in a large conference room, allowing everyone to walk around and examine them. Negotiators from each table decided which tables would combine to merge their respective designs that had been posted on the wall. Eventually, only two main design options remained. The entire group reconvened to understand the differences and similarities between the two design options. The "treasures" people wanted to retain from both designs were put on one list, and the key differences between the designs were put on another list. The community debated the differences, and the pro's and con's of each design, and creatively resolved their differences, agreeing on a final structural design.

Unresolved differences, and other considerations, were handed over to the Redesign Integration Team, which was entrusted by the group to decide how to handle any remaining issues. Obviously a lot of time and energy was devoted to coming to a large group consensus on a final design. Typically, Participative Design sessions are held with groups of twenty-five to thirty people, not hundreds. In this case, another day was set aside to bring people back together to deal with implementation issues, and to develop changes for their new structural units. This follow-up session included having groups work on defining their mission, setting work unit goals, and defining the scope of team authority and core member roles.

Reflecting on the design process, one senior manager noted, "Well, we were looking to empower the workforce, and we sure did it. All the dialogue that went on had everyone's full attention and created some real passion for the future of this business." This, in a nutshell, is what Participative Design is all about.

CHAPTER 10

DESIGNING THE SELF MANAGING ORGANIZATION

The Transformation of Syncrude Canada

> Not the autocracy of a single stubborn melody on the
> one hand. Nor the anarchy of unchecked noise on the
> other. No, a delicate balance between the two; an
> enlightened freedom.
>
> —Johann Sebastian Bach

Located near Fort McMurray in northern Alberta, Syncrude Canada Ltd. was created during the 1970s, as a joint venture among several oil companies and governments, to mine oil from the Athabasca oil sands. Syncrude operates the largest oil-sands crude-oil production facility in the world, producing over 12 percent of Canada's total oil requirements. The Athabasca oil sands in northeastern Alberta have 307 billion barrels of recoverable oil—more than all the known reserves in Saudi Arabia, and enough to meet Canada's energy needs for centuries.

Syncrude is a one product company: it produces a light, sweet synthetic crude oil known as Syncrude Sweet Blend. Innovation is geared toward doing one thing—producing that oil—and doing it better, faster, and cheaper. The key business drivers are safety, operating costs, production volume, and reliability. In 1989, Syncrude employed 4,700 people and subcontracted its noncore work to an additional 350 different unionized contractors, employing an additional 2,000 people on site. Today, Syncrude has 3,500 employees and an average of 1,000 maintenance contractors.

The company mines oil sand from a surface mine, extracts the raw oil, or bitumen, using steam and hot water, and upgrades it into crude oil by fluid coking, hydroprocessing, hydrotreating, and reblending. The final product is sent down a pipeline to three Edmonton-area refineries and to pipeline terminals that ship it to refineries in eastern Canada and the United States.

In this chapter we illustrate some of the innovative ways in which Syncrude accomplished a large-scale Participative Design restructuring of their entire operation. We will highlight the close relationship between strategic design and the operational design process.

Top Management Decides to Support Participative Design

In 1978, when Syncrude began production, its executives decided to create the most innovative form of work organization available. The entire operation was set up in a team format, with pay for skills and minimal supervision. However, supervisors didn't stay long enough to transfer their skills

---

The Syncrude operation is divided into four major areas: Mining, Extraction, Upgrading, and Utilities. The power plant is capable of supplying electricity for a community of 300,000. Every day 400,000 tons of ore are mined and processed. Since the mine opened in 1978, more soil has been moved than was required for the Great Wall of China, the Suez Canal, the Great Pyramids, and the ten largest hydroelectric dams in the world combined.

Four hundred thousand tons of oil sands produce 200,000 tons of a strange black tarry syrup known as bitumen. Extracting the oil from the sand is a complex technical process. First, all the overburden and topsoil is cleared and set aside for future land reclamation. Draglines (each is twenty-five stories high; the bucket is the size of a two-car garage), trucks (loaded with ore weighing as much as a Boeing 747), and hydrotransports move the actual oil sands.

The raw oil sand passes through large tumblers, where it is mixed with hot water and steam to produce an oil-sand slurry. The slurry is sent to settling vessels, where the bitumen floats to the surface as froth. At another site, the water is removed and the concentrated bitumen enters the Upgrading plant as a mixture of naphtha, water, and bitumen. The naphtha is removed and recirculated. The bitumen is processed through either the cokers or the LC-Finer, and then through the secondary-process units, where it is upgraded into a light sweet crude.

to teams, and technicians left at an alarming pace, undermining team integrity. When turnover reached 36 percent in 1980, management jumped in to restore order by installing a good, solid command-and-control system. Senior managers hired strong-willed supervisors and technicians, whose crisis-management skills stabilized the faltering organization.

Ralph Shepherd, Syncrude's CEO in the late 1980s, had been plant manager of an Exxon facility in Rotterdam; there he guided a highly successful redesign effort that created a team-based workforce. Shepherd piloted a redesign at Syncrude's electric utilities plant in 1986, at a time when business improvements were needed.

Unfortunately, the Utilities redesign bogged down, taking three years to implement, and was a disappointment in management's eyes. As with most expert-driven designs, a design team received a good deal of training, spending over a year in isolation figuring out how things *should* work in great detail. The approach focused on the social side of work, providing every employee three weeks of training in human relations skills—meeting effectiveness, teamwork, conflict management, and so on.

Syncrude learned that when a design team was placed in the expert role and made responsible for changing everyone's job, it was less able to generate enough excitement and ownership to drive implementation and diffusion of the new design. Even worse, the three hundred people in the Utilities organization resisted the new design and delayed its implementation.

This episode convinced Syncrude's senior management to find a design approach without the cost and long cycle time, one that would be simpler, would be more user friendly, and would produce good business results. Shepherd's consultant in Rotterdam, Hans van Beinum, was now running a management institute in Canada; he recommended that Shepherd hire Don de Guerre. De Guerre's prior expertise with Participative Design, along with his political skills in helping management lead large-scale change, would be instrumental in making change happen at Syncrude. De Guerre's task was to build a capable group of internal consultants and to work with Syncrude's executive group with processes for improving business performance and productivity.

The Business Case for Participation Design

Syncrude was in a tough spot. The cost of producing a barrel of oil had to be brought down to be competitive with traditional petroleum companies.

The only way this could be accomplished was by improving efficiencies in Syncrude's operating departments: Mining, Extraction, and Upgrading.

Ralph Shepherd believed that changing Syncrude over to a self-managing organization was one way to respond more effectively to oil-price volatility. He had seen impressive results generated at the Rotterdam refinery when a compliance organization was redesigned for high commitment.

Improvements had to come directly from the workforce, since there were not going to be any technical or economic changes to bail out Syncrude's long-term future. Syncrude was operating on $80 to $90 million of annual investment, just enough to maintain its baseline. No capitalization projects could be foreseen on the horizon.

Participative Design Produces Dramatic Results

Between 1989 and 1995, production of crude oil shot up from 54 to 74 million barrels of oil per year. The cost of producing one of those barrels of oil dropped to $13.69 Canadian. At the same time, total workforce productivity (thousands of barrels per employee) shot up by 76 percent (see Table 10.1 below).

These results can be attributed to the massive cultural-change effort that involved over 2,500 employees directly in a Participative Design process. The new high-performance organization—which Syncrude's employees designed themselves—is making everyone act like they are owners of the business. And that isn't just rhetoric. The new design insti-

Table 10.1 Results Achieved Through Participative Design at Syncrude Canada (Canadian currency)

Measure	1989 (before PD)	1995 (after PD)		1997	
Production (Mbbls)	54	74	↑37%	76	↑40%
Revenue ($M)	$1174	$1764	↑50%	$2107	↑79%
Operating Costs (as spent $/bbl)	$17.17	$13.69 $US 9.90	↓20%	$13.78	↓20%
Workforce	4,704	3,672	↓22%	3,513	↓26%
Productivity (Mbbls)	11,500	20,200	↑76%	21,550	↑84%

tuted a gainsharing compensation program, which distributes 30 percent of the economic gains that exceed a budget baseline. Now executives see that even more is possible. Syncrude's goal for the year 2000 is to drive down the production cost of a barrel of oil to $12.00 Canadian.

"Today, the men and woman of Syncrude think and act like they own the business," says Eric Newell, Chairman and CEO of Syncrude Canada, "and with the recent royalty trust offerings, many of them do." Newell goes on to say, "We truly have created a culture that fully engages people and motivates them toward realizing our vision. And, very importantly, we try to give them the tools they need to succeed. That's how we've brought our costs down so impressively, how we've made big strides in technology development, how we've lessened our impacts on the environment, and how we'll continue to make progress in all these areas—by directly involving our people in creating solutions."

What is even more remarkable is that the productivity gains at Syncrude were achieved with fewer people, and with the technology already existing throughout the site. And the redesign process was handled in a very humane way. As Eric Newell promised in one of his site-wide meetings with employees before the redesign effort was launched: "No one will lose their job as a result of Participative Design. Some people will lose their positions and roles, but there will always be a place for people willing to change, adapt, and increase their knowledge and skills. However, there is no place here for people who want to resist change and maintain the status quo." This promise was essential, not only to gain employee commitment to the redesign effort, but also to ensure that they would be willing to eliminate non-value-added work. Overall, between 1989 and 1995 the workforce was reduced by 21 percent, mostly through attrition and early retirement programs.

Overcoming the Inertia of Success

In 1990 there was little sense of urgency for change. Syncrude was doing well, but senior management had the foresight to keep moving the organization forward. Historically, in order to attract and keep good people in Fort McMurray, which can be quite a harsh environment in the winter, Syncrude paid its workers and supervisors particularly well. Employees were provided opportunities they couldn't get in any other organization. Northern Canada has seven months of winter that mimic the severe weather patterns found on the summit of Mount Washington—the cold-est, windiest place in the continental United States.

Syncrude's workforce perceived a secure future ahead of them. After all, in their eyes, Syncrude was sitting on black gold. Syncrude employees worked in an operation that historically had always made money. Every year they broke their previous production records; they lived in a bubble econ-omy where Fort McMurray was always booming. Even when the national economy was in the tank, Syncrude technicians with high-school educa-tions were earning good money. Life was good. It wasn't going to be easy to raise the sense of urgency for change.

Raising the Level of Urgency

In this uncertain environment, Syncrude Canada's senior management developed a new vision and a values statement: "Securing Canada's Energy Future with the vision to lead, the knowledge to succeed, the commitment to do better, and the heart to win the race. We will achieve this by encour-aging learning in everything we do; pushing the limits of what technology can accomplish; working together to make Syncrude the best place to work. In this way we will be safe, reliable, and profitable and all of our stakeholders will want to invest in the future."

Syncrude's executives convened a number of Search Conferences. In these conferences functional, departmental, and divisional managers examined the changing business environment, envisioned a more desirable future, critiqued the executives' vision statement and discussed whether it made sense, and made their own plans to help Syncrude to begin to change. As a result of this process, many managers in Syncrude's depart-ments and the divisions came to believe that the status quo was unaccept-able and that change was needed.

Providing Strategic Leadership for Participative Design

A group of senior managers began educating themselves on the principles and methods of self-management. They were introduced to the design principles, and for a little over a year they spent much of their time reading materials, attending workshops, holding dialogue sessions, and visiting other organizations. Senior management invited Fred Emery and Merrelyn Emery, the pioneers and inventors of the Participative Design and Search

Conference methods, to Syncrude to help the Syncrude people understand how these methods could be used to improve the business.

Senior managers decided that a Participative Design approach could help Syncrude become competitive with the traditional oil giants. As the guiding coalition for an enterprise-wide change process, they wanted people to work in self-managed teams that recorded, analyzed, planned, and performed their own work, without being dependent on supervisors. All eleven of Syncrude's departments would be encouraged to work in this way. At the same time, senior executives decided they would not insist or force departments to use any particular approach. The choice of how the change would be led was up to each department's leadership team.

Developing a Vision of Change

Syncrude's leadership made it clear to department managers that each of them would have to rethink their own business direction in line with the corporate vision, generate a map for their own redesign process, use Participative Design (or some other method) to examine every aspect of their operation, and implement the new work system. The goal was providing employees the capability to self-manage their own work, to improve reliability, safety, and timeliness, and to reduce costs.

The formulation of a vision to direct the change effort and the strategies to accomplish it is a complex issue in its own right, one which can also be democratized. Most of the divisions within Syncrude decided to use Search Conferences to formulate their strategic direction. A number of areas used traditional planning and design approaches and did not include the workforce in their discussions.

Syncrude's senior managers felt that an overarching "macro-design" for the organization ought to precede the operational design work in the divisions. For example, one of the concerns of the senior managers was to move toward a product-focused organization; this meant that some of the divisions, such as the engineering, human resources, technology, and information-systems organizations, would need to be largely decentralized into the field, where they could more closely support the core work process. Once the macro-design was in place, division managers would conduct Participative Design sessions for redesigning the work within various unit operations. In these Participative Design sessions operational details related to workflows, business processes, resources, reporting relationships, team structures, and human resource practices required would be worked out. This approach was a generative learning process to build the capabilities of the workforce.

Following the design pathway, one of the early steps in the process is to conduct a comprehensive organizational assessment that reviews the business strategy, the performance gaps, and any opportunities for improvement. Once a sound business strategy is in place, every organization has to address a number of critical questions: "How do we organize to transform this business strategy into operational reality?" "How do we create a culture that has the capacity to continuously redesign itself to accommodate rapid changes in business strategy and direction?" And in Syncrude's case, "How do we bring collaboration, teamwork, and end-user involvement into the management of large projects?" In Syncrude's industry—where the price of the finished product has fluctuated wildly over a twenty-year period—addressing these questions was key to securing a competitive advantage.

Mining, Engineering, Extraction, and Upgrading functions are very different technical operations. Even within each function, different divisions have their own unique subcultures. Participative Design was employed differently in each unique context. Further, as its experience with Participative Design grew, Syncrude's capacity to learn improved. In point of fact, Participative Design would be done differently today, based on the organizational learning that occurred then. Our intention in the rest of this chapter is to selectively focus on particular aspects of the Participative Design process at Syncrude. We chose two critical areas of the business: Mining Operations and the Upgrading division. We will describe how these two areas designed and implemented a large-scale Participative Design process where the scope, depth, and degree of participation were wide, deep, and direct. Our intention is to enable readers to take away some ideas and apply them to their own situation.

PARTICIPATIVE DESIGN OF THE MINING ORGANIZATION

In early 1990, the general manager of the Mining function was concerned that one of the divisions in the mine was experiencing a shortfall in production goals. He asked Mike Noon, an internal consultant at Syncrude, to interview people and diagnose the problem. Noon found that policies and procedures were stifling workers' ability to meet production targets. To remedy the situation, Noon recommended that workers and managers meet periodically to talk about what was wrong and develop solutions. Noon's approach worked. Employees offered numerous ideas and suggestions for improving the work process. Their advice was taken seriously. When production shot up and remained high, the general manager of Mining became convinced of the power of employee participation. He soon became an advocate for a fundamental shift into self-management.

The general manager sent Noon off to talk with the other six divisions at the mine, hoping that he would be able to replicate the productivity improvements he had achieved in the production area. The Syncrude mining organization was a typical command-and-control hierarchy, grouped into separate divisions—Mine Production, Mine Maintenance, Mine Overburden, and Mine Mobile—with several support functions, such as Mine Reliability and Mine Technical. Noon soon discovered that the magnitude of this task required a more system-wide approach if process and work improvements were to result.

Using a Search Conference to Develop a Vision and a Guiding Coalition

A Search Conference was used to kick off the Mining redesign effort. In this conference, the mine management team discussed and grappled with the need for change in the mine organization, and agreed on a set of strategic initiatives and stretch goals that would guide the redesign effort—all with the explicit purpose of improving business performance. After the Search Conference, the mine management team and several internal consultants agreed to meet twice a month to plan a system-wide change process for all 1,300 employees in the mine. The group was highly influential because its members included the line managers, the internal change agents with the Participative Design expertise, and many of the department's proven leaders whose credibility could not be questioned. One of the guiding coalition's objectives was to become a cohesive team capable of modeling the desired changes to the rest of the organization. Most divisions in the mine used the Participative Design method to involve employees directly in the process of redesigning their own work areas. Each Participative Design effort in the mine was customized to fit the unique situation and demands of the various divisions involved.

Participative Design of the Reliability Division

As a member of the guiding coalition, the general manager of the Reliability Division sanctioned the first Participative Design initiative in the mine. The Reliability Division was responsible for inspecting all the equipment in the mine, as well as for conducting predictive maintenance tasks. Personnel in the division included tradesmen (a Canadian term meaning skilled workers: welders, plumbers, etc.), metallurgists, information-system technicians, and planners, as well as mechanical and electrical engineers. In 1991, a division-wide meeting was held in preparation for the Participative Design effort. Different specialists in the division were brought together for the first time to learn about what the change to self-management would entail. As the dialogue progressed, a tradesman stood up to make a point. He was frustrated that the requisitions he had sent to Engineering to get equipment redesigned had vanished *again*. There wasn't even any way to trace lost requisitions. The engineers who were supposed to handle it were, at least on paper, in his same division and they both reported to a common boss—but this was the first time this worker had ever met the engineers face-to-face. Prior to this meeting the tradesman hadn't even known that the engineers and he worked in the same division. "Welcome to bureaucracy," said one of the participants.

A series of Participative Design sessions were held for all Reliability Division employees. These Participative Design sessions used mirror groups to broaden organizational learning between different departments and groups. By using mirror groups, each department could better understand and challenge the designs of other departments. Different departments were paired off in Participative Design sessions, allowing every group to raise questions, challenge assumptions, and offer constructive criticisms when any other group presented its proposals for redesign. Design proposals from every consecutive session were posted on a wall in a large conference room. Everyone in the Reliability Division was encouraged to walk through and examine the various designs.

After all the Participative Design sessions were finished, a town-hall meeting was held with all employees. Employees engaged in vigorous debate and dialogue before they finally reached a collective decision on a new organizational structure and work arrangements. As it turned out, the manager of the Reliability Division decided to stay home, to show his workforce that they—not he—really were in control of the final design decision. He made it known that so long as the new design made the best business sense, he would endorse it. Workers within the Reliability Division viewed this as a highly courageous act—a significant departure from the traditional command-and-control managerial culture.

Initially, the workforce selected an ambitious design that called for placing 80 percent of the employees in front-line support teams. When this proposal was made, several professional, white-collar work groups got cold feet and were less than enthusiastic about joining teams in the field. The majority of the workforce, however, ratified the design that called for field-based work teams. Four levels of supervision were reduced to two, devolving many of the traditional supervision responsibilities to the teams. However, the professionals were among the strongest advocates against teams. Tradesmen were not pleased when their preferred design, which relocated professionals into front-line support teams, was voted down. Professional employees, at least for the time being, would remain geographically separate from the field.

One year later, a cross-section of employees, selected by their peers, revisited the design to see if it could be improved. This group was pleasantly surprised when an uninvited representative from one of the professional engineering groups walked into the first meeting and said: "We've talked it over and have decided to join the field teams for the benefit of this organization." This set the tone for a truly innovative design that put engineers out in the field. The new design made it possible for engineers to become part of technician teams, management teams, and so on. Relocating specialists closer to tradesmen in the field made a huge difference in productivity.

As we can see from this example, Participative Design is a generative learning process. It requires getting everyone involved in assessing, planning, and implementing change, and experimenting with new work arrangements. In practice, it requires a great deal of planning, colearning from the experience, sharing of best practices, and progressive refinement of work arrangements and organizational designs.

Participative Design of the Overburden and Mine Mobile Maintenance Divisions

In this section we will look carefully at the Participative Design process that was conducted in several divisions of the Syncrude Mining operation.

This case provides a good overview of a complex and large-scale Participative Design process, including the unexpected twists and turns that typically occur. In 1993, the general manager for the mine told the managers in the Overburden and Maintenance divisions that they needed to integrate the 650 people from these two divisions into one organization. These two divisions had different work cultures, methods of working, and technical skills. Twenty senior and midlevel managers, ten from each division, hashed out guidelines for the design task. Managers decided the new organization needed to be designed around whole-task, self-managing teams with a strong customer focus. The new design would be expected to reduce the extensive overtime costs that had been occurring within these divisions.

A small task force of seven people was formed to orchestrate a Participative Design process (see Figure 10.1 below) encompassing the two divisions. The task force proposed that the design effort begin with a series of four Search Conferences. These conferences would be used to build a sense of urgency among employees, and to create a shared vision for the desired future for integration of the two divisions. Thirty-six people, representing

MINE MOBILE PARTICIPATIVE DESIGN PROCESS

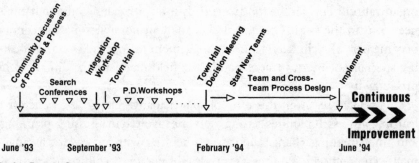

Design Process Steps:

- Over 300 employees participated in four meetings to discuss and approve the design process.
- Four Search Conferences and an Integration Workshop led to a Town Hall meeting. Key principles and parameters for Participative Design are established.
- A series of Participative Design Workshops are convened to create new designs for the division.
- Another Town Hall meeting is held to decide the final design for Mine Mobile Maintenance division.
- Employees bid and apply for new team positions.
- Self-managing teams designed and negotiated goals, roles, and procedures and cross-team processes.
- Implementation to self-management begins in June 1994.

Figure 10.1

a diagonal slice of employees from the two divisions, were included in each conference. Key questions were addressed in the conferences: "Where is the company headed if we just continue to do what we have always done?" "What is our strategic direction?" "How can we work together?" "Where are the performance gaps and how do we close them?" "What are the actions for which we will be held personally accountable?"

Initially, some of the front-line workers and supervisors didn't understand why they were being asked to scan the external environment and to consider questions that were normally reserved for upper-level management. "Why are you asking us to do this? My job is to work in the cab of a 240-ton truck," said one operator on the first day. But by the end of each conference, employees came to understand why their involvement and knowledge were critical to the design process. A great deal of trust-building occurred in these conferences between managers and employees.

Following the four consecutive Search Conferences, a two-day integration meeting was held to synthesize the results and findings. Six people from each of the four just-held Search Conferences attended this meeting. Several themes for the shape of a new organization emerged. These themes included the need for leadership and new structures, the benefits of multi-skilled teams and the need for training, and the need to provide clear boundaries for decision making and to hold people accountable for results. People wanted direct involvement in vibrant communication processes, a work system that allowed them to keep up with a rapid pace of technological change, and tools to eliminate non-value-added work. Employees were particularly impressed that management continued to uphold a long-standing tradition that places safety concerns ahead of production. Environmental concerns also surfaced, as many employees wanted to see the land on the Syncrude site returned to a pristine state. Numerous environmental restoration initiatives were discussed. There was also a strong sentiment among conference participants that financial rewards should be provided for performance improvements.

Large-Scale Participative Design Sessions

With a clear vision for the future of the business in sight, the next step involved convening a series of eleven consecutive Participative Design sessions. A seven-person task force was assembled to orchestrate the Participative Design process. Approximately thirty-two employees were involved in each Participative Design session for different work areas. For example, when the work of technicians was being redesigned, the session was composed of twenty-eight technicians and four supervisors. When management-level work was redesigned, most participants were managers, along with a few technicians. Several workshops included internal customers and suppliers to serve as mirror groups. One Participative Design session was held with only technicians, and one with only supervisors, as some were a bit hesitant to speak their minds with managers present. Information from each session were made public to all employees.

Early on, some employees expressed a lot of anxiety that Participation Design might lead to possible reductions in the workforce. The task force soon realized that they needed to devote more attention to this issue before employees attended the Participative Design sessions. Information meetings were held prior to each Participative Design session to address job-security issues. The long-term strategic plan and business forecast was shared in these sessions, which emphasized that Syncrude would likely be adding, not cutting, jobs in the future.

Over the course of several months, half of the workforce in the two divisions had participated directly in generating new designs for their areas. The eleven Participative Design sessions produced a total of forty-eight design proposals. During this phase, a new task force was formed: the implementation team. The first task this team faced was to devise a process by which the forty-eight design proposals could be reviewed and evaluated. The implementation team settled on a process for sorting through the designs, grouping them into common categories. Their charge was not to actually choose, change, or alter any of the designs, but to simply study the designs and group those with similar features into logical clusters. The implementation team also created a weekly newsletter to keep the workforce informed. Implementation-team members also met with formal and informal leaders on each of the work shifts to answer their questions.

As it turned out, only three of the forty-eight design proposals called for integration of the Overburden and Mine Mobile Maintenance divisions. It then became obvious to the general manager that consolidation of these divisions didn't make organizational sense. Employees were telling the implementation team, "We are two distinct divisions and there aren't any real synergies if we join forces." At that point, the two divisions split up to continue the redesign process as separate entities.

Redesign of the Mine Mobile Maintenance Division

The implementation team turned its attention to the redesign of the Mine Mobile Maintenance division. After reviewing numerous design proposals generated by the Participative Design sessions, the implementation team grouped all the design options into three clusters. The first design option was based on a maintenance-shop/field split. The mechanics in the field would form a team to work on equipment, as would the mechanics in the shop. According to the implementation team, the second design option amounted to nothing more than a dressed-up proposal for keeping the status quo; the basic structure was not significantly different from the current organization. The most ambitious design was to be found in the third option. This design called for a customer-based organization. Traditionally, maintenance is designed around specific equipment, where trucks are repaired in one shop, bulldozers are repaired in another, and so on. This more unusual design called for relocating equipment in maintenance shops aligned around customers.

Additional employee meetings were held to gather more input and details for each of the three design options. At the end of this process, the second design option was pulled from consideration by the implementation team because it failed to meet management's design criteria, which forbade status quo designs.

The Town-Hall Meeting

In order to reach a consensus among all employees in the Mine Mobile Maintenance division, a large group town-hall meeting was convened. Two weeks before the town-hall meeting, the implementation team met with each of the work shifts to explain the two designs and how the town-hall meeting would be conducted. Both design options were explained in detail, so each employee had an understanding of where he or she would fit in. Employees were informed that the town hall was a large-group decision-making meeting based on consensus. The implementation team continued to listen to employee concerns. The uncertainty associated with the new designs for Mine Mobile frustrated some employees. Many believed that the division general manager had "a hip-pocket design" that he would pull out later at the town-hall meeting. But dialogues with the workforce made it possible for people to really understand the new designs and where they fit into them before they arrived at the town-hall meeting.

During the town-hall meeting, the implementation team was willing to modify the designs, but wasn't willing to subjugate the will of the majority to the will of the few. Three hundred people attended the town-hall meeting, seated around some thirty tables. Everyone was there to make a decision, not to debate the designs, or to even reconsider why redesign was being done. Employees could choose either design, or any combination of the two designs. Similar to the process that occurs in selecting candidates at political party conventions, each table group of employees was polled for their final design decision. As it turned out, 270 employees supported a modification of the shop/field split design. The top five reasons for supporting each group's preferred design were also posted on a viewscreen.

Sam Salter, an affable engineer who facilitated the town-hall meeting, queried the small minority of employees who didn't favor the shop/field split design to see what they needed to be able to support the new design. During this process, those who wanted to speak or express disagreement were handed a wireless microphone and were allowed to voice their concerns. Through such skillful facilitation on the part of Salter, employees talked through some further modifications that led to a consensus on a final integrated design.

We should point out that before final consensus was reached, the division manager got up and made a last-ditch plea for the customer-based design. He was a lonely voice in the wilderness. It suddenly dawned on employees that the meeting really was about democratic decision making. The most senior manager really wasn't going to impose his preferred "hip-pocket" design, and employees were elated and excited.

News of the town-hall meeting spread like wildfire throughout the Syncrude grapevine. Employees who had been sitting on the sidelines were starting to believe this stuff was real. "We have a voice in how this business is run and can make a difference," said one participant. "Once you start this process, if you follow the principles, there is no way you can control the outcome. If I wasn't comfortable with that, I wouldn't do this," said Gord Ball, then the division manager.

Staffing the New Design

The next step involved staffing the new Mine Mobile Maintenance design. Numerous staffing decisions needed to be made to fill positions on newly formed self-managing teams within the division. The implementation team devised a process by which employees would apply for the jobs they wanted. The workforce was unsettled at having to reapply for jobs in the new organization. A lot of effort and thought went into the process to ensure that staffing decisions were handled fairly, openly, and equitably. Employees could apply for any job for which they felt qualified. Each employee was required to submit a first, second, and third choice for his or her preferred job. An appeal process was also created, in case anyone was placed in a job that didn't match one of his or her choices.

In a matter of days, all the teams were staffed up. Ninety-five percent of employees received their first- or second-choice position. Nearly 85 percent of employees were placed in their first-choice job. For the remaining open positions, a conference call was held with the electricians and riggers, who initially were not satisfied. When it came to selecting management roles, senior managers' opinions carried the highest weight.

Final implementation tasks fleshed out the details related to developing systems to support the teams. Teams needed to have the information and resources to control their own work. Tools were developed so that every team could analyze its own work process, and develop the procedures for how work would be controlled and coordinated within each team. Each team was also trained in technical workflow analysis and process mapping, to better understand variances and how to control them within each unit. During the transition to the new design, the implementation team also played a liaison role between the new teams, helping teams to negotiate their boundaries and to decide how coordination was going to occur. Implementation went smoothly and fine tuning of the designs continues to this day.

Self-Management in the Mine Mobile Maintenance Division

The Mining facility at Syncrude is a twenty-four-hour, 365-days-a-year operation. In the previous design, there was no overlap between successive work shifts. For example, workers starting the afternoon shift didn't cross paths with their peers leaving the day shift. In the new design, coordination mechanisms between shifts were developed. Similarly, managers in the old maintenance organization rarely cooperated or communicated with each other. Now these individuals support the division as a team. Managers now focus their attention on customer lines. For example, one manager is accountable for the entire Overburden area, another for the tailings operation. These managers are now totally dedicated to looking after the equipment that belongs to each area of the mine.

Seven functional managers have responsibilities encompassing the whole division. These responsibilities include dealing with safety, technology, human resources, and work environment issues. Below them are seven former shift supervisors, who now support all the teams on the shifts. Their new role is mainly to help the teams develop their self-management capabilities. In the old hierarchical organization, shift supervisors used to put a lot of energy into protecting their own turf. A shift supervisor would typically have the attitude, "The guys in this repair group are all mine and no one else can utilize them." Now teams and resources are shared according to varying workloads and customer needs. As its teams become more comfortable with taking on responsibility, this group has taken on more of a specialized resource role.

Front-line teams are focused along shop (intensive repair work) and field (minor repairs to keep equipment running) lines. At the team level, there are two shop-team leaders and two field-team leaders who are chosen by their peers and management. A development-team leader is responsible for transferring management capabilities into the groups. For example, this individual works with the teams to increase their skills in problem-solving, scheduling, planning, data-tracking, record-maintaining, and process-improvement work.

Paul Wohlgemuth, a leader from the heavy-duty-truck shop, was an engineer before the redesign. In his old job he used to sit in front of a computer most of the day doing calculations and working on one project at a time. Now he deals with value investigations and personnel issues, and works with teams to help them develop performance measures. "I am helping teams create measures they can monitor and relate to, so they can track their impact on the business. My role is mainly to help teams develop appropriate metrics to manage their own work," says Wohlgemuth.

The light-duty-truck-shop team has already saved the company over half a million Canadian dollars, and wants to save more. And they have no supervisor. Little remains of the old hierarchical organization. This team created a special role for handling work orders. Team members rotate jobs every four or five days. "The rest of the supervisory role, we split it up to three people like loss management, inspections, and computerizing our work," says team member Pat Bong. "We decide among ourselves who is going to do what job," mechanic Karen Menon points out. "There is no formal planner position because the team decided to manage its own planning."

Consider how work used to be managed in the light-duty-truck area. When a breakdown occurred out in the field, a functional manager would call down from the office and dictate to the mechanics that that job in the field should be their top priority. Then a supervisor in light duty would follow up with a promise: "I'll put my best man on it right now." Unfortunately, this best man (who happened to be a woman mechanic) was usually already working on another so-called top-priority job. Menon remarks, "It seemed like common sense to us to say, we've got two top-priority jobs, so let's drop some of the work we are doing so we can focus on these urgent repair jobs." The workers had known how to improve the work-order system for years, but didn't have the authority to act. Any time the mechanics confronted the supervisor and tried to change the system, the supervisor took it as an affront to his authority.

PARTICIPATIVE DESIGN IN THE UPGRADING DEPARTMENT

Upgrading is a complex technological operation that converts bitumen to light, sweet synthetic crude oil. In 1992, the general manager of Upgrading at the time, Murray Smart, gathered his management team to begin a process for making operational improvements. Smart and his team agreed that the Upgrading department's business direction needed to be better aligned with Syncrude's corporate strategy. The old organization structure in upgrading was functionalized into five silos, with twenty-six specialized functions focused on narrow segments of the bitumen-conversion process.

Over the course of several months, the management team revisited their mission statement, established key business objectives, drew a detailed wall map of the department's core work processes, and had an extensive dialogue about the need for a higher quality-of-working-life for all employees. This initial organizational assessment confirmed that a total redesign of the Upgrading division was in order.

Formation of the Upgrading Core Planning Team

A core planning team for the design process consisted of a number of senior managers and a cross-section of employees from the Upgrading workforce. Except for senior management, planning-team members were nominated through a peer-selection process. One business-unit manager stressed the importance of using a peer-selection process to choose planning-team members: "Peer selection is very important because it allows the workforce to put their most trusted people, who represent their views, on the planning team." The planning team believed in using widespread employee involvement for the redesign process, but they also had a concern that it be manageable. Nearly eight hundred people would be involved, making this the largest Participative Design project in the company. Three main steps for conducting the Participative Design process were mapped out by the planning team: (1) creating a strategic-level organization design; (2) creating an operational-level design; and (3) staffing and implementation of self-managing work teams.

A Strategic Organization Design for Upgrading

The first Participative Design session involved senior managers and a deep slice of the workforce; it produced a strategic organization design for the entire Upgrading department. This new design was product focused, collapsing the five previous operating units into two integrated operating units (Bitumen Conversion and Syncrude Sweet Blend production), along with an additional support unit (Plant Services), reducing the number of division management positions from five to three.

Creating an Operational-Level Design for Upgrading

As design shifted to the operational level, the composition of the core planning team changed. Some members who had been on the planning team returned to their regular jobs, and new members from the operating ranks were recruited. "Our role wasn't to get into actual design, but to map out how to get the majority of the Upgrading workforce directly engaged in Participative Design," says Doug Crowler, a process operator in Upgrading. Members of the core planning team were trained and educated in the Participative Design method, and served as the main change agents for the redesign effort at the operational level.

Senior management provided employees a conceptual framework for guiding local design decisions. The redesign guidelines for the operational-level Participative Design sessions appear below.

THE DESIGN GUIDELINES DRAFTED BY UPGRADING MANAGEMENT

1. **Business Requirements.** People will redesign to meet the department's mission and accomplish the strategic objectives. All 780 people in Upgrading will understand the business to increase the management capability in our workforce. Redesign efforts are to focus on the core business of making oil. Each team will establish performance benchmarks with clear criteria for success so improvements in business performance, resulting from redesign, can be measured and tracked.

2. **No-Layoffs Policy.** There will be no layoffs as a result of redesign. We guarantee everyone will be gainfully employed, but not necessarily in the same job. Retraining may be required in some cases. In order for employees to be willing and interested to look at doing work in different ways, division managers feel employment security needs to be guaranteed (excluding early retirement and attrition).

3. **Work Design.** Every team's focus will shift from a functional to a product/service focus. The macro-structure we have designed consists of three business units that will be operated in an integrated manner. In other words, people can't just go off and optimize each unit. They must take into consideration the products and services that are being transferred between units. The thrust of the redesign process is to get away from a functional organization with mechanical, chemical, and process engineers, millwrights, process operators, quality assurance, and metal inspectors. The objective is

to come up with an organization designed around multifunctional teams who can complete a whole work task together.

By adopting a Participative Design process, we create a significant amount of discomfort among the traditional decision makers who will be transferring some of the management function into teams. Each team will have a leader. Training for leaders and teams will be provided to support the new work arrangements.

Eventually pay-for-skills-held programs will be designed and aligned to support each team's ability to complete whole tasks—for example, if a process operator wanted to pick up a certain level of millwright skills to perform some basic maintenance on a pump or valve.

4. Managing the Redesign Process. Implementation of redesign will take place without business interruption. A work-flow analysis is to be part of the process. Redesign will be applied consistently across Upgrading. The process and proposed changes will be shared, understood, and worked through with all the affected groups. This includes groups within the Upgrading division and outside groups such as utilities, extraction (who feed bitumen into the upgrading process), accounting, and so on.

The core planning team formed additional task forces made up of volunteers. Task forces were created to involve more people in design activities, since not all eight hundred of Upgrading's employees could be included in the Participative Design process directly. Task forces were involved in education and preparation activities, team and leader development, design tasks, implementation, work-analysis training, implementation planning, and benchmarking. Many of the task forces interfaced with work shifts prior to redesign, to respond to employee concerns and questions. Task forces used a share file on the Local Area Network and e-mail to post key information about the design. Face-to-face dialogue with workers generated good questions and proved to be the most important education component.

For example, the education task force met with shift workers to talk about the business need for redesign, Syncrude's and Upgrading's strategic direction, the operating principles for self-managing work, and the design guidelines which would be used in the Participative Design sessions. The most critical activity in these sessions was the opportunity for employees to put their fears and concerns on the table. Concerns were centered on the ambiguity of the process and the issue of whether management could be trusted. Employees were initially quite skeptical and suspected that there must be some kind of "hip-pocket design." "We heard comments like . . . okay, you want us to change. But what is the new organization going to look like? Tell us the answer," said one education task-force member. But there was no answer . . .

The whole concept of a team managing its own work was totally alien to some people. One worker recalls being unable to imagine having a team without a supervisor, "You're going to let the children run the family. We thought of ourselves as children back then." Trust was going to have to be earned, and dependency wasn't going to disappear overnight.

The large number of task teams created a coordination challenge. To address the issue, the core planning team formed an eighteen-person integration task force to provide continuity through the phases of redesign and to manage the transition from one task team to another. Since each task team had different volunteers, it was necessary to help successive task teams get up to speed without reinventing the wheel. The integration task force ensured timely and relevant communication to the people in the department and interfaced with Upgrading's management.

Before the operational-level Participative Design sessions were held, a critical question had to be answered. Should managers be included in the sessions? A former member of the core planning team recalls the debate on whether to include or exclude the managers. "In the early 1990s we hadn't worked through our suspicion and mistrust of management. The winning argument was management shouldn't be involved in any way, shape, or form. We set them up as spectators."

This decision would later come back to haunt the planning team. "After doing the Participative Design sessions, we had a group of people who were excited and had ownership of their designs," recalls a planning team member. "But the managers had veto power." The problem came when the managers, who had been excluded from the Participative Design sessions, had difficulty fully understanding some of the designs. "It was hard to see the logic of some of the designs if you didn't participate directly in the session . . . it is one of those things where you had to be there." There was a similar problem for participants in the sessions who had trouble interpreting the meaning of management's design guidelines. Only a handful of workers had participated in the management meetings where the design guidelines were constructed. For most employees, the design guidelines seemed abstract, vague, and too general to be of any use.

Participative Design Sessions in Upgrading

Twelve Participative Design sessions, involving a total of 325 people, were conducted in Upgrading. Each session was three days long. Participative Design sessions were held for each of the twelve areas within Upgrading. Each of the twelve Participative Design sessions generated three to four design proposals for a new organizational structure. There was a lot of excitement about the process, and a feeling of ownership of the designs.

However, many design proposals coming out of the Participative Design sessions lacked sufficient detail on paper. Consequently, management had a difficult time evaluating whether or not a design proposal met their design guidelines. Management eliminated half of the thirty-six design proposals. When this occurred, employees felt that management had made arbitrary decisions. In hindsight, it was probably a mistake to exclude managers totally from Participative Design sessions, as simple verbal summaries of the designs at the end of each session couldn't convey the richness and complexity associated with each design. Most of the understanding and meaning associated with each design proposal was encoded in the oral knowledge and community of practice that had developed over the course of three days of intense analysis, debates, and conversations after work at the local pubs. Yet management was expected to make critical evaluations of the various design proposals by walking into the session at the end of the last day.

Even after half the designs were eliminated, there was still the challenge of integrating some eighteen different design proposals. Against the advice of Syncrude's internal consultants, a design-integration team was formed to synthesize proposals into a cohesive design for the whole department. The decision to turn the design process over to a representative group was a crucial mistake that compromised the Participative Design effort. As you might recall, one of the cardinal rules of Participative Design is that no designs can ever be imposed. Handing off the Participative Design process to a representative integration team transformed it from a high-involvement democratic process into something akin to a forced change.

The eighteen-person design-integration team wasn't even truly representative. Most of the members were selected by management, including several employees who were close to retirement. Since these soon-to-be-retiring employees would not have to live with the consequences of the new design, their selection as representatives for the workforce did not engender a great deal of confidence or trust. In effect, the integration group became for all practical purposes a classic design team with all of its typical problems. As one design-integration team member recalls, "We took bits and pieces from what other people had done and pasted them together into a design which made sense to us." This piecemeal approach elicited a negative response from the workforce community. Employees resented having representatives making key design decisions. Suddenly, employees were much less willing to implement a new design, because it was not the product of their direct participation. It took a lot longer to secure the trust and commitment of the workforce with this design-team approach.

During implementation, several days were set aside for newly-formed teams to meet and clarify their goals, roles and objectives. After this session, every team member understood his or her performance goals and how his or her outputs were going to be measured. Each team had developed a system of mutual accountability to ensure that performance goals were met and for making quality decisions. "Team-on-team" meetings were encouraged to support coordination across team boundaries, and the role of managers changed to support the new organization design.

Syncrude's business results have been extraordinary. A 75 percent improvement in productivity is impressive, but what if everything had gone perfectly? Perhaps productivity improvements on the order of 100 to 200 percent are possible if self-management is fully implemented at every level, and in every area of the organization. With the benefit of hindsight, what might Syncrude have done differently to transform its operations into a self-managing organization?

Lesson 1: Combine top-down with bottom-up change. Syncrude needed a combination of top-down as well as bottom-up approaches to Participative Design and change leadership. A good model for change leadership can be found in John Kotter's (1996) book, *Leading Change*. Management is about coping with complexity, while leadership is about coping with change. Syncrude's senior executives provided the vision, but left each area free to do its own thing. De facto, the Participative Design process became more of a bottom-up effort. While Syncrude's executives were quite sincere, and spent a great deal of time developing a vision and corporate strategy for the redesign effort, they overestimated the extent to which it was clearly understood at all levels of the organization. But as Kotter points out, this shortcoming is quite common to many cultural change efforts. Many executive-management teams do a great job in creating a vision at the top of the organization, but declare victory too soon.

Simply convening all-employee communication meetings is not enough. It is one thing to hold meetings with several layers of management, show viewgraphs and slides, and provide boilerplate answers to employee questions. It is quite a different matter to engage people in a genuine dialogue where they can collectively come to feel the pinch of the future threats facing the organization. Employees in the trenches have to feel the competitive environment in their bones. They have to discover the competitive realities and business demands first hand, through their own direct perceptions.

As one division manager recalls, "We never gave the general population the long-term perspective on redesign. We communicated that to most managers, but not to the workforce. There could have been a greater degree of executive involvement in the redesign, and our senior managers could have done a big education piece up front. If they had, we'd be a lot better off today."

Lesson 2: Self-management is not only for the operatives, but includes management. When middle managers believe they are exempt from redesigning their own work, the organization will get stuck in the middle, retaining a traditional dominant hierarchy with teams on the bottom. If the general manager still tells his direct reports what to do, and expects them to be on top of operational details that should be the purview of the teams, it will weaken an already fragile structure. Division leaders and area supervisors (middle management) will quite rightly hold on to direction-giving roles, and team leaders will jump when they come looking for numbers that will make them look good. Consequently, authority and responsibility are not transferred to teams, systems to support team-based decision making are not created, and team members will soon become frustrated over the fact that they have little ability to control and coordinate their own work.

The bottom line is that unless senior leaders can understand the change, embrace it, and see it as changing their world, not just the world of the workforce, the future of self-management will be in jeopardy. The typical scenario is that five years down the road, competitive pressures or a new management team will revert the organization back to a traditional dominant hierarchy.

Lesson 3: Middle needs to play an integrator role in the Participative Design process. Middle managers need to be involved right from the inception of the Participative Design process. They take on the role of integrators, tying together the support and human-resource systems that make it possible for teams to make their own decisions. Support systems concern things like standards, measurement and feedback, accounting, budgeting, and information systems. Human-resource systems include roles and policies, selection and orientation, appraisal, compensation, skill development, and training. System integration cannot be accomplished from isolated piecemeal efforts by a few middle managers.

At Syncrude, middle managers are now developing strong peer-group relationships that will allow them to transform support and human-resource systems throughout the organization. For this to occur, middle managers need to conduct their own Participative Design sessions, and invite senior managers from operating groups to join them. By integrating themselves into a self-managing team responsible for putting all the pieces together and making them work, middle managers can transform their role in the hierarchy too.

Syncrude is now operating with 50 percent fewer middle managers. This was achieved through early retirement and attrition, and through a management redesign, has shrunk its administrative jobs even more. The remaining middle managers have the critical knowledge needed to make the system work effectively. Middle managers need to conduct their own Participative Design sessions to redesign the middle-management role. Middle management needs to be carefully prepared to participate through dialogue about what is possible in their new role, and how it could be more rewarding and add value to the business. Omitting this step leaves them in a high-stress environment where they have too much to do and not enough time to do it. Resistance to change can be expected when managers are well aware of what they are being asked to give up, but largely unaware of the new role they can take on.

In a self-managing organization, the middle-management role has unlimited potential. As at Syncrude, middle managers are now the ones who improve processes, lead change, help establish a connection to the customer interface, manage critical boundaries, and get the proper resources to work teams.

Lesson 4: Include every stakeholder group in the Participative Design process. In the journey from bureaucracy to self-management, sometimes certain groups are excluded from the Participative Design sessions. Exclusion occurs either when groups with the least power are ignored, or when there is lack of trust between levels of management, specialists, and departments. All stakeholders need to be included in planning, deciding on, and implementing an optimal design.

In the early 1990s, many employees were suspicious and didn't trust management at Syncrude. Consequently, in some instances, management was excluded from Participative Design sessions. But how can managers be expected to understand employee-generated designs and contribute to the redistribution of authority, if they are not involved until the very end?

However, even in cases where managers were included in Participative Design sessions, they ended up helping employees with their shop-floor designs. Consequently, these managers didn't rethink how their own management roles and responsibilities would be handled in the new organization. For example, before redesign the Upgrading maintenance organization had hundreds of employees, whose work was coordinated by thirty to forty maintenance supervisors and planners. These supervisors did long-range planning, ordered equipment, organized the work flow, and scheduled the maintenance of highly specialized equipment. The Participative Design process eliminated these traditional supervisory roles, along with the role of the shift supervisor. These supervisors were gradually phased out of their traditional roles over the course of eighteen months. Some supervisors and planners decided to seek other jobs in the company, taking on special assignments, joining project teams, and so on. During this transitional phase, more attention could have been given to developing what the new role of supervisors would be in the self-managing system. Holding special Participative Design sessions to address the changing roles of supervisors in Upgrading would have been particularly helpful.

SUMMARY

The Syncrude case demonstrates that even when Participative Design efforts to produce a self-managing organization are less than perfect, powerful business results can be achieved (75 percent productivity improvement) and a highly committed workforce can be developed. As we can see from this case, Participative Design requires an extraordinary commitment from senior and middle managers, who must lead the effort. Senior managers often struggle before they reach the point of being willing to change the fundamental design principle of the organization. Senior managers also need to model the behaviors they advocate if the middle and operational level are going to be able to take the concept of self-management seriously. Further, if senior and middle management are willing to change the design principle, they face the challenge of finding ways to guide the design process at a fast enough pace so that the organization can survive.

The power of Participative Design is in the intense learning and the extraordinary commitment generated by the people in the design process. With the traditional approach, isolated design teams are given a year or more to develop a new design for the entire organization. But many failed Reengineering projects have demonstrated that such designs more often than not stay on paper and rarely get fully implemented. In contrast, with Participative Design employees are involved directly in the design process. Employees develop a depth of understanding, a detailed design, and a skill level far more advanced than any isolated design team could ever accomplish.

For example, last year, Syncrude launched a Participative Design initiative for the start-up of a new mine. The new mine would be organized from the ground up as a fully self-managing operation. The mine would also be staffed with people from existing operations. The general manager for the new mine reflected on the Participative Design process: "We selected people from Mining, Engineering, Extraction, and Utilities who had been through redesign before and had some success with it. They understood why we were there and what we had to do. It was a tremendously satisfying experience and we were able to come up with a great design and staffed up the new organization quickly and effectively."

CHAPTER 11

THE ROLE OF MANAGEMENT IN A SELF MANAGING ORGANIZATION

You must be the change you wish to see in the world.
—Mahatma Gandhi

Many organizations have had success with implementing self-directed work teams at the operational level, but have struggled with the idea of implementing self-management at the managerial levels. In the self-managing organization, all levels of work are redesigned, relocating responsibility for control and coordination at an appropriate level that allows people to perform their tasks effectively without external supervision or hierarchical interference. In traditional organizations, managers often find it difficult to cooperate with their peers in other departments, and those above them at higher levels of management may not provide much help. Hence, middle managers often feel isolated, having to fend for themselves in a system that does little to foster lateral communications and integration between functions.

Although there is a plethora of literature about work teams, there are few examples and little information for managers to draw upon to make self-management work at their level. Even when managers espouse getting rid of bureaucracy and value the idea of empowerment, they often have trouble uprooting the old ways and liberating themselves from dominant hierarchical structures.

In self-managing organizations, the role and structure of management need to change dramatically to support and embody the democratic design principle. This chapter begins by first illustrating the typical organizational dynamics associated with the role and structure of management in a traditional dominant hierarchy. Then we provide a counter illustration of the role of management in a self-managing organization. Finally, we end with a case study of how a medical-products company implemented self-management within its management ranks.

STRUCTURAL PREDICAMENTS IN A TRADITIONAL HIERARCHY

The Executive-Level Predicament

John is a successful CEO of a global corporation with sales in the billions of dollars. After graduating from Harvard Business School in the early 1970s, John worked for a prominent strategy-consulting firm before being recruited by his current employer for a position in sales and marketing. He rose rapidly through the ranks of his company, spending the bulk of his career in the finance organization, where his predecessor groomed him for CEO.

As the year 2000 approached, John saw a number of problems affecting his organization. There was an underlying lack of trust and cooperation between executives and their managers. The senior staff simply didn't buy into the strategic plan. There was very little constructive and voluntary discussion. The leaders of each of the five strategic business units held their cards close to the vest and couldn't collaborate on the issues that cut across their organizational boundaries.

Consequently, the five divisions had no interlocking initiatives among them to improve their competitive position in the marketplace. As John put it: "We manage in thirty-day increments. This is to the detriment of quarterly, annual, and five-year plans. A Herculean effort is put into the strategic plan, but we get off track when one of the numbers heads south— like sales projections, production figures, or revenue targets—and then we stay off track."

Division managers were self-interested, and showed little concern for the common good of the whole organization. These executives didn't share critical information and actually competed with each other for resources and customers. Relationships among them were acrimonious, characterized by a good deal of backbiting and finger pointing. Instead of being capable of partnership, they actively worked to defend themselves from one another. And—no surprise—their direct reports knew how to take a hint and repeated the same pattern across business lines and even with their peers.

How could John get people to look beyond their own narrow divisional perspective and see the big picture? What would it take to get each divisional leader to put more energy and initiative into improving the whole organization as a system? How do people move beyond lack of responsibility, excuses, blaming others, and righteous indignation toward collaboration and cooperation?

Like that of CEOs everywhere, John's world has become more complex and difficult to manage. The rate of market and technological change is high, product life cycles are compressing, and knowledge has become the critical resource. John feels burdened with the responsibility to please institutional investors and the capital markets. It often seems that there is too much to do and not enough time to do it. Seventy-five- or eighty-hour workweeks are the norm. Other stakeholders such as customers, suppliers, employees, and the community clamor for his time and want to be put on top of the CEO's attention list.

John hungers for more time to focus on the things that truly count. There are alliances and partnerships to build, and new dynamic relationships with customers and suppliers that need to be developed. He would like to involve people in rewriting the rules, conventions, and boundaries of competition; rethinking the skills the business should be building; and considering how to organize for opportunities, which are inhibited by the present structure. He knows that assumptions based on past success are hard to change because they are embedded in places like policy manuals, capital budgeting, accounting, and information systems.

As CEO, he would like more complete information to work on critical decisions. He would like to empower the division executives and middle managers to have more responsibility and entrepreneurial initiative. He would like their support to get critical strategic initiatives implemented. And it would be great if his sense of isolation and feeling of being out of touch with operations could somehow be alleviated.

John is just getting comfortable sharing power with the workforce. He is also getting used to an empowered board of directors, who monitor corporate and management performance, and expect him and other top managers to keep performance on track. John fears losing control while still being held responsible. If responsibility and accountability are pushed downward, will others be as skilled, responsible, and committed as John has been? Will middle managers be capable of coordinated and coherent action to improve the business? Won't it simply take too much time to involve, train, and develop them so they can be responsible?

How many executives can relate to John? Like John, many senior leaders face the challenge of creating responsibility and accountability in others while remaining responsible and accountable themselves for the success of the business. They hunger for a self-managing organization where the patterns of "us and them" are replaced with a desire by middle managers to reduce complexity and internal competition. They are eager to find a way for their people to share responsibility for the success of the whole enterprise.

The Middle-Level Predicament

Joan is a middle manager in one of the company's five divisions. Her boss, Richard, the division manager, reports to John, the CEO. Joan graduated from MIT's Sloan School of Management, where her master's thesis was on information-systems management in a high-technology workplace. She was recruited by her current employer to work on designing information systems for teams in a Total Quality environment. Her efforts helped the division win the state quality award and led to her promotion to Information Systems vice president.

As her division seeks to meet ambitious growth goals, Joan finds herself torn between wanting to please her boss and wanting to support front-line work teams in continuous-improvement activities. Joan's boss continues to want to know exactly what is going on every day, down to the minutest details. At the same time she is hearing complaints from quality-improvement teams, who feel they are being stifled by unnecessary data requirements demanded by higher-ups. Getting information to the teams and having open information systems is not an easy or inexpensive task. And the teams are beginning to question whether this empowerment rhetoric is really a load of bull.

As Joan strives to help her organization go for the Baldrige National Quality Award, she sees a number of obstacles impeding efforts to change and become less bureaucratic. It seems her counterparts in marketing, sales, product development, research, accounting, operations, human resources, and finance are feeling micromanaged by Richard, the division manager. She notices that John, the CEO, calls Richard on the carpet and asks for an explanation whenever a business problem exists. Then Richard jumps all over her and her peers. Joan wishes that Richard would model empowerment by being willing to talk openly with his team about the ways in which his personal behavior is either enhancing or thwarting efforts to foster ownership and accountability.

She feels a sense of separation and isolation from the other members of the division management team. In her mind, she and they have very little in common with each other. The way performance evaluations are done causes her to compete with the other functional managers and win points at their expense. Joan finds herself evaluating her peers—how they dress, speak, whether they are too emotional or rational—and finding them lacking. She doesn't socialize with them, preferring her own staff's company, and doesn't believe there is any benefit in working with peers to deal with common problems.

How could Joan get herself and her counterparts, the other functional VP's, beyond their assessments that they have little in common; beyond their competitive and evaluative behaviors; and beyond their belief that there is no point in working together to coordinate improvement projects across their turfs and territories? What would it take to get each functional leader to face the possibility that this collection of misfits could become a powerful and effective force in the division? How could they become a useful support system for each other, so that Richard really valued them as a team and the workforce would see them as providing effective and coordinated leadership?

Like that of middle managers everywhere, Joan's world has become more complex and uncertain. Two layers of middle management were removed in her division, spans of control have increased, and Joan, like her colleagues, is expected to partner with Richard and get closer to her internal customers. She has been told to share Information Systems (IS) knowledge with others, to train, coach, and delegate, to think beyond her functional role, to be a team player, to develop managerial as well as technical competency, to think strategically, and to help the division GM get a clear picture of the larger organizational issues. Joan wants to let go of control and spend more time planning strategy and working outside her function, but fears not having the instant answers demanded by Richard. She also isn't fully confident whether she can trust her people. As a result, she spends much of her time bean-counting details, pestering her employees for information, and being angry with the division GM when he criticizes her for doing lower-level work.

How many middle managers can relate to Joan? When people are given a middle-management role in a command-and-control environment, whether they want to or not they often become isolated from each other, focus on their own turf—the needs of their unit—and may be seen by workers as uninformed, weak, and unintegrated. Since the work of middle managers is fragmented, employees may notice differing practices among them and judge this to be unfair and inconsistent.

In Joan's division, Richard feels burdened with the responsibility for integrating functional efforts toward common business goals. As division GM, he judges his middle managers as lacking entrepreneurial spirit and feels that his strategic initiatives disappear into a middle-management black hole.

Joan and Richard have something in common. They hunger for a self-managing organization where the middle role is transformed. Richard, like Joan, is a middle manager, sandwiched between the CEO and his divisional management team. Both Richard and Joan could benefit from having a supportive peer group. Imagine if the divisional GMs could put the past behind them, work with John to create a compelling vision, and support each other in pursuing corporate-wide strategic initiatives!

Imagine if Joan and her peers could create regular meetings to share information, help support each other, and work on improvement projects! If both these groups of middle managers were focused on what their own division or function needs, as well as on the larger system, both John and Richard could be released to work on the things that truly matter.

Richard recently took Joan and his functional leaders on a bench-marking trip to an organization that had won the National Quality Award and came back inspired and excited. They saw functional managers meeting at the beginning and end of each work period, without the division GM, to share information, identify issues they needed to work on, and coordinate improvement initiatives across their boundaries. Richard began to wonder whether this might not be a good idea for the five division GMs in his own company to do themselves on a quarterly basis.

Despite time demands from the GM, the workforce, and customers, the quality-award winners saw their time together as sacred and continued meeting to coordinate work across functions. When Joan and Richard sat down with the award winner's president, he said: "First, I thought these meetings would go nowhere. But the truth is they've become an effective team and its taken a big burden off my shoulders." Workers felt that having the functional managers coordinate work together had eliminated backbiting and poor communication and had led to strong, knowledgeable, and consistent leadership. Results like these intrigued Richard and his staff.

The Operational-Level Predicament

Clayton is a systems analyst reporting to Joan in the Information Systems function of Richard's division. He was hired by Joan to help Product Development create common platforms and protocols so information could be shared more readily during product development. His efforts have helped physicians, scientists, manufacturing engineers, FDA officials, and operators work more closely to cut product-development cycle time.

Clayton sees a number of problems with the quality effort and the team concept: "Management hasn't shifted its basic views about people. Both these programs were forced on us. They are still over-controlling and micro-managing our work. Richard and the senior management group forced us into teams and didn't change anything else in the organization. Self-directed teams have a lot of potential, but managers are having trouble relinquishing control. We need organization-wide changes in reward systems, in work design, and in the resources available to the teams. It's a mess here. And it's not likely to change, so it will probably disappear like the other programs did."

Clayton sees Joan as confused and wishy-washy, with no firm opinions of her own. Sometimes he feels that she is on his side and championing the cause of the systems-development team with Richard. Other times he feels that Joan is Richard's clone, making unreasonable demands that simply don't make sense. He believes Joan is competent but feels that she adds very little value to the IS group. "She just seems uninformed, powerless, and inconsistent. I'm very disappointed with her and with the GM," says Clayton, in confidence. He is sick and tired of all the changes that have occurred in the division: downsizing, reorganizations, the Quality program, self-directed teams, and Mickey Mouse team-pay schemes, to name a few.

Clayton sees the merit associated with these changes, but he is resentful that such changes were done *to* him, not *with* him. He feels oppressed by higher-ups. First, he's told to be on a team; now the analyst team is being broken up and its people dispersed into support groups. He's pissed. Health and retirement benefits are being cut. A process orientation will be the next initiative. Clayton feels vulnerable and unable to see the big picture behind these changes. He has very little grasp of the competitive situation, doesn't really see how his work fits into the whole, and never seems to get enough feedback to figure out how to do better.

Clayton sees John and Richard on a podium twice a year during division-wide meetings where they spout platitudes, show viewgraphs, talk about the business's performance in glowing terms, and ask everyone to sacrifice and persevere in a tough competitive environment. He feels Richard is out of touch with the workforce and resents his multimillion-dollar salary and his stock options.

Richard is viewed by Clayton and much of the workforce as insensitive, callous, focused on numbers, and only marginally concerned with the topic of his latest speech: "The most important aspect of the business is our people." It's clear to Clayton that the GM is in charge and can dump whatever policies, programs, structural changes, and new technologies suit his whims on "those of us who do the real work."

And Richard, the division GM, rightly wonders, can Clayton and his colleagues get out of the comfortable role of having someone else to blame for their misfortunes? Can they escape the victim mentality and their "I'm not responsible" attitudes? Is it possible for the front-line workforce to become co-creators of the organization's future? Can a workforce that doesn't seem to be willing to accept responsibility really accept the mantle of self-management?

Meanwhile, like others at the bottom of their organizations, Clayton's coworkers are waiting for the higher-ups to shove the next initiative down their throats: "What's next? What are they going to do to us next?" Whining, complaining, and feeling put upon is the order of the day. After all, the history is there. During previous change efforts, people were asked to fill out surveys and give "input." Nothing they really wanted came to pass. Internal consultants interviewed them, soliciting their ideas and opinions. None of this alleviated their feelings of vulnerability, their fear of being oppressed, and their antagonism toward management.

When the workforce talk in muted whispers in Richard's organization, they belittle management. Cliques of workers have developed that reinforce the group's unspoken norms and attitudes. There is little or no individual action beyond the minimum effort that's required. Workers are scapegoated, shunned, or ostracized if they dare to voice differing opinions. Unique talents, experiences, skills, and interests stay submerged. Competencies atrophy, while creative and committed workers never step forward to go the extra mile.

Clayton hungers for a self-managing organization where Richard would invite him and the rest of the workforce to have a say in reorganizations, physical space changes, change initiatives, and the design of new information systems. He believes there is a creative tension in the workforce waiting to be unleashed. It would be nice if there was a partnership around the future of this business. He would love to have a meaningful vision he could commit to and some genuine contact with the division GM. "Richard needs to hear some of the things we can see that are wrong," says Clayton. He would like to be able to see himself and his coworkers as central players with the capacity to affect the future of the division and the tools and systems to manage their own work.

The Patterns That Connect John, Richard, Joan, and Clayton

What can we learn from John, Richard, Joan, and Clayton? Their stories demonstrate the typical patterns of relationship that occur between tops, middles, and bottoms in any organization. When you rely on command-and-control management, this is what you get. If at each level of management a supervisor is held responsible, tells people what to do, and figures out how to put all the pieces of their direct reports to work together toward common ends, then these patterns of behavior will be reproduced indefinitely. In other words, no matter how much communication, leadership, and team training occur in a dominant hierarchy, it will not fundamentally change these underlying patterns of behavior.

This is a blind, uncomfortable, and unconscious game that no one wants to play any more but almost everyone is still stuck playing. In our new economy, where almost 60 percent of the workforce are knowledge workers and 80 percent of the new jobs are in information-intensive areas, a radical rethinking of the nature and function of management must occur.

And yet the old patterns continue to play out like tired old recordings stuck on the replay button. At the top of the organization warfare erupts over and over again. Over what? Turf and boundaries. Leaders take on too many responsibilities and find it difficult to create accountability in others. Each can handle his or her own affairs, but there is a struggle when it comes to developing common goals that can be pursued by all senior managers.

Those who are stuck in the middle never seem able to work together, learn from each other, or direct their energies to strengthen the whole system. They are forever alone and isolated, torn between the demands of those who are above them and the desires of those who are below them.

The minions at the bottom of the pile become frozen in group-think, view differences as insurmountable, and can't seem to decide anything on their own. When management tries to tell them what to do, they resent it. They become like passive sheep, dependent on management, reluctant to take on ownership and responsibility.

Finding a Better Way

Imagine that you bent down and scooped a fish out of the water and cast it on the bank. In a few moments the fish would be aware that it is suddenly in a new environment, quite different from the one where it has spent its entire existence. When managers are involved in the transformation to a self-managing organization, they too suddenly realize they are being cast out of the comfortable environment of a dominant hierarchy.

Although fish are doomed if they are taken out of water, managers can change and adapt when placed in a new environment. A fish has a physical structure (gills) adapted to extract oxygen from water and not from air; its genetic and evolutionary makeup won't allow it to survive on land. Throughout their careers, managers are conditioned to work within a dominant hierarchy. The further up the chain of command they go, the more they take for granted and deeply internalize the values, beliefs, and behaviors that a dominant hierarchy demands. While their values and beliefs can change, it isn't always an easy task.

Phil Noble is an internal consultant at Storage Technology, a company located in Colorado that designs and manufactures computer storage devices. He persuaded middle managers in one of the departments at Storage Technology to use Participative Design to redesign the middle management function. In this session, middle managers would discover to what extent their work could be devolved and transferred to work teams.

During the Participative Design session, managers made a long list of the knowledge, skills, and abilities required to do their work. Noble asked them to underline all the tasks that could eventually be relocated and assigned to self-managing teams. Managers underlined close to 90 percent of the tasks on the list. The tension in the air was suddenly obvious—it was not unlike the reaction of a cast-up fish when it realizes its gills cannot extract oxygen from air.

"Why, there are only eight things left for us to do!" said one manager. A cloud of gloom filled the room. "I guess a lot of us would lose our jobs after the teams reach the high-performance threshold," said another. As people looked at all the skills they would eventually have to give up, they had the same glazed look as Alice in Wonderland when she careened through the looking-glass and found herself in a world where all the old rules no longer applied.

Social scientist Ronald Lippitt (1983) studied group problem solving and found that when people focus only on problems, they get depressed; their energy for change diminishes below the threshold where meaningful action could occur. Lippitt also found that groups that first develop a compelling vision of their future are more likely to have more energy and motivation for solving problems along the way. The same challenges don't seem so daunting and sustainable energy is available for change when people have a clear idea that there *is* a desirable future ahead of them. Noble learned his lesson the hard way. When he worked with the next group of middle managers at Storage Technology, they were given time to brainstorm their new roles in a self-managing organization. Noble found that managers were more eager to move forward, and subsequently more willing to give up their old roles in the dominant hierarchy.

In their new role, middle managers now listen to customers and change products and distribution systems to meet customers' needs. They have their own team whose mission is to look for "red-flag" trouble spots: slow customer response times, rigid systems, internal frustrations, or patterns of customer dissatisfaction. Middle-management teams now involve the workforce in problem solving to meet competitive challenges. Many managers are subject-matter experts in certain areas, and they bring that expertise to all the teams to help them do their work.

What is on the other side of your looking glass? Will each level of your management be able to employ their current talents and skills in roles that are as satisfying and dynamic as before? Isn't it true that many people in the middle will lose power, status, and in some cases their jobs? What is the nature of self-management and the role of the top, middle, and bottom of the management hierarchy in a self-managing organization?

THE ROLE OF MANAGEMENT IN SELF-MANAGING ORGANIZATIONS

The shift to a democratic design principle is system-wide in scope; everyone in the organization, at all levels, is affected. However, managers are unlikely to make the journey toward self-management unless they have some understanding of how their roles at different levels will change. The self-managing organization is based not on a hierarchy of perceived superiority, but on a hierarchy of professional competence. There is still a need for hierarchy in self-managing organizations, but it is a competency-based hierarchy. Any dominant hierarchy—where there is always a designated boss responsible for supervising the work of subordinates—is completely dismantled.

Redundant control mechanisms—managerial positions whose only real purpose is to check on and oversee the work of others—are eliminated. What remains is a hierarchy of accountability, where each level has authority and responsibility over its own set of tasks. Unlike a dominant hierarchy, where there are clearly demarcated status differences between "superiors" and "subordinates," relationships between levels in a competency-based hierarchy are more egalitarian and complementary, with high degrees of participation between them. A management hierarchy still exists in self-managing organizations (albeit with fewer levels), but its character is radically transformed.

In a competency-based hierarchy, each level is provided the conditions for increased autonomy and self-regulation. Each level in the hierarchy—from the top to the bottom—has clear roles, responsibilities, and objectives, and is free to manage its own affairs, within designated and mutually negotiated boundaries. A competency-based hierarchy is also designed to increase accountability, by enhancing the capabilities and skills of every employee to manage his or her part of the business. The objectives of every department and level of the hierarchy are aligned with the corporate strategy. Further, each level of the hierarchy performs a specific value-added function. Most importantly, the traditional role of management shifts its primary attention from internal control and coordination tasks—from

COMPETENCY-BASED HIERARCHY

Adapted with permission from John Duncan.

Figure 11.1

bossing others around—to managing across internal and external boundaries of the company.

A hierarchy based on competency will prize, nurture, and reward innovation. When risk taking is no longer punished, human creativity and initiative can flourish. And the talents and insights of people throughout the organization can be brought to bear on providing higher levels of value for customers.

One of the hallmarks of a competency-based hierarchy is a higher level of employee participation. Over time, everyone (managers, professional staff, and workers in the trenches) is emancipated from centralized planning and control over their work by bosses in favor of jointly negotiated decision rights. This is what Charles Koch, CEO of Koch Industries, learned as he hacked his way through command-and-control structures to turn a $177-million-a-year oil company into a $30-billion-a-year business bigger than Intel, Boeing, or Motorola. Many of his ideas for growing Koch Industries were inspired by Abraham Maslow, the father of humanistic psychology. Maslow spent the summer of 1962 at Non-Linear Systems, a company that made voltmeters. The owner, Andy Kay, regrouped his workforce into teams, each being responsible for an entire product. In an airport hangar turned production facility in Del Mar, California, Maslow found workplace conditions where people were working at their full potential—and productivity soared. Maslow wrote, "The more influence and power you give to someone else in a team situation, the more you have yourself." Charles Koch confers decision rights on employees based on people's knowledge, skills, and demonstrated competence. Success expands decision rights and the scope of those rights varies depending on who holds which jobs.

And as the Non-Linear Systems example indicates, one component of self-management, multiskilling, was already a defining characteristic of self-managing teams decades ago. Multiskilling continues to be appropriate in many operational environments that involve low to moderate skill complexity and high task interdependence.

For a competency-based hierarchical organization to work, every team needs a clear direction—but should *not* be told how to achieve it. Teams need meeting spaces, tools, training, computers, and access to support groups that can help them operate effectively. Every team needs to have clear and well-defined decision rights to manage and control its own work. Managers cannot intervene in the work of these teams. As teams mature and become more capable of self-management, the scope of their decision rights is expanded. Challenging performance goals are set that are consistent with the organization's objectives, and that can be completed within a specified time.

In essence there are four fundamental criteria for successful competency-based team structures:

1. All self-managing teams need common goals.
2. A real self-managing team has genuine interdependence. Stick with traditional supervision if this isn't present.
3. Teams are effective when there is a philosophical willingness to work together and collaborate.
4. Mature teams need to be jointly accountable for their own results. In other words, commensurate with differences in salary levels, team members ought to suffer equally when performance slackens and be rewarded equally when performance is outstanding.

Role of the Strategic Level

The role of the strategic level is primarily to manage the relations between the organization and its environment. Managers at the strategic level are focused on understanding changes and opportunities in the industry, changing and aligning the enterprise to delight customers, and championing innovations that will bolster the firm's competitive advantage. All the activities at the strategic level are oriented toward enhancing the organization's capabilities for speed, flexibility, and innovation. And because self-managing organizations expand the degree of self-regulation within and between various departments, managers at the strategic level of the enterprise have more time and freedom to concentrate their attention on strategic opportunities.

Interaction between managers is more frequent at the strategic level than in traditional hierarchical organizations. Strategic-level leaders use space to promote a free exchange of ideas. For example, in the Kao Corporation, an innovative Japanese firm, conference tables are out in the open. When executives sit down to discuss the business, anyone who feels he can contribute may sit down and contribute his ideas on any topic. Spontaneous discussions occur just as readily as planned meetings, and participants are treated as equals regardless of their formal role in the hierarchy.

It is important to note that we don't refer or equate the strategic level to senior management. In self-managing organizations, those who occupy managerial positions at the strategic level may often be quite junior. The strategic level is staffed by managers who are adept at creating and inventing value-added products and services, who have a proven track record in building organizational capabilities, and who have an intimate knowledge of their industry. Such qualifications for promotion to the strategic level are not based simply on seniority, i.e., managerial experience gained by rising through the ranks of a corporate hierarchy. Instead, the competencies needed for strategic-level management resemble those of creative entrepreneurs who have successfully managed one or several small start-up companies. Those who reach the ranks of the strategic level in self-managing organizations are not necessarily "career managers." In many cases, the best and the brightest will emerge from the young upstarts who are at the edges of the organization. New strategy-creation processes—like the Search Conference—are used to tap people who have relevant knowledge and ideas that can be used to reinvent the business strategy.

Strategic-level managers are the stewards of the corporate vision, the arbitrators of resource allocation conflicts, and the guardians of the operational philosophy. They work together to ensure that the company has the necessary core competencies to build future businesses. Most of their time is spent envisioning new possibilities for enhancing the firm's economic health. Another important role the strategic level plays is to create cooperative synergies among business units with complementary skill sets for new markets. Sustaining growth may require new technology, expansion of the business to global markets, or seeking out new relationships through strategic alliances, partnerships, joint ventures, and acquisitions.

When the strategic level does turn its attention inward to more operational issues, it is always with a future focus. The strategic level sponsors change-management initiatives, and thereby puts flesh on the bones of the corporate strategy. They may sanction large-scale strategic organization-design initiatives such as Search Conferences and Participative Design. More importantly, the strategic level is responsible for determining the scope, depth, and internal consistency of such change initiatives. Will the whole organization shift to permanent self-managing work arrangements as much as possible, or will the organization be allowed to drift into a state of laissez-faire—which will necessitate a return to command and control?

It is up to the strategic level to make a clear and conscious choice to change the organization-design principle in order to prevent the proliferation of inconsistent and competing initiatives throughout the organization. Further, transformation to a competency-based hierarchy requires that all levels be redesigned to support higher degrees of self-management. A competency-based hierarchy is not reserved only for the operational level. Self-managing teams cannot be implemented at the operational level of the business, or in an isolated geographic area, while top-down directives still keep flying around like Scud missiles.

In a self-managing organization, the strategic leaders of the business learn how to cooperate with each other. They typically use Participative Design to redesign their own work, and for orchestrating the major change initiatives that cross the old boundaries and demarcation points. Strategic-level managers work together to identify the strategic challenges facing the organization. Strategic challenges are often highly ambiguous in nature, where past routines have little relevance. The role of the strategic-level team is also to diagnose symptoms of disequilibrium, performance gaps, and the social dynamics that underlie performance problems throughout the organization. They must generate the will and sense of urgency needed to jolt the organization out of its complacency. They will identify the primary stakeholders—the parties who have the keys to improving business performance—and invite them into the dialogue. When each stakeholder view is represented, each part of the system can begin to join in the diagnosis of performance gaps and generate solutions for business improvement.

Role of the (Middle) Growth Level

The shift to a self-managing organization radically changes the content of middle management's task. The task of middle management is reoriented toward managing for growth and innovation. The growth level is sandwiched between the strategic and operational levels of the business. We don't like to refer to this level as "middle management" any more, because their role is not merely to occupy an administrative space between the top and the bottom, but to grow the business.

With the deployment of self-managing teams at the operational level, the number of growth-level managers required to run the business is significantly reduced. However, the tasks that remain become more demanding. Eventually, many former duties—like putting out operational fires, working on budgets, or struggling with problems generated by employees or customers—are capably handled by self-managing teams. Therefore, managers' attention at the growth level shifts from fighting and competing with each other to being on teams that harness, channel, and align their collective energy toward common business goals.

It is no longer appropriate for these managers to retain their tunnel vision by waiting for those above them to set the ship's course. As part of the growth level, these managers now assist the strategic level in crafting compelling business strategies by participating in strategy formulation and deployment. Growth-level managers need to understand the competitive environment, the strengths of the business, what adds value for customers, and how their piece of the operation fits into the big picture. The role of the growth level fundamentally shifts from supervising and overseeing the work of the operational level to translating the organization's strategic intent into the operational level of the enterprise. In other words, they solve unique problems, which strengthens the business's ability to gain and please customers. They also design, maintain, and strengthen the support systems that allow true self-management to persist over time.

In practice, this means that growth-level managers become the integrators of the workplace, working together as a strong middle group. Working as an integrator means sharing information and solving problems across functional boundaries. It involves joint planning and strategizing for the organization. Growth-level managers do two things well: They work cooperatively as a middle group, and they manage information flows and negotiate goals with self-managing teams within their own departments.

Growth-level management is developed through democratic dialogue, negotiation, and strong leadership. Functioning as internal boundary-spanners, these managers interpret and translate strategic-level objectives, control principles, and current policies for application in operations. Their role changes from prescribing goals and handing down orders to negotiating targets and developing plans in collaboration with self-managing teams. In a democratic work organization, the functional managers become a self-managing team in which members are judged and rewarded as much for effective cross-functional coordination as for their ability to achieve functional objectives.

An important step toward self-management in the middle ranks occurs when they are able to consistently work together to solve intractable problems, combining their unique talents. Consider the role of Lisa Zackman, vice president of human resources at Wearguard, a company that makes rugged work clothes in Norwell, Massachusetts. The company had self-managing teams throughout its call centers and on the production floor but had a middle management that simply didn't buy into the participatory culture.

Zackman put seven middle managers in charge of cross-functional groups to deal with special problems. Her own team included an accounting manager, a manufacturing director, and a call-center manager. Working together, they solved a persistent problem that occurred every fall: Four hundred temporary workers, hired to help take and fill 20,000 orders a day during the peak selling season, quit at a high rate as they found better permanent jobs. This annual pattern affected quality, training costs, and efficiency. The middle-manager group came up with an innovative and effective solution: Partner with another business whose peak selling period occurred at other seasons; link the telemarketing systems together so people could stay on their respective sites; and cross-train call-center personnel in both workforces to handle each other's business during the alternating peak seasons.

As this example from Wearguard illustrates, when growth-level managers work together, a unique synergy can occur. Each individual manager has detailed knowledge and experience in a particular area. When they join together as peers and colleagues, they have the potential of generating creative and innovative solutions to business problems.

Self-managing teams are self-regulating. Growth-level managers can't resort to traditional command-and-control forms of influence. Rather, they must work collaboratively with self-managing teams to arrive at jointly negotiated objectives. Individual managers may be assigned to work with several teams, or, if they have particular expertise, with all the teams in a particular domain. In many organizations they form support teams that work with struggling self-managing teams to help them reach maturity and higher performance levels. The role of managers at this level shifts to providing relevant knowledge, information, and training to ensure that teams are focused in the right direction. Clearly, growth-level managers must provide direction to help self-managing teams align their work with organizational goals and corporate strategic objectives. They must communicate the big picture to self-managing teams on an ongoing basis. In addition, these managers are responsible for enabling the operational level to perform its tasks with a minimum of outside interference and external disruptions.

The role of the middle is essentially to protect the self-managing teams' boundary conditions so that the teams can continue to control and coordinate their own work. Such protection is not paternalistic, as would be the case in traditional organizations. Rather, growth-level managers play a critical support role, acting as resources and consultants to the teams. Furthermore, growth-level managers allow self-managing work teams to deal more directly with external constituencies, realizing that by doing so they will have more time to focus their attention on long-term planning and other tasks that can add value to the business. Thus, the time span of responsibility for growth-level management is also expanded.

Since self-managing teams work close to the customer or production process, they may have special training needs or important information that could be of strategic interest to the company. The growth level plays a critical brokerage role in making sure that such information is utilized, while also leading teams to understand the logic and demands of the strategic level's objectives. The development and maturation of self-management at the operational level depends on how much support and training the growth level makes available during the early phases of a redesign effort. Such support will also determine the degree to which the growth level reduces its involvement in operational-level tasks. As the operational level acquires the relevant knowledge and skills to become more autonomous and self-managing, the growth level is released from having to focus its attention on operational-level issues.

We can summarize the role and activities of growth-level managers that support teams at the operational level by stating that growth-level managers:

- negotiate goals with teams.
- assist with development plans for teams to grow and mature in their capabilities for self-management.
- help teams develop protocols and policies for performance issues.
- design metrics to support self-managing teams.
- remove obstacles and provide sanctioning so that innovative reward and compensation systems can be implemented.
- coordinate the activities across various teams.
- provide a clear business direction.
- steward the teams' performance in line with strategic goals and business objectives.
- lead by providing support and mentorship to enable the teams to achieve their mission.

In most cases, growth-level managers will also need training and practice to be able to take on these new roles. This is a particularly important activity. Without proper training, only a few isolated middle managers will have the capability to design the systems and processes that help teams evolve and grow. And these individuals will be resented by their peers instead of embraced as role models for creating sustainable self-managing organizations. This is where many efforts at self-management are stopped in their tracks.

A mature, capable growth-level management will have the capacity to work effectively together. They must be deployable to assist with management crises wherever they exist in the enterprise. When pooled, their spare time becomes a valuable reserve for higher management.

The payoff of an effective growth level is great for these managers and an extraordinary benefit for the business. Effective managers at the growth level sustain the self-managing organization. They free strategic-level managers from having to manage internal problems, which is a diversion from their primary task of managing the interface between the organization and its competitive environment.

Self-Management at the Operational Level

The operating level controls and coordinates routine production and service-delivery activities. The operational level solves day-to-day problems, applying real-time measures to eliminate errors in current work processes while making continuous improvements. Workers at the operational level initiate improvement projects within their area of control using a mix of hard and soft techniques. They also participate with the growth level of the hierarchy in diagnosing broader organizational needs for change that impact the whole system or one of its business processes.

Operational-level people use quality tools (fishbone and scatter diagrams, control charts/graphs, histograms, statistical process control, etc.) to help evaluate whether a process is under control. They seek to ensure that production or service delivery runs smoothly, and that the whole process is streamlined and redesigned to prevent recurring errors and variances. Identifying internal and external customer needs, and providing superior customer service, is a primary work focus.

The operational level helps select, operate, troubleshoot, and maintain equipment; analyze and redesign the workflow in its functional area; and integrate technical improvements into its work. They also set and track success indicators, develop operational guidelines and goals, plan workloads, manage projects, and work with customers, vendors, and the public. The operational level may also assist the growth level in analyzing markets, understanding competitors, and identifying customer needs.

We have already examined what happens to the operational level in a dominant command-and-control hierarchy. Workers feel vulnerable and invisible. Change is done to them. Senior management mandates programs and forces new flavors every month upon them. Mergers, great; strategic alliances, sure; reengineer core business processes, you bet; rightsizing, thanks for the memories. Lower-level employees in traditional organizations can't see the big picture—they have no vision they can commit to, they don't get feedback on their work or see how it fits into a larger whole. Lacking a connection to the purpose of the enterprise, and stuck in fragmented work, lower-level employees are often disillusioned, alienated, and powerless.

When operational-level groups become self-managing, they are not independent and autonomous. They become part of a larger system and must be integrated into that system. The growth level of management is responsible for setting the operational strategy, pay rates, overall quality goals, and managing boundaries—both between teams at similar levels and between core processes. At the lowest level of self-management, operational groups may simply have the right to decide on working methods and the allocation of work among team members. At a somewhat higher level, operational teams may control some of the conditions from which they start—membership of their groups, equipment and tools, maintenance, support arrangements, responsibility for their own quality control—as well as many other tasks that were formerly in the hands of managers or staff specialists.

At an even higher level, operational teams may be involved in the longer-range concerns of the organization: product development, knowledge discovery and knowledge creation, change processes, coordination of work activities with external customers and suppliers, and so on. For some companies, this amount of control devolved to employees represents a quantum leap.

REDESIGNING THE MANAGEMENT HIERARCHY AT MEDICAL PRODUCTS, INC.[1]

Background

The parent company of Medical Products, Inc. is based in Europe and has sales in excess of $8 billion. Medical Products is one of the leading enter-

---

[1]Medical Products, Inc. is a pseudonym. We are grateful to the senior mangement team for allowing us to observe and interview managers at all levels on their changing roles in a self-managing organization.

prises in their industry with subsidiaries all over the world. The North American subsidiary of Medical Products began operations five years ago. This operation is staffed with a high percentage of Ph.D.'s—geneticists, medical researchers, organic chemists, and process engineers. It has maintained a 40-percent-per-year growth rate since its inception, and is expected to continue this rate for some time.

Medical Products' mission is to dominate the markets they serve by providing outstanding value to customers. The unique competency of the business comes from the products they produce combined with a very close relationship with key customers, who contribute to product innovations. The organization has a very sophisticated quality program and a management team that, in early 1995, was beginning to shift its orientation toward a high degree of employee participation.

Despite its current success, Medical Products' new president felt that the competitive environment was changing so rapidly that the business couldn't afford to rest on its laurels. Any pause in business performance would jeopardize the future of this company. Medical Products was managed carefully, relying on a classical chain of command with seven levels of management. The common problems associated with this form of management were becoming a drag on flexibility and competitiveness. These challenges included lack of trust, suspicion between knowledge workers and management, poor lateral-communication flows among technical professionals in different departments, and a slower market-response time than was needed in a highly fluid global environment.

If you had walked through Medical Products, Inc. in 1994, you would have seen fancy multicolored metrics all over the walls to keep track of performance and foster improvement. Unfortunately, few people actually used the metrics. Most employees were not devoting much attention or energy to continuously improving their work. The onus of responsibility was always on the managers. Work groups were dependent on them for guidance and directions. If a manager was absent, people avoided making decisions and tried to get the next-higher-level manager to solve problems.

The traditional chain of command presented problems with role clarity because functional chiefs and midlevel managers were constantly waging turf wars. Confusion existed at the top, middle, and bottom of the business about the types of decisions people needed to make and who ought to make them. Executives sometimes took on middle management roles, and middle managers sometimes took on first- or second-line supervisory roles. Consequently, front-line workers complained they were constantly being asked to reorient priorities, and they resented the firefighting atmosphere in the work setting.

The management team wanted to recapture a competitive focus and achieve a faster market response time in order to sustain the growth curve. Their first step was to cut the levels of management from seven down to three, which only increased the stress and pressure on people. Many complained that their new roles were unclear. The general manager wanted to change the mindset and behavior of management, and began searching for a way to get every manager to begin thinking differently about the nature of his or her work.

In the search for new methods that might help him achieve a transformation of Medical Products, the general manager learned about Search Conferences and Participative Design from a colleague in another organization. He felt that these approaches could help the business set a clear strategic direction and establish a competency-based hierarchy.

A Competency-Based Hierarchy: Remolding the Top Group

The general manager at Medical Products, along with the management team, went through a Participative Design session to redesign the organization structure, their roles, and their working relationships. The general manager's role changed toward being an interface between the outside world and the enterprise. He was no longer going to be the one responsible for giving immediate direction to his department heads. The functional managers, as a group, would share responsibility for running the company. They would negotiate their coordination and performance goals for the business with the general manager. These goals were specifically designed to adapt the enterprise to the changing business environment.

For example, the production, marketing, and R&D directors worked together on a project to improve innovation and cut development-cycle times. Several cross-functional improvement groups helped to structure jobs with overlapping responsibilities, set up work areas so people could actually see each other's work, and received permission to base the majority of rewards on team performance. Information-systems professionals collaborated with Quality personnel to establish systems that shared information more quickly and in a more useful form across the functions.

The general manager conferred decision rights on the functional managers, giving them considerable latitude. In the new design, the general manager would intervene only in extreme performance-problem situations. If the strategy was not aligned with the competitive realities, the general manager would step in to reorient the middle group to changes in the competitive environment. He would also intervene if critical work that needed to be done to stay competitive was not being done. In the latter case, the general manager would initiate a strategy review, using techniques like the Search Conference, to create a new framework for operating policies to respond to the competitive threats.

Another situation that might call for his intervention was if certain functional leaders were unwilling or unable to cooperate with their peers. In fact, the general manager did have to step in and intervene on one occasion, when middle-level managers were having difficulty in forging cooperative partnerships. The message to the middle level was clear: We are going to adopt self-management and a team orientation. Anyone who doesn't want to play ball will no longer have a role in the management hierarchy.

Moving Self-Management Deeper into the Business

After the strategic level learned to become a cohesive self-managing team and started modeling new behaviors, they turned their attention to redesigning the organizational architecture. Strategic-level managers at Medical Products were interested in running the organization so that each management level worked with peers in a spirit of cooperation and mutual dependence, eliminating the backbiting and acrimony that existed under the old command-and-control hierarchy.

The strategic level's vision called for a high-performance organization where people were willing to learn, were energetic and optimistic about their work, and could be creative and decisive in solving problems. The idea was to base the organization around the self-managing-team concept. The general manager wanted self-managing teams to set goals for their work areas, linked to the business strategy and backed up with strong metrics. Metrics would give teams clear feedback on their contribution to business goals, like market share and cost reduction; operational goals, like responsiveness, quality, and outputs; and team-maturity goals, like cross-training, customer service, and changes in team membership. The middle group of managers would be charged with helping teams take on more decision rights.

Strategic and growth-level management, as well as seasoned technical professionals who were close to the customer, participated in a Search Conference to conduct a thorough scan of the changes happening in their industry. The conference was held to ensure that key stakeholders were aware of the competitive realities, and to diagnose whether the organization was aligned with the business strategy. These strategic thinkers generated three-year objectives and committed to deploying the plans. In the Search Conference they decided that a major realignment was necessary: the organization needed to change from a functional to a process-based design. This strategic shift meant that the roles and structures of management would be changed significantly. The strategic level of the enterprise, which included only the general manager and the business team, would be reformed along business lines and process ownership.

Following the Search Conference, senior managers, technical professionals, and a deep slice of the workforce went through a three-day Participative Design session to create a new strategic-level design. The challenge was to get rid of functional barriers and establish a process orientation. The general manager wanted to proceed cautiously by first creating a process-based design, then moving deeper to democratize the work. As the general manager recalls, "If we were going to replace command and control, we didn't want a structure where people can do whatever they like, resulting in complete anarchy. Our goal was for everyone to know their role and be able to respond rapidly to customer demands. When people grab the end of the hose, we want them to be very clear about whether they were going to the fire or the hydrant. The management function also had to be geared toward leveraging our core competencies, generating highly flexible behavior, and increasing our ability to respond fluidly to change in the competitive environment."

The central point here was that the new, competency-based hierarchy would reflect the different roles at the strategic, growth, and operational levels. A hierarchy based on different competencies meant that people would have complementary roles and would no longer be dominated by the next-higher level of the hierarchy. But this didn't mean that traditional supervision would disappear. Far from it. The general manager and his team knew there would be several instances where people were simply not mature enough for self-management. Those groups of people would have traditional supervisors selected by management.

It became very easy for participants to redesign the workforce along business-unit lines once everyone had the benefit of collective reasoning. The business-line model established in the strategic-level Participative Design sessions made sense for several practical reasons. For example, there was no production equipment that was shared by all the potential business lines. Some technical resources were shared, but this was easy to work out in the design process. The other important advantage was that only a few customers used two or more of the business lines; infighting and internal competition were unlikely.

Redesigning the hierarchy at every level of the business reoriented people for continued success. Three people who had the skill sets to help guide the organization through the maze of opportunities and threats—presented by customer imperatives, potential partnerships, and competitor advances—were invited to become members of the strategic management level. These people became business-line leaders. Their peers—middle managers from various other technical disciplines and departments—chose them. Senior management simply gave middle managers criteria for selecting the best people, then asked them to nominate peers who they felt could most ably perform the duties of business-line leaders. Senior management sat down to review the recommendations and discovered that a very clear consensus existed for those three individuals, whom they subsequently endorsed as strategic-level managers.

Ten individuals were also selected as process managers, since the redesign involved reorienting along business-process lines. Seven of those individuals were already part of the strategic level and three became strategic-level members once they assumed their new roles.

Strategic-Level Roles Added After Redesign

The strategic level of Medical Products, Inc. is now responsible for corporate objectives and relations with the parent company. This group maintains a two-way flow of information on strategy, business goals, competitive challenges, needs, and capabilities. Every quarter the strategic level hosts a meeting to discuss current issues with the growth-level management team and representatives from the work teams.

Strategic-level managers assess whether Medical Products, Inc. is meeting its mission and business objectives, help ensure that business processes are being effectively carried out, and make sure everyone's behavior remains consistent with the team concept. They monitor the performance of the boundary spanners—the growth-level management group—by working with them to set clear objectives. These objectives remain within the framework of corporate objectives, and are subject to change when new competitive realities emerge.

The growth-level management group consists of eighty people. They are organized into seven different teams. Each growth-level management team sets three to seven objectives for the current business quarter, and develops an operating plan that includes a budget for the next year. These are negotiated with the strategic level and tied to key business drivers. For example, the growth level is working on strengthening the support systems that make teams viable; it has several six- to eighteen-month objectives in this area.

Performance goals are explicitly defined and objectively assessed. They have to fit the growth-level team's decision-cycle time and ensure timely feedback so that these formerly isolated middle managers can make their own midcourse corrections. Growth-level teams often coordinate across the different boundaries by making a map of all the sections of the organization that share similar objectives. Procedures for coordinating the work and sharing information are created to keep important responsibilities from falling through the cracks.

An important distinction was made between maintaining day-to-day performance standards and developing new ways of working. For example, in order to support continuous improvement, task forces are often charged to come up with new ways of working. These teams are temporary. The strategic level found that staffing them with the stakeholders who will have to implement the change ensures that these people will be motivated to make the needed changes. This replaced the prior approach of passing new ways of working on to teams, who then didn't implement them.

The Redesign Process for the Business Lines

"After thirty of us created the high-level strategic design, we involved the entire workforce from each business line in the Participative Design sessions for their area," said the general manager. This was a whole-system approach, where all the stakeholders were represented in each design session. Stakeholders developed the operating-level structure for each set of business processes in separate Participative Design sessions.

A special Participative Design session was held for management to establish the three levels of management for the core business processes. Participative Design sessions were also held for redesigning essential support and ancillary activities. During the Participative Design sessions, a lot of work was put into defining which were growth-level activities and which were operating-level activities. Roles, responsibilities, and reporting relationships had to be clearly defined in order to create an effective organization design.

The Shift from Middle Management to Growth-Level Management

A transition plan was created to facilitate the role change from middle managers to growth-level managers. The growth-level group is held responsible for cross-boundary activities in the new process-based design. They pool their resources and are located together on one floor in an open area in sight of each other, similar to floor plans in Japanese offices. All seven of the growth-level management teams are located on the same floor.

Growth-level managers have seen their management duties change dramatically and increase in complexity. Sam Chen, a member of the growth-level team, is awed by the change in his management role. He is now responsible for three process teams, who take responsibility for the outcomes of their own work. Before the redesign, Chen was rewarded for dealing with day-to-day tasks and activities. Not any more. Chen now spends a lot of his time helping each team develop the skills they need to deal with the day-to-day work. As Chen recalls, "We now spend a great deal of time managing the boundaries between teams and the organization. My colleagues and I, on the growth-level management team, are working on several processes teams can use to deal with their own hiring, training needs, and performance problems. One current issue is the individual-merit pay system. We are pushing the strategic level to support team-based rewards, not individual or mixed rewards, because research indicates team rewards are more effective in sustaining self-management."

Some teams are not up to spec yet. Chen is helping out other teams that aren't as far along. He now works side by side with his middle-management colleagues to help each team to improve its performance and maturity in handling team-related issues.

The growth-level management team is strongly supportive of the way they are working together, and most managers, if you talk to them now, would tell you that they think their work is significantly better than it was in their previous position as isolated middle managers. Many found the transition and the learning process of taking on new roles as difficult and painful for them as it was for the teams. "This is not a picnic," said one manager, "and I would have chosen not to do it in the beginning, but once it's in place and you've gotten used to it, it makes the business better and it's more fun to work this way."

Self-Managed Teams in Operations

Participative Design sessions were conducted for each of the new product-line groups in the company. Each product-line group set itself up in self-managing teams; these teams are completely accountable for measurable business results. Roles were defined so teams of knowledge workers could be clear about which of their activities were growth-level and which were operational-level responsibilities.

In addition, each team defined its new roles, reporting relationships, and team-based procedures for working. Performance measures were established so team members could continue to monitor what they were doing and make needed changes.

Self-managing teams in the core-business and business-support operations chart their own metrics, seek data on how well they are doing, and alter their performance strategies as needed. They meet with other teams to benchmark best practices, take action to solve their own internal problems, and regulate the way each member contributes to the work.

The organization is still working on developing solid performance measures. How do we monitor what is happening? How do we change what we are doing? As one of the strategic-level managers commented about the shift to self-management: "Each of us has learned more in the past three years than in the previous twenty years combined. And we are not done yet."

Many organizations fall down on performance measurement or performance management, but not Medical Products, Inc. Their previous history of evolving the tools, strategies, and processes to strengthen quality was drawn upon to create an integrated self-managing system. As another growth-level manager commented: "Participative Design fits in quite nicely with a TQM orientation and builds on our participative culture. When you place self-management on top of an established TQM program, it accelerates the benefits derived from both."

SUMMARY

Medical Products, Inc. is one of the few examples of integrated self-management at all three levels of the management hierarchy. One reason this case is disguised is that the corporate parent in Europe is still organized in a traditional command-and-control hierarchy. The shift to self-management changes the way work is done and is often difficult for experienced managers since it involves, as we have illustrated, unlearning much of what management has been for the last two centuries. It also means a sense of loss for some managers. Giving up some power and control in exchange for increases in flexibility, speed, innovation, and performance can be a painful learning process for some.

Change is usually associated with some kind of loss (at a minimum, giving up the way it was). Exercising leadership means moving people through that period of loss. The strategic-level managers must lead people through the changes demanded by the business environment. They must provoke a sense of urgency, providing people with opportunities to discover for themselves the demands and pressures of current and future competitive realities. Strategic leaders do not protect people from threats; rather, they help people to feel the pinch of the threat so that they can develop the energy and motivation to change.

A period of tension is unavoidable during the transition to a competency-based hierarchy that relies on high degrees of participation. For a time, some managers at each level of the hierarchy will be reluctant to let go of what they know best: traditional command and control. Their voices will compete with those who are more enthusiastic about self-management. It is important for the organization to be aware that the manner in which the change is brought about is just as important as the final design of a self-managing organization.

In this chapter we have sought to facilitate the unlearning and relearning process by providing a clear description of the management patterns that exist on the command-and-control side of the looking glass, and what the world is like for those organizations which are bold enough to take the leap and create an integrated system of self-management in their own enterprise.

DEMOCRACY AT WORK IN THE TWENTY-FIRST CENTURY

> Everybody's for democracy in principle. It's only in practice that the thing gives rise to stiff objections.
> —Meg Greenfield

DEMOCRATIC WORKPLACE REFORM: A NEW SOCIAL MOVEMENT

For the last half-century we have been witnessing an evolutionary movement away from the industrial logic of bureaucracy and toward more self-managing organizations. The recent fashions of work teams, empowerment, Total Quality, and even Reengineering—despite their problems and flaws—are not merely passing fads. Instead, these trends show that the evolution toward a new paradigm of work is already under way and is here to stay. Reengineering, Total Quality Management, and the Human Relations movements, however, attempted to transform organizations by working within the logic and strictures of the existing corporate order. The Quality movement, for example, lost its momentum and transformational power when it was reduced to a set of management tools and consulting techniques. Whenever social movements for reform are corporatized they lose their spirit and power to effect fundamental change. Change agents and social activists for reform lose heart as they find themselves becoming obedient technicians and consultants who are expected to follow the standard administrative logic. Such reforms eventually become enshrined in a method—a set of tools and techniques—which are deployed in an orderly, programmatic, and well-controlled manner. Once a movement for reform is reduced to technique it is effectively depoliticized, rendering such approaches impotent to effect transformative change.

Democracy at work—whether it be in the private or public sector—

might become a new social movement, one where common citizens will band together to abolish employment contracts and work structures that bar them from being full-fledged members of their enterprises. People can only derive a sense of membership when they are given responsibility for controlling and coordinating their own work—when they have a real share of the voice in the organization. We need to take back our inalienable right to democratic self-governance. We did it when we were fed up with English rule, and perhaps we will do it again, only this time in the economic sphere. But this will require a new declaration of interdependence between those who work in the firm and those who provide the capital, a new social contract based on mutual obligations and mutual responsibilities. Charles Handy agrees:

> Membership is a way of thinking about the psychological contract between an individual and the organization. If the individual is seen as an instrument, even an "empowered" instrument, he or she is there to be used by others for their purposes. Such an instrumental contract, no matter how well intentioned or how benevolently interpreted, is a denial of democracy. Our economic well-being and the continued success of capitalism depend on efficient and effective organizations of all types. One way, perhaps the only way, to match our needs for democracy in our critical institutions with our need for efficiency is to think of our organizations as membership businesses. (1995, p. 192)

Moreover, the source of capital is shifting away from physical and financial assets to having access to human assets. Indeed, the real source of strategic competitive advantage is located inside the head of the knowledge worker. Wealth creation is now derived from intellectual property. But here is the paradox: Investors don't really own, nor can they really control intellectual property, since that property is embedded in the network of interactions within a community of knowledge workers. Intellectual property must be viewed, at least to some extent, as being part of the organizational commons. Knowledge development occurs in the public domain, in public spaces, where ideas can be shared freely and widely. Unlike ordinary private property, which we usually regard as sacrosanct—a scarce possession that we need to hoard, protect, and defend—knowledge expands the more it is shared. This is all very counter-intuitive, but knowledge sharing increases the value of knowledge. It's based on the principle of increasing returns and self-reinforcing mechanisms. Knowledge has to move, circulate, and connect for it to develop and add value. A good example of this is the Shareware movement, where millions of copies of software have been given away free to users. Revenue streams were generated from the technical support and service spin-offs that were tied to the use of the software. Netscape followed the same strategy, giving away more than four million copies of its browser. Knowledge has properties that are more ethereal in nature; like the Internet, knowledge is created through a web of connections—nobody controls it, nobody owns it, but everybody benefits. Intellectual capital defies the laws of physical commodities and classical economics.

Participative Design is not merely a tool or a technique; it is a movement that gives people back their rights to control their own affairs at the workplace. What we have traditionally is an employment contract where those who work in organizations hand their membership status and rights to manage and govern themselves over to the employer. Along with this transfer of rights comes a transfer of responsibilities. The employer is made ultimately responsible for the welfare of the firm, yet the employer is a representative of the owners, who have a very different set of interests and priorities from those who work in the firm. And employees, having transferred their rights to manage over to the employer, have also dissociated themselves from the goals of the organization. As a consequence of this arrangement, both shareholders and employees feel little sense of emotional connection or loyalty to the enterprise. Shareholders are only interested in maximizing their return on investment (in the short term), and employees are only interested in maximizing their wages. Neither party has a deep emotional connection or sense of commitment to the long-term welfare of the enterprise.

This absence of loyalty is a recipe for disaster in an economy where the only strategic competitive advantage is access to brainpower. Firms need a new social contract that provides a credible basis upon which to build loyalty. Otherwise, how will firms expect to attract and retain knowledge workers? How can a community of interests be forged to provide conditions for loyalty to be rebuilt? Under the current adversarial scheme, that is virtually impossible, because the system is designed to maintain asymmetrical power relations between stakeholders, with the shareholders as the Number One beneficiary. John Dasburg, CEO of Northwest Airlines, realized that this arrangement was unbalanced and needed to be overhauled. Dasburg led the crusade to save Northwest Airlines from imminent bankruptcy, forging an unprecedented creative partnership with the company's many unions. As part of the deal, the unions gave up $900 million in wage and work-rule concessions, and the owners gave labor three seats on the corporate board, along with 30 percent ownership in the company. Dasburg argues, ". . . we've had enough experience in the twentieth century with national socialism and with Stalin, Bolshevikism and on and on to conclude that—that the utopian model is flawed. My concern about the capitalist model is that—that while it seems to work and we're all involved in capitalism in an incredibly existential way—the fact of the matter is that there is, in my view, the need for some type of balance. Democracy didn't work without certain rights being guaranteed—what we call the Bill of Rights. And in my view, there is somewhat of a Bill of Rights to capitalism. You just simply must take into consideration all of the various interests in a society in an enterprise. And if you fail to do that, capitalism will fail."

Putting worker representatives on corporate boards is a step in the right direction, but it is not enough. True democratic workplace reform calls for putting democracy directly where the action is—in the hands of the people who do the work. People must be given the legal structures and decision rights that allow them to participate and control their everyday affairs. Some may argue that this form of democratic governance within private enterprise is not an inalienable right. Private enterprises, like private individuals, are free to choose how they govern their own affairs. In the privacy of our own homes, we may choose to be dictatorial or democratic with our spouses and children—and its nobody else's business. Although some parents may, either by choice or by character, be dictatorial with their children, that doesn't justify a dictatorship for all other human relations. We, as a people, certainly detest and do not tolerate modern dictatorships or totalitarian governments. We, as a people, have decided that citizens in a democracy *do* have an inalienable right to govern themselves. As Robert Dahl (1985) argues, "*If* democracy is justified in governing the state, then it must *also* be justified in governing economic enterprises; and to say that it is *not* justified in governing economic enterprises is to imply that it is not justified in governing the state." The argument that democratic governance is not an inalienable right, but an "option," that it should be a "free choice," doesn't hold water, since how can one choose if one is disempowered? Any human association for which democratic principles are valid has an inalienable right to be governed by such principles. It doesn't really matter whether that human association exists in the public or the private sphere.

If we as a people truly believe that every citizen has an inalienable right to life, liberty, and the pursuit of happiness, how can we then say with any kind of legitimacy that that right doesn't apply in the workplace? The right to participate in decision making, the right to have some reasonable degree of control over one's own affairs—these are inalienable rights. To disallow them or to take them away is an immoral act. A lack of motivation at work, employee alienation, and employee apathy—these are not psychological problems. Rather, these "problems" are a displaced and muffled form of civil disobedience, a demonstration against a system of governance that has long denied individuals their inalienable rights to control and coordinate their own affairs.

For years we have operated off a misdiagnosis of the problem, attempting all sorts of remedies and panaceas—human relations programs, pep talks, job enrichment, team building—all to no avail. Since the human relations movement, we have had this warped idea that if only employees could be persuaded or trained to *think* that their interests were the same as management's, everything else would fall into place. Yet this yearning for harmony is a pipe dream, since it is impossible to harmonize a system that is designed along undemocratic lines—a system that for all practical purposes disenfranchises and disempowers its corporate citizens. It's hard to feel that one belongs, it's hard to identify with the goals of the organization, if one has only resident-alien status. The problem, like a gaping and infected wound, will never be healed with these Band-Aid solutions. We need the real medicine now: democracy at work.

Perhaps it is time for us to put an end to the charades and face up to the fact that we can't integrate people into the organization unless there is a substantial change in the distribution of power. Perhaps it is time to cut through the pretense of management-controlled "empowerment" and cooptive participation programs. We need to aim higher than simply humanizing the organization, which is relatively easy to do, and which often amounts to nothing more than a better treatment of the human commodities. Instead, we need to democratize the organization so that people can become full-fledged members, where their rights to participate are protected and their capacities for participation are developed.

For years we have also tried to justify empowerment, high involvement, and employee participation based on their consequences and potential benefits. Other organizational reformers have followed this path too—the Human Relationists, the Socio-Technocrats, the Reengineerians—all to no avail. Human Relationists, with their exaggerated claims, said, "Reform the supervisor, and everyone will work together like one big happy family!" Socio-Technocrats, in their studious way, said, "Match technology with the people doing the work, and then everyone will benefit!" The Reengineerians, with their hype and hoopla, said, "Don't automate, obliterate the silos and performance will improve dramatically!" We now face the prospect that Participative Designers will attempt to justify the self-managing organization by asserting their own set of overinflated claims: "Democratize the hierarchical structure, and productivity, commitment, and flexibility will be enhanced!"

To some extent we have made such claims in this book. Yes, self-managing organizations have proven to be more economically viable, as evidenced by lower costs, lower overhead, higher productivity. Yes, self-managing organizations are more effective in terms of being able to adapt and respond to changing demands. Yes, self-managing organizations provide good work that enhances employee commitment and involvement. Yes, self-managing organizations unleash creativity and free people up to be more innovative. Yes, self-managing organizations foster a partnership culture built on norms of equality and trust. Yes, self-managing organizations—because they provide good work and treat people as adults—might even make sense simply because they are the right thing to do. But none of these claims or appeals for self-management need to be defended when participative democracy at work is justified as an inalienable *human right*.

Should we expect the self-managing organization to miraculously transform the character of human beings? No, not their character, not their personality; but it can transform their *behavior*. The fact is that when people are placed in structures that provide them with responsibility to control and coordinate their own work, dramatic behavioral change is often the result. We are now in a period of punctuated equilibrium where all the rules of engagement are in flux. Under these conditions, even a small change may lead to a ripple effect that transforms the way people think and behave throughout society. Social change may happen much more rapidly than we can imagine. But whether such transformation takes several years or several generations, self-management is still the right thing to do.

Democratic workplace reform begins when one lonely, isolated individual—out of his or her inner conviction—dares to speak up and becomes an advocate for fundamental change. As we look at the 1990 outbreaks of democracy in Eastern Europe and the former Soviet Union, along with the 1989 student uprisings in Tiananmen Square, we can see that a democracy movement begins when one courageous individual speaks up for the rights of the people. A new social movement is born when isolated individuals who harbor similar aspirations for reform discover that they are not alone. Right now, there are many senior executives, middle managers, employees, and, yes, even unionists in every organization who share similar hopes and dreams for a more spirited and productive workplace. These individuals simply haven't gone public—they haven't shared their innermost concerns and values. There is a pro-democracy contigency in every organization, but it often remains dormant because nobody is willing to take the risk to lead the change. A conspiracy of silence and collusion with the existing corporate order keeps people immobilized. But there comes a time when an enlightened leader, in an act of integrity, steps forward to break the code of silence. When that moment occurs, the inner truth of the leader's moral convictions for democratic reform are made public, this deeply resonates with the inner truths of the populace, and the movement begins. Democracy at work spreads one person at a time, but it takes an act of courageous leadership to get it started. The movement gains momentum as more and more people within organizations band together to work for a common cause.

As a new social movement, democracy at work can help to rehabilitate society, reinvigorating many of our cherished ideals, which were founded on the belief that all people are created equal, that all people deserve to live in freedom and with a measure of dignity. Bringing democracy to the workplace is a noble cause. Such a movement can help to reverse many of the debilitating and regressive trends in society by empowering people to take responsibility for their actions, and for the common good. How can society expect people to be responsible citizens if they are alienated and disenfrachised for the duration of their working lives? Active citizenship in society requires employees who can participate in decision making. Through active participation, democracy at work can increase people's sense of political efficacy, enlarging their capacity to take responsibility for their own affairs. Through Participative Design, people can redesign their workplace so that it meets their higher-order needs and their psychological requirements for good work. In sum, self-managing organizations can restore pride of ownership, tapping the deep source of integrity where people can find meaning in what they do.

The diffusion of democracy at work requires, then, that we view and use Participative Design as more than just another management tool or consulting technique. The movement toward democracy at work needs to be embodied and lived through Participative Design sessions. Participative Design provides a legitimate forum in which people engage in real dialogue to redesign organizations to align them with their highest democratic ideals.

However, we must remember that democracy has never been a popular form of government. During the course of civilization, democracy has been more the exception than the rule, and it has a fragile history. Like other significant social movements, democractic workplace reform will encounter significant resistance and anti-democratic sentiments. "Democracy may work for the Boy Scouts, and I'll fly my American flag on the Fourth of July, but Not-In-My-Corporation (NIMC). Can't you read the sign? Private Property, No Trespassing. Democracy at work? Over my dead body." These are the attitudes and sentiments that we have to contend with. Resistance to democracy in private and public institutions is to be expected. After all, why should those in positions of power be willing to support such a fundamental reform if they stand to lose the most from such a change? The job of traditional management in a dominant hierarchy is to preserve and protect the prevailing organizational order.

One of the basic features of self-managing organizations is the absence of a dominant command-and-control hierarchy. Democratization of work creates a climate where ideas and people can flow freely, without censorship. Dissent is tolerated, and those who wish to challenge the status quo do so without fear of reprisal. Democratic organizations don't "shoot the messenger" when bad news is made public. Conflict is seen as necessary to the creative process. Those who express minority or unpopular opinions are viewed as the "loyal opposition," rather than as traitors or disloyal antagonists whose views must be squelched and made to conform to the party line. For these reasons ideas, which are necessary for transforming the status quo, for shaking the organization out of its set routines and habitual patterns—for creating change and stimulating innovation—have more chance of making an impact. Democracy at work brings about a corporate *glasnost,* creating a culture of openness that allows a rapid acceptance of breakthrough ideas. Similarly, as people are given more responsibility for controlling and coordinating their own work, they also come to accept more responsibility for the consequences of their own decisions.

We can see why democracy at work might appear threatening to managers, who find comfort and safety in a corporate aristocracy that buffers them from the rough-and-tumble realm of public scrutiny. Conventional wisdom and our training tell us that change and revolution will come by rejecting and overthrowing the existing order. But trying to pit a small group of reformers directly against the entrenched patterns of corporate power is surely an exercise in futility. Many enthusiastic advocates for democratic workplace reform, many change agents have been stopped dead in their tracks when they tried such a direct approach. And when these change agents encounter resistance, they become rigid and defensive. Indeed, many change agents are their own worst enemies—self-righteously blaming, attacking, and cajoling managers into accepting their doctrinaire ideologies for reform. After banging their heads against the corporate wall of bureaucracy too many times, these change agents eventually fall into despair and become cynical, diminishing their hopes, aspirations, and expectations for fundamental change.

Resistance to democratic workplace reform should be looked upon not as a setback, but as a good sign that we have touched a nerve. Shaking people out of their complacency and complicity with the status quo will always evoke an emotional response. Resistance is a critical success factor, a useful indicator and form of feedback that tells us that we are challenging deep and fundamental assumptions. In fact, change agents should welcome resistance—the more, the better, since we can use it to constructively plot indirect alternative ways to make deeper inroads into the organization. Change agents for democratic workplace reform must free themselves from having to draw their sustenance and support from a dry well—the existing corporate power structure. To strengthen the movement, reformers need to form regional networks and national coalitions, not only to help diffuse "best practices" and "share learnings," but to build a community of support. Change agents can turn to these centers of support to replenish their source of power, sustenance, and inspiration.

FULFILLING THE PROMISE

As we enter the postmodern age, the idea of progress—that society is moving inexorably toward a more promising future—is no longer a guiding myth. With so much uncertainty in the air, for many people the promise of a more fulfilling future is questionable. Furthermore, as the nature of work becomes more abstract and symbolic, as more and more people spend their working lives in cyberspace, people will crave a real and authentic connection to the purpose of the enterprise. Without an overarching and compelling purpose, people may fall prey to an existential despair.

Democratic business organizations won't solve all the world's problems, but they will be places where people can find meaning in their work. Work becomes meaningful when people have attained real membership status, when work is restored to its rightful place, which adds value to both the customer and to the worker, and when people are shapers and co-creators of the organization's future.

We hope that the ideas in this book have planted a few seeds that may help democracy at work to take root. It is now up to you to take them and cultivate a grassroots movement in your own organization. Someone like yourself must break the code of silence and take the first step. If we worry that we are not the ones who should come forward, we only undermine the power of democracy. We may doubt our own strength and leadership abilities, but we can still act. We can honor our inner convictions and can go forward with others. Perhaps change is not as difficult as we have imagined and have been led to believe.

REFERENCES

Chapter 1: The End of Management

Bennis, W. 1997. "Cultivating creative genius." *Industry Week*, August 18, pp. 84–90.

Cabana, S. 1995. "Can people restructure their own work? How HP, Syncrude and others use Participative Design and the Search Conference to unleash organizational power." *Target*, November–December, 11 (6):16–30.

Cusumano, M., and R. Selby, 1995. *Microsoft Secrets*. New York: The Free Press.

Davenport, T. H. 1996. "Why reengineering failed: The fad that forgot people." *Fast Company*, January, pp. 69–74.

Dumaine, B. 1994. "The trouble with teams." *Fortune*, Sept. 5, pp. 86–92.

Emery, F. E. 1977. *The Futures We Are In*. Leiden, Holland: Martinus Nijhoff.

Emery, F. E., and E. Thorsrud. 1976. *Democracy at Work: The Report of the Norwegian Industrial Democracy Program*. Leiden, Holland: Martinus Nijhoff.

Emery, M. 1993. *Participative Design for Participative Democracy*. Canberra: Australian National University.

Emery, M., and R. E. Purser, 1996. *The Search Conference: A Powerful Method for Planning Organizational Change and Community Action*. San Francisco: Jossey-Bass Publishing.

Fessler, C. 1997. "Rotating leadership at Harley-Davidson: From hierarchy to interdependence." *Strategy and Leadership*. July/August, pp. 42–43.

Follet, M. P. 1965. *Dynamic Administration*. London: Pitman.

Gould, S. J. 1993. *Eight Little Piggies: Reflections in Natural History*. New York: Norton.

Handy, C. 1992. "Balancing corporate power: A new Federalist Paper." *Harvard Business Review*, November/December, pp. 59–69.

Heckscher, C., and A. Donnellon. 1994. *The Post-Bureaucratic Organization: New Perspectives on Organizational Change*. Thousand Oaks, CA: Sage Publications.

Hoerr, J., M. Pollock, and D. Whiteside. 1986. "Management discovers the human side of automation." *Business Week*, September, pp. 70–76.

Hurst, D. 1997. "When it comes to real change, too much objectivity may be fatal to the process." *Strategy and Leadership*, March/April, pp. 6–9.

Hurst, D. 1995. *Crisis and Renewal: Meeting the Challenge of Organizational Change*. Boston: Harvard Business School Press.

Jesitus, J. 1997. "When catastrophe threatens: Turning the corner: How new CEO David Weiss is retooling StorageTek." *Industry Week*, August 18, pp. 102–108.

Kanter, R. M. 1997. *Frontiers of Management*. Boston: Harvard Business School Press.

Katzenbach, J. R., and D. K. Smith. 1994. *The Wisdom of Teams*. New York: Harper-Collins.

Koch, R., and I. Godden. 1997. *Managing Without Management: A Post-Management Manifesto for Business Simplicity*. London: Nicholas-Brealey.

Levering, R., and M. Moskowitz. 1998. "The 100 best companies to work for in America." *Fortune*, January 12, pp. 84–95.

Macy, B., and I. Hiroaki. 1993. "Organizational change, design, and work innovation: A meta-analysis of 131 North American field studies—1961–1991." In R. W. Woodman and W. A. Pasmore eds., *Research in Organizational Change and Development*, Vol. 7. Greenwich, CN: JAI Press.

Magretta, J. 1997. "Growth through global sustainability: An interview with Monsanto's CEO, Robert Shapiro." *Harvard Business Review*, January–February, pp. 79–87.

Mason, R. 1982. *Participatory and Workplace Democracy: A Theoretical Development in the Critique of Liberalism*. Carbondale, IL: Southern Illinois University Press.

McKenna, D. 1997. Personal interview.

Petzinger, T. 1997. "The front lines: Self-organization will free employees to act like bosses," *The Wall Street Journal*, January 3, p. 1.

Purser, R. E., and A. Montuori. 1998. *Social Creativity*, Vol. 2. Cresskill, NJ: Hampton Press.

Purser, R. E., and W. A. Pasmore. 1992. "Organizing for learning." In R. Woodman & W. A. Pasmore, eds., *Research in Organizational Change and Development*, Vol. 6. Greenwich, CN.: JAI Press.

Sheridan, J. 1997. "The world's 100 best managed companies: The best versus the rest." *Industry Week*, August 18, pp. 70–82.

Shipper, F., and C. Mantz. 1992. "An alternative road to empowerment." *Organizational Dynamics*, Winter, pp. 48–61.

Slater, P. 1991. *A Dream Deferred: America's Discontent and the Search for a New Democratic Ideal*. Boston: Beacon Press.

Stross, R. 1996 *The Microsoft Way*. Reading, MA: Addison-Wesley.

Taninecz, G. 1997. "The state of manufacturing: Analysis of the U.S. industrial base and the competitive factors impacting success, best practices and performances." *Industry Week*, December 1, pp. 24–47.

Vogel, A. J. 1997. "Simple, yes. Easy, no. A controversial thinker (Margaret Wheatley) talks about the biology of organizations." *Across the Board,* January, pp. 19–24.

Vogel, A. J. 1996. "The latest chapter: The head of the world's largest defense and aerospace company knows a thing or two about the laws of business." *Across the Board,* June, pp. 21–26.

Waldrop, M. M. 1992. *Complexity: The Emerging Science at the Edge of Order and Chaos.* New York: Touchstone.

Wheatley, M. 1993. *Leadership and the New Science.* San Francisco, CA: Berrett-Koehler.

Woodman, R., J. Sawyer, and R. Griffin. 1993. "Toward a theory of organizational creativity." *Academy of Management Review* 18:293–321.

Chapter 2: The Road Less Traveled

Bartlett, C. A., and S. Ghoshal. 1994. "Changing the role of top management: Beyond strategy to purpose." *Harvard Business Review,* November/December pp. 79–88.

Best Manufacturing Practices. 1995. Center For Excellence For Best Manufacturing Practices. *Report of Survey Conducted at Lockheed-Martin Government Electronic Systems, Moorestown, New Jersey.* Requests for copies of recent survey reports of best manufacturing practices can be obtained by contacting the Best Manufacturing Practices Program, 4321 Hartwick Road, Suite 400, College Park, MD 20740. Attn. Mr. Ernie Renner, Director. Telephone 1-800-789-4267.

Emery, F. Personal communications, 1995.

Graham, Pauline, ed. 1995. *Mary Parker Follet—Prophet of Management: A Celebration of Writings from the 1920's.* Boston: Harvard Business School Press.

Gunn, R., and M. Burroughs. 1996. "Work spaces that work: Designing high performance offices." *The Futurist,* March/April, pp. 19–24.

Hequet, M. 1994. "Teams at the top: Why is it that teams are blossoming just about everywhere—except in the executive suites?" *Training,* April, pp. 7–10.

Katzenbach, J. R. 1998. *Teams at the Top.* Boston: Harvard Business School Press.

Katzenbach, J. R., and D. K. Smith. 1994. *The Wisdom of Teams.* New York: Harper-Collins.

Kinni, T. B. 1996. *America's Best: Industry Week's Guide to World-Class Manufacturing Plants.* New York: John Wiley & Sons.

Martin, R. 1993. "Changing the mind of the corporation." *Harvard Business Review,* November/December, pp. 81–94.

Miller, W. H. 1994. "Cover story: America's best plants." *Industry Week,* October 17, pp. 25–28.

National Baldrige Award. 1997. Criteria for performance excellence, Baldrige National Quality Award application, finalist: Lockheed-Martin Government Electronic Systems.

Quality New Jersey. 1995. Lockheed-Martin, Government Electronic Systems: 1995 New Jersey Quality Achievement Award Winner, award application, confidential internal document.

van Eijnatten, F. M. 1993. *The Paradigm That Changed the Workplace.* Assen, Holland: Van Gorcum.

Walton, R. 1982. "The Topeka work system: Optimistic visions, pessimistic hypotheses and reality." In R. Zaeger and R. Rosow, eds., *The Innovative Organization.* New York: Pergamon.

White, J. B., D. Clark, and S. Ascarelli. 1997. "Program of pain: This German software is complex, expensive: SAP's R/3 helps coordinate all aspects of business." *Wall Street Journal,* March 4, p. A-1.

Womack, J. P., and B. T. Jones. 1996. *Lean Thinking: Banish Waste and Create Wealth in Your Company.* New York: Simon & Schuster.

Chapter 3: Away with Experts

Ackoff, R. 1994. *The Democratic Corporation.* New York: Oxford University Press.

Emery, F. E. 1959. "Some characteristics of Socio-Technical Systems." In L. E. Davis and J. C. Taylor, eds., *Design of Jobs.* Harmondsworth: Penguin Books, 1972. (Originally published as Tavistock Document T125.)

Emery, F. E. 1976. *Futures We Are In.* Leiden, Holland: Martinus Nijhoff.

Emery, F. E. 1996. Personal communications.

Emery, M. 1993. *Participative Design for Participative Democracy.* Canberra: Australian National University.

Fayol, H. 1949. *General and Industrial Administration.* London: Sir Isaac Pitman.

Hammer, M., and J. Champy. 1993. *Reengineering the Corporation.* New York: HarperBusiness.

Ketchum, L. D. 1975. "A case study of diffusion." In L. E. Davis and A. B. Cherns, eds., *The Quality of Working Life,* Vol. 2. New York: The Free Press.

Ketchum, L. D., and E. Trist. 1992. *All Teams Are Not Created Equal.* Newbury Park, CA: Sage.

Kuhn, T. 1970. *The Structure of Scientific Revolutions,* 2nd ed. Chicago: University of Chicago Press.

Lancaster, H. 1995. "Reengineering authors reconsider reengineering." *The Wall Street Journal,* January 24.

Macy, B., and associates. 1993. "Organizational change, design, and work innovation: A Meta-analysis of 131 North American field studies—1961–1991." In R. W. Woodman and W. A. Pasmore, eds., *Research in Organizational Change and Development,* Vol. 7. Greenwich, CN.: JAI Press.

Mumford, E., R. Hendricks, R. Lumb, and M. Oram. 1996. "Business process re-emerging RIP: Failure of a management fad," *People Management*, May 2, 2(9):22–27.

O'Toole, J. 1974. *Work in America*. Cambridge: MIT Press.

Pasmore, W. 1988. *Designing Effective Organizations: The Sociotechnical Systems Perspective*. New York: John Wiley & Sons.

Taylor, F. 1911. *Principles of Scientific Management*. New York: Harper & Row.

Trist, E. L. 1971. "A Socio-Technical Critique of Scientific Management." Paper presented at the Edinburgh Conference on the Impact of Science and Technology.

Trist, E. L., and H. Murray. 1993. *The Social Engagement of Social Science*. Volume 2: *The Socio-Technical perspective*. Philadelphia: University of Pennsylvania Press.

Trist, E. L., C. Higgin, H. Murray, and A. Pollock. 1963. *Organizational Choice*. London: Tavistock Publications.

Womack, J. P., and B. T. Jones. 1996. *Lean Thinking: Banish Waste and Create Wealth in Your Company*. New York: Simon & Schuster.

Chapter 4: Going to the Roots

Adams, S. 1995. "Managers journal: The Dilbert principle." *The Wall Street Journal*, May 22, p. A-12.

Adams, S. 1996. *The Dilbert Principle*. New York: Harper Business.

Bennis, W. 1993. *Beyond Bureaucracy: Essays on the Development and Evolution of Human Organization*. San Francisco: Jossey-Bass. (Originally published in 1966.)

Davis, L. E. 1971. "The coming crisis in production management technology and organization." *International Journal of Production Research* 9:65–82.

Drucker, P. F. 1989. *The New Realities*. New York: Harper & Row.

Dumaine, B. 1991. "The bureaucracy busters." *Fortune*, June 17, pp. 36–37.

Edleman, K. A. 1997. "Open office? Try virtual office," *Across the Board*, March 7, p. 34.

Emery, F. E. 1977. *Futures We Are In*. Leiden, Holland: Martinus Nijhoff, 1977.

Gabriel, T. 1997. "Scaling corporate heights without going over a cliff." *New York Times*, June 1, p. D-10.

Hentoff, N. 1984. *Jazz Is*. New York: Limelight.

Jaques, E. 1990. "In praise of hierarchy." *Harvard Business Review*, January/February, pp. 127–133.

Katz, R. 1978. "The influence of job longevity on employee relations to task characteristics." *Human Relations* 31:703–725.

Kraines, G. 1996. "Hierarchies bad rap." *Journal of Business Strategy* 1(4):13–15.

Kuhn, T. 1970. *The Structure of Scientific Revolutions,* 2nd ed. Chicago: University of Chicago Press.

Lancaster, H. 1996. "Managing your career: Those rotten things you say about work may be true after all." *Wall Street Journal,* February 20, p. B-1.

Land, E. Quoted in P. C. Wensberg. 1987. *Land's Polaroid.* Boston, MA: Houghton Mifflin.

Lewin, K. 1947. "Group decisions and social change." In E. Macoby, ed., *Readings in Social Psychology.* New York: Holt, Rinehart and Winston.

Liebowitz, S. J., and K. T. Holdern, 1995. "Are self-managing teams worthwhile? A tale of two companies." *SAM Advanced Management Journal,* Spring, pp. 11–17.

Magretta, J. 1997. "Growth through global sustainability: An interview with Monsanto's CEO, Robert Shapiro." *Harvard Business Review,* January–February, pp. 79–88.

McCarty, S. 1995. "Airline industry's top ranked woman keeps Southwest's small fry spirit alive." *Wall Street Journal,* November, 30, p. B-1.

Papanek, V. 1985. *Design for a Real World: Human Ecology and Social Change.* Chicago: Academy Chicago Publishers.

Petzinger, T. 1997a. "The front lines: Self-organization will free employees to act like bosses." *Wall Street Journal,* January 3, p. B-1.

Petzinger, T. 1997b. "The front lines: How Lynn Mercer manages a factory that manages itself." *Wall Street Journal,* March 7, p. B-1.

Purser, R. 1991. "Redesigning the knowledge-based product development organization: A case study in sociotechnical systems change." *Technovation* 11(7): 403–416.

Purser, R., and A. Montuori. 1994. "Miles Davis in the classroom: Using the jazz ensemble metaphor for enhancing team learning." *Journal of Management Education* 18(1): 21–31.

Purser, R., and A. Montuori, eds. 1998. *Social Creativity: Creative Organizations and the Organization of Creativity.* Cresskill, NJ: Hampton Press.

Purser, R., W. Pasmore, and R. Tenkasi. 1992. "The influence of deliberations on learning in new product development teams." *Journal of Engineering and Technology Management* 9:1–28.

Quinn, J. B. 1985. "Managing innovation: Controlled chaos." *Harvard Business Review,* May–June, pp. 76–83.

Rehm, R. 1998. "Democratic workplace design." Unpublished paper.

Reich, R. 1987. "Entrepreneurship reconsidered: The team as hero." *Harvard Business Review,* May/June, pp. 77–88.

Salner, M. 1988. "Introduction: Metaphor and understanding." *Saybrook Review* 2(2):1–20.

Savage, C. 1990. *Fifth Generation Management: Integrating Enterprises Through Networking*. Boston: Digital Equipment Press.

Schrage, M. 1995. "Managers journal: Notes on collaboration." *Wall Street Journal,* June 19, p. A-10.

Senge, P. 1990. *The Fifth Discipline: The Art and Practice of Organizational Learning*. New York: Doubleday.

Slater, P. 1991. *A Dream Deferred: America's Discontent and the Search for a New Democratic Ideal*. Boston: Beacon Press.

Stein, M. L. 1996. "Reporting teams seek new creativity." *Editor and Publisher Journal* 129, no. 45 (Nov. 9):22.

Stewart, T. 1996. "The great conundrum—You versus the team." *Fortune,* November 25 pp. 165–66.

Taninecz, G. 1997. "Census of manufacturers: The state of manufacturing and best practices and performances." *Industry Week,* December 1, pp. 24–43.

Wensberg, P. 1987. *Land's Polaroid*. Boston: Houghton Mifflin.

Witte, J. F. 1980. *Democracy, Authority, and Alienation in Work: Workers' Participation in an American Corporation*. Chicago: The University of Chicago Press.

Chapter 5: Revolutions Gone Sour

Alvesson, M., and H. Wilmott. 1996. *Making Sense of Management: A Critical Introduction*. London: Sage.

Argyris, C. 1957. *Personality and Organization*. New York: Harper & Row.

Argyris, C. 1964. *Integrating the Individual and the Organization*. New York: John Wiley & Sons.

Baritz, L. 1960. *The Servants of Power: A History of the Use of Social Science in American Industry*. Middletown, CN: Wesleyan University Press.

Bell, D. 1956. *Work and Its Discontents*. Boston: Beacon Press.

Bushe, G., and A. B. Shani. 1991. *Parallel Learning Structures*. Reading, MA: Addison- Wesley.

Deming, E. W. 1986. *Out of the Crisis*. Cambridge, MA: MIT Press.

Drucker, P. 1954. *The Practice of Management*. New York: Harper & Row.

Elden, M. 1986. "Socio-technical systems ideas as public policy in Norway: Empowering participation through worker-managed change." *Journal of Applied Behavioral Science* 22(3):239–255.

Emery, F. 1995. Personal communications.

Emery, M. 1993. *Participative Design for Participative Democracy*. Canberra, Australia: Australian National University Press.

Famularo, J. 1986. *Handbook for Human Resource Administrators*, 2nd ed. New York: McGraw Hill.

Hammer, M., and J. Champy. 1993. *Reengineering the Corporation: A Manifesto for Business Revolution.* New York: HarperBusiness.

Juran, J. M. 1964. *Managerial Breakthrough.* New York: McGraw-Hill.

Kalgaard, R. "ASAP interview with Michael Hammer." *Forbes,* Sept. 13, pp. 69–75.

Keeley, M. 1988. *Social Contract Theory.* South Bend, IN: Notre Dame University Press.

McGregor, D. 1960. *The Human Side of Enterprise.* New York: McGraw Hill.

Montuori, A. 1997. "Creative inquiry: From instrumental knowledge to love of knowledge." In J. Petranker, ed., *Light of Knowledge: Essays on the Interplay of Knowledge, Time and Space.* Berkeley, CA: Dharma Publishing.

Perrow, C. 1979. *Complex Organizations: A Critical Essay.* Glenview, IL: Scott Foresman.

Scott, W. 1962. *Human Relations in Management: A Behavioral Science Approach.* Homewood, IL: Richard D. Irwin.

Talmon, J. L. 1952. *The Rise of Totalitarian Democracy.* Boston: Beacon Press.

Trist, E. L., and H. Murray. 1993. *The Social Engagement of Social Science: The Sociotechnical Perspective.* Philadelphia: University of Pennsylvania Press.

Chapter 6: Democratizing the Strategy Creation Process

Beckhard, R., and R. Harris. 1977. *Organizational Transitions: Managing Complex Change.* Reading, MA: Addison-Wesley.

Cabana, S., and J. Fiero. 1995. "Motorola, strategic planning and the Search Conference." *Journal of Quality and Participation,* July/August, 18(4):22–31.

Emery, M., and R. E. Purser. 1996. *The Search Conference: A Powerful Method for Planning Organizational Change and Community Action.* San Francisco: Jossey-Bass.

Hamel, G., 1997. "Killer strategies that make shareholders rich." *Fortune,* June 23, pp. 70–84.

Hamel, G., and C. K. Prahalad. 1989. "Strategic intent." *Harvard Business Review,* May–June, pp. 63–76.

Hamel, G., and C. K. Prahalad. 1994. *Competing for the Future.* Boston: Harvard Business School Press.

Liedtka, J. M., and J. W. Rosenblum. 1996. "Shaping strategic conversations: Making strategy, managing change." *California Management Review* 39(1):141–157.

Lippitt, R. 1983. "Future before you plan." In R. Ritvo and A. Sargent, eds., *NTL Manager's Handbook.* Arlington, VA: NTL Institute.

Prahalad, C. K., and G. Hamel. 1990. "The core competence of the corporation." *Harvard Business Review,* May/June, pp. 79–91.

Senge, P. 1990. *The Fifth Discipline: The Art and Practice of the Learning Organization.* New York: Doubleday.

Trist, E., and F. E. Emery. 1960. "Report on the Barford conference for Bristol/ Siddeley Aero-Engine Corporation." Document no. 598. London: Tavistock Institute.

Chapter 7: The Search Conference

Bank, D. 1997. "Microsoft moves to cut off Sun's JAVA with new program-writing technology." *The Wall Street Journal,* September 24.

Dodge, J. 1997. "Is Microsoft waiting for the JAVA bubble to burst?" *PC Week,* April 7, p. 3.

Emery, M., and R. E. Purser. 1996. *The Search Conference: A Powerful Method for Planning Organizational Change and Community Action.* San Francisco: Jossey-Bass.

Gaudin, S. 1997. "Microsoft questions cross-platform viability." *Computerworld,* March 3, p. 4.

Hamel, G. 1997. "Killer strategies that make shareholders rich." *Fortune,* June 23, pp. 70–84.

Hamel, G., and C. K. Prahalad. 1994. *Competing for the Future.* Boston: Harvard Business School Press.

Hamm, S., A. Cortese, and C. Yang. 1997. "Microsoft refines its net game." *Business Week,* September 8, p. 126.

Purcell, K., and E. Dunn. 1996. "Using search conferences for creating Microsoft's consumer division strategy." Presentation at the Large Group Intervention Conference, Town & Country, MO: ACTS (audio cassette).

Purser, R. E., and W. A. Pasmore. 1992. "Organizing for learning." In R. Woodman and W. A. Pasmore, eds., *Research in Organizational Change and Development,* Vol. 6. Greenwich, CT: JAI Press.

Radosevich, L., and B. Trott. 1997. "Caught in the web?" *Infoworld,* July 21, p. 1.

Ramo, J. C. 1996. "Winner take all." *Time,* September 16, p. 56.

Reid, Robert. 1997. *Architects of the Web.* New York: John Wiley & Sons.

Schlender, B. 1995. "Whose Internet is it, anyway?" *Fortune,* December 11, p. 120.

Schlender, B. 1996. "Software hardball." *Fortune,* September 30, p. 107.

Taninecz, G. 1995. "Gates wins respect." *Industry Week,* November 20, p. 12.

Trott, B. 1997. "Ballmer: Sun is Microsoft's top foe." *InfoWorld,* August 11, p. 41.

Chapter 8: Democratizing Work

Ackoff, R. 1994. *The Democratic Corporation: A Radical Prescription for Recreating Corporate America and Rediscovering Success.* New York: Oxford University Press.

Ackoff, R., and F. E. Emery. 1972. *On Purposeful Systems*. London: Tavistock Publications.

Beer, S. 1985. *Diagnosing the System for Organizations*. New York: John Wiley & Sons.

Cabana, S. 1995a. "Participative Design works, partially participative doesn't." *Journal of Quality and Participation*, January/February, 18(1):10–19.

Cabana, S. 1995b. "Can people restructure their own work? How H-P, Syncrude and others use Participative Design and the Search Conference to unleash organizational power." *Target*, November/December, 11(6):16–30.

Cabana, S., F. E. Emery, and M. Emery. 1995. "The search for effective strategic planning is over." *Journal of Quality and Participation*, July/August, 11(4):10–19.

Emery, F. E., and E. Thorsrud. 1969. *Form and Content In Industrial Democracy*. London: Tavistock Press.

Emery, M. 1993. *Participative Design for Participative Democracy*. Canberra: Australian National University, Center for Continuing Education.

Kepner, C., and B. Tregoe. 1965. *The Rational Manager: A Systematic Approach to Problem-Solving and Decision Making*. New York: McGraw Hill.

Trist, E., and H. Murray. 1993. *The Social Engagement of Social Science: A Tavistock Anthology*, Volume 2: *The Socio-Technical Perspective*. Philadelphia: University of Pennsylvania Press.

Van Eijnatten, F. 1993. *The Paradigm That Changed the Workplace*. Assen, Holland: Van Gorcum.

Chapter 9: Participative Design of Business Processes

Cabana, S. 1995. "Participative Design works, partially participative doesn't." *Journal of Quality and Participation*, January/February, 18(1):10–19.

Cabana, S., and J. Duncan. 1997. "A whole-system change process which is self-managed and autonomy based rather than hierarchical and centralized: The Sequa story." *Work Teams Newsletter*, Center for the Study of Work Teams, University of North Texas, Spring, p. 1.

Davenport, T. H. 1993. *Process Innovation: Reengineering Work Through Information Technology*. Boston: Harvard Business School Press.

Emery, M. 1993. *Participative Design for Participative Democracy*. Canberra: Australian National University, Center for Continuing Education.

Emery, M., and R. E. Purser. 1996. *The Search Conference: A Powerful Method for Planning Organizational Change and Community Action*. San Francisco: Jossey-Bass.

Harrington, H. J. 1991. *Business Process Improvement: The Breakthrough Strategy for Total Quality, Productivity, and Competitiveness*. New York: McGraw Hill.

Hayes, R. H., S. C. Wheelwright, and K. B. Clark. 1988. *Dynamic Manufacturing: Creating the Learning Organization*. New York: The Free Press.

Kaplan, R. S., and D. P. Norton. 1996. *The Balanced Scorecard: Translating Strategy into Action.* Boston: Harvard Business School Press.

Lawler, E. E., S. A. Mohrman, and G. E. Ledford, Jr. 1995. *Creating High Performance Organizations: Practices and Results of Employee Involvement and Total Quality Management In Fortune 1000 Companies.* San Francisco: Jossey-Bass.

Perry, L. T., R. G. Stott, and W. N. Smallwood. 1993. *Real Time Strategy: Improvising Team-Based Planning for a Fast-Changing World.* New York: John Wiley & Sons.

Pepitone, J. S. 1995. *Future Training: A Roadmap for Restructuring the Training Function.* New York: AddVantage Learning Press.

Porter, M. E. 1985. *Competitive Advantage: Creating and Sustaining Superior Performance.* New York: The Free Press.

Rummler, G. A., and A. P. Brache. 1990. *Improving Performance: How to Manage the White Space on the Organization Chart.* San Francisco: Jossey-Bass.

Chapter 10: Designing the Self-Managing Organization

Ghosal S., and C. A. Bartlett. 1996. "Rebuilding behavioral context: A blueprint for corporate renewal." *Sloan Management Review,* Winter, pp. 23–35.

Emery, M. 1993. *Participative Design for Participative Democracy.* Canberra: Australian National University, Centre for Continuing Education.

Hurst, D. K. 1995. *Crisis and Renewal: Meeting the Challenge of Organizational Change.* Boston: Harvard Business School Press.

Kershaw, D., J. Buckles, and D. McNeil. 1996. "Success through collaboration on large scale change projects at Syncrude." Presentation at the "Creating Canadian Advantage Through Project Management" Conference, May 13–15, Calgary, Alberta, Canada.

Kotter, J. P. 1996. *Leading Change.* Boston: Harvard Business School Press.

Nadler, D. A., and M. L. Tushman. 1997. *Competing by Design: The Power of Organizational Architecture.* New York: Oxford University Press.

Chapter 11: The Role of Management in a Self-Managing Organization

Butler, C. (S. Ghoshal, supervisor.) 1992. Kao Corporation case, INSEAD-EAC.

Cabana, S. and C. Parry. 1996. "Leadership for turbulent times: The challenge of integrating authority and leadership." *Journal for Quality and Participation,* March, 76–79.

Duncan, J. 1997. "Contextual Concepts in Support of Redesign for High Performance: Organizational Readiness." (Unpublished paper) The Duncan Network, Inc.

Emery, M. 1993. *Participative Design for Participative Democracy.* Canberra: Australian National University, Centre for Continuing Education.

Hackman J. R. 1987. "The design of work teams." In J. W. Lorsch, ed., *Handbook of Organizational Behavior.* Englewood Cliffs, NJ: Prentice-Hall.

Iwasaki, Y., and J. Nakane. 1995. "Downscaling to adapt to your environment: Mayekawa Manufacturing Company, Ltd." *Target,* July/August, pp. 9–17.

Kanter, R. M. 1997. *Frontiers of Management.* Boston: Harvard Business Review Press.

Lippitt, R. 1983. "Future before you plan." In R. Ritvo and A. Sargent, eds., *NTL Managers Handbook.* Arlington, VA: NTL Institute.

McDermott, L. 1992. *Caught in the Middle.* Englewood Cliffs, NJ: Prentice-Hall.

Noble, P., R. Leiker, and E. Granata. 1996. "The library change process at Storage-Tek." In T. Chase, ed., *Large Group Interventions For Organizational Change: Concepts, Methods and Cases, Conference Readings.* Northwood, NH: Organizational Development Network.

Oshry, B. 1995. *Seeing Systems: Unlocking the Mysteries of Organizational Life.* San Francisco: Berrett-Koehler Publishers.

Parry, C., M. Darling, and S. Robbins. 1997. "Putting best practices into practice." *The Systems Thinker* 8:10, 1–5.

Petzinger T., Jr. 1996. "The front lines: Lisa Zackman solved her staffing woes with a wacky plan." *Wall Street Journal,* June 21, p. B-1.

Petzinger, T., Jr. 1997. "The front lines: Self organization will free employees to act like bosses." *Wall Street Journal,* January 3, p. B-1.

Epilogue: Democracy at Work in the Twenty-first Century

Petzinger, T. Jr. 1997. "The front lines: radical work by guru of leadership takes thirty years to flower." *Wall Street Journal,* April 5, p. B-1.

Dahl, R. A. 1985. *A Preface to Economic Democracy.* Berkeley, CA: University of California Press.

Ellerman, D. P. 1990. *The Democratic Worker-Owned Firm: A New Model for the East and West.* Boston: Unwin Hyman.

Handy, C. 1995. *The Age of Paradox.* Boston: Harvard Business School Press.

Purser, R. E., and W. A. Pasmore. 1992. "Organizing for learning." In R. Woodman and W. A. Pasmore, eds., *Research in Organizational Change and Development,* Volume 6. Greenwich, CT: JAI Press.

Stacey, R. 1992. *Managing the Unknowable: Strategic Boundaries Between Order and Chaos in Organizations.* San Francisco: Jossey-Bass.

INDEX

ABOUT THE AUTHORS

RONALD PURSER is Associate Professor of Management in the College of Business at San Francisco State University and Adjunct Professor of Organizational Inquiry at Saybrook Graduate School. He is the author of over fifty articles and book chapters, and has conducted research on issues related to high-performance work systems, organizational learning, management of new product development and knowledge work, systems theory, social creativity, and industrial ecology. Some of his major corporate clients have included Amoco, Andersen Consulting, Eastman Kodak, Exxon, General Electric, Polaroid, Procter & Gamble, Progressive Insurance, Storage Technology, United Airlines, Whirlpool, and Xerox. He has also worked with the Calgary Board of Education, Chicago Empowerment Zone, Educational Commission for the States, Mississippi Commission for Volunteer Services, The Nature Conservancy, Illinois Board of Education, Symphony Orchestra Institute, U.S. Office of Personnel Management, and the Environmental Protection Agency. To learn more about the concepts and methods for designing *The Self Managing Organization,* see Professor Purser's website at: http://userwww.sfsu.edu/~rpurser/ Or you may contact him at: San Francisco State University, College of Business, 1600 Holloway Ave., San Francisco, California 94132. Telephone: 415-338-2380. His e-mail address is: rpurser@sfsu.edu

STEVEN CABANA works with organizations to help create, improve, and sustain their competitive advantage. He is the managing principal of Whole System Associates, a consulting firm that specializes in the design of change processes that make team-based organizations work effectively. Mr. Cabana is a recognized expert in aligning work structure to corporate strategy. He specializes in processes which engage people in revitalizing their own work and which connect their teams to the larger organization. Drawing on seventeen years of experience leading large-scale change efforts in high tech, manufacturing, government, service, and health care, he helps organizations make strategic change happen. Mr. Cabana has worked with organizations around the world including Cabot, Fidelity, Monsanto, Merck, United Technologies, Education Commission of the States, and

Boston Medical Center. He is the author of the first North American articles introducing the principles and practical tools described in this book.

Whole System Associates offers one-day overviews of the principles of self-management, intensive training courses for experienced change leaders, and consulting services to build high-performance workplaces. Visit our website at selfmgmtorgs.com, or contact us at 888-547-1695 or info@selfmgmtorgs.com.